NEW GILL HISTORY OF IRELAND
3

Seventeenth-Century Ireland: The War of Religions

BRENDAN FITZPATRICK

GILL AND MACMILLAN

Published in Ireland by
Gill and Macmillan Ltd
Goldenbridge
Dublin 8
with associated companies in
Auckland, Delhi, Gaborone, Hamburg, Harare,
Hong Kong, Johannesburg, Kuala Lumpur, Lagos, London,
Manzini, Melbourne, Mexico City, Nairobi,
New York, Singapore, Tokyo
© Brendan Fitzpatrick 1988
Index by Helen Litton
Print origination in Ireland by Graphic Plan
Printed in England by Camelot Press, Southampton

British Library Cataloguing in Publication Data

Fitzpatrick, Brendan, *1953–*
    Seventeenth-century Ireland: the war
    of religions.—(New Gill history of
    Ireland)
    1. Ireland — 1603–1691
    I. Title
    941.506

ISBN 0-7171-1576-3 Hbk
ISBN 0-7171-1626-3 Pbk

Contents

Introduction   1

1. Identities and Allegiances, 1603-25   5

2. The Crown and the Catholics:
   Royal Government and Policy 1625-37   36

3. Fateful Ideologies: The Stuart Inheritance   59

4. Wentworth and the Ulster Crisis, 1638-9   77

5. On the Eve of Revolution, 1639-41   109

6. 1641: The Plot That Never Was   133

7. Insurrection and Confederation, 1641-4   168

8. In Search of a Settlement:
   Ormond, Rinuccini and Cromwell, 1645-53   188

9. Theology and the Politics of Sovereignty:
   Jansenist, Jesuit and Franciscan   209

10. Ideologies in Conflict, 1660-91   227

References   257

Bibliography   261

Index   279

IRELAND

Inishowen Peninsula

Coleraine

Derry

Carrickfergus

Belfast

ULSTER

Enniskillen

Sligo

Dundalk

CONNACHT

Drogheda

Battle of
Aughrim (1691)

Battle of
the Boyne (1690)

Athlone

R. Shannon

Galway

LEINSTER

Dublin

Wicklow

Limerick

Kilkenny

Clonmel

MUNSTER

Wexford

Waterford

Cork

Principal Uplands   ------- Provincial Boundaries

Introduction

THE sixteenth century was the century in which the Gaelic Irish came face to face with the reality of English conquest. Although it seemed to them that the nature of this conquest was military, time was to show that it was, more than anything else, legal. Government troops were used to restore order to an area in revolt, but it was the legal confiscations that followed which determined the future. Such confiscations could not have taken place within the law if the Gaelic Irish had not signed away their independence under a policy generally known as 'surrender and regrant'. The process whereby a Gaelic chief expropriated the property of his people could not itself have taken place if Henry VIII had not become King of Ireland in 1541. Before this date Ireland had been a lordship in which the power of the law was as much dependent upon physical geography as it was upon Gaelic acquiescence. After 1541 Ireland had a sovereign ruler and it became imperative that the government of the country should reflect that new abstract uniformity.

There were many reasons why Ireland exchanged the status of a lordship for that of a kingdom, but the most telling aspect for the future was Henry VIII's break with Roman Catholicism. With this break came the need to assert political sovereignty for the very reason that politics and religion were inextricably entwined and Ireland had now become a security problem in a way that it had not been hitherto. The ground was prepared before 1541 by the introduction of direct rule; that is to say the Lord Deputy would henceforth refer to London rather than to local magnates in governing the country. The Anglo-Norman community (hereafter referred to by their later name of Old English) handled this momentous change with the same degree of political sophistication that they had shown throughout their own rule. They retained their Roman Catholicism while at the same time acknowledging the political reality of the new Protestant Church of Ireland. Their reward for doing so was very significant: they accepted monastic property in return for their allegiance.

The Old English bought a very substantial amount of security by acknowledging, if not adhering to, the king's new religion. Because they stressed their English race, with its English political heritage of urban and rural government, their loyalty could not easily be questioned. Not so with the Gaelic Irish, who had equally accepted the new political sovereignty. Their race and culture was not descended from the king's, nor did they have the tradition of law and politics behind them as did the Old English. What this meant in effect was that there were vast estates in Ireland to be had by hard-nosed Englishmen who could successfully demonstrate that the Gaelic Irish were a political, military and religious threat. The easiest way to do this was, of course, to drive the Irish into such a position where their expropriation became a matter of necessity. The pioneers of this new method of aggrandisement became known as the New English, but they had little in common with the old colony. Their religion was the keenest of all: a pragmatic (and theologically strained) mixture of Anglicanism and Calvinism which gave them unrivalled access to claims on sovereign authority.

In this respect the New English were more adaptable than the Tudors themselves, who were obliged to confront the political reality of the Reformation. The Anglicanism of Henry VIII was followed by the Calvinism of Edward VI and the Roman Catholicism of Mary until a settlement was achieved under Elizabeth. The New English did not suffer the Tudor monarchy's religious problems, however, because the political framework of Ireland lay outside that of England and the type of conformity required was different for that very reason. Although Ireland became a kingdom, its king never resided there. The country was ruled in the king's name by his deputy. This clarified official sovereignty where the deputy's power was concerned, but it did the opposite for the subjects of the new realm. Although matters were simplified for the New English, they became increasingly complicated for the Old English and quite impossible for the Gaelic Irish. This was because whole identities, with all the historical complexities that went with them, could be reduced by the Dublin government to a question of loyalty. It was politically impossible to demonstrate qualified loyalty to a sovereign. Loyalty was either unconditional or it was potentially traitorous. While Scotland under the Stuarts and England under the Tudors underwent considerable turmoil because the religion of their indigenous monarchs was often at variance with that of their subjects, a great deal of political evolution had taken place by the end of the sixteenth century. During this time Ireland remained a country of conditional loyalties and localised resistance.

The Old English adherence to Roman Catholicism under a Protestant monarch split the concept of sovereignty down the middle. It was this divide which the New English exploited so successfully, first against the Gaelic Irish and those Gaelicised lords such as the Desmonds, and then, in the seventeenth century, against the Old English themselves. It was the latter's inability to keep control of the government that made the fate of Ireland's Roman Catholics all but inevitable in the face of the pristine loyalty of the New English. This raises the question of why the Old English did not convert to the king's new religion or to the religion of Edward and later Elizabeth. The answer is simply that they were not required to do so for the very reason that they no longer represented the royal government, and once this fall from power had taken place (after 1534) the New English had no intentions of encouraging their competitors to regain control. The religion of the New English was well suited to this situation. They gained and retained their estates by unqualified political loyalty to the crown, while at the same time they tended towards a Calvinistic exclusivity which freed them from the problem of converting the opposition.

The Gaelic Irish existed on the outer fringes of the Old English compromise, but because they were politically deprived (by the Old English themselves) they were inarticulate and often resorted to arms as the only way to reach the bargaining table where land confiscation was being discussed. This was a vicious circle because it demonstrated exactly what the New English continually warned the crown about.

These were not rebellions against English sovereignty—this point cannot be emphasised enough. Throughout the sixteenth and seventeenth centuries European republican government was born out of Calvinistic struggles for independence—conditions which represented the very opposite religious position of either the Gaelic Irish or the Old English. Because of its hierarchical structure, Roman Catholicism was always sympathetic to monarchical government, so there was never a question of Ireland's Roman Catholics replacing the English king with a presbyterian-style democracy. What was at issue was not religion but expropriation based upon religion, and this fundamental post-Reformation flaw in Ireland's loyalty could always and ever be exploited by newcomers.

The Catholics of Ireland were destined always to be on the wrong side for as long as the crown remained Protestant, but the country's history has often been interpreted retrospectively to show that the

oppressed and the rebellious were first republicans and then nationalists as far back as the late sixteenth and early seventeenth century.
Within this view, it has proved hard to explain how, for example,
Rory O'Donnell was raised to the earldom of Tyrconnell at the end
of the Nine Years' War; how the great Earl of Tyrone was supported
fully at court by Mountjoy; how Sir Cahir O'Doherty resorted to
arms on the same day as his request for a place at court had been
granted; how the loyal towns 'revolted' after the war was over in
1603; how the rising of Roman Catholics in 1641 was impeded by the
question of whether loyalty was better served by resorting to arms in
the king's defence or by assiduously keeping the peace; how, after the
Confederate collapse in 1649, the Catholic Primate set about facili-
tating Cromwellian rule in return for religious toleration—a policy
pursued to its limits by his successor under the restored monarchy.

In this context modern republicanism could never retrace its steps
back into early modern Ireland, nor could the nineteenth-century
form of nationalism built around the concept of a nation-state. The
Gaelic Irish had been a nation without a state; the Old English had
been a semi-state but were never a separate nation; the New English
had been political grafters who survived because they had no
indigenous identity whatsoever. The famous 'Irish question' evolved
out of this hotchpotch struggle for survival, but the question itself
cannot be answered unless it can first be asked. What follows is an
attempt to examine how the Catholics of Ireland attempted to reconcile themselves to the Stuarts as their only defence against the New
English. The attempt failed, and the latter (who were often considerably less loyal than the Catholics) retained control and saw to it
that Catholicism became synonymous with the 'hidden Ireland' of
the eighteenth century.

It is intellectually naïve, and has often caused great confusion, to
believe that modern Irish republicanism or nationalism is the product
of a continuous Catholic struggle which can be traced back to the
early seventeenth century. The year 1603 was indeed a great watershed, but so also was 1691. Between these two dates much took place
which had the most profound effect on the crisis of identity which
Ireland has perpetually undergone; but that is not to say that the
century saw the beginning of a great struggle for unity. For as long as
Ireland's history is written backwards—that is, in order to justify one
particular conclusion over another—the concept of unity will have
no meaning. Indeed, the 'unity' of Ireland may well be its greatest
myth.

Identities
and Allegiances, 1603-25

O N 30 March 1603 Hugh O'Neill, Earl of Tyrone, surrendered to Lord Deputy Mountjoy at Mellifont. Tyrone was not informed that Queen Elizabeth had died six days earlier. Had he been privy to this information, he might have improved the terms of the treaty, but he could not have undone the manner of his defeat. After several years of the most serious rebellion in Ulster the country was conquered by a blanket policy of destruction. The Battle of Kinsale itself was a notably indecisive event: the bulk of the Irish forces were not engaged, while the entire Spanish contingent was neutralised by siege. Tyrone may have been outwitted by superior tactics, but his inability to retaliate had little to do with military power and everything to do with policy. Mountjoy had followed up his victory at Kinsale not by waging war against Tyrone but by devastating the country itself, destroying crops and livestock with indiscriminate efficiency. When the defeated earl abandoned his stronghold at Dungannon and took to the woods Mountjoy did not pursue him. Instead he burnt the year's harvest in Ulster, causing three thousand people to die of starvation on the earl's land alone. Mountjoy had told the Privy Council that famine would be the only effective means of ending the war, and he proved true to his word. Moreover, his policy was combined with a military and political campaign that was to see Ulster garrisoned for the first time, the presidency of Munster secured, and the country ready to receive the legal and administrative changes that were to follow.

Tyrone's defeat and the end of the Nine Years' War has often been seen as a great blow to the Catholics of Ireland and the last great stand of a national culture which would not rise to prominence again until the nineteenth century. According to this view, Tyrone was the first great leader to recognise what was at stake when he claimed, during his rebellion, 'that they that are joined with me fight for the Catholic religion and the liberties of our country'.[1] Unfortunately, both for Tyrone and his adherents, the island contained another type of Catholicism, practised by a group whose definition of 'liberty' was quite different. By the end of the sixteenth century the Catholicism of Gaelic Ulster looked firmly to Spain for its support, just as that of the Old English looked to England and France. Spanish Catholicism had been forged over many centuries in the face of a double-edged threat from Arab and Jewish cultures. There was little room or need for compromise. Cut off as it was geographically from northern Europe, Spain developed institutions such as the Inquisition which saw compromise not just as a type of weakness but as a clear indication of guilt. Set against this rigid adherence to orthodoxy were those countries where compromise between the powers of the king and those of the pope was deemed necessary for political survival. What characterised the Gallicanism of France and the Anglo-Catholicism of England were definitions of loyalty which sought to reconcile the temporal and spiritual powers.

It was from within this balance that the largely urbanised Catholic Old English of Ireland derived their political and religious identity. They had ignored Tyrone's claim that he was the defender of their faith, but they had not done this unwittingly. At what was perhaps the height of his power the earl had addressed the towns from his headquarters at Dungannon in November 1599. It is clear from what follows that he himself was under no illusion as to the obstacles he faced, but his address is also interesting as an indication of how things might have gone for the non-Gaelic Catholics under a Gaelic king (if such a development had been possible). To the Catholics of the towns of Ireland Tyrone had this to say:

> Using hitherto more than ordinary favour towards all my countrymen who generally by profession are Catholics, and that naturally I am inclined to affect you, I have for these and other considerations abstained my forces from tempting to do you hindrance, and because I did expect that you would enter into consideration of the lamentable state of our poor country, most tyrannically oppressed, and of your own gentle consciences, in maintaining, relieving and helping the enemies of God and our country, in wars infallibly tending to the promotion of heresy. But now seeing you are so obstinate in that which hitherto you continued of necessity, I must use severity against you (whom otherwise I most entirely love), in reclaiming you by compulsion. My tolerance and happy vic-

tories, by God's particular favour doubtless obtained, could work no alteration in your consciences, notwithstanding the great calamity and misery whereunto you are most likely to fall by persevering in that damnable state into which hereunto you have lived. Having commiseration on you, I thought it good to forewarn you, requesting every of you to come and join with me against the enemies of God and our poor country. If the same you do not, I will use means not only to spoil you of all your goods, but according to the utmost of my power, shall work what I may to dispossess you of all your lands, because you are means whereby wars are maintained against the exaltation of the Catholic faith.

Lest there be any doubt among the Catholics of the towns as to precisely what the earl had in mind, he concluded that he was

in conscience bound, seeing God hath given me some power, to use all means for the reduction of this our poor afflicted country into the Catholic faith, which can never be brought to any good pass without either your destruction or helping hand.[2]

The Catholics of the towns did not rise in support of the earl. They did not do so for the simple reason that since the coming of the Normans in the twelfth century the townsmen had adhered to the very legal system which was at the heart of the crown's thrust against the Gaelic chiefs. The power of the Anglo-Norman towns of Ireland was based on the charter. This was a legal agreement which amounted to a local constitution and which was developed from the twelfth to the sixteenth centuries to include all powers exercised within a municipality by the consent of both subject and monarch. It was here, however, in the definition of a subject, that the real differences between the Gaelic Irish and the Catholic townsmen were to be found. The town proper was a Norman contribution to life in Ireland. Intrinsic to its structure was a legal constitution which looked back to European, to Roman and ultimately to Athenian notions of citizenship and representation. A citizen was known as a freeman, and he had the right to stand for office or vote in the municipal elections; he had the right to practise a trade under protective conditions; and having paid his taxes, he had the right to expect the public maintenance of his town or city. As the country's capital, Dublin was the model town not just because it was the largest municipality but also because it was the seat of the English government in Ireland. This meant in effect that the old Norman traditions could not be allowed to degenerate in the presence of the crown's representative, the Lord Deputy.

What characterised these Norman traditions as much as the municipal structures themselves was the official antipathy of the citizenry to all things Gaelic. The 'native Irish' resided in the areas immediately outside the municipality, that is to say in the liberties. They were allowed to enter the city to trade on certain appointed days, and in this respect they were often used by the ruling council to force prices down on basic commodities such as bread. As the Irish could not legally inhabit the city, they could not become freemen, and consequently they had no chartered rights whatsoever. In this respect the towns were an expression of the old Norman culture. Naturally proximity to Dublin, or the lack of it, had a great effect on the formality of the municipal life, and even in the capital a great deal of interaction between the two races took place but it was not official.

———————

Within weeks of the conclusion of the Nine Years' War and Tyrone's surrender the very towns to which the earl had appealed for support, and which had remained stubborn in their loyalty to the crown, suddenly revolted in a mass profession of their Catholicism. However, this was clearly not to be identified with the religion of Gaelic Ulster. This was a form of Catholicism whose adherents professed loyalty to a Protestant monarch. The revolt of the towns in April 1603 is perhaps the first indication of what will be a vital consideration throughout the century: the history of the Old English Catholics is not to be confused with that of their co-religionists, the indigenous Gaelic Irish. What precipitated the revolt of the towns was not the threat of extinction which faced Gaelic Ulster, but rather the new political prospects posed by the accession to the throne of James VI of Scotland as James I of England.

The revolt of the towns in 1603 can be seen in the context of a belief in the king's sympathy for Roman Catholicism, but also as a demonstration to his perhaps Puritan advisers that the towns needed to be treated with respect. Ireland had, and was to continue to have, a long history of such 'loyal' rebellions. The religious divisions of Scotland within which the king grew up were, in the main, those of Roman Catholic *versus* Presbyterian. James was raised as a

Protestant and, it was hoped, as a Presbyterian. As a king who believed in the divine right of monarchy, however, he inclined to a hierarchical rather than a Presbyterian view of society, although on his accession little was known in England of his intentions. There was nothing spontaneous, however, about the blatant and illegal profession of Catholicism by the inhabitants of loyal towns such as Kilkenny, Drogheda, Waterford, Cork and Limerick. In defence of their actions the townsmen claimed not only that James was secretly a Catholic, but also that he was directly descended from a true line of Irish kings. There was certainly more method than madness in this approach, despite its lack of subtlety. Moreover, it proved to be the first of many attempts at adaptation which would eventually push the Old English into taking arms in 1641, professing not only their loyalty but a relationship with the king that placed the onus upon them to protect him from his enemies. When Mountjoy moved against the towns in April 1603 matters were considerably more simple, however. By the time he reached Waterford, four days after his departure from Dublin, the towns of Kilkenny, Thomastown and Wexford had already submitted themselves humbly to the government once its displeasure had been made known. Waterford remained obstinate for two days, but the smaller towns such as Cashel and Clonmel did not even offer resistance.

Yet this exercise in demonstrative disobedience would be wasted unless at least one town could hold out long enough to emphasise the peculiar nature of the protest. Cork was chosen for this purpose largely for geographical reasons. When the mayor protested his loyalty and said that he was 'like the slavish Duke of Venice and could not rule the multitude'[3] he was referring to the fact that the town was built on an island and was only accessible across three bridges which were easily closed. The President of Munster, Sir George Carew, had left the province in the hands of a commission on his departure to England. The task of dealing with Cork fell to the most senior member of this commission available at the time, Sir George Thornton. His duty was clearly to insist that the municipal corporation proclaim the accession of the king according to the Lord Deputy's instructions, sent to the town on 11 April. The corporation delayed for as long as it could, claiming blandly that it was too early to commit itself. Nor was it affected by the information that the king had already been proclaimed elsewhere, not least in Dublin and London. A full twenty-four hours passed in negotiation and prevarication before Thornton himself took the initiative and proclaimed the accession outside the town walls. Although the corporation followed suit, the resistance of the townsmen had really only begun. When Sir Charles Wilmot, head of the commission, arrived from Kerry a week later he found the recalcitrant citizens in the process of demolishing a government fort which stood at the entrance to the town's harbour. After Wilmot had put an end to the demolition shots were exchanged, with the loss of one life. The town was fired upon briefly, and a truce was made five days before the arrival of Mountjoy. The Lord Deputy occupied and garrisoned the town, after which he exercised his martial powers and executed some of the ringleaders. He found it impossible, however, to empanel a jury that would find the town's recorder guilty of treason. Indeed, in addition to these local loyalties, Mountjoy was confronted with a more vital obstacle to pacification. Opposition was united around the long-standing rights granted by the crown to the towns. Before it conceded, Waterford had argued that King John's charter allowed it a specific degree of autonomy—not enough to refuse the Lord Deputy entry to the town, but enough to close its gates to anyone else. Mountjoy replied that he would cut King John's charter with King James's sword—a prophetic sign of things to come, as it turned out.

In response to this organised revolt, the government decided to demonstrate its attitude to the towns by singling out the very town which had offered no resistance and whose loyalty was more assured than all the others. If opposition was to be broken and charters amended, then the obvious place to start was Dublin, the strongest town with the strongest charters. The accession of James provided a good opportunity for the government to act, because of the necessity to update all municipal agreements. In July the Irish government wrote to London requesting that

> the corporations may be restrained to due limitations, such as may stop their former presumption and leave them no ground to interpret themselves to be so peremptory and absolute as they now do: for upon the well-tempering and moderating of the charters of the corporate towns will depend a great moment for the better ordering of the other parts of the kingdom.[4]

This was coupled with another significant request, made in the previous month, from the Protestant Archbishop of Dublin and Bishop of Meath to the effect that 'by some moderate co-actions' the populace might be forced to attend church because they would not do so otherwise.[5] Here were the two weapons which were about to be used against the towns in general and Dublin in particular. Battle would be joined over the next decade on the questions of religious loyalty and chartered independence in such a way that the Old English would be forced to expose the weakness in that loyalty and so undermine their entire future.

The enforcement of the Oath of Supremacy could be decided upon by the government at any time and whenever it wished to force the Old English onto the defensive. It did so in the case of Alderman John Shelton, a Catholic elected to the mayoralty of Dublin in July 1604. Shelton was to take the oath before the barons of the Exchequer on the assumption of his new office; however, the lords had left the city to avoid the plague which was then rampant. The city council did not waste this opportunity and improvised in such a way that the new mayor was installed without taking the oath. According to Sir John Davies, Solicitor-General and later Attorney-General, 'the manner of the refusal was worse than the refusal itself'.[6] The Lord Chancellor and Chief Baron of the Exchequer were commissioned by Sir George Carey, Mountjoy's replacement as Lord Deputy, to investigate the matter. They had the oath read to Shelton, who did not then refuse it but instead asked for time to consider. Consultation with a 'learned divine and a zealous Protestant' assured the mayor that his integrity would be unaffected by the oath, and he gave notice that he was now willing to comply. That Shelton was only playing for time can be seen by the fact that no Catholic could possibly take the Oath of Supremacy, with its declaration that the king was the only head of the church. On his arrival at the Exchequer, therefore, and contrary to the government's expectations, the mayor set about defending his refusal. He argued that the oath referred to the queen and was invalidated by her death. When it was put to him that 'the politic royal body' did not die he conceded the point, but then produced an altered form of the oath which he said he was prepared to take. The Lord Deputy was informed that Shelton had again refused, and the city council was instructed to elect another alderman to the mayoralty. Davies was of the dubious opinion that Shelton had been manipulated by the Catholic clergy, but that he had repented his refusal afterwards—thereby indicating to Davies that the root of the problem was the presence of religious in the city.

All other Catholic aldermen in line for the mayoralty refused to serve if the oath was to be enforced. Eventually the office was bestowed on Alderman Robert Ball, a Protestant, who was awarded the £300 fine imposed on Shelton. Other aldermen then began manoeuvres to avoid the oath (usually on the grounds that they could not support the office of mayor financially). The government responded by an order to the city's recorder to take the oath. Sir William Talbot, a leading recusant, refused and was removed from office. The scene was now set for an open confrontation in which both sides had declared their position. The predicament of the recusants quickly became apparent in so far as the Irish government would always have the initiative and therefore the first call upon the king's attention. James was requested by the government to put an end to all speculation about religious toleration and thereby force the recusants to face the paradox of their situation. Whether the king was a crypto-Catholic, an Anglican or a Puritan makes no difference in the context of early seventeenth-century Ireland. The fact of the matter was that when asked to declare for the New English interest in Ireland he did so consistently. This is hardly surprising in view of the huge losses which Ireland had caused the crown and which English investors were most anxious to recoup. Ireland may have been secure militarily after the defeat of Tyrone, but it had not yet been exploited financially. In order to do this, it would be necessary to overcome all opposition, and in particular the complex variety of attitudes that passed as loyalty. Consequently the king put an end to Catholic hopes with a proclamation, published in October 1605, which ordered all Catholic clergy to be out of the country by 10 December. In doing so James quashed any expectation of religious toleration and reminded the populace of its legal duty to attend Protestant worship. It might at first seem that this last aspect of the proclamation, namely the attendance at divine service, was somewhat incongruous if there were no religious services being held in the country for the people to attend. The condition of the Church of Ireland left a great deal to be desired, but it was still possible to attend service in most of the towns and ostensibly in the territories inhabited by the Old English. Thus it was specifically at the Old English and not the Gaelic Irish that the proclamation was aimed. Some months earlier, when he prorogued the English parliament, the king gave a clear indication of how he perceived issues of obedience. What is notable about the king's view is its affinity with the niceties of the Old English Catholic position. James might have been addressing his loyal Catholic subjects in Ireland when he told his English parliament:

There is no man half so dangerous as he that repugns against order, yet some which make scruple I would use with clemency; but let them meet me with obedience. To discreet men I say, they shall have their desires by grace, but to all I profess they shall extort nothing by violence.... Only I wish you had kept a better form. I like form as much as matter.[7]

The king, however, did not reside in Ireland, and access to his presence entailed dealing first with his government in Dublin, who were not always as subtle as their master. When a deputation of the Pale gentry requested the suspension of the proclamation until they had put their case to the king they were promptly arrested and imprisoned. Following this, the principal citizens of Dublin were chosen for exemplary punishment by the government, now headed by Sir Arthur Chichester (who would remain in office until 1615). The city itself was perceived by Chichester as 'the lantern of the whole kingdom and in that matter the only place whereupon the eyes of expectation of all the rest were earnestly fastened'.[8] Five aldermen and three others, two of whom were merchants, were fined and imprisoned for their refusal to attend divine service. Proceedings were brought against a further five citizens, all of whom were fined and imprisoned. In a letter to the English government Davies summed up the position:

> The multitude was ever made comformable by edicts and proclamations; and though the corporations ... and certain of the principal gentlemen stood out, and the multitude only by their example, yet if this one corporation of Dublin were reformed the rest would follow; and if those gentlemen that were in the Castle were reduced, the whole Pale would be brought to conformity.[9]

There are two points of interest here. The first is the disingenuous view that the people would respond to legislation where matters of religion were concerned. It can be taken for granted that Davies knew this to be an over-simplification of the situation. Yet it was necessary for the government to feign belief in the efficacy of a hardline policy, if only to carry out the initial stages of its implementation. The second point of interest is that it was not the country at large that was to be converted by force; it was not even the loyal towns that had recently rebelled. It was to be the capital itself. As the seat of government, the wealthiest and the most loyal of the towns, Dublin

provided the best target. That the majority of its aldermen were un-
questionably loyal further enhanced the political significance of the
attack (e.g. between March 1599 and December 1600 the city had
granted a loan to the crown which totalled £62,000). The message was
plain: Catholic allegiance would always be questionable, and those
who professed it could not complain if they were attacked for an
anomaly which it was in their power to correct.

Opposition to the government's policy was all the more organised
and coherent as a result of the pointed nature of the attack. When Sir
Patrick Barnewall pleaded the case to the king's secretary Cecil (later
Earl of Salisbury) he warned of a future rebellion which might be
fuelled by the bitterness that had recently been created. The response
of the English Privy Council was to instruct Chichester to moderate
his course sufficiently to enable the lesson to be learned without too
great a loss to the crown of Old English support. It is significant,
however, that part of this middle course of action still entailed the
admonition of some of the principal townsmen. The government
pressed on with further proceedings against two more aldermen and
one merchant. Barnewall had earlier warned Cecil about Lord Chief
Justice Sir James Ley, who had made it his custom to deprive the
accused of a copy of the indictment. In February 1606 a petition of
complaint was drawn up to this effect by some of the recusants who
had been tried by Ley. Meanwhile the response of those aldermen
already fined and imprisoned was to attempt a transfer of their
property to other members of the city council who had not been
accused. This was dealt with in the prerogative Court of Castle
Chamber on the same day as the petition of complaint was signed: the
deeds of transfer were ruled to be null and void, and the participants
in the scheme were committed to jail. Davies described the scheme as
'a most manifest collusion and mockery to all the world' and
explained that the widespread support for the offenders was the
result of a generally held belief that the English government would
intervene on their behalf as a result of Barnewall's influence.[10] While
the Irish government hoped that, on the contrary, a public example
would be made of Barnewall, it had every intention of continuing its
course of action, and in May three more recusant aldermen were
fined and imprisoned.

Legal actions against the recusants continued, although it was by
no means a foregone conclusion that the English Privy Council
would censure Barnewall, whom they committed to the Tower of
London. The case he presented was twofold: he complained of the

measures taken to enforce conformity through the use of the great seal (i.e. the royal prerogative), and he attacked the behaviour of Chief Justice Ley. Thus by a combination of particular and general grievances Barnewall had increased his chances of achieving at least partial success one way or another, and the prevarication of the English government in response to his case must have confirmed him in this approach. This was the first time that the king was confronted with a united Old English opposition, and he could not afford to ignore it. In defence of his government, Chichester professed the more general hope that gains might be made with the populace at large, and shifted the blame for the situation from the recusant citizens to the presence in the country of the Catholic clergy. The recusants were sentenced, he said, because of their 'outward disobedience' both in relation to the king's proclamation and in their refusal to attend Chichester himself at religious service on Sundays. This was, in effect, to say that it was a matter of conformity and not of conscience. The Lord Deputy was no doubt anticipating the moderate policy that would be proposed by the Privy Council, and his intention was to let his government off its own hook. After some hesitation the recusants submitted to this more general accusation; their fines were reduced, and they were released from jail. Yet if the steam was taken out of the immediate situation, the prosecutions continued until April 1607, when the English Privy Council finally issued a direct order to the government to change its policy from one of enforcement to one of moderation.

When this policy is viewed in the context of a move on the part of the English government to break the power of the municipal corporations in the vital areas of economics and politics, it is more explicable in practical terms than such oscillation would suggest. The loyalty of the towns to the English crown was not a matter of degree, but rather one of definition. The basis upon which the towns perceived this loyalty was their charters and the mutual fulfilment of agreements. These charters had been strengthened and reinforced over a period of several hundred years, and no direct assault could be made upon them if the loyalty of the citizens could not also be impugned. This could as easily be done by dramatic measures as by covert erosion. The imprisonment of the recusants, therefore, allowed the government to question this loyalty as a matter of obedience and not religion and, as such, the real effect of this attack was not immediately felt. Likewise, the government's attitude to conversion should not be misunderstood. It made no attempt to hide the distinction between conversion and conformity. Thus it made no pretence at spreading the Protestant faith, but rather held that

> The very action itself is in the abiding in church during divine service, which containeth no spiritual action therein, for he is not commanded to hear or give attention, to pray or yield adoration; only he is commanded to behave himself soberly and modestly, which he ought to do at all times and in all places.[11]

With regard to the towns the situation is similarly straightforward when examined over a period of time. The reason for this is that the religious question can be related to the attacks upon the merchant guilds, the financial independence of the municipal corporations, their liberties, trading privileges and the very charters upon which these were based. They were not co-ordinated attacks in the sense that they were acknowledged as such; they did, however, occur simultaneously. If the question of conformity and conversion in matters of religion can be put to one side, therefore, policies of moderation and enforcement might be seen as more subtle and successful means of destabilisation where the towns were concerned. The fact that the citizens conformed in so far as they attended church, or the fact that they were fined if they did not, was less significant than the simple fact that the municipal corporations had been attacked directly and doubts cast upon their loyalty for the first time. Nor is it incongruous that this loyalty had gone unquestioned by the state throughout previous periods of instability and yet aspersions could now be cast at the time of greatest conquest and military security.

The reaction of the English government to developments in Ireland is one example of how a policy of enforcement could quickly be altered to one of moderation. In its instruction to Chichester to pursue toleration the Privy Council reminded the Lord Deputy that the loyalty of the towns had been a vital bulwark in the past and that to further question this loyalty might well provoke a violent response. This advice was particularly applicable to the President of Munster, Sir Henry Brouncker, who had pursued the question of enforcement with such vigour that the king himself remarked that 'his zeal was more than was required in a governor, however allowable in a private man'.[12] Brouncker's death early in 1607 made it easier for Chichester to implement the new policy, but the President's treatment of the municipal recusants in Munster had provoked a response from the merchant communities which had little to do with religion. Many merchants and others had abandoned the towns under

Brouncker's jurisdiction and threatened to cease trading altogether rather than allow Brouncker to profit from the impost on wines at their expense, and, furthermore, 'they would incur any infliction of the law in that case rather than he should gain any glory or commendation in the work which he intended'.[13] Brouncker's apparent religious zeal had actually exposed the economic factors in the whole religious question more quickly than might otherwise have been the case.

In April 1606 two Englishmen, Thomas Hibbots and William Long, were granted exclusive rights to the export of specified quantities of wheat, wool, sheepskins, hides, tallow and woollen flocks. Although this agreement was only one aspect of the English government's general plan to resume the trading rights of Ireland, and was therefore not intended to be final, the licencees were also granted rights of search and confiscation which should have alarmed all municipal towns. The provisional acceptance by the Privy Council of a scheme proposed by the Earl of Nottingham for a farm of the Irish customs was a clear indication that the role of those who held these customs, namely the towns, was about to change. Another possible cause for alarm was the fact that, apart from the obvious economic gains to be made by both the crown and its speculating supporters, there was a new view of the port towns and their inhabitants which, when held by a New English administrator, automatically excluded them from participating in the new schemes. The views of Sir Thomas Ridgeway, Vice-Treasurer of Ireland, illustrate the point. Besides the reputed idleness of the people of Ireland, and besides the scarcity of money throughout the realm, Ridgeway put forward two other possible reasons for 'the decay of trade and bare intercourse of traffic'. These reasons are significant in that they illustrate how an Englishman working in the Irish administration could view the towns and their inhabitants in such a way that a policy of financial exploitation could be justified. One reason for the low return of the customs was stated to be

> the overruling privileges of most or all of the port towns, where, upon the arrival of any ship whatsoever, they enforce the merchant to stay fourteen days at least without selling any part of his wares to any other, and afterwards at his leisure and their own poor and dilatory manner of payment, the townsmen engross it to themselves, which all merchants naturally abhor.[14]

A categorical distinction is made here between 'all merchants' and 'the townsmen', as if the latter were not merchants. If this view was myopic, it was also paradoxical in so far as the other reason for the decay of trade which Ridgeway put forward took cognisance of the very merchants he had just excluded. He noted

> a wilful peevishness and perverseness in the popish and hollow-hearted merchants themselves (grown as they say upon urging of the Oath of Supremacy and coming to church), rather to desist from trafficking than by their adventures to bring in anything that may prove any way beneficial to the English.[15]

The connection is well made here between the enforcement of a tough religious policy and the alienation of customs rights from those who could not deserve them. Brouncker's extremism in Munster had already made this connection clear, but it was a gross overstatement of the case to suggest that the merchant community would go into a decline rather than see the crown benefit. The interests of the two had for centuries been the same, and it was this symbiotic relationship that had given rise to the very structure of the Anglo-Norman town. Thus it can be seen that the only way in which the Old English could be dispossessed in the immediate future was to call into question a loyalty which was legally defined through chartered agreements. Ridgeway rightly indicated that the insistence upon the Oath of Supremacy had resulted in merchant opposition. What he did not admit was that it was necessary to create this opposition in order to defeat it more successfully. The Old English were well aware of this, but there was little they could do so long as the initiative was with the government. Indeed, the whole question of economic exploitation was to become even more complex when the wealthy members of the Old English (both gentry and townsmen) came to realise that not everything new was undesirable. Ridgeway's proposed solution for Ireland's economic problems left a good deal of scope for the rich to become richer. He suggested that

> There must be an act of parliament that all strangers and others may freely come and trade in all parts of this kingdom, notwithstanding any former charters, privileges, prescriptions or usages to the contrary.[16]

This recommendation was indeed put into effect before the rebellion of 1641 to such an extent that by the mid-1630s the trade of Dublin had increased manyfold, though at the expense of its municipal independence. Yet this change took place in a wider

European context which ought not to be forgotten. Ridgeway's suggestions could, for example, be used to support the view that the struggle between corporate power (either municipal or guild) and 'free trade' was essentially a struggle between the medieval and the modern, the static and the dynamic. There can be no doubt that urban government which was based upon corporate power did in fact portray itself as essentially static. Appeals to charters, formalities, traditions and precedents were intended to support or reinforce a structure whose existence was, of necessity, self-enclosed. Yet such appeals cannot be taken at face value without contradiction. Divided loyalties meant, for example, that while the merchant monopoly was attacked from outside the guild, it was not uncommon for the merchants themselves to support the government with financial loans. The reason for this was straightforward enough. The wealthier inhabitants were compensated for the loss of their privileges by the increase in trade which followed the abolition of guild monopolies. This was not true for the less well-off citizens such as the butchers and bakers who depended upon their market stalls for a living and who now had to compete with newcomers on an equal basis. The net result of this was to be a division among the Old English along economic lines which even affected the type of religious allegiance which had hitherto been united. On the one hand, the wealthy Old English were obliged to be flexible in the face of the Protestant threat; on the other, the ordinary tradesmen had no incentive to do likewise and increasingly found themselves in alliance with a more uncompromising and unilateral form of Catholicism.

All this lay in the future, however, and in the meantime nothing could be done unless the minutiae of all municipal agreements were examined with a view to finding the necessary loopholes. To this effect Chichester was ordered to carry out an inquiry into all existing charters and privileges and to examine those who claimed to hold them. This was promptly done, and proceedings were commenced against Dublin and Limerick. It was the opinion of Sir John Davies that it would be a matter of months before all opposition would be overcome, despite the fact that the corporations were planning to defend themselves. This defence was to be in two parts: first it was hoped to establish that customs and subsidies were not the same thing and, secondly, that the charters in question did indeed confer the disputed rights upon the towns involved. Whether the corporations were aware of the fact or not, the outcome of these proceedings had already been decided upon in advance by the English government. It was pointed out to the Lord Deputy that the essence of the scheme was to change the Irish customs operation along the lines of the new English model, and not the confirmation or renewal of existing privileges. Although Ridgeway had earlier acknowledged that the citizens of Dublin, Waterford and Drogheda were free of poundage under the act of 15 Henry VIII, the English Privy Council instructed the Lord Deputy to express views to the contrary and, as an incentive to compliance, to offer exemption from payment ('of great sums') of arrears. On the presumption of a considerable degree of gullibility on the part of the towns, the Privy Council instructed the Dublin government to promise that the inhabitants would not be 'left in the power of any subject' and would be treated 'as becomes merchants in their honest trade'. It was not to be made known, however, that this treatment of honest merchants would not include recognition of their traditional status or that the government had been ordered to 'diligently investigate the claim of a certain privilege called the Trinity guild, which those towns pretend to their own prejudice'.[17] In response to this situation, the agents for the towns ('making show of good conformity')[18] agreed to put the king's case to their respective authorities in view of the promised remittance of arrears and a stay on the *quo warranto* proceedings.

Whatever the response of the towns, it was necessary for the English government's purpose to maintain the initiative, and to this end a new book of rates for the Irish customs was compiled in 1608 without any consultation with those who were to be affected. It was received by Chichester in March and published immediately. Following this, Salisbury wrote to the customs officers of Chester to inform them that Dublin merchants were no longer permitted the custom-free trade which they had been granted hitherto. Duty was to be paid on all commodities with the exception of small wares intended only for trade within the limits of Dublin city. Such a concession was similar to one made in the same month when the king instructed Chichester to grant 'new charters, with such enlargement of franchises as shall appear convenient', retaining for the crown simultaneously the great and petty customs together with tonnage and poundage (thereby withholding everything the towns actually wanted).[19] Opposition to these measures had mounted to such a height by this time, however, that it was deemed necessary to remove the judicial hearings to London. In view of Recorder Richard Bolton's strong defence of the Dublin privileges there, it is clear that the government had found a favourable decision impossible in any but the London courts.

The proceedings against Dublin will serve to illustrate how things went. The first question concerned a proviso in the act of 15 Henry VIII and was whether the city had been exempted from the payment of poundage or whether this could be claimed by the crown on the basis of common law. Bolton had anticipated the argument and produced evidence to show that the grant of poundage was in fact based upon common law and merely confirmed by statute; the judges were obliged accordingly to find for Dublin. The second issue to be decided upon involved the petty customs to which, Bolton admitted, the city had no recognisable claim. He avoided making the claim at all, however, and with some skill he showed instead that the city 'owned' the river and maintained the port, and that for this they had always charged foreigners 3d in the pound. In other words, by showing that it was not necessarily the petty custom (although that was also 3d in the pound charged to foreigners for the use of the port) the issue could not be decided on the basis of that custom at all. The way was open for compromise, and the court was willing to recognise Bolton's claim if he in turn conceded the petty custom. He did so with the result that foreigners would henceforth be double-charged. The final issue concerned the great custom and revolved around an interpretation of the words *theoloneum* and *consuetudo* which were central to a grant made by Henry II to the citizens of Dublin. Bolton was driven to use St Matthew's Gospel to validate his use of *theoloneum* as an early equivalent of the word *custom*. The court, however, was not impressed, and the claim was overruled. Similarly, the judges held that the word *consuetudo* meant 'the usage in a place' and not custom. Bolton disagreed in a report to Dublin:

> I hope to change their opinions in that point, for I have since searched the records of the Exchequer here in England, where I find the word *consuetudo* was used for the revenue custom in the time of Henry II, Richard I and Henry III, and the word *customes* (which the judges hold to be the proper word for revenue custom) was never intended till the time of Edward II.[20]

Once again, however, the judges disagreed, and the claim was simply overruled. The final result, therefore, was that Dublin retained the right to impose poundage, as did the other major ports of Drogheda, Waterford and Galway; it was agreed to duplicate the petty custom, and the great custom was conceded to the crown.

The four principal ports continued to withhold poundage, however—an action which not only defied the government but threatened to draw trade away from the remaining ports which had earlier agreed to pay. Likewise, resistance was offered by individual traders who now refused to pay duties and who thereby forced the Dublin government to take proceedings against them. The response of the English Privy Council was unequivocal: an additional custom of 12d in the pound (i.e. identical to poundage) was imposed on the ports in question. The king had threatened as much in March 1611, and Chichester acted accordingly in October when it was established that the port towns were not amenable to persuasion. By July of the following year the country's entire customs network was farmed out, and it was clear that as far as the towns were concerned the issue was lost.

The loss to the towns of their vital trading rights was a slow process the effect of which did not become obvious until the reign of Charles I. While the struggle over these rights was taking place a more brisk and dramatic struggle was taking place in Ulster. The Ulster plantation which began after the 'flight of the earls' and the rebellion of Sir Cahir O'Doherty in 1608 was undoubtedly the principal undertaking of James's government in Ireland. The idea had been considered even before the surrender of Tyrone as part of the larger question of how Ireland was to be governed after the war had ended. Unlike the rest of the country, Ulster had maintained its distinctively Irish culture, and it was this very success in survival that obliged the government to think in radical terms. Apart from a policy of plantation, the only other option open was to bring about a gradual conversion of the province to the socio-economic and legal framework within which the rest of the country operated. After the Treaty of Mellifont it appeared that this latter policy was to be pursued. The province was divided into nine counties to which were appointed sheriffs, justices of the peace, coroners and constables. The first assize was held in Donegal in December 1603, and this heralded the beginning of an administrative structure which, it was hoped, would wean the native Irish from the protection of their chiefs and secure for them greater rights under the law.

Yet there was no reason to expect that those chiefs who had so recently declared war upon the crown would tolerate the erosion of their power without opposition. It was the potential of this opposition to erupt, once again, into rebellion that caused the government its greatest concern. Tyrone had been defeated in a tactical battle, and the north had been decimated by Mountjoy's famine, but the Irish had won too many battles not to know that their collective strength was renewable. Such was their awareness of this fact that the king and Mountjoy openly cultivated the goodwill of both Tyrone and O'Donnell. Both were received at court with honour (much to the acute vexation of the English public), and the earldom of Tyrconnell was conferred upon Rory O'Donnell on his return to Ireland in September 1603. Throughout the period which followed Mountjoy proved himself to be the staunchest supporter of Tyrone when the latter set about adapting to the spread of English administration in his territories. Tyrone did this so successfully and exploited the terms of his pardon so adroitly that he actually established a wider control than he had ever enjoyed previously. In this, however, as in many other respects, Tyrone was unique.

Both Davies and Chichester were totally opposed to this policy, but it was clear that unless they could work within the confines set by the king and Mountjoy, they would be unable to counter the growth of the earl's power. They did this through a long-standing dispute which Tyrone had with Donal O'Cahan, chief of Iraght O'Cahan or County Coleraine (later Londonderry). O'Cahan had gone over to the government side in July 1602 while Tyrone was still in rebellion. The loss to the rebels of his territory was considered critical when combined with the defections of two other chiefs, Sir Niall Garbh O'Donnell, Rory's cousin, and Sir Cahir O'Doherty of Inishowen. When O'Cahan submitted to Sir Henry Docwra he relinquished his claim to certain lands which the crown had need of for military purposes. In return he was granted the remainder, with the promise of a patent. The agreement was signed by O'Cahan and Docwra and then ratified by Mountjoy. It had never been the Lord Deputy's intention, however, to uphold O'Cahan's claim against Tyrone. The latter sought rents and services from O'Cahan and began to quarter troops on his land with the open support of Mountjoy. Davies saw his opportunity here to dispossess Tyrone legally and encouraged O'Cahan to bide his time until the case could be settled in his favour. Unfortunately for O'Cahan, his friends were even less trustworthy than his enemies, but he took their advice and made a temporary agreement with Tyrone pending a judicial decision. Tyrone himself was most anxious to have the matter settled as soon as possible, but he was not in a position to do this until he had consolidated his recent gains.

In more ways than one Tyrone was playing against time. Although he had the king's support through Mountjoy, who was now in London, he was opposed implacably in Ireland by Chichester and Davies. The Irish government persuaded the king to publish a proclamation in March 1605 which declared that all of the people were his 'free, natural and immediate subjects'[21] and that in this respect they were under no obligation to lords or chiefs. The proclamation was aimed specifically at the inhabitants of Ulster and emphasised that all freeholders would be unaffected by post-war agreements made between the king and the chiefs. Davies also persuaded the king to appoint a commission to examine all boundaries in the province and to redraw these wherever the crown's interests would be served by so doing.

Two of the largest landholders suffered considerably at the hands of the commission. Rory O'Donnell, now Earl of Tyrconnell, was obliged to witness the division of his territories between himself and his hated cousin Sir Niall Garbh O'Donnell, a staunch ally of the crown and a claimant to the entire O'Donnell territory. He also lost land to the MacSweeneys and O'Boyles in the north and west of Donegal. Unlike those of Tyrone, Tyrconnell's estates were not well managed, and indeed were mortgaged to such an extent that his total income from rents was no more than £300 per annum. His real problem, however, was the support given by the commission to Sir Niall. During the war the latter had joined the forces of the crown on the agreement (made, like O'Cahan's, with Docwra) that he would be granted full title to Tyrconnell, This was to be a fight to the finish within the O'Donnell clan itself, and Sir Niall had proved his determination by killing with his own hand his cousin Manus, Rory's younger brother. The commission knew well what it was doing, however, and Sir Niall was furious that Rory was to retain sufficient power to continue the struggle. Thus both sides were alienated and encouraged to destroy each other. The same treatment was meted out to the Maguires of Fermanagh. The territory was split between its chief, Cuconnacht Maguire, and a kinsman, Conor Roe. Described by Chichester as 'a desperate and dangerous young fellow',[22] Maguire was rumoured to be in contact with potential allies on the continent with a view to another insurrection. The evidence is equivocal on this point and also on Tyrconnell's alleged support and involvement. What is clear, however, is the desire on the part of both of these young men first to preserve their freedom from imprisonment, and then perhaps to bring pressure to bear upon the government. Neither possessed Tyrone's genius for manoeuvring or his long experience in dealing with the English. Their only choice was either to stay and negotiate with a government that was openly supporting their enemies or to flee to the continent and there to decide upon the future.

To understand the 'flight of the earls', therefore, it is necessary to be aware of the separate struggles for survival that were taking place simultaneously. Tyrconnell and Maguire could get no help from Tyrone when the latter was desperately trying to establish himself before Chichester and Davies could plant a president in Ulster. Tyrone urged Tyrconnell not to jeopardise everything by a sudden flight to the continent, but to go to London instead and have his case heard there. It must have been clear to them both, however, that at best Tyrone himself was the only individual with sufficient status to be relatively sure of his safety in London. Tyrone had every reason to deflect Tyrconnell in his plans to escape: if such an event was to occur before he had secured his own estates and titles, he would be implicated automatically in the claims of treason that would follow. He knew well that the Irish government would not spare him above all people if the province was to be opened up for plantation. It was vital, therefore, that he should take the initiative in his dispute with O'Cahan while there was still time. Chichester later recalled that right up to the end Tyrone was earnestly preparing to go to London to have his case settled, 'not withstanding he held himself much bound unto His Majesty, that so graciously would vouchsafe to hear and finally to determine the same, yet that it much grieved him to be called upon so suddenly when, as what with the strictness of time and his present poverty, he was not able to furnish himself as became him for such a journey and for such a presence'.[23] What led Tyrone to being 'called upon so suddenly' to put his case can only be described as bad luck. In keeping with his support of the earl, Mountjoy had recalled O'Cahan's only ally, Sir Henry Docwra, early in 1606, but this was followed by the sudden death of Mountjoy in April. The old balance of power between Tyrone's support at court and the Irish government's threatened attacks in Ulster could no longer be maintained. Tyrone's position was suddenly desperate, and he was now forced to risk all in the hope that he could gain a settlement before the exodus of Tyrconnell and Maguire.

Whether or not he believed possession to be nine points of the law, his solution was to invade O'Cahan's country and seize his cattle. This was done in October, and Davies looked on with keen interest, describing it as the first 'notorious violent act'[24] committed by Tyrone since the ending of the war. O'Cahan's response was equally dramatic: he offered to surrender all his land to the king in order to have it regranted and his title established. The death of Mountjoy, however, had changed everything. O'Cahan had already lost his ally in Docwra, and now Tyrone was without his own support. The only beneficiary could be the government itself and the policy of plantation being pursued by Chichester and Davies. The case was never heard in London because Maguire left for the continent in the following summer to secure a boat large enough to take himself, Tyrconnell, their family and servants, and Tyrone himself if the latter had not secured his position by then. It is extremely unlikely that the government would have tried Tyrone's case in the knowledge that Maguire could return at any time and thereby put the earl in an intolerable position. Tyrone must have known this once Maguire left the country. Without Mountjoy there was little he could do but hope perhaps that Maguire would never return. It was, of course, vital to both Tyrconnell and Maguire that the latter return as quickly as possible before the government could act against them. Tyrone was with Chichester at Slane on Thursday 28 August 1607 when he received the news that he least wished to hear: Maguire had returned, and they were leaving immediately. Later in Rome, Tyrone described his options at that time in simple terms: it was 'better to be poor [in Rome] than rich in a prison in England'.[25] He said nothing of Maguire's return to his host, but it was recalled later that 'he took his leave of the Lord Deputy in a more sad and passionate manner than he used at other times'.[26] He left Slane for Mellifont, the scene of his surrender to Mountjoy, and the house of his friend Sir Garret Moore. On leaving the following day Tyrone 'wept abundantly, giving solemn farewell to every child and every servant in the house, which made them all marvel, because in general it was not his manner to use such compliments'.[27] On Monday he arrived at his house near Dungannon, where he spent two days preparing for his departure. By Friday of the same week he had joined Tyrconnell at Rathmullen in County Donegal, where Maguire had landed. Ninety-nine persons took part in what became known as the 'flight of the earls'.

If there was any doubt on the part of those involved that they had acted wisely, it would have been dispelled immediately when they heard of the fate of Donal O'Cahan, ally of the crown and the government's principal agent in opposing Tyrone. Chichester had him arrested on the absurd suspicion that he had intended to join his enemies in flight. He was imprisoned in Dublin Castle and later removed, in 1609, to the Tower of London, where he died in 1628. He was never tried upon any charge for the likely reason that he had committed no offence; his lands were declared forfeit and became part of the proposed plantation. If such treatment appeared ruthless, it was at least well reasoned. O'Cahan's problem was that no demonstration of loyalty on his part could alter the fact that before his submission in July 1602 he had been an independent Gaelic chief. He was thus of the old order as far as the new schemes were concerned, and his fate would have to be that of the old order itself if his lands were to be opened up. There were two other allies of the crown in almost identical positions to O'Cahan, namely Sir Niall Garbh O'Donnell and Sir Cahir O'Doherty. Just as Tyrone had lost the support of Mountjoy, so these three loyalists had lost the support of their staunch ally Sir Henry Docwra. With the exodus of Tyrone and Tyrconnell, the government had no further need of these chiefs, or indeed to maintain any large Gaelic landholder of their stature. O'Doherty was in the process of securing a place at court in an effort, somewhat similar to Tyrone's, to counterbalance the power of the Irish government. It was made abundantly clear to him, however, by Docwra's replacement, Sir George Paulet, that he would enjoy no such privilege. The failure of Tyrconnell and Maguire to survive had forced Tyrone to act with little initiative or hope. Now the flight of the earls forced O'Doherty into open rebellion as his only method of defence. His hope was undoubtedly to put himself into a bargaining position and perhaps then to retire to court. That he was not unrealistic in his aim can be seen both in the favourable treatment of Tyrone as a rebel and in the fact that he did indeed enjoy support in London. On the very day he chose to launch his rebellion the Irish government received an order from London that O'Doherty should be restored to his former position. It was, however, too late. In a short insurrection he seized the fort of Culmore and burnt Derry, but he was killed shortly afterwards in a skirmish in July 1608.

It is debatable whether Sir Niall Garbh took part in the struggle, but he was accused of doing so immediately. He shared O'Cahan's fate in that he was arrested and accused of treason. There were more grounds for the government's case against Sir Niall in so far as he was a friend of O'Doherty and would no doubt have sympathised with one whose fate he was now likely to share. He was tried in Dublin in June 1609, but the jury could not be persuaded to find him guilty despite their being locked up without food for several days. As a consequence of this, he was transported to the Tower of London in the same boat that took O'Cahan. He died there without further trial of his case in 1626.

The plantation of Ulster which followed these events was a logical continuation of the large aims of the Irish government. There were, however, differences of opinion as to the best method of dealing with Gaelic opposition in the province. Chichester was of the view that the native Irish must be contained as a recognised group within the new arrangement. Davies maintained a contrary view, namely that there was no place for a people who could only cause trouble in the future. Both were agreed that to succeed the plantation must maintain itself in such a way that cultural superiority would eventually win the day. From the beginning, however, it was not matters of culture which determined the course of events but matters of efficacy. The government survey which was carried out during the summer of 1608 found the counties of Armagh, Cavan, Coleraine, Donegal, Fermanagh and Tyrone to belong to the crown. This was done in spite of the assurances given to freeholders before the earls' departure that their titles were secure. Clearly it was the more thoroughgoing policy of Davies which was to hold sway. He himself was appointed to a committee in London which prepared an overall plan, completed in January 1609, that was carried out in the following year. All the native inhabitants were to be removed from the areas which were assigned to English and Scottish undertakers. The Irish were to be allowed to remain on the holdings granted to the church, the servitors (i.e. military officers who had served against Tyrone) and the small number of Gaelic landholders who were to be included in the plantation. The land grants were to be of three sizes, each with an addition of bog and woodland which was to be rent-free. The 'great proportion' comprised 2,000 acres, the 'middle proportion' 1,500 acres, and the 'small proportion' 1,000 acres. The entire county of Coleraine was granted to the city of London largely because its military and commercial importance necessitated its colonisation on a more systematic footing than the other areas. Land was first assigned to the Church of Ireland, to Trinity College, and to the authorities whose task it was to establish a school in each county. Following this, approximately one-third of the land was distributed by the English and Scottish Privy Councils to those undertakers who agreed to fulfil the conditions of plantation. In theory these conditions were quite straightforward. Rent was fixed at £5 6s 8d per 1,000 acres; a five-year residence was required, together with the settlement of twenty-four males from a minimum of ten families of English or Lowland Scottish origin. The Oath of Supremacy was obligatory, as was the erection of at least one building capable of storing arms and defending the settlement. No Irish tenants were permitted, nor was land to be alienated in any way to the Irish by the undertakers. It was the task of the government in Ireland to approve applications made by both servitors and natives. Conditions for the former were similar to those for the undertakers except that they were permitted to take Irish tenants on payment of a 50 per cent surcharge. The native Irish were excused the Oath of Supremacy but obliged to fulfil all other conditions, in particular those relating to the introduction of English methods of agriculture and management. By the end of 1610 the distribution of land within the framework laid down by Davies and the committee was complete. Owing to inaccurate surveys, profiteering and the manipulation of loopholes, however, the proportions allotted were far in excess of the intended acreage. The net result was that approximately one hundred undertakers (a little over fifty per cent of whom were Scottish) received a quarter of the land granted; the servitors (who numbered about fifty) received a fifth; the native Irish who received grants and those who were exempted from plantation (who numbered about three hundred in all) received approximately a fifth; the remainder went to the Church of Ireland, Trinity College and the Lord Deputy (who received a grant of the entire peninsula of Inishowen, which had recently belonged to Sir Cahir O'Doherty).

The initial stages of the plantation scheme went smoothly enough, but the crux of the matter lay in the difference between the proposals of Davies and those of Chichester. Davies was a relative newcomer to the scene and tended to see the crown's options with greater clarity and simplicity than was suggested by reality. Chichester, on the other hand, was an ex-soldier and administrator who tried to bear in mind the long-term consequences of any innovatory policy. He was not happy with the basis of the plantation, with its emphasis on racial segregation and exploitation. There were other models, not least of which were the non-escheated counties of Antrim and Down where colonisation had proceeded along individual lines and where Chichester himself was one of the three principal landholders (the others being James Hamilton and Hugh Montgomery). The problem was, and would remain, the native population. In practice it was not feasible to force the inhabitants off their traditional areas of occupation, and even if this could be done, it would be impossible then to prevent their return. Consequently the government was dubious about its abilities in this respect and came to condone unofficially the tendency of the planters to engage natives on their lands. The undertakers did this not only for convenience, in so far as it provided them with the labour they would otherwise have had to import, but also because the Irish were willing to pay double rents in order to remain in their own areas. Looking on from London, Lord Chancellor Sir Francis Bacon summed up the situation: 'Take it from me that the bane of a plantation is when the undertakers or planters make such haste to a little mechanical present profit, as disturbeth the whole frame and nobleness of the work for times to come.'[28] He and Chichester were not the only ones who saw danger in the erection of an unstable base. Sir George Carew went so far as to prophesy a union of disaffection between the native Irish and the Old English forged by the unsophisticated methods being used to disinherit both groups—a prophecy that was amply fulfilled by events in the 1640s.

In order to secure the plantation of Ulster, it would be necessary for the crown to summon a parliament for the attainder of those who had fled the province and for the acknowledgment of the king's title to the escheated lands. The Old English at this time could still see no cause which might be common to both themselves and the Gaelic Irish; consequently they were anxious to avail of the opportunity of confirming the attainders to demonstrate their loyalty. The Gaelic Irish, for their part, would prove slow to forget this. As the Old English saw it, however, they too had been roughly handled since 1603, and it would be imperative that they use the parliament to exert some control over the government. The crown, however, was simply not willing to bargain with the Old English. Moreover, it had a dramatic plan to deal with the problem posed by the large majority of Catholics who would be elected to parliament by the Old English. The plan was consistent with all that had happened since the beginning of the reign. A sufficient number of boroughs would be created in which the Oath of Supremacy would be obligatory for election. Thus the traditional majority of the Old English in what they considered to be their own representative body would be ended at a stroke; and so it was. The plan was not put into effect until the last minute, while the Old English busied themselves with the question of their right to participate in the drafting of legislative proposals. Whether or not they were disarmed by the relatively mild programme put forward by the government, they went ahead with their preparations for the election of their members. The programme was completed by September 1612 and contained no measures likely to force the Catholics into a confrontation. By the time the writ was issued for summoning the parliament in March of the following year, however, thirty-eight new seats had been created in Ulster, eighteen in Munster, sixteen in Leinster, and twelve in Connacht. Many of these 'boroughs' were not even villages, and the Old English protested to the king 'that by the votes of a few elected for that purpose, under the name of burgesses, extreme penal laws should be imposed upon your subjects'.[29] They were, however, missing the point. The aim of the parliament was not to impose 'extreme penal laws' but rather to consolidate the gains recently made and to do so by neutralising the Old English Catholics in the process. The plan bore fruit when the election results were declared: the old boroughs had returned a Catholic majority of two to one, but when the eighty-four new boroughs were added to this the government had an overall Protestant majority of thirty-two.

The opposition mustered by the Old English to this barefaced manoeuvre was indicative of their peculiar dilemma. They could only protest within the rules, but in doing so they would have to recognise the king's right to create as many boroughs as he pleased. When parliament met on 18 May 1613 the peers absented themselves as a demonstration of their discontent. Further protest was made by the Commons, who objected to the artificial majority of Protestants. A scuffle broke out on the election of a Speaker when the government's nominee, Sir John Davies himself, was physically lifted up by his supporters and deposited in the lap of the Catholic Sir John Everard, who had been installed at an opportune moment in the chair. This type of impotent action was indicative of the frustration of the Old English, bound as they were to respect the rules. They withdrew indignantly from the chamber, forcing the government into an adjournment. Negotiations were likewise adjourned pending an appeal to England, and parliament was prorogued on 17 June.

The king indicated his feelings by appointing Chichester as head of a commission to investigate matters in August. Not surprisingly, the commission found that the Catholics had in fact no grievances whatsoever. James expressed as much to a delegation sent to him in April 1614, but when he gave his final judgment in August he was more conciliatory. Some of the new boroughs had been granted charters after the writ of summons had been issued, and he ordered that these returns should be cancelled, thereby diminishing the Protestant majority to six. He also instructed the government not to put forward two bills aimed at the expulsion of Jesuits and seminary priests and the prohibition on the education of Catholics abroad. The opposition accepted these concessions because they had no choice. They claimed victory over the government, but it was not difficult to see that such a move could never be made again. In any further parliament the right of the new boroughs to elect members could not be questioned. Indeed, even in the concessions granted to the Old English it became apparant that the king had merely shifted his ground. In place of the new legislation against Catholics he ordered Chichester to revive the enforcement of the Oath of Supremacy in the county commissions of the peace and the municipalities, to pursue the disqualification of Catholic lawyers, and generally to enforce a more earnest policy with regard to recusancy.

The response of the Catholics when parliament reassembled on 11 October 1614 was all the more marked by the fact that they found themselves temporarily in a majority. Their behaviour was exemplary, and a good deal of the government's programme was passed, including the acknowledgment of the king's title and the attainder of the rebels. Parliament was subsequently prorogued in November and convened again in April 1615, when it dutifully passed the subsidy. A certain amount of negotiation went on with regard to the religious question, but this did not affect the business of the house, and during the recess following the prorogation of 16 May parliament was dissolved. The legislative programme of the only Irish parliament of the reign was practically harmless as far as the Old English were concerned. The king and his government were not only acting within the letter of the law, they could also argue that they had not even contravened its spirit. The Catholics might respond that it was not the spirit of the law which had been contravened, but rather the spirit of parliament itself, that unique institutional form of their collective identity. Yet neither the government nor the king had taken advantage of this historic eclipse of Catholic power; the response of these loyalists was therefore simply one of indignant frustration.

In the meantime the government reinforced its plantation policy by extending its scope to include areas in Wexford, Longford, Ely O'Carroll and Westmeath. Although in each case conditions were different, the essential aim was to solidify government support through the creation of permanent interest groups. Thus there were often no rebels to disinherit, but the policy was nevertheless enforced as if there were. In Wexford, for example, the agreement had been straightforward in theory. Landholders would submit their titles to the crown and have them regranted within the terms of the new agreement. As soon as this surrender had taken place in 1610, however, the titles themselves were called into question. Almost all of the proprietors were Gaelic Irish and consequently were treated in the same way as their Ulster counterparts had been. One delegation of petitioners who travelled to London, for example, were simply arrested and shipped off to Virginia. While the practice of transportation itself was not uncommon (thousands of able-bodied males had been shipped to the continent since the war), it was not fully realised by the petitioners that the government's ends were predetermined and any means would suffice which brought these about. The eventual outcome was that approximately one-quarter of the original title-holders were granted land, while the remainder were dispossessed in favour of the undertakers. Local conditions varied in each area, but the overall effect was the same, and when the commission of 1622 reviewed the progress of these plantations it found that little or nothing had been done to alter the character of the areas. Those of the 'mere Irish' who could not resist or defend themselves against the legalities of defective titles had either lost their property or had become small leaseholders. A few had fared better and had managed to gain the freehold to their allotments, but these were in the minority, and even this freehold was subject to the continued goodwill of the government.

The plantations of Wexford and the midlands belong in the wider context of the post-war conquest of the country. The primary factor throughout this period was the continued government support for any measures which would further establish its control. Thus by the time Chichester was recalled in 1615 the opportunity had already been taken to follow the parliamentary gains with a new assault upon the recusant towns. In accordance with the king's instruction that the old anti-Catholic legislation was to be revived, the new Lord Deputy, Sir Oliver St John, found on his arrival that more than eighty of the principal townsmen in Leinster and Munster were in prison for their refusal to take the Oath of Supremacy. The corporation of Dublin had removed itself from the front line by electing Protestant aldermen to the mayoralty whenever it foresaw trouble. The provincial towns had no such resource, however; and where the capital had earlier been used for a demonstration of the crown's new policy, it was now the turn of Waterford. The Catholic corporation was asked to do the impossible, namely to administer the Oath of Supremacy to its mayor. A refusal was inevitable, and although St John himself would have liked to enforce the oath on all corporations in this way, he settled for the exemplary reduction of one of the oldest loyal towns. In July 1616 the mayor-elect refused to take the oath and so began a legal battle which took approximately two years to run its course. The government did not hesitate to use all means necessary to reduce the townsmen; the case was referred to the English Privy Council, while attempts were made simultaneously to empanel a local jury that would find for the crown. By March 1618 both lines had converged: a compliant jury had brought in the desired verdict, while a commission of inquiry had concluded that the municipality's charter should be revoked. Consequently the town was 'reduced to be a mere disfranchised village'[30] in the face of its inhabitants' stubborn, if helpless, resistance. The net effect of this confrontation was not actually in the government's favour. The revocation of the corporation's charter relieved the Catholics from a most unwelcome struggle and placed the onus on the government to make all the remaining moves in this public example of confiscation. In keeping with the crown's general policy of confrontation and plantation, it was decided to invite a sufficient number of worthies from England to inhabit, as it were, all the necessary municipal offices. The idea was not only inane, it was a significant example of the simplistic determination of a government which saw all opposition merely as so many obstacles to be either overcome or bypassed, it made no difference which. In the event the corporation of Bristol rejected the proposal that it should send thirty of its principal families to Waterford and the plan was abandoned. As a result of the dispute, Waterford remained without a charter or a municipal corporation for the rest of James's reign. What was particularly clumsy about the government's heavy-handed approach was that it could not mete out similar punishment to the other recusant towns without immobilising the economy, while at the same time it had by now caused a considerable degree of ill-will among the Old English, who were not likely to overlook such a blatant attack.

Meanwhile the collection of fines for non-attendance at divine service was stepped up and extended to include women. Similarly, the system of collection itself was altered and the onus placed upon the Primate and his appointees to administer it. Another lucrative source of finance which was reorganised at this time was the control of wardships. A commission was appointed in 1616 to update procedures, and this culminated in the establishment of a Court of Wards in 1622. Both the collection of recusancy fines and the Court of Wards, with its arbitrary exactions, had become increasingly important as a means of moving Ireland in the direction of financial self-sufficiency. The king's minister behind this aim was Lionel Cranfield, Earl of Middlesex, on whose appointment as Lord Treasurer of England a commission was dispatched to Ireland in 1622 to investigate ways and means of achieving this rectitude. A considerable reorganisation of the entire administrative structure was begun as a result of the commission's recommendations, but Cranfield himself fell from power in 1624 and all initiatives were gladly dropped by the government in Ireland. One result of this attempted reform which took effect, however, was the recall of St John and the appointment of Henry Cary, Viscount Falkland. From the beginning of his period in office St John, now Viscount Grandison, had been at odds with the council in Dublin, and it was hoped that his replacement would facilitate government reforms without acknowledging the conflict which Grandison himself had brought about by his zeal.

Orders were issued in June 1623 for the enforcement of the Oath of Supremacy on the election of municipal officials, but all initiatives were then suspended temporarily pending the outcome of the attempts to arrange a marriage between Prince Charles and the daughter of the King of Spain. A Spanish match would alter the position of the Old English (and even the Gaelic Irish) to a considerable extent, because the future queen would, of course, be a staunch Catholic. Indeed, the Irish recusants waited in great anticipation, and in some rural areas the marriage was actually proclaimed to the relief and joy of the populace. All hopes were dashed, however, when Charles returned in October 1623 to announce the rejection of his suit and his great indignation as a consequence. England prepared for war with Spain, and the immediate effect of this dramatic shift in alliance was the temporary suspension of anti-Catholic policies in Ireland. The death of James I in March 1625 and the accession of Charles I was of less significance to the Old English than the war with Spain. Suddenly their loyalty and their financial support was in demand, and the English government's fear of a Spanish landing in Ireland was now more real than it had been at any time since the flight of the earls. It appeared that, at last, the balance of power in Ireland was about to shift.

The Crown and the Catholics: Royal Government and Policy, 1625-37

IMMEDIATELY after his succession to the English throne Charles married Henrietta Maria, the sister of the Catholic King Louis XIII of France. This was the first of three Catholic marriages which the Stuart Kings of England were to embark upon, and its significance cannot be overestimated. The seventeenth century in Europe witnessed the decline of Spain and the simultaneous rise of France. One of the principal effects of this new balance of power was the development of a concept of monarchy which, although absolute, was unlike the Spanish model in that it sought independence from the papacy. It also sought independence from those political forces within its own realm, and for Charles this meant the control of the English parliament. Historians will continue to debate the nature of the constitutional conflict which arose in the early part of the century and erupted into war in the 1640s. What is clear, however, is that from the beginning of the reign of James in 1603 until the final defeat of his grandson at the Battle of the Boyne in 1690 the Stuart kings took the initiative against their enemies more times than not, often in the face of impossible odds. The links from mid-century onwards between this form of dynamic kingship and that of Louis XIV of France are many, but it must also be pointed out that the trends were present during the reign of James I. Certainly by the accession of Charles I the policy of testing the king's power through confrontation was established in the principal areas of politics and religion. In general it can be said that the Old English in Ireland were supporters of the crown in this contest both through their own natural sympathies and the antipathy of the English parliament towards them. This, however, was merely the potential for mutual support between the crown and its loyal subjects. What proved to be the impediment was the fact that rarely, if ever, could the king put the affairs of Ireland before those of England. This meant in effect that the Old English could only win by default; in other words, events in England must first turn in their favour before any local success they might achieve could be taken advantage of.

In the summer of 1625 the English parliament refused to back the government's policy of fortifying Ireland at England's expense, the cost in question being approximately £3,000 per month. The Old English were only too pleased to supply the king if in turn he would facilitate them in their demands. In September Charles agreed that the Old English should raise their own forces, but this caused an immediate protest from the New English Protestants in the country, and the plan was dropped by the following spring. Here was the conundrum in its simplest form. The Old English wished to express their loyalty; the New English perceived this as an attempt to take the initiative and responded by casting official doubt on the loyalty of Catholic subjects to their Protestant monarch. There is no doubt that the Protestants in Ireland did indeed feel threatened by the possibility of the country being garrisoned by the Old English, but their attempts to discredit their opponents' loyalty when the king himself was naturally sympathetic was disingenuous to say the least. Discussions took place throughout the summer between the government and the representative of the Old English, Sir John Bath. A compromise of sorts was arrived at whereby the Old English agreed to fund the expansion of the army to 5,000 foot and 500 horse in return for twenty-six 'matters of grace and bounty' offered by the Lord Deputy on behalf of the crown. These were forerunners of what were later known as the Graces. The most important were the suspension of the collection of fines for recusancy and the abolition of the Oath of Supremacy where inheritance, the practice of law and the holding of official office were concerned. In November Lord Deputy Falkland convened a meeting with the Old English representatives to discuss the terms of the proposed agreement. It was put to him that the reintroduction of trained bands would indicate government confidence and confirm its good intentions. Anxious to avoid committing himself to anything so concrete at this point, however, Falkland suggested an assembly along the lines of a parliament in which these matters might receive the full approval of the Old English throughout the country. This assembly convened in April 1627 and reaffirmed categorically the demand for trained bands in return for the subsidies promised.

It was necessary for the New English to be included in these arrangements, but they were reluctant participants. In the more exalted language of their clergy, their disquiet was expressed in sermons preached by the Bishop of Derry, George Downham, and James Ussher, Lord Primate and Archbishop of Armagh. The sermons stressed the point that toleration of Catholicism in exchange for money should be strongly condemned. In keeping with this, a request was then made by the Irish government to re-commence the recusancy fines, just as the assembly was in the act of disbanding. The Earl of Westmeath, who was associated with Bath in his discussions with the government, responded by a similar request that the negotiations be transferred to England, and in June the king agreed to meet an elected delegation of the Old English. The months from July to November were taken up with the conventions throughout the country and the election of this delegation. In January 1628 eight representatives of the Old English and three of the New English met the king.

Fifty-one Graces were agreed upon in return for three successive subsidies of £40,000 English, to be paid quarterly. As part of the agreement a parliament was to convene in November to legislate for the new Graces, but in the meantime the first of the subsidies was to be collected. To protests from the Irish government Charles responded by compromising himself immediately and gave a reassurance that the proposals for the army were to be subject to council approval. He further ignored the intent of the agreement itself by enlarging the army at one stroke to its proposed capacity of 5,000.

The assassination of the king's chief adviser, the Duke of Buckingham, was followed by an immediate foreign policy reversal which considerably weakened the bargaining position of the Old English. Peace negotiations were opened with France and Spain (and were concluded respectively in April 1629 and November 1630). The government could now halve the Irish army and afford to collect the subsidy over an extended period. The diffusion of foreign conflict meant in effect that Old English compliance or support was no longer necessary to the king. The change was indeed abrupt. While pre-parations were under way to hold a parliament Falkland was informed by the English government that the requirements of Poynings' Law had not been met and that consequently parliament could not convene as planned on 3 November. The displeasure expressed by the Old English at this treatment was predictable; what was more notable, however, was that they continued to pay the subsidy. Their credibility at the bargaining table was further weakened when Falkland was instructed to issue a proclamation against Roman Catholics and ordering the dissolution of religious houses throughout the country. The proclamation was issued on 1 April 1629, two weeks before the Lord Deputy himself was recalled (as a result of his loss of patronage on Buckingham's death). He was replaced by Lords Justices Cork and Loftus in October, an appointment which signalled nothing but discomfort for the Catholic population. The following year saw the closure of religious houses throughout the country and the suppression of religious observance. The most famous incident took place in Dublin, and it illustrates the divisions within communities which were being caused by the short-term pragmatism of crown policy. On the surface, the occurrence which took place in December 1629 was straightforward enough. Dublin's Protestant mayor, Christopher Forster, the sheriffs (both conveniently Protestant) and the Protestant archbishop were instructed by the Lords Justices to disrupt the celebration of a mass on St Stephen's Day. This they dutifully did and with military support arrested two friars and confiscated the chalice and vestments; a riot broke out immediately during which the perpetrators were chased through the streets by a large mob who forced them to release the priests.

Yet the mayor's signal and sectarian action would be inconsistent with the interests of his Catholic fellow-aldermen if there was not an additional motive behind the provocation. An anonymous Catholic member of the municipal government commented upon the disruption:

> You desire to know whether this act was by direction out of England. No, it was by direction of council table here and, as we conjecture, it was done of purpose to draw the soldiers on the city; for we stood out that we would not give the soldiers lodging nor fire and candlelight, and now have we two companies both forced on us, whereof we are constrained to pay one hundred pounds, sterling, for this three months past. We were on sending of an agent for England and have provided two hundred pounds, sterling, for this and he was to go away the Monday before Christmas, and the justice, hearing thereof, had sent for the mayor and, after communication with the justice, our mayor would suffer no agent to go, so as after we had made out instruction and fitted all things with the consent of the mayor, recorder, all the aldermen and commons, we were

dashed; so as you now may perceive, it was a plot to dash our agent and to draw the soldiers on us.[1]

The writer was undoubtedly a member of the staunch Catholics within the city council (probably William Bellew, one of the 'sheriffs' peers') who had an order passed in the Easter assembly to the effect that the city would no longer support the soldiery, and that what money it would make available was to be looked upon by the government as a loan. This could only be construed as an insult likely to provoke an antagonistic reaction. The aldermen who favoured compromise cannot have approved this action, but the Catholics among them could equally not have supported the crown without exposing themselves severely to the citizenry. The meeting between the mayor and Lords Justices produced a solution. A conflagration would be necessary to invoke the power of the crown behind which the mayor and aldermen would then be obliged to stand. All that was needed, therefore, was a catalyst.

Charles Lord Wilmot was appointed as general of the army in Ireland by the crown in August 1629. On taking up the office he wrote to Forster informing him of the city's duty to house some fifty soldiers. The 'mayor and citizens' refused, which caused Wilmot to refer the matter to England with the comment that

> Such conduct must not be tolerated; if it is, the action of Dublin will be made a precedent and all the other towns of Ireland will stand upon their charters. It is really the gravest question of the time.[2]

The aldermen would no doubt have agreed with this assessment, but did not wish to support the government just yet. The real issue as far as the Irish government was concerned was not the billeting of soldiers but the source of the warrant for such billets. After the riot Wilmot wrote to the English government in January:

> If [the Catholic religious in the city] do not go, we must send for a greater garrison to reside amongst them. None of the papist aldermen stirred to assist the mayor in his danger; six of them have been committed thereof and as many of the common people as the Lords Justices could lay hands on. They cannot proceed, however, without more soldiers, whom I have sent for.[3]

Yet Wilmot could not be content with the capitulation of the city council because the aldermen, in doing so, had ensured that their action would redound not to his benefit but to that of the Lords Justices. Thus outmanoeuvred by an alliance between the government and the aldermen, he complained that

> At last, after three days' dispute, they [i.e. the municipal government] said they would obey the warrant of the Justices if it were sent to them. To allow such a system would be a great disservice to the king. If I were abroad or in the field, should every warrant for accommodation of my army have to be sent to Dublin for the signature of the Justices? If such a concession is made in Dublin it will be insisted upon elsewhere.... The stiff urger of this disobedience was one Catelyn, recorder of the town, a serjeant-at-law and the king's counsel.[4]

Catelyn's role had been to draw Wilmot's anger away from Cork and Loftus so that no open breach could ensue. Although convicted for instigating the disturbance, the recorder protested that he had, in fact, defended the warrants of the Lords Justices, which had never been, nor would be, ignored by the city. To conclude the affair it was necessary to extend the logic of the government's position. Six of the aldermen were arrested; their release a few days later was counterbalanced by an order that they be obliged to witness the seizure of the major religious houses in the city. The closures took place without incident, so that Cork could report: 'This is a great triumph for the good cause.'[5] Although it was necessary to sacrifice Catelyn's position (he was temporarily suspended at Wilmot's behest), the Lords Justices were not constrained in their expression of thanks to the mayor, whom they knighted for his defence of the king's religion and in compensation for the odium which he had brought upon himself as a result. The Franciscan house in Cook Street was demolished in order to indicate to all concerned the government's serious attitude to religious conformity.

What was significant about the successful execution of this scheme was the manner in which the aldermen had achieved their aims. The arrest of six of their Catholic members, together with 'as many of the common people as the Lords Justices could lay hands on', was an ingenuous, if not barefaced, amalgamation of two disparate groups: the common people, to be charged with the active defence of their clergy, and the aldermen, to be charged with doing nothing. As a result of the opprobrium which was conferred upon them, the aldermen were freed from any imputation of betrayal by the commons or citizenry. If the Lords Justices were particularly amenable to a set-up such as this, it was because of the peculiar nature of their interim government.

The government of Loftus and Cork could never have been more than interim, if only for reasons of finance. The agreed subsidies were due to come to an end and would either have to be re-negotiated or other sources tapped. The Lords Justices, because of their own interests, could not have managed the parliament promised to the Old English and which was necessary to the agreement of a new subsidy. Instead they proposed the rigorous collection of recusancy fines, a suggestion which itself indicated the narrowness of their government policy. The king, however, had already decided by the end of 1631 that Thomas Viscount Wentworth should take up the reins of government in Ireland.

———

One of the great Lord Deputies of the century, Wentworth was a re-markable man in many ways. At a time of increasingly bitter divisions in English society between the king and his parliamentary subjects Wentworth had changed sides more than once, yet seemed to do so with great conviction. Before Charles had deprived him of a seat in the parliament of 1626 he had already been rebuffed by the king on two occasions when he had offered his services to the crown. He then not only succeeded in gaining a seat in the parliament of 1628, but also became one of the two leaders of the House of Commons. Having already spent a brief period in prison for his refusal to pay the forced loan demanded by the king, Wentworth was seen by his con-tempories not only as a committed parliamentarian but also as one of considerable political skill. Under his leadership (and that of the renowned common lawyer Sir Edward Coke) the Commons drew up a Bill of Rights aimed at attacking the growing and dictatorial powers of the king. If support from the House of Lords had been expected for this bill, it was not forthcoming; a compromise was agreed upon and a Petition of Right drawn up instead. A severe political attack was also made upon the favourite Buckingham and upon the king's support for the High Church policies within the Anglican com-munity which were known as Arminianism.

Why Wentworth changed his allegiance towards the end of 1628 has never been established beyond dispute, and it is still possible to argue that the enmity between Charles and the Commons was not such that loyalties could only be unilateral. One thing is certain, however: Wentworth's conversion coincided with the death of Buckingham and the opening of the government to a great number of men who would not otherwise have had such access. He accepted a peerage and was soon appointed as President of the Council of the North. Here he developed the theory of government which he later described as 'thorough' and which meant in effect that there could be no compromise where the king's will was concerned. Although it was said that his appointment to the deputyship of Ireland was brought about by his enemies, there can be little doubt that his qualities both as a leader and an administrator suggested him for the job of putting the country on a more permanent and firm financial footing.

Charles announced his decision to appoint Wentworth to Ireland in January 1632, but the new Lord Deputy was not sworn in until July of the following year. In the meantime the king was not pleased with the direction of his government under Loftus and Cork. He wrote to them in April expressing his annoyance that no arrangements were being made for a continuation of the subsidy. If the Old English were not eager to fulfil their duties in this respect, then the recusancy fines might justifiably be renewed; an order was included for the publication of the letter itself. The king's intention was clear, and it is an indication of the animosity felt by the Lords Justices, particularly by the Earl of Cork and his party, towards the Old English that they ignored his demand for the negotiation of a new subsidy and instead put into effect his threat with regard to the fines; moreover, Cork had the letter suppressed rather than published.

This precipitous action on the part of the New English allowed Wentworth to side with their Catholic opponents. It is likely, however, that even without this impetus he would have sided with the Old English for two basic reasons. Their sympathies were with the king and his attempts to bring about a stronger Catholic element within the Church of England. The sympathies of the New English, on the other hand, were far more with parliament and its opposition to this Arminianism. Secondly, and of more vital significance for the course of events, the Old English had already indicated the area of their greatest weakness. They had continued to pay the subsidy even though the king had reneged on his part of the bargain. They had been obliged to do so, and it is more than likely that Wentworth knew they would have to do so again if circumstances demanded it. The Old English hoped, however, that this could be avoided by successful negotiation and, above all, by convincing the Lord Deputy that his interests were also theirs.

———————

Before he set foot in Ireland Wentworth had arrived at a formula for government which proved to be the keynote of his administration and in some respects of his political life. In January 1633 he wrote of his new task: 'The truth is, we must there bow and govern the native by the planter and the planter by the native.'[6] Short of complete ineptitude, the formula could not fail where Ireland was concerned because it implied a system of spoliation in which the recipients had no choice but to compete against each other. However, as the basis of a policy it contained two flaws which should have been evident even on paper. Ireland was divided not into two camps, but into three. When Wentworth used the term 'native' he did not mean the Gaelic Irish but rather the Old English. To the latter group the term 'native' was an insult to their historical orthodoxy akin to being described as 'mere Irish' (meaning 'of pure Irish descent'). The distinction was vital: what their 'Englishness' amounted to was an agreement with the crown as to how the country should be governed, and in this sense they were not 'natives' but 'planters'. Moreover, to describe them as natives left no room in the formula for the natives themselves. The Ulster plantation was a settlement which required successful government throughout the country; failure to achieve this would create an opportunity which might be availed of by the dispossessed, who would not then confuse their own condition with that of the Old English. As for Wentworth's use of the term 'planter', the inconsistency is equally significant. The New English could surely take it for granted that they were not just 'planting' civility in Ireland, but that this entailed the genesis of a culture which was specifically that of the king in matters of religion, politics and economics. That is to say that they were supposedly at one with the king in a way that it was not possible for the Old English to be since the Reformation. No one was under any doubt, however, that this was not the case. Most important of all where the rule of Ireland was concerned, the New English did not share the king's growing commitment to High Church Arminianism. In short, if their own test of loyalty was one of religious conformity, they were increasingly to be found on the wrong side of the king himself. Thus they were not Wentworth's natural allies which, as English Protestants in Ireland, they might have been.

The second flaw in Wentworth's political formula was not one of distinction but one of foresight. It is true that the king was cutting a new path through the English constitution, and we can only presume that he expected to arrive at a new consensus with his own powers increased and with the active participation of those who had hitherto been his opponents. What this implied, more than anything else, was a redistribution of power which would ultimately result in a new constitutional equilibrium. Loyalty to the crown would be the cornerstone of the agreement, but it would be essential that such loyalty should be taken for granted and not, as Wentworth intended, used as a means of division. In other words, a divisive policy of alienation could only work in Ireland if the king succeeded absolutely in England. If he did not, Ireland could be used in a new and dangerous way by the king's opponents. That this is what would happen if Wentworth's Irish policy were to fail could hardly be surprising; that Wentworth himself was aware of the risks would seem somewhat doubtful. It is not ironic that the first instrument to be used by the new Lord Deputy to free the king from his own parliament was the Irish parliament itself. Wentworth was not building a model for future rule in England, as has often been suggested. He was expending his power absolutely in a way which could never be possible in England. If the immediate consequence of this expenditure was a growth in the king's income, then all would be justified. In the final analysis, Ireland was subject to the military rule of all England, both king and parliament (as would become clear all too soon). Ireland did not have an independent power which the king's representative need respect. Ireland was a kingdom without a king; Wentworth was to be a ruler without consensus.

In this respect Wentworth has been treated separately by Irish historians at the expense of those aspects of his policy which were more typical of Stuart government in Ireland since 1603. Wentworth did almost nothing that was new, exploited no weakness that had not already been exposed, and succeeded only because he acted as Mountjoy had done before him and Cromwell would do after—that is to say, without reference to the niceties of a conflict in which there was no power higher than his own. The fact of the matter was that there was no political, religious or ethnic unity on the island, and there was always a vital lack of sympathy among one or other of the groups in any given conflict. When Tyrone was defeated the Old English passed a parliamentary act of attainder; when the aldermen were imprisoned the towns accepted the punishment; when their trading privileges and customs were taken arbitrarily they adapted at the expense of their weaker brethren; when Wexford, Leitrim and Longford were planted the Old English accepted grants of land that had belonged to their Irish neighbours; when the king broke his promise over the Graces the subsidy was continued in full. Wentworth is usually accused of a lack of political insight when, in the plantation of Connacht, he included the Old English county of Galway along with the more Irish counties of Mayo, Sligo and Roscommon. Grave injustice was claimed for the whole plantation scheme, yet the protest was limited to the Galway area. Moreover, Wentworth took on one of the best-established families in the country, headed by the Earl of Clanricard, whose English, as well as Irish, status was acclaimed universally. It is unlikely that Wentworth would have risked his government for County Galway if he was not certain of the king's support.

It has been this failure to see Wentworth as an instrument of Stuart government in Ireland that has led to the view that he was a political aberration. What he sought was fiscal rectitude, and the means he employed were well established and, ultimately, condoned by his critics. It so happened that the greatest political crisis in England's history was taking place at this time, and Wentworth's success depended entirely upon the king's readiness to back him.

The composition of Wentworth's first Irish parliament was largely the result of the creation of new boroughs in the reign of James. The House of Commons comprised 142 Protestant members, one-third of whom were office-holders, 94 Old English, and eight representatives from native Irish areas. There was a large Protestant majority in the House of Lords as a result of the many peerages created by both James and Charles. It was the balance of power in the Commons, however, that would determine how things would go, and this was established immediately in a vote over non-resident members which clearly went the government's way. Wentworth then encouraged the formulation of bills designed to confirm the Graces on the condition that they be voted on only after parliament had satisfied the king's financial requirements. This was done on 18 July, a mere four days after the opening; six subsidies were voted and passed into law by the end of the session, by which time Wentworth had also succeeded in having a bill passed which would confirm the powers of the commission for defective titles. It was a measure of Old English trust that they did not foresee the use to which this law might be put. The light, however, was about to dawn. On 19 August the Commons committee whose job it was to oversee the preparation of legislation on the Graces was called before Wentworth and told that none of the Graces which might compromise the king's powers could be passed. The most important of those which would not now be approved was the statute of limitations protecting estates of sixty years' occupancy. The new legislation strengthening the commission for defective titles was cited as having made the proposed statute unnecessary.

Wentworth was playing a game with the opposition which he could not lose. When they opposed minor pieces of legislation during the next session the Lord Deputy encouraged them to be conciliatory by promising to increase the permitted Graces from four to ten, but at the same time he accused the opposition of being papist and declared that the king was not obliged to make any concessions to such a group. This view had an immediate appeal for the Protestants in the house, and Wentworth was assured of a majority, despite Catholic opposition, for the remainder of the parliament. The most pointed of the laws passed were those modifying inheritance in favour of the crown, measures for the collection of debts outstanding to the government, and a new system which set the subsidy in advance of collection and in accordance with ability to pay. The approximate divisions of the subsidy were: Leinster £13,000, Munster £11,200, Ulster £10,000, and Connacht £6,800—proportions which were clearly weighted against the Old English.

Although quite happy with the way matters had gone, Wentworth was not content to leave the number of Catholic seats in parliament as it was. Writing to Coke, he pointed out:

> We might well overthrow at least twenty of these old corporations who all sent, and so will still, mere Irish and papists, the most obstinate senseless creatures I am persuaded of the world, who had no more wit nor will than to do just as their Jesuits and friars appointed them.[7]

Coke replied giving the king's approval:

> [In parliament] the excessive multitude of corporations and burgesses will always increase faction, especially when the greatest part remain so ill-affected. The remedy then which you

propound, by a legal proceeding against old corporations that have usurped upon the crown, is very well approved; and His Majesty requireth you to pursue it with care and diligence, in such way as in your wisdom you find best.[8]

Wentworth did indeed proceed with care, and although we know of at least seven boroughs which were disfranchised, it would seem that he picked those which were weakest, and consequently the issue was not brought to the forefront.

He did, however, openly attack privileges within the municipal corporations both in an attempt to weaken them and also to open their monopoly of trade to wider interests. Dublin was again used as an example. As clerk of the market it was the mayor's duty to fix and regulate commodity prices. It was equally the custom that certain profits accrued to the mayor through the rates which were set in addition to the collection of other tolls. When he lowered the price of coal below the king's rate Wentworth employed a double-edged tactic: he would immediately gain the support of the city's inhabitants, while at the same time it was an open challenge to the mayor, Sir James Carroll, to maintain the standard rate. In addition to this, it was an attack upon the clerkship of the market itself as one of the last of the municipality's major privileges. The immediate consequence of its loss would be a rapid shift of emphasis from the interests of the citizen to those of the trader, free or not. It would follow from this that guild representation in the municipal assembly would be less effective, and consequently the role of the guilds themselves would be weakened. This in itself was central to Wentworth's economic policy of increasing trade in order to exact greater levies.

Nor was such a policy at odds with the changes that had already taken place in Dublin since the beginning of the century. By 1635 the citizens were outnumbered by non-freemen. By this time the city's merchant elite had come to accept such change, and indeed to profit from it. It had been in Carroll's mayoralty ten years earlier that moves had been made by Falkland's associates to gain the clerkship of the market in the face of aldermanic indifference but against the wishes of the Commons. By appearing to side with the underdog Wentworth was thus in a position to outmanoeuvre all sides. A proclamation was issued in January 1635 which announced the lowered rates with a pointed instruction to the mayor to acknowledge them. Carroll continued to adhere to the customary procedures and was charged accordingly with disobedience. 'And the said mayor, being demanded what he could say in his defence, alleged nothing for himself in excuse or extenuation of his said offences, only pretended he knew not at all of the said proclamation and that he took up coals by privilege and custom, as he had done in the former times of his mayoralty.'[9] Carroll was fined £1,000 sterling, imprisoned during the Lord Deputy's pleasure and debarred from ever holding office again. As a response to Carroll's defeat the aldermen chosen to be mayor for the years 1635 and 1636 stepped down in favour of Sir Christopher Forster, who served continuously from June 1635 until October 1637. He was mayor again in 1638, and was succeeded by his brother Charles in 1639. Apart from Charles Forster, the only alderman elected in the quarter assembly after 1634 who actually took up office was the Protestant James Watson. Between 1634 and 1640 five Catholic aldermen were elected to the mayoralty and not one of them served in the office. Apart from removing the religious option from Wentworth's choice of initiatives, however, the response of the aldermen was weak in two respects: first, the initiative itself would remain with the government; and secondly, it provided no protection from the Lord Deputy's invidious use of the commission for defective titles. Attempts were made where possible to cast doubt upon city property titles and those of the religious guilds, the predominant beneficiaries of which had always been the city's elite, both Catholic and Protestant.

On the positive side, Wentworth's government was committed to an increase in trade, if only for the additional revenues it would bring the crown, but in this respect he was against all restrictions, whether practised by Catholics or not. In 1634 Sir George Radcliffe, one of the new customs farmers and a close associate of Wentworth, wrote from Dublin to Sir Arthur Ingram:

> The new company of soapers in London have got a restraint of vending tallow here, themselves to have it all, which if it go forward will destroy many of our Dutch merchants, whereby we shall lose at least £4,000 per annum. The parliament has been sensible of this, and both houses have petitioned about it. Besides, we have the king's covenant that this and all other commodities shall be free.[10]

It is significant that Radcliffe could refer to the Dutch as 'our' merchants—a view which contradicts the impression given by many commentators that national divisions had a crucial effect upon the economic policy of the English government. Indeed, Radcliffe's (and we may presume Wentworth's) view could be used to support the notion that the struggle between corporate power (either municipal or guild) and 'free trade' was essentially a struggle between the medieval and the modern, the static and the dynamic. Urban government throughout Ireland which was based upon corporate power did in fact portray itself as essentially static. Appeals to charters, formalities, traditions and precedents were intended to support or reinforce a structure whose existence was, of necessity, self-perpetuated. Yet such appeals cannot be taken at face value, as the Lord Deputy himself would have known well. Divided loyalties meant, for example, that while the merchant monopoly was attacked from outside the guilds, it was not uncommon for the merchants themselves to support the government with financial loans.

On a more practical front, piracy was a constant problem for the merchants throughout the early decades of the seventeenth century. Chichester had complained of it in 1610, and an act for the punishment of pirates had been passed in the Irish parliament in November 1614. It was not until Wentworth focused his attention on the problem, however, that it was effectively dealt with. Before his arrival it had been reported that all trade with both Europe and England had been stopped by pirates, to the great detriment of the merchant community and the country as a whole. While a certain amount of exaggeration may be allowed for here (it was said of the merchants that they 'cry out before they are hurt'), the Irish government was obliged to take action when ships were actually chased into Dublin harbour. A Dutch ship was hired temporarily to clear the port, but the government complained that the work was hindered by a prohibition on the employment of locals. In 1632 the problem had grown to such an extent that pirates were anchored on the river itself, to the indignation of the Privy Council. Two months later a group of Dublin merchants lost a cargo valued at £3,000 to a pirate named Nutt, who seized it half a league from Howth. The ships in question were taken by Nutt in the full view of onlookers who watched from the shore. Wentworth (himself a victim of piracy in 1633) was familiar with the problem, as it was almost endemic in the north of England. By September 1635 he could report that the pirates had been banished and trade revived through all the ports. Less than a year later, as he reviewed the state of the country, he could add that, with one minor exception, there had been no trouble whatsoever and no losses sustained by the merchants, and that he was determined that, despite a renewed threat from Turkish pirates, no expense would be spared to maintain the security of trade.

Wentworth's economic policy lacked any coherence apart from the financial expediency of raising revenue. In this respect he never actually gained the goodwill of those who benefited from his government, but instead was always looked upon as a threat simply because of his indifference to any local interests which did not serve his own. During his period in office there was a remarkable increase in the yield from the customs farm due in part to his restructuring of the customs administration (but also, it must be said, from an international increase in the volume of trade). The profit from the farm in 1636/7 was almost equal to the total yield for 1632/3, but as far as Wentworth's critics were concerned the distribution of that profit spoke for itself: administrative costs were £3,000; the king's rent was £15,500; while the profits of £21,500 were divided in such a way that five-eighths (£13,500) went to the king, one-quarter (£5,400) to Wentworth, and one-eighth (£2,600) to his assistant Radcliffe. As far as Wentworth was concerned, however, there was no case to answer. As he himself had undertaken the administrative reforms necessary to produce such profits, he was justified in taking his share. In many cases, however, the increased yield was in fact due to greater efficiency rather than to the extraction of moneys from those who would not otherwise have expected to pay. This was not the case with another of Wentworth's great projects, the plantation of Connacht.

At a political level, the plantation of Connacht migh be seen as the further extension of New English control. In this respect it followed on the plantation of Ulster and those of Leitrim and Longford, the completion of which had removed the strategic significance of Connacht itself. The 'composition' or financial settlement of Connacht had been agreed upon in 1585, but its yield in the early part of the seventeenth century was only £3,000 and there was much scope for improvement. The difference between the earlier plantations and that proposed by Wentworth was that Connacht was a loyal province under the protection of the Earls of Clanricard and Thomond, while the county and city of Galway were peopled mainly by Old English. Not to distinguish betwen the loyal Old English and the loyal Irish was seen as a grave signal that security of tenure was a thing of the past. In a comment made in November 1635 Wentworth indicated that he was more than aware of this: 'They within the Pale begin now to find His Majesty hath the same title to a great part of Meath which he hath to Connacht and that many other places amongst them also are upon other fair and just claims subject to plantation.'[11]

Wentworth himself presided at three sessions held at Boyle, Sligo and Ballinrobe in which he met with no opposition. This was largely because the juries had been properly chosen to produce the required verdicts and were mostly Protestant and New English; thus by the end of July 1635 title had been found for the king for the counties of Roscommon, Mayo and Sligo. The Lord Deputy's management of the juries had as much to do with his reputation as with the veiled threats which he made. In these three cases opposition was possible but not feasible because there was no organised support of the type that Galway was about to demonstrate. The essential difference is worth noting: even within the law the legalities were irrelevant; it was the identity of the group under threat that determined the type of response and the degree of success achieved. The 'law' in Ireland was only theoretically based on those principles being fought over in England at this time, where the balance of power within the political constitution was supposedly under the protection of the judges. No such niceties could exist in seventeenth-century Ireland, nor had they really existed in the preceding period when the Old English abandoned constitutional questions and looked instead to the more pragmatic protection of their possessions. As far as the resistance in Galway was concerned, therefore, the law must not be relied upon, but rather the jury must be packed. Wentworth sent the county sheriff a list of his nominees, but this was rejected in favour of a list drawn up by the defendants. It would be on the determination of this jury to resist, and not on any point of law, that the case would be decided. Equally, failure on Wentworth's part would be a failure of authority, of ability, and of the thrust of his government in Ireland. Moreover, it would indicate for the first time a crucial loss of the king's confidence in him. This was to be a trial of strength, not a trial of law. He chose as his residence in Galway, and the court's location, Clanricard's house at Portumna. This was a most pointed gesture of assertion, intended to illustrate Wentworth's awareness that the matter would really be decided at court between the earl and himself. As a natural extremist the Lord Deputy seemed happiest fighting on all fronts simultaneously, but this was indeed a daring gesture in view of the possibility that the king might waver. Clanricard held an English title (that of Viscount St Albans) and was no Irish cipher where court loyalties and connections were concerned. For Charles to act publicly against Clanricard would be to signal to his English (and Scottish) subjects that it was ultimately his, and not Wentworth's, policy which was being implemented. More importantly, he would also be indicating that he approved of the manner in which Ireland was being governed.

Wentworth's treatment of the packed Galway jury which he found on his arrival at Portumna was indicative of this very support. Some members had failed to appear and were quickly fined £200 each. Evidence was presented over a period of three days, after which the jury would only acknowledge the king's title to those lands which had reverted to the crown on the deaths of William de Burgo, Earl of Ulster, and Lionel, Duke of Clarence. The Lord Deputy had them bound over and the sheriff fined £1,000 for drawing up what was now clearly a jury bent upon recalcitrance. Others involved in the defence were similarly fined or bound over to appear in the Court of Castle Chamber in Dublin. Battle-lines had now been drawn; both sides were committed to a test of strength, and agents were appointed by the Galway landholders to plead their case at court. Significantly, they were joined by a similar group appointed by the Palesmen; this anticipation of an attack upon the best land titles in the country said a great deal about the urgency of the situation. For the lords of the Pale to draw attention to themselves at all in this contest, let alone expose their belief that the fate of Galway might be their own, was to narrow the ground considerably.

For his part, Wentworth's response was equally pointed: he requested that the Galway agents should be ordered to make their submissions in writing, after which they should be arrested and returned to Ireland on a charge of conspiracy against the crown. That this signal course of action was taken by the king indicates the degree to which he supported his deputy. Before that, however, the agents were given a formal hearing in November 1635 at which they put forward a two-part and futile defence. They suggested first that the jury had not found for the king because they had not been presented with sufficient evidence by the government. Unfortunately this was taken to be a criticism of Wentworth, while the second defence was seen as an affront to the king himself. The claim was made by the agents that a legitimate agreement made in 1615 between James I and the landholders of Connacht was secured by Article 25 of the Graces (which made additional provision for the systematic confirmation of existing titles). That is to say that the spirit of the Graces, if not the law itself, still bound the king to his promise. The claim could only be made, however, by a feigned unawareness of the fact that the Graces had been denied by the king intentionally and were to all practical purposes a dead letter. It was a defence which the king could not countenance, nor was it in keeping with the more naked corollary offer of double rents made by the agents. To make matters considerably worse, the death of Clanricard, which took place precisely at this point in the negotiations, removed any personal misgivings which Charles might have had about pressing ahead with the plantation. The agents were dismissed and ordered to return to Dublin, where they were to be handed over to the Lord Deputy as requested. They appealed for their own safety, but by March of the following year only one, Martin Darcy, had succeeded; all the others were arrested and imprisoned on their return to Dublin.

Darcy managed to remain in England because he had another commission; although less dramatic, it was equally illustrative of the course of affairs in Ireland. Acting now on behalf of the New English, he proposed that the king resume and re-farm the Irish customs in which Wentworth had a large stake. The proposal was rejected out of hand, but it was consistent with the offer of double rents. That is to say that the only way in which Wentworth's government could be safely criticised was to suggest that the Lord Deputy himself was not acting in the king's interest and to follow this with an offer of money. This offer was not made within an Irish context only, however. A joint attempt was being made in England to remove Wentworth from his central position as chief beneficiary of the dramatic rise in customs revenue. His chief opponents were Sir Arthur Ingram in England and Lord Mountnorris in Dublin.

Mountnorris was one of the last surviving allies of Wentworth to go into opposition as the New English attempted to retain their influence in the administration. Mountnorris had more than one axe to grind. As Vice-Treasurer he had held the most important administrative office within the Dublin government. His alliance with Wentworth was prompted by expediency rather than sympathy. He was a principal farmer of the customs and a member of the Court of Castle Chamber. It was this very position of power, however, that made a clash inevitable. As a result of Wentworth's reorganisation of the customs administration and his efforts to control Castle Chamber, relations between the two men deteriorated sharply. It was clear to Mountnorris, as it was clear to the New English generally, not only that the Lord Deputy was proving himself unconcerned about their special position within the government and the country, but also that he was portraying them to the king as a narrow and self-interested group with Puritan sympathies. In other words, they were being represented as not only dispensable but as fundamentally despicable. Mountnorris lost his position as Vice-Treasurer on what can only be described as a dramatic technicality. He had complained about a reprimand his brother had received as an officer in Wentworth's troop of horse. As an army captain Mountnorris was arrested, charged with sedition by a council of war and sentenced to death; on Wentworth's recommendation the sentence was commuted. The action itself was not necessary in that Wentworth followed it with a report on Mountnorris to the king which in turn resulted in the Vice-Treasurer's dismissal. The extraordinary charge of sedition was not intended to be taken at face value; it was a pointed insult designed to demonstrate not only the power of a Lord Deputy but also the very precarious foothold of the New English in Ireland. It was Mountnorris's position within the customs farm, however, that brought about the real struggle for power which took place at the same time as Wentworth was dictating to the Connacht landholders. The security of Wentworth's position within the customs farm may be seen from the increase in yields which followed his arrival in Ireland.

A new book of rates for the customs had been struck in April 1632, three months after the king had announced Wentworth's appointment; the coincidence was not accidental. New farmers were appointed: Sir Arthur Ingram and Robert Cogan had previous interests, while Mountnorris and Sir George Radcliffe, Wentworth's secretary, were to represent the new initiative. Ingram and Cogan had been in since 1613 when the crown had finally wrested control of the customs from the towns. The yield since then had not been great, but the investment was made with an eye to the future. The farm itself changed hands several times before Wentworth took it over, and while there are no returns for the period, the modest yield was reflected in the fact that the rent, which stood at £6,000 in 1613, had not changed by 1631. The new farm was to be a projection of new profits, and the rent was increased to £15,000, with an additional outright payment of £8,000.

Wentworth did not disappoint his backers: profits rose from approximately £5,000 on his appointment to £8,373 in 1633/4 and £20,019 in 1634/5. The aim of the reforms which produced this increase was central to Charles's own government: the king had committed himself to rule without the financial support of the English parliament, and he needed this money. Moreover, he needed ventures such as this one to succeed in order to show that the initiative would remain with the crown and that it would do so through the success of his policies. In other words, there had been a major shift of emphasis in the function of the customs farm since 1613. Before that it had been the bulwark of town finances; after its revision it had become a source of patronage for James (who granted the farm to Buckingham, whereby it was inherited by his widow); now, under Charles and Wentworth, it was to be a pivot of royal independence. It was understandable that Mountnorris and Ingram should want to improve their position in view of the dramatic increases, but an attack upon Wentworth was more than an attack upon a fellow-beneficiary.

At a time when it would be judged a sign of weakness by the Galway landholders for the Lord Deputy to leave the field of battle, this is precisely what he did. At the end of May 1636 the Galway jury were arraigned on a charge of refusing to find legitimate title for the king, found guilty, fined and imprisoned, while Wentworth left for England. The purpose of his visit was undoubtedly to give an account of himself to the king, but its effect could be seen in the removal of Mountnorris and Ingram from the customs farm and their replacement by Wentworth himself, and also in the new arrangements made for the distribution of profits in favour of the king and his servants. His return to Dublin at the end of November was followed by the complete capitulation of the Galway jury, which was in turn followed by the complete and humble submission of the Galway landholders, with the plea that they might be treated as generously as those who had submitted willingly in Mayo, Sligo and Roscommon.

———————

The plantation of Connacht was never completed, and Wentworth's plans never developed any further than the stage at which they were in the late 1630s. The new Earl of Clanricard appealed to Charles on the basis of his loyalty and his aristocratic status, and the king exempted his lands from confiscation. After 1637 the king's position changed dramatically, and Wentworth came to realise painfully what Charles had always known: that the king could and would decide every issue according to his own immediate interest. It so happened that until Charles came into conflict with his Scottish subjects, during and after 1637, his interests were also those of his deputy in

Ireland. By the late 1630s, however, it was becoming clear that the central issue of Charles's whole reign was the political-religious unity of his Anglican headship.

Wentworth had taken the view that the king's religion was a political matter which was directly bound up with the government of the realm itself. The finer points of Puritan theology did not concern him once loyalty to the king was demonstrated willingly. In this respect Wentworth differed vitally from his master. The Lord Deputy was an administrator, and as such he referred every issue to the question of whether it would impede or enhance the royal government. Thus it was his deeply held belief that Charles should not meddle with the Scots when it could only provoke a costly confrontation. The king, on the other hand, was consistent in his determination that his three kingdoms should profess one religion only. Nor was this religion a static form of Anglicanism inherited from the Elizabethen settlement. Charles was brought up by a father who had been King of Scotland for almost forty years before he came to the English throne, and Charles was to take the religious question of Scotland as seriously as he took his own life.

By contrast, Wentworth's religious policy was similar to the other branches of his Irish administration: matters were judged on the basis of the king's wishes and the extent to which these were observed by his subjects. The New English in Ireland were largely Puritan in their outlook, and the Lord Deputy was aware of the limitations which this must necessarily place upon them. However, the king himself was under no illusions as to the general direction religion must take throughout his three kingdoms. The appointment of William Laud as Bishop of London in 1628 and then as Archbishop of Canterbury in 1633 made it clear to all that Charles was bent on strengthening the Catholic elements of the Anglican church at the expense of the Elizabethan settlement, and the effects in Ireland were consistent with this. Wentworth's chaplain, John Bramhall, was made Bishop of Derry in 1634 when he replaced the Puritan George Downham. This was to be the pattern throughout Wentworth's period of office. George Webb, chaplain to the king, was appointed to the bishopric of Limerick in 1634; the Arminian Henry Leslie succeeded to the bishopric of Down and Connor in 1635; while in the same year Wentworth's nominee, John Atherton, succeeded to Waterford and Lismore. William Chappell, the Laudian Provost of Trinity, was appointed to Cork and Ross in 1638, and similar appointments were made to Kilfenora and Elphin in 1638 and 1639 respectively. By the end of Wentworth's period in office the Church of Ireland had changed outwardly from being almost wholly Puritan to representing the High Anglicanism of the king, and in this respect Ireland was the only one of the three kingdoms to do so smoothly. The change was achieved easily because for all groups, Catholic or Protestant, the Irish administration was essentially a local government, and as long as the official nod was given a great deal could take place off the record. This could never be the case where a king resided among his people, because there the line of authority was direct and personal. The only group who had never had the chance to get the official nod were the Gaelic Irish because they had never held office. The complete exclusion of their religion because of its alien Spanish connections was to have the most profound consequences upon the whole history of Britain and Ireland. Charles I had eventually married a French Catholic, but not before he had hiked incognito (complete with false beard) to Spain to have a look at his Spanish prospects. Spanish Catholicism held no fears for Charles I. As the 1620s progressed into the 1630s the symbolic false beard was carefully clipped away, and with every year that passed Charles became more like himself.

Fateful Ideologies: The Stuart Inheritance

THE Tudors had, by a process of political evolution, arrived at a compromise which had taken England from the Henrician break with Rome through the Puritanism of Edward VI and the Roman Catholicism of Mary to the compromise instituted by Elizabeth. Both Catholic and Calvinist extremes had proved unworkable precisely because of the existence of their opposites within the immediate Tudor family, and hence the possibility for each side of a sovereign religion. By her unwillingness to commit herself Elizabeth had prevented a conflict which might have arisen from the tendency of each side to confront and attempt to subdue the other. If it did nothing else, the establishment of the Anglican church, and the queen's own longevity, provided England with a stability which for its time was sophisticated but artificial. For as long as the queen did not delcare for either side there would be peace. This was not the case in Scotland, the home of the Stuart monarchy.

There was no compromise in Scotland between Protestantism, there manifesting itself as Presbyterianism, and Roman Catholicism. In the political sphere the reason for this was quite simple. In its attempt to maintain independence from England, Scotland had always attached itself in diplomatic alliance to the French court. One crucial benefit which Scotland's alliance produced was the one which had always characterised the Gallican church; in 1535 Pope Paul III had granted James V of Scotland the right to nominate his own bishops. It was on this issue that France had fought for its political independence from Rome, and on which the Vatican had been split for many centuries between the unyielding Spanish church and its northern neighbour. The significance of the French alliance for Scotland cannot be overestimated. The Stuarts did not experience the political clash with Rome over the control of their own clergy, and consequently the Roman Catholic Church in Scotland was independent and remote in a way which made its degeneration almost inevitable. Added to this, the tribal nature of Scottish society meant that the monarchy itself depended on immediate family alliances and the exclusion of others from power. The Lutheran Reformation had little to offer the Scottish malcontents because it preached that the religion of the ruler should be that of his people. Calvin had altered this rule-of-thumb to suggest that where great corruption existed it was conceivable that pressure might be brought to bear upon the king to reform. When John Knox had returned to Scotland with this doctrine he informed Mary Queen of Scots (James I's mother) that the people would be justified in removing their monarch if he or she was not godly.

Added to this uncompromising formula was the fact that Scottish political tradition demanded the monarch's direct involvement in a conflict, and this often resulted in the death of the king and a long minority; consequently faction was very common. Thus when James IV died in battle at Flodden in 1512 his son was seventeen months old; James V died in 1542 and was succeeded by Mary Queen of Scots, who was then six days old; when Mary was forced to abdicate in 1567 the new king James VI, later James I of England, was less than one year old. The regencies which spanned these periods were as much dependent on the physical possession of the monarch as they were about policy. A high proportion of nobles died violently in this game of power if only because there was no overriding sovereign authority to settle disputes. Apart from the destructive feuds which resulted, another consequence of Scotland's unlucky history in the sixteenth century was that there tended to be only two parties—the ins and the outs. When the Lutheran Reformation reached Scotland it was not well received by the Catholic monarchy because the pro-French Stuarts had already a great deal of independence in church affairs. However, it was only a matter of time before those nobles and lairds who were continually banished from the centre of power saw in the Calvinist Reformation a vital criticism which they might use as a lever to shift the monarchy, namely that its autocratic support for the church obliged it to condone corruption. In this respect Scotland inherited its Calvinism from France (Calvin himself was French), where the Lutheran Reformation in the independent German principalities had little relevance. Lutheranism was a mild doctrine when it came to political matters (because unlike Calvinism it was not forged in the heat of threatened extinction), and it was this very temperance which prompted a Calvinist political opposition to grow around religious questions in a Scottish environment of almost natural extremism. (There are many cases throughout early Scottish history of the attainment of ceremonial office by an individual who was then unceremoniously killed by his opponents. After the Stuarts came to England the most notable example of this was the assassination of the Duke of Buckingham as the only means of altering the king's course. The English never allowed this characteristically Stuart phenomenon to reoccur.)

Although geographically Scotland was isolated, politically it stood between French Catholic resistance to the Lutheran Reformation and the Anglicanism initiated by Henry VIII of England. Where hitherto Scotland had always used France to protect itself against the English, it was now inevitable that a pro-English party would grow around the new Lutheran doctrines. It is ironic, however, that the nature of Scottish Catholicism, influenced as it was by France, was flexible on questions of dogma. In other words, in matters of religion a mild Lutheranism on one side was opposed by a politically sophisticated and independent (or, as some would say, corrupt) Catholicism on the other. No contest was more ripe for the entrance of a truly revolutionary and uncompromising doctrine, that of John Calvin.

What characterised the two great Calvinist, or Presbyterian, leaders of Scotland, John Knox and Andrew Melville, was their undoubted fearlessness. While Knox had informed Mary Queen of Scots personally that monarchs were to be judged, Melville spelt it out for James:

> Sir, I must tell you, there are two kings and two kingdoms in Scotland. There is Christ Jesus the king and his kingdom the Kirk, whose subject King James the sixth is, and of whose kingdom not a king nor a lord nor a head, but a member.[1]

The famous tenet of 'no bishop, no king' by which James summed up his own stance was in perfect opposition to Melville's religious equality. According to James, the king was the fount of authority through which God ruled his people, and as such the monarch was himself bound up in a godly rule. If, however, the king was not all that he might be, it was not given to his subjects to criticise or indeed object to his law. For James, the law derived from the power of the king, whether or not that law was made in parliament or by royal fiat. As far as church organisation was concerned, Melville wished to see power wielded by groups of presbyters or elders, whereas the king insisted that this be the domain of the bishop. The essential difference between the two as far as the political constitution was concerned was that the bishop was appointed by the king, whereas the presbyters were elected by the congregation.

The Black Acts of 1584 decided the matter in the king's favour by re-establishing the authority of the bishops, not just at the expense of the presbyters but also at that of the general church assemblies which the king wished to see replaced by the bishops in parliament. Not even James, however, could legislate against a system of church government which was by now an integral part of Scottish life, and by the end of the sixteenth century a compromise had been reached, albeit one which did not question the king's right to institute further changes. These he did not undertake until after his accession to the English throne. This was due not to an increase in zeal but to the greater authority which his headship of the Anglican church now gave him. As a Scottish monarch James was obliged to recognise beliefs and practices which he did not personally adhere to. Consequently he left behind him many statements on religious matters which were later to be used in an attempt to undermine him. As the King of England, however, James became head of that established church which had never abolished episcopy, and indeed which considered it a pivot of the reformed religion. Thus after his accession he was faced with the central question which Charles I would later feel obliged to answer: how can subjects be forced to conform to the religion of their king?

Unfortunately for the Stuarts, their own concept of the divine right of kings had evolved in a context far less sophisticated than that of their new home. Elizabeth had never made such divine claims and so never had to defend an abstract position in any concrete political context. James now had two kingdoms on one island; his English throne had depended on toleration (albeit grudgingly) for stability, while the other was composed of two sides anxious to gain any ground that might further entrench their doctrine.

James decided to ally his own concepts of hierarchical religion to those of the Anglican church and impose, or attempt to impose, these on Scotland. In 1606 he attempted to impose permanent moderators on the Scottish presbyteries, but the move was rejected by the synods. He overcame this opposition by convening a nominated assembly which agreed to his proposals and which he then used to claim that permanent moderators of synods had also been approved. Coupled with these moves in 1606 James pushed through a parliamentary bill which restored the estates of bishops and effectively returned them to their old political status so that by 1610 episcopy had to all intents and purposes been restored in Scotland. A royal proclamation issued in 1614 ordered the Easter celebration of Holy Communion. In the following year the proclamation was extended, and the University of St Andrews was ordered to observe the major Christian festivals, and colleges in general were ordered to use the Book of Common Prayer at certain times. Other moves were equally significant. In 1616 new liturgical changes were proposed in what became known as the Five Articles: these entailed private baptism, private communion, kneeling at communion, the confirmation of children by bishops, and the observance of the Christian year. James was granted the power to legislate in church matters by the parliament of 1617, but the bill was withdrawn on the advice of the bishops; by November the Five Articles were rejected by an assembly summoned at St Andrews. In response the king put into practice his 'divine right' to proclaim, by royal edict, certain days as Christian feast-days. Two factors were of vital significance in this apparently innocuous order: the first was that a feast-day or holiday had to be observed physically, regardless of the observant's personal religious beliefs; the second was the king's crucial use of his own legal powers to make law in spiritual matters. In other words, James was now treating the Scottish Presbyterians in the way that the Tudors had always treated the Irish Catholics: official religion was to be a matter of physical observance rather than personal belief.

The characteristics of congregation and religious practice which were shared by all types of Christianity in the seventeenth century were both essential to the survival of each religion, or sect, but ironically they were the easiest aspects to legislate against. That is not to say that legislation could ever cancel the existence of a religion. In most, if not all, cases it consolidated and confirmed the Christian belief in satanic and wordly opposition, and the Christian concept of martyrdom as a most desirable victory. Tragically for the history of Europe throughout the sixteenth and seventeenth centuries, the legal solution had only ever enhanced the problem. What lay at the heart of the conflict was the form of worship and whether the individual related directly to God (with the aid of the Bible) or whether ritual and intercession were effective (and affective). The practice of Protestant salvation was opposed to the practice of Catholic adoration. Both religions were self-confirming and consequently could only be certain that the other was mistaken. What was not understood in the seventeenth century was that both modes were equally justified experientially.

In his attempt to outlaw Presbyterianism and replace it with a Scottish form of Anglicanism, James was bringing on himself and his heirs a conflict which centred on his own right of kingship. This situation was the opposite to that of Ireland, where serious religious change, or indeed conversion, was never undertaken. The difference was that although Ireland had been declared a kingdom in 1541, it never had a king; its government could always be altered or replaced without any reference to those being ruled, and consequently there was no direct constitutional relationship between the king and his subjects as had existed both in Scotland and England. Ireland suffered more from the technicality of the Oath of Supremacy than from any drive to convert its Catholics.

The Scottish conflict was only partly disguised because the Presbyterians actually did believe in the need for a godly king, as opposed to a Roman Catholic one who left all spiritual matters in the hands of Rome. Thus, since the Stuarts were no longer Roman Catholics, they were never completely abandoned by the Scottish Presbyterians. There can be no doubt that had James been a Roman Catholic like his mother, Scotland would have produced something similar to the English civil war in the second half of the sixteenth century. As it was, the king was compromised by his own long minority, but he made up for it slowly, and the direction was always towards autocratic or, as it was to be known later, absolutist monarchy.

Following his proclamation of January 1618 establishing the festivals of the Christian year, James convened an assembly at Perth in which his own nominees were in the majority. His Five Articles were passed, and consent was given for a new liturgy. There was great personal hostility in Scotland to these moves, but in particular to the requirement to kneel at Holy Communion. The significance of kneeling was whether the worshipper was to stand erect before God or whether he should bow or bend before a person or object (priest or tabernacle) as intermediary.

Although a new liturgy was introduced into Scotland, it was never formally observed, and a good deal of compromise was achieved towards the end of James's reign. The reason for this was one of political and constitutional balance. As well as being King of England for more than twenty years of his life, James had been the resident King of Scotland for almost forty years before that. He had not achieved the sophistication of Elizabeth's religious settlement; but then, Elizabeth's solution was inherently English, whereas the Scottish problem could be viewed as a conflict between imported

French Catholicism and its equally imported French Calvinist opposite. It should have surprised no one that the last of the Stuart kings could end (literally) in the pay of the great French absolutist Louis XIV.

When Charles I took up his father's work in converting the Scots to what was now straightforward Anglicanism they did not perceive it in the same way that he did. The king held the view that uniformity of religion was a requirement of a properly governed state, while the Scots simply viewed the issue as an attack on their religion, which in effect, if not in intent, is exactly what it was. In the first year of his reign Charles issued an act of revocation whereby all crown property granted since 1540 was resumed. This had been traditional Scottish practice in the monarch's twenty-fifth year, but the secret way in which the new king went about it and the intention which lay behind it, namely to find new income for the Established Church, was a foretaste of what was to come. The 'lords of erection' were those nobles who had, by one means or another, acquired church lands and who were consequently at the king's mercy in so far as all ecclesiastical property ultimately belonged to the crown. In one act, therefore, Charles indicated clearly to his subjects that they enjoyed their security of tenure at his discretion alone. Furthermore, it would be difficult in the extreme to oppose the policy of allocating the proceeds towards the king's religion when the power to resume the lands itself could not be challenged. This mode of action was to become typical of the new regime: prerogative power would be wielded in the political area, while the benefits would be applied in the religious. The two could be linked simply by finance, and it was this, the search for income, which would be the ultimate test of Charles's policy. It was undoubtedly aggravating to see the king playing his trump card, but it was to become unbearable that those who lost should also be obliged to foresake their religion as part of this non-bargain.

Part, if not all, of the king's political problem stemmed from his religion, which, as events were to show, he placed above his own life. After the Scots broke the back of the king's power (by simply resorting to superior physical force) Charles compromised all the way to the scaffold, but always after a defeat and consequently always too late for any initiative. What was beyond dispute, however, was the king's single-minded determination to establish a Catholic (albeit non-Roman) form of worship throughout his three kingdoms. What is generally known as 'the rise of Arminianism' was in fact the re-emergence and reassertion of the already existing Anglican religion. The question of whether or not Arminianism aspired to union with Rome (as the Puritans claimed) has no meaning in any narrow context apart from some generally isolated facts (such as the offer by the Vatican to make the Anglican Archbishop Laud a cardinal). What is beyond doubt, however, and what can only be seen by a long-term view of the Stuart monarchy, is that there was a natural and logical progression in both political and religious outlook from the ambivalence of James I through the Anglicanism of Charles I and that of his son Charles II (who died a Roman Catholic) until the culmination in the public profession of Roman Catholicism by his other son, James II. In other words, the constitutional crisis began with James's declaration of 'no bishop no king', which is precisely what was tried during the Puritan regime when the political pendulum swung to one extreme. The restoration of the Stuarts was necessitated by the very failure of the Puritans to draw up a con-stitution broad enough to be stable—a failure which forced them ultimately to offer the crown to Oliver Cromwell. Yet the restoration brought only a brief respite as the conflict that had begun in the late 1550s between the Scottish Protestants and the Stuart monarchy took on a more international dimension when it became linked with the rise of Louis XIV. In the end the English were obliged to expel James II in a quasi-legal attempt to expunge a constitutional problem that seemed to have no other solution.

Charles took up the question of the liturgy where James had left it, with the proposals of 1618. Between the late 1620s and his Scottish coronation in 1633 he made preparations to issue an official declaration on the subject. The king's delay in being crowned in Scotland has been put down to, among other things, the lack of finance necessary to perform the ceremony. It may also be suggested that Charles waited until he was in a position to mark his coming to the throne with a clear signal of what his kingship would entail. The ceremony spoke for itself, with as much ritual and vestment as could be displayed. Also symbolically, the church of St Giles, in Edinburgh, which had been divided into three separate churches, was reconstructed and the divisions demolished to produce one cathedral. In certain parts of the country the king ordered the use of the English Book of Common Prayer, and the Archbishop of St Andrews was soon afterwards promoted to first subject as well as Chancellor of Scotland. In the year after his coronation Charles ordered a whole new liturgy to be drawn up based on the English model. While this was in preparation a new code of canons was published in January 1636 which embodied the Five Articles and went a good deal further. Most significantly, the new canons pointed to the new liturgy and required its acceptance, even though it had not yet been completed. This was not just the arbitrary use of the prerogative; it implied that the king's Scottish subjects could simply be willed into obedience without regard to their own beliefs. When the new liturgy did appear in 1637 it left no doubt as to the king's determination to follow his own course; a royal proclamation accompanied the book commanding all to use it. Perhaps it was this command as much as the content of the book itself which provoked the Scottish opposition and began a chain reaction which went rapidly beyond the king's control.

———————

Since the beginning of Charles's reign, therefore, the initiative was taken constantly by the crown, and there could have been little doubt among the Scots that this situation would continue. What had characterised the compromise between the Presbyterians and King James was that the nature of that compromise was first and foremost political. What James had managed to do was to pull Scotland out of the potential chaos of regencies and clan factions while at the same time strengthening the Catholic style of his government. Because this worked it was accepted, but the king also made major philosophical concessions to Calvinism in his own writings which Charles I could never have conceived of doing. So while James preached the divine right of kings he balanced his inclinations with equal, but opposite, acknowledgments of Calvinist theology. Within this compromise, however, the Roman Catholic religion was not only tolerated by the king but viewed as essentially friendly within the political arena. Moreover, the very strong links between the Gaelic Irish Catholics of Ulster and the Gaelic Scots Catholics of the Western Highlands became increasingly significant after the accession of James to the English throne.

While the government in Ireland or in Scotland might at any given time be in the hands of officials with Puritan leanings, the irony was that the religion of the 'undesirables' was more sympathetic to the king than those who were upholding his law. Because Ulster had remained Gaelic while the rest of Ireland came to terms with the Anglo-Norman inheritance, the politics of the north were more in keeping with the extreme divisions in Scotland than with the fine debates of the Old English on constitutional matters. Nor were the Catholics of Ireland themselves under any illusions about the traditions and form of worship which separated both camps. From the arrival of the Normans onwards there was hostility between the clergy involved in the mission to the Gaelic Irish and the orders who served the Anglo-Normans or Old English.

While this division in Ireland was cultural as well as racial, the origin of the religious divide itself was to be found in the wider European split between the constitutional forms of northern Europe and the militant form which came out of Spain. Thus the Anglo-Norman church in Ireland looked to England and France for its traditions, whereas the principal order ministering to the Gaelic Irish, the Franciscans, looked to Spain. The essential difference between the two camps as far as religious worship was concerned was the difference in emphasis placed by the Franciscans on matters of faith and by the Anglo-Norman church on the problematic constitutional relationship of the church to both king and pope. In the final analysis, these traditions developed outside Ireland as a result of the political modes in both England and France on the one hand and Spain and the Holy Roman Empire on the other. The Anglican and Gallican settlements had a great deal in common when compared with the more zealous church of Spain. Although the Franciscans themselves were not a Spanish order, they quickly adopted Spain as their spiritual homeland. In this respect the Franciscans belong to the Spanish tradition which produced the Dominicans and the Jesuits. At different times and in different countries these orders became spearheads in a movement which saw the essential threat in the humanistic traditions of the north of Europe.

The Jesuits undertook their European Counter-Reformation work in those areas where the intellectual threat was greatest, in France, England, Germany, etc., while the Observant Franciscans concentrated upon those groups who were less threatened by the Reformation because it had passed them by. (There were deep theological reasons for the different missions of the Jesuits and the

Franciscans, but these only became vital to Ireland in the late 1640s.)

Thus the Gaelic Irish of Ulster and the Gaelic inhabitants of Western Scotland had a natural affinity for the Franciscan mission. The constitutional question of the king's relationship to the pope and the religious implications of this had no meaning for a social group that had no constitutional history whatsoever. The essence of Gaelic power was not the written charter or the practice of the king's religion as a legal matter; it was the tribal allegiance owed to a chief. This arrangement was not a written one, but was based on the exercise of power. Gaelic society in both Ulster and the west of Scotland stabilised itself through warlike conflicts into hierarchies which depended solely upon the chief's ability to prove himself.

It was in the second decade of the seventeenth century that the Roman Catholic Church in Ireland began to divide along these very different lines. This was to become a conflict of the most vital importance for Ireland's later history, since the failure of one group meant the unbridled success of the other. The conflict was a straight-forward one between the secular clergy and the Observant Franciscans. It was no coincidence that when the Catholic hierarchy was re-established in Ireland (instead of residing at Rome) as part of the Counter-Reformation mission to the Old English, it was accompanied by the establishment in 1619 of a new and most vigorous Franciscan mission not only to the Gaelic Irish of Ulster but also to their kinsmen in the Western Highlands of Scotland.

This new Franciscan mission had everything to do with the rise to prominence of the first Earl of Antrim, Randal MacDonnell (created earl in 1620). The Irish MacDonnells of Antrim with their Scottish MacDonald cousins best portray the political and religious ties between Ulster and the west of Scotland. The Franciscan mission began in 1619 and was based in the Bonamargy friary in the extreme north-east of Antrim, a few miles from the coast of Kintyre in Scotland. The friary became the burial place of the MacDonnell Earls of Antrim and a symbol of the interconnectedness of Scots-Irish politics. MacDonnell history can be summed up quite simply. At the end of the fourteenth century the MacDonalds enjoyed their posses-sions in the Western Highlands. A brother of the head of the clan married the heiress of the Glens of Antrim and thereby established what became the MacDonnell branch of the clan in north-east Ulster. The Scottish MacDonalds declined in the face of incursions made into their territories by various competing clans, in particular by the Campbells of Argyll. It became the ambition of the now well-

established MacDonnells of Antrim to regain their former possessions in the Western Highlands. This struggle was typical of the
dynamic of Gaelic society, with continual shifts of power and a great
deal of intrigue through family alliance and allegiances. Thus when
Chichester arrested a group of Gaelic Irish conspirators in 1615 he
was aware that their planned rebellion was related directly through
their leader, Alexander MacDonnell, to the rising which took place in
the Western Highlands in 1614-15 led by Coll MacDonald and in
which Alexander's brother Sorley was a principal. The Scottish
rebellion failed and the Ulster conspiracy was thwarted, but despite
their leadership and involvement the Antrim MacDonnells were not
called to account (Chichester's sorry handful of culprits being of the
Gaelic Irish alone). This immunity was due to the support of King
James himself, who saw both branches of the clan as a bulwark
against the increasingly successful (and unreliable) Campbells of
Argyll. This was the way in which clan power operated and
which characterised so much of Scottish history. Those who were
losing ground (often literally) could be boosted for the price of their
loyalty. Not surprisingly, this often produced a very unbalanced
political scenario because some clans owed their decline to their own
inabilities and consequently the crown often cultivated those who
would otherwise have not earned such success. Nevertheless, as far as
the history of the seventeenth century was concerned, what mattered
was that credence was given to the MacDonnell–McDonald clan
which had a profound effect on the nature of rebellion and the key
question of whether a group might rise out as an expression of loyalty
to the Stuarts. Thus the stepping-stone between the Ulster–Scottish
rising of 1614-15 and the Ulster Irish rising of 1641 was the attempt
to rise once again in 1626, when Coll MacDonald appealed to Pope
Urban VIII to support a Catholic conquest of the Highlands which
would be undertaken in conjunction with a similar Irish rising in
Ulster.

This appeal is highly significant because it followed a major
political change in the Vatican with the death in Rome in 1625 of
Peter Lombard, the Old English Archbishop of Armagh, and his
replacement first by the Gaelic Irish Franciscan Hugh MacCaughwell
and then, after his death in 1626, by the Bishop of Kilmore, Hugh
O'Reilly, who had been Tyrone's nominee. Although of Old English
stock, Lombard had set himself the task of serving the interests of
Hugh O'Neill until such time as the latter's failure caused Lombard
to return to his own side. He was Tyrone's successful nominee for the

archbishopric of Armagh in 1601, when the earl's influence was so strong that he had just secured (in 1600) the archbishopric of Dublin for his personal envoy, the Spanish Franciscan Mateo de Oviedo. (Oviedo had been a prime mover in the Catholic crusade of James FitzMaurice FitzGerald in 1579; he was resident in Ulster during the Nine Years' War and accompanied the Spanish forces at Kinsale one year after his appointment to Dublin.) At that time Lombard had worked ceaselessly but unsuccessfully among the Spanish faction in the Vatican to urge Pope Clement VIII to make disloyalty to Tyrone a matter for excommunication. Pope Paul V had continued to countenance Tyrone's influence with the appointments of the Franciscan Florence Conry to Tuam and Eugene MacMahon to Dublin. The flight of the earls, however, had not only revealed the weakness of Gaelic resistance to the legal proceedings of Davies and Chichester, it also revealed to Lombard the inadequacy of a religious policy which did not have the support of the most powerful group in Ireland, the Old English. The defeat of his erstwhile patron saw Lombard shift his politics to the other faction in the Vatican. Elizabeth had been a Protestant monarch for whom the practice of Catholicism of any variety had been a threat. It was not surprising that Lombard had chosen to support the most aggressive and militant version nurtured in Spain, because it might, after all, win the whole of Ireland for Rome. After the defeat of Gaelic Ulster there was nothing to do but explore the more constitutional possibilities, as practised by the Old English, of obedience to James in return for religious toleration. (This policy was to be taken up again in the 1650s after the war.) In other words, Tyrone had aimed at that which the Old English had never even countenenced, the taking of the country by force; as head of the Catholic Church in Ireland Lombard had nothing to lose and everything to gain by supporting O'Neill. Equally the total defeat of Tyrone left the archbishop no choice but to change sides and explore the prospect of toleration under a king whose earlier Scottish experience had taught him that Catholics were at heart closer to his theory of divine right than Puritans. By and large Lombard succeeded, and the years between Tyrone's defeat and the Primate's death were not marked by religious persecution. The mandates controversy at the beginning of the reign was indicative of the problems encountered when the Old English were forced to resist Chichester directly. This was not the mode of operation they had cultivated successfully since the Reformation, and Lombard had no option but to acknowledge this in the later years of the reign. Lombard died at an appropriate time. Had he lived, he would have witnessed the break-down of that political constitutionalism which had hitherto worked for the Old English, and he would have witnessed the slow but certain reorganisation of post-Tyrone Gaelic resistance both in Ulster and on the continent.

The Roman Catholic Church, under the unrelenting influence of the Spanish, was never at ease with the Old English tradition of compromising with a heretical monarch; nor was it happy with the Anglican and Gallican deviations. Spain had inherited the Holy Roman Empire and was accordingly obliged to see all the territories which it did not rule as a threat to itself. It was hardly surprising that the Spanish Catholic Church saw the Vatican as the centre which, when controlled, could determine the form of religion (and so the politics) of the Catholic flock.

The net effect of this division as it was expressed within the Irish Catholic Church was that there was little or no sympathy between the Gaelic Irish and the Old English. The latter defined themselves and their religion within the context of the political constitution, while the Gaelic Irish defined themselves as a race. It is not an idle observation to suggest that the mode of response among the Gaelic Irish as a nation was emotional, while that of the Old English was intellectual.

This division was essentially one of tribal community *versus* the post-Renaissance civility which gave the European state a new and abstract definition. Gaelic Ireland had not been conquered by the Romans and had remained outside this European tradition, some-times to advantage and sometimes not. What was clear from the Tudor attempt to conquer the Gaelic Irish, however, was that the English perceived law, religion, politics and even social culture as a question of civility, that is to say as matter contained within a definition of the political state. The period abounds with instances of this anti-Gaelic and anti-barbarous perception, but certainly one of the most pointed examples was the attack made on Tyrone as a Gaelic chief by the zealous Sir John Davies. Moreover, Tyrone was exceptional at this form of adaptation and survival, but in the end he could display the same emotional touchiness which the English found all too easy to needle in the Gaelic Irish. It was commonplace for Gaelic chiefs to protest at personal insults to their dignity while seeing no great danger in signing documents which gave the monarch ultimate and legal right to their lands.

The problems posed by republicanism for Irish history have caused present-day historians to treat very gingerly the reorganisation of resistance in Gaelic Ulster. The fact is that those who led the Ulster rising of 1641 were also those Gaelic Irish who had fought against Tyrone and who, when they rose out, insisted emphatically on their loyalty to the crown. Republicanism *per se* developed out of the constitutional conflict which Calvinists found themselves in when ruled by a monarch who did not share their religion. Such a development was not just predictable, it was inevitable. In this Calvinists shared a fundamental predicament with the Old English in Ireland. Anglican Catholicism and Gallican Catholicism had given the Old English their origins. These Anglican and Gallican settlements had evolved within the political framework as it was defined by independent monarchies. However, both England and France contained uncompromising Calvinists, and both countries underwent republican revolutions as the extreme response to the extreme Catholic absolutism which had followed the Counter-Reformation. By the end of the sixteenth century the Dutch Calvinists had already broken the Spanish imperial hold on the Netherlands and established the first great Calvinistic republic born out of revolution. In short, it might be said that the history of revolution in post-Reformation Europe begins in Calvin's Geneva, free as it was from monarchy. It was applied in the crucible of Scotland, and the British revolution against Catholic monarchy was the result. The Calvinist revolution in the Netherlands was followed by the Calvinist revolution in England. Those Calvinists who fled to America found themselves in a free environment to develop not just the theory of religious toleration but the political corollary of this which came to be known as democracy.

All this might appear to be a far cry from the position in which the Old English in Ireland found themselves under Charles I. This is not the case, however, because their constitutional dilemma was precisely that of the rights of the subject (both religious and political) under a Catholic monarch. Had Charles been a Roman and not an Anglican Catholic, the later history of Ireland would have been a great deal less tragic than it was. Because Anglicanism acknowledged the Reformation, Charles was also, in the broad sense, a Protestant. This meant that the established Church of England could always play both sides against the middle. As a consequence of the split in Irish Catholicism in the seventeenth century and its ultimate loss of political power, the Catholic Church settled for the souls of its flock and left their physical government to the English. Perhaps there were many benefits in this split for the Irish people, but loyalty to the Protestant parliamentary tradition of London, taken together with loyalty to the Roman Catholic heirarchical tradition of the Vatican, meant that the essential split between matters constitutional and matters of unquestioned faith produced the famous 'Irish question' which would seem never to have been asked, let alone answered.

The constitutional development which began in Ireland among the Old English was taken up after their complete disappearance by the Protestant Dissenters of the eighteenth century—the very group who had opposed them most. The link between the two, however, is the same characteristic which will allow us to view Gaelic resistance as truly nationalistic and Old English resistance as constitutional (although not republican). The New English in Ireland tended to profess Calvinism because this was the doctrine which the landed Roman Catholics could not get round. The Gaelic Irish could be viewed not merely as religious idolators but also as racially inferior; hence they saw physical force as the best means of articulating their exclusion. The Old English could not be considered racially inferior and were also more than able to articulate their exclusion, but they could not get round the use, at any time, of the Oath of Supremacy as a test of loyalty. It would seem to follow from this that the New English would make no attempt to convert either group and thereby forfeit a unique opportunity for themselves to become landed gentry. Also consistent with this picture is the fact that the New English Puritans saw land in Ireland, rather than commerce, as the ticket to wealth. A Catholic landowner could be dispossessed by court order in a matter of minutes and the income from his land transferred immediately to his Puritan displacer. Not so with the Catholic merchants of the towns, because a business could not have been expropriated and then continued without experience. Thus the eighteenth century has often been portrayed as having a stagnant, landed and Low Church Protestant ascendancy defined by the penal laws,

while in the towns and cities a considerable number of successful
Catholics continued to trade.

The most crucial year in Ireland's history, the year in which the die
was cast for the first and last time by the Old English, and which, it
might even be said, made the remainder of Ireland's political history a
footnote, was 1641. When they were forced into the Ulster rising of
the Gaelic Irish, centuries of constitutional and religious complexities were reduced to a position of win or lose—a position with which
the Gaelic Irish had lived since their conquest was first begun by the
forefathers of the Old English themselves, the Anglo-Normans. The
Old English found themselves in a constitutional trap by the end of
1641, and the only solution was to be found in the answer to a single
question. Could they rebel against the Puritan government in Dublin
as a demonstration of their loyalty to the ultimate head of that
government, the king?

The answer was to be found within the origins of the rising itself.
Why they should have had to ask this question in the first place is the
essence of the constitutional crisis posed by the Stuart monarchs.
Historians of the English civil war have not, as a rule, been
conversant with Irish history in any detail. (Indeed, this might also be
said of the lack of importance given to Scotland's crucial Stuart
history.) If the Ulster rising and its Scottish connections are not
taken into account on the one hand, and if an explanation of why the
Old English joined that rising is also not included, the major
questions of the English civil war cannot be fully answered. The
reason for this is simple enough. The term 'English civil war' implies
that the war was one fought within the English *civitas* or state.
Unfortunately Charles was, separately, King of Scotland and King of
Ireland. If the 'English civil war' was the result not of an English
Puritan revolution but of an attempt by the Stuarts to alter the
constitutional basis of their kingship at the expense of all non-
Anglican (and later under James II non-Roman) Catholics, then the
history of the seventeenth century would seem to be a lot more
straightforward. Charles I was accused by the Puritans throughout
the war of sympathising with the Catholics of Ireland, of having
attempted to use an army of Irish Catholics against his English
subjects and, most important and least considered, of having had a
hand in the Ulster rising of the Gaelic Irish. It is this last claim which

historians have judged most ridiculous, although the first two can now be seen as historical fact. The claim has been dismissed largely because of the huge gulf which ostensibly existed between the refined Anglican monarch and the barbarous Gaelic Irish tribes. However, by ignoring the Scottish basis of the Stuart monarchy historians have also ignored the use which might have been made of clan politics by the monarch. The ignorance is forgivable because the basis of the clan power which bridged Ulster and the Western Highlands was that of personal allegiances and alliances which were seldom if ever dependent upon written agreements. Yet no sense can be made of the wider picture unless the Ulster dimension is fully accounted for. This has not been possible because of two fundamental mistakes made hitherto by historians of the seventeenth century. The first was to discount the possibility that Charles might have used the politics of Ulster and the Western Highlands as part of his wider plans for Scotland and, consequently, England. If Charles did indeed have a hand in the Ulster rising, then it could not have been a rebellion, and it would only be a matter of time before the Old English were obliged by their very loyalty to join the fray. Quite reasonably, historians have pleaded a lack of evidence for the origins of the Ulster rising; but they have hitherto compounded the problem by their additional error in accepting literally and at face value evidence of an event which did not take place but which nevertheless had a profound influence on the Old English decision to take up arms, and indeed on the subsequent course of events. This non-event, which has been generally accepted, even by contemporaries, as having actually occurred, was the alleged attempt to seize Dublin Castle on the morning of Saturday 23 October 1641 as part of the rising that began on the previous evening in Ulster.

4

Wentworth and the Ulster Crisis, 1638-9

THE significance of the relationship between the Earl of Antrim and Charles I in the late 1630s could not be greater. Even if the evidence is assessed purely at face value (a thing usually impossible in the myriad dealings of the king), Antrim succeeded in arming parts of Ulster for the king immediately before the rising. Moreover, he did so under the highest royal authority (that is, the king's expressed command) and received permission to use the great seal in his efforts. Antrim was not only a Roman Catholic, he belonged to the little-known world of the Ulster-Scottish clans which were viewed by the New English in Ireland (and by many subsequent commentators) as being barbarous and uncivilised. The perception is, of course, a mistaken one, but it has played a major part in clouding what would otherwise be quite clear. Throughout the 1620s and 1630s the Franciscans were working strenuously not merely to retain north-east Ulster for their order, but to expand into the Western Highlands and extend their mission to the Catholic clans there. This was in effect a great cultural revival of the Gaelic form of Catholicism, which had suffered as much from the Old English adherence to the Counter-Reformation as it had from the policies of the New English. What Franciscan thinking had in common with Charles I was the maintenance of that form of strong allegiance which was opposed to the compromise of constitutionalism. The later seventeenth century was to witness this internal Catholic battle over the jurisdiction of the Franciscans and the diocesan clergy; it was a battle mainifestly fought between the emotional faith of the Franciscans, based in the Gaelic tradition, and the administrative and legalistic diocesan bishops implementing the Counter-Reformation in the true spirit of the Old English. In the 1630s, however, there was everything to play for under a king determined, apparently at any cost, to push back Calvinist gains.

Antrim acted of his own accord in what follows, but he also acted on behalf of the Gaelic ringleaders of the Ulster rising. He made no secret of this and added the names of his 'friends' to a demand to Wentworth in March 1639 to furnish him in the king's name with men, arms, support and the great seal itself. The names he appended to this list included Sir Phelim O'Neill, the leader of the rising, Conor Lord Maguire and Hugh MacMahon, both of whom were arrested in Dublin for their alleged attempt on the Castle. Thus there can be no doubt that, as well as representing his family interest in the perpetual MacDonnell–Campbell feud, Antrim was the front man in a far bigger business.

The evidence for Antrim's design comes largely from his correspondence with Wentworth beginning in July 1638. Wentworth's reluctance to countenance these plans until he was ordered to do so by Charles throws considerable light on the Lord Deputy's outlook and what must have been his very painful recognition that he and his master did not share the same views. That Wentworth was used by Charles in a quite blatant way could not have dawned on the Lord Deputy until he realised how far the king was willing to go in his support for the Catholic chiefs of Ulster—those who represented for all Englishmen, Anglican or Calvinist, the least civilised people in western Europe.

In July 1638 Antrim wrote to Wentworth to tell him that he had been informed by the Marquis of Hamilton that Lord Lorne (Antrim's Campbell rival who became the eighth Earl and first Marquis of Argyll) had sided with the Scots assembly against the king and that it was possible he would invade Antrim's territories in Ulster. Antrim appealed to Wentworth for arms to defend himself. As if to reinforce this request, Archbishop Laud wrote to Wentworth in the same month concerning a rumour that the Scots had made a list of their supporters in Ulster and that the total number was believed to be 40,000. Wentworth wrote to the king on 28 July that 'the Earl of Antrim shall be observed as Your Majesty hath directed', but he cast doubt on Antrim's ability. He told the king that he could not inform the Dublin council of Antrim's request because they saw the earl simply as the grandson of Tyrone. Anway, to store such arms would be unsafe if the Scots were to revolt and the rising were to spread to Ulster; as Wentworth put it, the Scots Presbyterians in Ulster 'might chance to borrow those weapons of his lordship for a longer time and another purpose than his lordship would find cause to thank them for. They are shrewd children, not won much by courtship, especially from a Roman Catholic.'[1] This straight talking was accompanied by a request for further instructions, and Wentworth then went on to talk about the strength of the army in Ireland. This was in answer to a request made by the king to let him know what support he might call for from Ireland should trouble break out with the Scots. Wentworth was not optimistic; he put the total strength at 2,000 foot and 600 horse, which he said was not even enough to secure the Irish government against the opposition to the various current plantation schemes. There was no doubt also that the Presbyterians in Ulster were against the king, so that to remove soldiers from Ireland would be asking for trouble; 'for howbeit the Irish might do very good service, being a people removed from the Scottish, as well in affections as religion, yet it is not safe to train them up more than needs must in the military way which, the present occasion past, might arm their old affections to do us more mischief'.[2]

This was the matter in a nutshell, and Wentworth was politely telling the king that within the Protestant conquest of Ireland there was no logical way of arming the Gaelic Irish. There is a crucial difference here between Wentworth and Charles which can only be accounted for by the king's dynamic push against the Calvinists. Wentworth wrote a long letter to Northumberland, the Lord High Admiral, two days after his letter to the king, expressing his own view of what should be done about the Scots. He advocated a cooling-off period during which the Scots would not be provoked, though at the same time their demand for a parliament would not be met. The Scottish ports should be blockaded, while a force of Scots loyalists could be raised, with a similar force in the north of England.

> The best part of the Irish army [Wentworth explained] might be drawn down into Ulster, close upon Scotland, as well to amuse those upon that side as to contain their countrymen amongst us in due obedience. The clergy of England and Ireland would be instructed to preach to the people against their disorder and rebellions, as they [the Scots Presbyterians] do most impudently against the Common Prayer Book and ceremonies of our church.[3]

The point here was essentially one of containment which was both logical and strong, but it ignored the fact that Charles did not want to leave the Scots alone until the uniformity of his religion had been established. Counter-preaching, as Wentworth here advocated, was not in the nature of a king committed to dicta. Yet the problem of the Ulster Presbyterians was as much Wentworth's as it was the king's, and he acknowledged to Laud that 'It is not to be kept secret that there are 40,000 Scots in Ulster able to bear arms; we hear the crack of it, if not the threat, every day in the streets.'[4]

In answer to a request from the king that he raise four troops of 100 horse apiece, Wentworth suggested in August that one troop be assigned to Ulster, 'close upon the Scottish plantations', another to go to Ormond, a third to his own brother Sir George, and the fourth to be ready for service in England. This division was to pre-empt the obvious:

> If the Earl of Antrim hear of the raising of these troops, Your Majesty will have him a suitor for one; but I beseech you he may not be admitted, as a thing that would be displeasing to all the English on this side. His religion, nor yet his descent (being the grandchild and son of Your Majesty knows whom) sort not well with it. And I am upon very probable reason for believing that in the way of pretending service, but doing nothing for Your Majesty, he attentively watcheth to do something for his own fortune and power.[5]

This pointed attack on Antrim was intended to spell out to the king that his Scottish policy was too close to the affections of Gaelic Ulster for safety. Wentworth was a civil servant, however, and was obliged to act under instruction; accordingly he wrote to Antrim in the same month that he would facilitate him in every way possible. His dilemma was acute; the very basis of his loyalty was obedience to the king's wishes, but hitherto these wishes had been largely for more money from Ireland. In other words, Wentworth's abilities had been exploited to the full in the administrative area, and when it came to political power games he had only to rely on his authority to override opposition. It had been unnecessary to develop an appreciation of Irish complexities—a circumstance which had often been the rock upon which foundered many a deputyship in the past. Where the Ulster-Scottish question was concerned, however, Wentworth was not being asked for his advice, but only to apply his famous administrative skills to raise troops. Most importantly, he was not being asked to advise the king on matters of religious commitment. Yet Wentworth's ground was safe enough in the sense that the king could not come out publicly and declare for Antrim. It was to be Charles's greatest problem that he could not declare exactly what he wanted or where he hoped his policies might lead. Nevertheless, his support for Antrim was only thinly veiled. He wrote to Wentworth at the end of August:

> [The Earl of Antrim's] professions have been so free and noble at this time that (as I have promised) indeed he deserves to be recommended unto you; which, at his coming over to you, I wish you to take notice of him. But to have the command of a magazine of arms, I leave to you and the council there to judge how far ye will trust anyone in that kind, of his profession in religion. To conclude this, I would have you favour and countenance him as much as anyone of his profession in religion.[6]

The Lord Deputy could hardly forget that Charles was married to a Roman Catholic, a fact which would serve to remind him that there was a great difference between legalism and loyalty. It is also clear that Charles was coupling Wentworth with the Irish Privy Council in a rather insulting way, with the implication that the Lord Deputy, famous for his personal power, might have to consult with his fellow-governors. The line of allegiance had been drawn by Charles, and the question was now whether Wentworth's own personal convictions would impede that allegiance or whether he could side with the king's increasingly Catholic policies.

It was the king's problems in Scotland which, more than anything else, continued to force the pace and indeed ultimately forced Wentworth himself to act. He was obliged to write to Charles in October and acknowledge that Lord Lorne had moved down into Argyll and built fortifications on islands not three hours away from Ulster. The key question was whether this activity was a defence against Antrim's designs or whether Antrim's designs were a defence against Lord Lorne (now eighth Earl of Argyll on his father's death early in October). Wentworth reported the presence on the islands of 'sixteen pices of ordnance, well provided and mounted in places of best advantage for the defence of his country, and people taught the use of their weapon'. This was to side with Argyll, but Wentworth could not ignore the fact that 'besides, his lordship causeth to be made a great many of flat-bottomed boats'. Yet Wentworth was determined not only that Antrim would not benefit from Argyll's aggressive activities, but also that these activities themselves would be blamed directly on Antrim:

What [Argyll's] motives or purposes may be herein Your Majesty will be best able to judge; but the reason which passeth over, and is given to us on this side is, that some of the Clandonalds had a design upon his country, and intended to bring in upon him Tyrone with his regiment of Irish in Flanders; that the Earl of Antrim declareth himself to be their patron; that they reported Your Majesty had given the earl your title; that the earl came to take it [i.e. Argyll] by strong hand; to which purpose three of Your Majesty's ships full of arms were appointed to bring and furnish him for the attempt.

After further casting doubt on Antrim's personal abilities, Wentworth pointed out bluntly: 'These preparations so near upon us, give great apprehensions to the well-affected in those parts.' The king responded simply: 'As for Argyll, look you there, I shall do here as well as I can.'[7]

Clearly Charles was separating Wentworth the man from Wentworth the servant, but if this caused the Lord Deputy any relief, he was misreading the king's relentless and impersonal tendency to use the abilities of his servants even at the expense of their lives, as Wentworth would find out to his cost shortly afterwards. Charles wrote calmly to Wentworth in October:

Some months ago I wrote to know of you what assistance I might expect from thence for to curb the rebels in Scotland; the expectation of which (because I found by your answer to be so difficult to be had, and likewise of no great consequence being had) I have relinquished so far as not to build much upon those hopes.

This was not to say that Charles had abandoned his hopes, but that he had abandoned the hope that Wentworth would actively participate in them. As part of his Scottish plan the king revealed that he intended to take Carlisle, but that he would also need Wentworth to raise 500 well-provided men in Ireland and to let him know how soon this could be done 'with caution of the highest secrecy, for you must find some pretext for the providing and transporting of those men'. He concluded blandly: 'So expecting a speedy and I hope a good answer to this letter I rest, etc.' In a postscript he added: 'If this be feasible lose no time in providing all things necessary, that ye may be ready at the first warning from me.'[8]

Thus the vital split between Charles and Wentworth took place invisibly. The Lord Deputy responded on receipt of the king's letter that he would indeed keep its contents secret and that he lived to obey the king's commands 'and trust they shall never find me so ill-provided again to fulfil them'. The civil servant had bitten the bullet, even if it went against all his better judgments. He told the king that the organisation of 500 men would present no problem and that they would be ready in two months 'without any great prejudice to these affairs'; but he added that to get it right he would need direction.[9]

That Wentworth fully appreciated the implications of the king's policy is clear. The man whose actions had always been literally above board and who had used that fact to intimidate all parties in Ireland was now about to suppress his own better judgment and enter the king's realm of intrigue, an area for which he was exceptionally unsuited. Arming any part of Ulster for the king at this time meant, in effect, supporting the Gaelic Roman Catholics against the Presbyterians, and this could not be done openly. The easiest way around the problem was to take Antrim's view that the Scots were indeed preparing an invasion. Moreover, the point had already passed in the conflict between Antrim and Argyll where one or the other could be seen as the aggressor. The difficulty for Wentworth now was to act a part that he neither believed in nor judged to be safe, but Charles had given him no choice. Intrigue was not his style, however, as is shown by his obedient but lacklustre response to the king's demand:

> The colour I give this levy shall be the putting of a garrison for five hundred men into Carrickfergus, the Derry and Coleraine, in regard I understand the Lord of Lorne fortifies on the other side, which not hearing to be Your Majestys command I understand not what to think of it; the rather also in regard, I am informed, the Scottish in these parts are observed all to ride up and down the country armed with swords, which formerly they had not been accustomed to. And, to cover the business better, I purpose so to handle the matter as the council here shall advise and avow these preparations for that end, which will be a means, I trust, to effect the service without the least thought of the true intent indeed. And this I adventure on of myself, in regard upon Your Majesty's letter seems to leave the pretence for me to take upon the place, that I am commanded to lose no time; and that all may be thus in the more readiness.[10]

Showing more of his true colour, he asked the king if he might have these 500 men when their immediate purpose had been served, 'and I durst with the peril of my life be answerable to contain all here in quietness; but then I must have present and full authority to take every little inclination in the first appearance of it, and to crush the serpent in the egg'.[11] What the Lord Deputy wanted was a restoration of the king's trust, and to achieve this he was first willing to view the Gaelic Irish as the king would seem to do. He advised Charles to rely on his English subjects, 'and, as for this subject, questionless the English (and native in this exigent) are most assured, no suspicion to be had of them at all'.[12]

Wentworth was effectually confounded by his own obedience. He was obliged to write to Archbishop Laud in November: 'Questionless this whole kingdom, not Scottish, would zealously live and die with the crown.'[13] It cannot be emphasised enough that not only was this not his real view, but that this was not the view upon which he had built his administrative success in Ireland since 1633. In short, Wentworth had never had to lie before. The crux of the matter, however, was that he had no sympathy whatsoever for the Presbyterians who challenged the king, but at the same time he appreciated fully that they would not concede if they were continually pushed. This left the door wide open for a real Gaelic revival on the sole basis of Catholic allegiance to the Stuarts. In the face of such a shift, Wentworth's so-called policy of 'thorough' would be neutralised by a group who held a higher card than his own. In other words, they could outbid him in the stakes for the king's all-important support. Just over a month after he had included all the Catholics of Ireland, Gaelic and Old English, among those who would live and die for the crown, he had to face the logic of his predicament in a letter to Sir Arthur Hopton:

> Your [letter] mentions the expression of [Hugh O'Donnell, the titular earl of] Tyrconnell's willingness to return and replant himself in his native soil. A treaty which hath been long in motion betwixt my lady his mother, here amongst us, and himself, as some letters which were to pass betwixt them sufficiently show; but it is much better he were as he is, for he looks for mighty conditions, such as might render him little less than a prince in Ulster, and consequently would be set up again to these natives as the altar whereon to lay and sacrifice all.

Such was the danger, and now came the impotent advice to Hopton: 'So as in my judgment, giving a civil hearing unto him, in conclusion it will be the best to put him off to solicit his restitution by his other friends, than for you to interest yourself in his business.'[14] Nothing could be simpler: a restoration of The O'Donnell (son of Rory, the first earl) would dismantle the conquest of Ireland, which now depended upon constitutional balance, by making him once again a Gaelic chief. On the other hand, there were those who were already working in this direction and who also had the king's approval; in such circumstances the best thing to do was to do nothing.

The king's problem was not what his plans or intentions were, it was that he had begun to move on the widest front before he had secured his own ability to do so. The great difference between Charles and his father in this respect was that James appreciated fully that a theory of kingship by divine right, or any other right, was nothing more than a theory. If it was not grounded in the power politics of the kingdom, it could not rely upon the naked self-interest of those who stood to lose if the king lost. The Reformation and Counter-Reformation had been used in this way since their respective inceptions, and very few monarchs could be found who had ever relied upon an ideal rather than physical support. This was simply because those who governed Europe throughout this period did so in the midst of their own subjects and could not have failed to appreciate their own relative strength on the ground. Charles, however, was ruling Scotland from the south of England, and as a result his rule was more abstract than anything else. This was the same problem faced by the Catholic Spanish monarchy when it had tried and failed to force the Netherlands to conform. The Lutheran Reformation itself had been incubated in the tensions which had existed both between the German principalities and Rome and between those principalities and the new Spanish Habsburg empire (after the German Maximilian had died in 1519). More than any monarchy, the Catholic Church had appreciated that there could be no Counter-Reformation if the essential basis of political or physical support was not there. The theology of divine right would be less than nothing if it was not grounded ultimately in physical support. In Ireland's case that support had been found largely by the Franciscans, among the Gaelic Irish in particular, but among any discontented groups in general. For example, the rebellion in the Desmond earldom was greatly facilitated by Franciscans who came to prominence in the Vatican at the same time as did the order's general Felice Peretti, who became Cardinal Montalto in 1570 and pope (as Sixtus V) in 1585. Such was the Spanish king's support for Peretti that he instructed his ministers at the Vatican to treat the pope's wishes as they would his own. The Spanish retained control over the papacy throughout the period of the Nine Years' War so that the politics of Spain and the mission of the Franciscans were united in the concept of a Catholic rebellion against a heretical monarch. However, Spanish control of the papacy came to an end with the election of the French candidate, Paul V, in 1605. The Spanish in the Vatican did not gain full control again until the election of their candidate Cardinal Pamfili, who became Pope Innocent X in September 1644. The mission to Ireland of the Arch-bishop of Fermo, Rinuccini, and his support for the Gaelic cause, must be seen in this light. (Sixtus V had himself held the see of Fermo.)

King Charles recognised that the Roman Catholic interest was sympathetic to his own, but whereas the Vatican always first secured the physical basis of its policy (whether it be the Spanish–Gaelic or Old English–French alliance) before it acted, the king was now advancing without this vital consideration. Wentworth could see it, but he was powerless to intervene because although the two men shared the same political outlook, they did not share the same faith. Wentworth was capable of changing sides, from being a leading par-liamentary opponent to being a king's minister, when there was a logical and clear course set out for him. In both cases he was a true civil servant who had altered course when he had altered his definition of where sovereignty lay in the state. Charles was adept at encouraging this type of servant, and what Wentworth shared with Laud was the humble nature of his origins. Both men owed their great power to the king, but both were to be disabused of any notion that this support amounted to familiarity. It was not until the very end that Charles granted Wentworth an earldom, which meant that the Lord Deputy was obliged to defer to the social rank of a great many of those in Ireland who were not sympathetic to him. (This was par-ticularly noticeable in Antrim's casual treatment of the intellectually superior Wentworth, and the latter's obligation to acknowledge his social inferiority.) When the Lord Deputy eventually achieved aristo-cratic status it was precisely to give him what he had by then lost, his authority. It was yet another example of Charles responding to a reaction which he had himself caused rather than anticipating that reaction by getting it right in the first place. The result was to give his opponents a very dangerous sense of where the king's weakness lay at any given time. The nature of this weakness was in the rigidity of the royal policy: Charles could not in conscience raise Wentworth to the peerage to increase his status when Wentworth's authority had been at the command of the king in the first place. To do so would have been to concede the principle of the royal authority itself. The king did not live in the same world as his subjects, however, and it was these subjects that Wentworth had been given the task of ruling.

It must be said on the king's side, however, that the practice of European kingship was changing in such a way that he was almost obliged to put his own authority before any local realities, as the Tudors might have done. By the late 1630s the old rivalry between France and Spain had altered as both monarchies realised that they were now far more at risk from Calvinist revolution and its political instrument, parliament, than they were from each other. The net effect of this realisation was the rise of absolutism in the face of this parliamentary threat. It also meant that for a politically naïve monarch, which Charles appears to have been, support could be gained from either camp without ever having to decide in favour of one. Thus in the late 1630s Charles set on foot a scheme in Ireland which had a profound effect on the country's perception of his intentions. He granted licence to some Irish and Old English colonels from the continent to recruit men in Ireland for service abroad. This made no sense to anyone unless it was a cover to raise and organise among the Catholics of Ireland an army which would then be turned against the Puritans (of Scotland, England, and not least Ireland). That is to say that there was now sufficient common cause among the seventeenth-century monarchs that Charles could use the Netherlands to hold forces whose sympathies had not hitherto coincided. For the moment, therefore, the Irish army on the continent could be fed from both Gaelic and Old English communities to be used in the struggle which was by now inevitable. The pretext which the Protestant Charles could use was the removal from Ireland of disloyal Catholic forces; no one, least of all the English parliament, was fooled by this, however. Thus what seems an inexplicable paradox is quite straightforward. The New English Puritan council in Dublin did not want these Catholic soldiers either to be recruited or taken out of the country, whereas the pro-Catholic king did. The issue, of course, revolved around the use to which these men would be put. If they really were to serve on the continent, then the New English would have fully encouraged their departure, as indeed they had done in the past after the defeat of Tyrone. If, on the other hand, the king was banking up his forces, then that was an entirely different matter and a grave threat. Moreover, it was known to all and sundry by the late 1630s that both groups of Catholics in Ireland were in constant contact with their military cousins on the continent. Wentworth had to swallow this unpalatable fact because it was his job to grant licences in the king's name to these recruiting officers. He wrote:

> [With regard to] the two Irish colonels and their regiments, I like that employment best that carries them farthest hence; their affections are altogether Irish, and by habit it is now their belief that they are more subjects to the Spaniard than to our master; yet by their favour, where they say that their recruits come for love of them without His Majesty's licence, in that they magnify themselves without reason; for without His Majesty's leave they would not have had many hundreds, which have passed since my coming hither, by my warrant pursuing His Majesty's direction to me in that behalf.[15]

The reality was not just unpalatable to Wentworth, it was tending increasingly to a revolution within the constitution; and it is in this context that the Ulster rising of 1641 is entirely explicable. Late in January 1639 Charles wrote to Wentworth informing him that he planned to move on Carlisle and Berwick on 1 April. Wentworth was instructed to have his 500 men in readiness. Nor was the king under any doubt as to where further support was to be drawn. He wrote:

> Lastly, I should be glad if you could find some way to furnish the Earl of Antrim with arms, though he be a Roman Catholic; for he may be of much use to me at this time to shake loose upon the Earl of Argyll. All of which particulars none of my secretaries at this time are aquainted with, wherefore that answer must come immediately to [me].[16]

The matter was coming to a head for Wentworth because the king was determined to bring it to a trial of physical strength with the Scots. Wentworth foresaw the enormous and disastrous consequences of this action, and he could also see that if the English parliament was drawn in directly on the side of the Scots, and if the king lost the contest, he (Wentworth) would lose his head. His reply to the king contains a note of protest mingled with some desperation:

My lord of Antrim doth not by one word make known his desire to me for arms, which is advisedly done, his lordship perceiving I am not ignorant of his great want of money, his credit to be so low as not able at this very instant to take up in this town poor three hundred pounds. Therefore his great undertakings are more like to be believed on abroad than they would be nearer home. I shall be able to furnish him with arms when the supply comes we have sent for into the Low Countries, if it be your pleasure to have it so; but I crave to know who it is Your Majesty purposeth shall pay for them.[17]

The Lord Deputy was here resorting to quibbles, but the pointedness could not have been lost on Charles, nor indeed could Wentworth's personal castigation of Antrim, who was, after all, married to the Duchess of Buckingham, widow of the king's great friend. Wentworth went on to spell out what was indeed the truth, namely that Antrim was not in any position to cause trouble to the powerful Earl of Argyll. If this was all the king had in mind, then, by pointing out what the whole kingdom knew, Wentworth was coming very close to the logical conclusion that the king was a complete fool. Wentworth was only too well aware by this time, however, that Charles knew exactly what he wanted, and that the instruction to help the Earl of Antrim was merely a euphemism for putting arms into Ulster. The Lord Deputy knew that he could not be acting treasonably if he was carrying out the king's instructions, but it was the secrecy of these schemes that seemed to imply the almost incomprehensible notion that the king was rebelling against himself. This was to remain the essential question for every single inhabitant of Ireland, and indeed the British Isles, throughout the civil war; it was to inform all the constitutional problems of the Commonwealth and was to surface for the last great conflict which followed the Restoration: where did sovereignty lie?

It was Wentworth, however, who was faced with a possibility which had not yet materialised, and he was obliged to plod on, in an increasingly dangerous way, and point out what the king knew very well. The implication of Charles's actions was that the king could commit treason if he was to act against the interests of his subjects. Wentworth tried to warn Charles:

The secrets Your Majesty gives me in charge shall never be discovered to any creature, yet that I be not thought upon for other men's faults, I here enclosed send a passage I myself read in a letter writ thence to Captain Byron, the writer is one Mr Daniel Neale, a very slight and busy person, his principal dependence on the Earl of Antrim and, if I be not mistaken, very conversant at Arundel House.[18]

If Daniel O'Neill (who proved to be a leading figure in the Ulster rising and Confederate war) was working in the Spanish interest and was dependent on the Earl of Antrim, then the king, once informed, would be obliged to avoid compromising his rule in such a vital area as Spanish influence and thus had no choice but to drop Antrim immediately. Wentworth was here resorting to the only means possible to address the king, namely that he was being misinformed as to the nature of his situation. That the king himself was fully conversant with the politics of Daniel O'Neill was something which the Lord Deputy could not bring himself to acknowledge.

If there was to be any constitutional solution to the problem of raising men, it should be done, Wentworth wrote to Windebank, under licence not to Spanish sympathisers but to the Old English on the continent, as represented by Colonel Preston, 'a gentleman of English race, well affected to the king, and in great emulation with these other two [colonels], who being native Irish and the sons of rebels, acknowledge indeed no other king but the King of Spain'.[19]

He again castigated Antrim to Windebank and said that, as far as he was aware, the earl had no forces; 'besides, it is common with the Irish to be more mighty abroad than they are found to be at home'.[20] Furthermore, Antrim had debts of £50,000, and if his conflict with Argyll came to blows, it would not be Antrim but Argyll who invaded, 'which, if not much mistaken, I judge to be the very true state of that business'.[21] The Lord Deputy was not willing to acknowledge that this was indeed the position which Antrim had been putting forward all along and which, unless the Irish government wanted an invasion from Scotland, was what could easily happen. In other words, Antrim's cover was actually legitimate, and it was only for this reason that he could continue to keep up his demand for aid.

Antrim could continue to put pressure on Wentworth as long as the king's problems with the Scots remained unresolved, and it began to seem to the Lord Deputy that there was a somewhat less than honest reason for this. Wentworth wrote again to Windebank in March 1639 that the earl was

pleased to desire my advice, to whom he never imparted himself concerning this action in all his life, that know not any part of his design: which makes me think his lordship is pleased either to be merry with me or covets to draw me blindfold into his business, so according to occasion either to take the glory of the good success to himself or cast the ill upon me, who neither envy him the one, nor shall willingly undergo the other for him.

Antrim had written to Wentworth telling him that he was not then able to give account of his forces, but that on instruction from the Lord Deputy he could do so—that is to say when Wentworth committed himself to the earl's schemes. Wentworth complained to Windebank that it was with great difficulty that he had raised the money sufficient for no more than 8,000 arms to furnish the stores for the whole country's defence, 'and at one clap his lordship demands 6,000 of them of free cost'.[22] Apart from the problem of replacing these arms, Wentworth wanted to know where the money for this purpose was to come from. Antrim had assured Wentworth that his aims were those of the king, but Wentworth reasonably pointed out that this could not become a reality until the earl was furnished not only with arms but with provisions as well.

As Antrim was becoming more confident, the Lord Deputy was becoming more desperate:

> Above all, I am astonished with his lordship's purpose of putting these men under the command of Colonel Neale, understood to be in his heart and affections a traitor, bred no other, egg and bird as they say. And I beseech you [he wrote to Windebank] imagine what a comfortable prospect it would be for all us English here to see 6,000 men armed with our own weapons, ourselves by that means turned naked, led by that Colonel under the command of Tyrone's grandchild, the son of old Randy MacDonnell, in the same country, formerly the very heart and strength of those mighty long-lasting rebellions? Indeed, for myself, I will put his lordship's conditional pro-position into an absolute conclusion, I shall never think of the Colonel more; since his lordship desire it, advise his lordship also to resolve of the same himself.[23]

The Lord Deputy's predicament, however, could not be so easily resolved by not thinking about it. He was in effect trying to behave as if he still retained the king's absolute confidence, and indeed when he had done so such an 'absolute conclusion' would have proved final. But even if those days had gone, Wentworth had not achieved his position as head of the Irish government by buckling in the face of adversity, and he was determined that if his own career (or indeed life) was to be on the line, then the king must come straight out and acknowledge what could only be interpreted as traitorous schemes. For as long as he was in control, and for as long as the central decisions were still his to make, the Earl of Antrim and his Gaelic allies would get no help from the government in Ireland. If the king wished to attack the Earl of Argyll from Ireland, then he had only to command his deputy and it would be done and, most importantly, it would be done in the king's own name. If there was advantage to be gained, then it should be the king's own; if not, then action should be avoided.

The Earl of Antrim responded to Wentworth's opposition by calling on him directly on 9 March 1639. Wentworth reported to Windebank 'the broken discourse which passed betwixt us, wherein you will find many uncertainties, small hopes, and to my poor judgment some various readings and impossibilities'. Yet this description was not true of the reported conversation which Wentworth himself gave. Antrim spelt out in no uncertain terms how things stood in Ulster, and, like it or not, the situation was beyond Wentworth's control. He reported Antrim as having said that

> instantly upon the receipt of His Majesty's letter [of support] he had sent to the O'Neills, the O'Haras, the O'Lurgans (if I mistake not that name), the Macgennises, the Maguires, the MacMahons, the MacDonnells (as many O's and Macs as would startle a whole council-board on this side to hear of) and all his other friends, requiring them in His Majesty's name to meet him with their forces, so as this business is now become no secret, but the common discourse both of his lordship and the whole kingdom.[24]

In a most aggressive way Antrim was confronting Wentworth face to face with the latter's utter weakness. No one could think that these Gaelic chiefs were now in league for the sole purpose of aiding Antrim in his family struggle with the Campbells in Scotland. What was being paraded before Wentworth was a rising, in the king's name, against the government of Ireland if that government was to oppose those chiefs. Antrim then maintained his invasion story (because otherwise Wentworth could have had him arrested for subversion) by telling the Lord Deputy that he had purchased some boards and had ordered the making of boats and would now like Wentworth's advice as to what he should do. In what must have been the low point of Wentworth's entire career, he replied that he would give whatever assistance he could, but as to advice, 'being a mere stranger to his design, wholly ignorant of the state of that country and people', it would be 'a great vanity (in plain terms) to abuse him and myself'.[25] Antrim seems to have lost his temper at this point and claimed that false information had been sent to England from Dublin that he was not able to fulfil his pledges to the king, but he wished to point out to Wentworth that if His Majesty wished it, he would raise 20,000 men to serve him. After these and other professions of loyalty on Antrim's part the real purpose of the interview became clear: having committed himself completely to the king and having demonstrated that the Gaelic Irish chiefs had done likewise, Antrim offered to give up the whole design if Wentworth advised him to do so and protested that he would keep nothing secret from him so that Wentworth would fully understand what he was advising Antrim to do.

In effect the earl was putting Wentworth into a truly impossible position, and the Lord Deputy had no choice but to fall back on his own feigned ignorance, which he did clumsily.

> As for imparting unto me his design [he reported himself as replying], it was not my custom to covet any man's secrets, but I held it high presumption for me so much as to inquire after those of His Majesty's, nor were it at all to the purpose for his lordship to acquaint me therewith, for howbeit as a private person I should credit all his lordship related, yet in my public capacity I could only understand my master in his own language, to wit, by his hand and seal, and otherwise in these important matters I gave myself no latitude at all.[26]

Wentworth then resorted to a simple but clever ploy: if Antrim would commit everything to writing, he would guarantee him a speedy reply. Antrim replied by playing the card he had already played: he gave a long discourse on the Isles of Scotland and the MacDonald problems there, but concluded by saying that since he could not make war alone, and since it was obvious that Wentworth was not interested in helping, he would not even go on with his plan to build boats. Wentworth retorted that it was not his fault if Antrim had decided to make war (which it must be remembered had started out as defensive measures) and no one could say anything of his own involvement when he knew nothing about it; the whole affair was undertaken on Antrim's responsibility to the king, and that was that. Antrim said that it was true that his own friends in England had tried to dissuade him from the plan, but that he had committed himself before he realised how far the Scots were willing to go. Now that things were the way they were, however, he must do his best for the king, but he could do nothing without 8,000 foot and 300 horse (100 of which would be needed as his personal bodyguard). Otherwise he could not set foot on the Isles. Antrim was here taunting Wentworth because the latter was insisting on remaining with the definition of the scheme as an invasion plan. It was obviously Antrim's intention to get Wentworth to compromise himself one way or the other: he must either support the Ulster cause or he must relinquish control to someone who would.

In this battle of wits Wentworth could only return to his offficial role; he told Antrim that this was indeed a great number of men and that he should apply himself diligently to the task of raising them, but in the meantime he must commit it all to paper and send it to the king, either through Wentworth himself or through a messenger of his own. Antrim then very skilfully conceded this point and said that he would indeed commit it all to writing. He then announced that he had only one more request, namely for a commission under the great seal to levy the men, as well as 6,000 arms and an allowance to cut wood for the boats.

This was the first mention of a great seal to be used by the Gaelic Irish in the king's cause. After the rising had begun the Irish did indeed produce a royal seal which they claimed had come from Scotland and which endorsed their actions. It has not been possible to prove the matter one way or another where the rising was concerned, but it can certainly be said that when Wentworth forced the king to pronounce upon Antrim's request Charles did indeed instruct him to grant a commission under the great seal. The Lord Deputy would not countenance the king's support for the Gaelic Irish under any circumstances, however, nor did he even wish to deny the request for arms on the grounds that they had not yet arrived (and thus reveal the weakness of the Irish government's position). For the moment his position was clear:

> The arms provided for the defence of this kingdom being not
> yet arrived, and myself utterly resolved not to give way to the

drawing so great a body of Irish together, under the command of those septs that now only remain of the Ulster rebels, without full and clear warrant from His Majesty, it was necessary to gain time rather than to discover [i.e. reveal] we were not able to furnish the 6,000 arms so suddenly, or myself in flat terms deny the levy, and so furnish a shift off and turn the failing on the king's part; two principal motives indeed, which caused me from the beginning to propound this way of putting the propositions into writing, and transmitting them over for a final and full direction thereon.[27]

The two adjourned at this point but met again shortly afterwards. By this time Wentworth had decided that if he was confined to the pretence that Antrim's schemes were for an invasion of Scotland, then he would exploit the obvious failure of the earl in this direction. It was not an ideal position, but it did at least give him some security. The result was a conversation which reads like a sequence of comic exchanges. Antrim was asked what provision he had made to feed his men, to which the earl replied that he had made no provision whatsoever but presumed that they would find sufficient provisions in Scotland; and besides, he intended to bring with him 10,000 cows to furnish his troops with fresh milk. He taunted Wentworth with the observation that this 'had been his grandfather (Tyrone's) play'. Wentworth expressed his curiosity as to what the earl would do if Argyll should enclose the cattle and lay waste the land; Antrim replied that he would feed his horses on the leaves from the trees and his men on shamrocks. The Lord Deputy pointed out that there were no trees in the Isles, but even if there were, they would not be in leaf yet, and so the earl should wait for one or two months before setting off. In the meantime he wondered what provision Antrim had made for the minimum two months' training in Ireland which his troops would have to undergo, and also whether he had considered the likelihood that they might have to wait for a favourable wind for anything up to two or three months. Antrim's response was that he had not given it any thought, but the Lord Deputy pressed the point. Eight thousand foot at 6d a day for victuals, plus 1s 6d for 300 horse, for a period of two or three months was no small undertaking. What officers had the earl chosen to lead and instruct his men? Antrim replied that he had not appointed any officers but rather hoped that Wentworth would furnish him with a hundred sergeants from the king's army in Ireland. Wentworth informed him that there were only eighty sergeants in the whole army and that even these were not capable of such a mission; the earl should therefore include the cost of recruiting officers plus their keep in his budget. Antrim said that he hadn't really intended 'to make a formal war of it', so the officers would not really be necessary, and besides, the islanders 'did so adore him (his very word)' that once he had landed, even if it was only with 300 men, they would all rally to his cause. Furthermore, if he had only 300, it would still be enough for him to 'do more than another should do with twenty thousand'. Wentworth rejoined smartly that if such was the case, then there would be no need 'of any these great and troublesome preparations', but his doubt was that Argyll would not easily quit his possessions. The earl conceded that Argyll had indeed erected considerable defences, but claimed that he possessed only £200 worth of land, the rest being the rightful possession of the MacDonalds for thirteen hundred years. Wentworth asked what arrangements had been made about powder, shot, ordnance, etc.; in this matter, Antrim blandly replied, he proposed to put himself in the Lord Deputy's hands. Wentworth observed that the earl would appear to have no detailed plan whatsoever and that the best general in the world could not work in this way. To the question of a landing place the earl replied that he hadn't decided upon one, whereupon Wentworth concluded the interview by asking Antrim once again to put it all down on paper. On his way out Antrim stopped off to talk to Sir George Radcliffe, Wentworth's secretary. He told Radcliffe that at first he had been dissatisfied with the Lord Deputy's attitude, but now that the latter had spelt out the ineptitude of his invasion plans he was grateful to him, and he admitted to Radcliffe in all confidence that he would be glad to be rid of the whole business.

That Antrim was making a fool of Wentworth is obvious from the conversation. That he was deadly serious about the position of the Gaelic chiefs upon whose behalf he was acting was to be seen from the written proposition he submitted to Wentworth two days later. It contained many detailed requests some of which were of great importance but none more than the first:

> I desire that your lordship will presently grant me a commission under the great seal for levying of three regiments, each regiment consisting of sixteen hundred foot and two hundred light horse, with power to make officers.

This was to put on paper what Wentworth had hoped Antrim would not claim. If that was not enough, however, Antrim's second request could only have been taken by Wentworth as an insult:

> I desire your lordship to send presently your several letters to
> my friends to encourage them to make up their books, and to
> have their men in readiness upon four or five days' warning,
> because your lordship knows the time limited by His Majesty
> to me is very short, whose names I here annex.

The names were a roll-call of those Ulster chiefs prominent in the
rising of October 1641: Lord Magennis and his uncles; Phelim
O'Neill and his brother; Conor Lord Maguire and his brother; Art
Oge O'Neill; Turlough MacHenry, his children and grandchildren;
Coll O'Hara, his son and grandchildren; and, finally, Hugh
MacMahon. Antrim went on to spell out his requirements in detail,
not least of which was a loan of £2,000, and to point out that, except
for the provision of boats, all would be granted at the king's expense.
In closing, Antrim apologised for his lack of preparedness in putting
forward his plans, but explained that the king's letter of support had
only reached him on 6 March and he was with Wentworth on the 9th,
'by means whereof I could not make my proposition sooner, and the
time being so short I was forced to make them of myself, without
consulting with men experienced in the like weighty affairs'.[28]

Wentworth finally capitulated. His only hope had been that
Antrim would not go public about his Gaelic Irish backers or that the
king would not have supported him had he done so. This hope was
now patently dashed, and the Lord Deputy had no choice but to
assist Charles in arming the Irish chiefs of Ulster. Wentworth's
dilemma was acute when he wrote to the king on 1 April 1639:

> I have, to my judgment, complied with that which in relation to
> his lordship was appointed for me. . . . [I] crave most humbly
> Your Majesty's directions express under your own
> hand. . . . Let me but clearly know what I am to do, and if I
> neglect my duty in the execution, let not only the shame but
> punishment light deservedly upon me.[29]

The key phrase in the letter was that which stated that Wentworth
had acted according to his own judgment. He did not specify how far
he had gone in meeting Antrim's demands, but confined himself to
reporting those measures he had taken to put the Ulster garrisons on
full alert. The matter might yet be one of life and death for the Lord
Deputy and it was on this basis that he appealed to the king to put
down on paper his instructions in his own hand and thus clarify the
issue for once and for all. The king's response spoke volumes:

> To ease my pains at this time (having very much business) I
> have commanded Henry Vane to make you full answers of
> yours of the 1st and 2nd of April. Only I will say this, that if it
> be possible, it is most fit that Antrim be set upon Argyll, and I
> shall no ways despair of the success so that you lead the design,
> whereof I find him most desirous. Therefore I desire you not to
> shun it, but to assist him all you can in it.[30]

This was as near to plain speaking as the king was ever willing to go
on the subject of his Ulster Irish supporters. He would not commit
himself in writing other than to stick to the euphemism of Antrim's
invasion scheme and his very clear desire that Wentworth should take
the point. Charles's reliance on his secretary to deal with Wentworth
is a good illustration of the awareness even of the king himself that
these matters might well be the subject of future investi-
gation—which is precisely what they proved to be. Both Wentworth
and the king paid dearly for the charge levelled at them that they had
cultivated the Catholics of Ireland against the Protestant people of
England. There can be no doubt from the evidence that Charles was
implicated in the Ulster rising of 1641, but there can be equally no
doubt that Wentworth did his utmost to prevent the king fulfilling
his designs.

From the moment Charles committed his authority to a contest
with the Scots, Wentworth's career and influence began to wane.
This is not, of course, how it appeared on the surface. To all
appearances the Lord Deputy's stock continued to rise, but it is
notable that the rise was characterised by an ever-increasing responsibility for policies which he himself would never have approved. By
the time Wentworth had been created Earl of Strafford and invited
by the king to head his government in England he had been placed in a
position from which there was no escape. The man who had begun as a
parliamentary leader and had gone on to make his reputation by
managing the Irish parliament could think of no other solution to the
king's problem than to call a parliament in England—a misjudgment
which must rank highly among the many great ones made on the
royalist side. It is hard not to gain the impression from Wentworth's
handling of the Ulster situation that he was a man of considerable
integrity, but one who was out of his depth, for the first time, in the
face of his own master's duplicity. This duplicitous tendency on the
part of the king was by no means confined to his dealings with
Wentworth; throughout the 1640s until his death Charles was to

prove time and time again that he kept his own counsel while encouraging different groups to fight on his behalf.

———————

In the meantime, in April 1639, control of the Ulster crisis had slipped completely from Wentworth's grasp. He received a letter on the 11th from Sir Henry Vane informing him that the king considered that it was time the Earl of Antrim received his commission under the great seal for the levying of troops against Argyll. As if this was not enough, the king now commanded Wentworth himself to take responsibility for the scheme,

> for without that, His Majesty having well weighed your lordship's dispatches...cannot frame any success of that lord's undertaking unless you will patronise the same. In confidence whereof I send your lordship His Majesty's letter to Antrim, in which he is graciously pleased to declare himself unto him, that if he will put over three or four thousand men into Argyll's country, or any other of the Covenanters, he hath given your lordship order to give him powers and assistance, that is, at his own charge; and whatever land he can conquer from them, he having pretence [i.e. claim] of right, he shall have the same.

Vane also instructed Wentworth to send 'a considerable part of your army' to the north of Ireland.[31] For his own part, Antrim kept up the pressure on Wentworth. He wrote on the same day telling the Lord Deputy that he had formally committed himself to his Scottish allies in the king's name and that the king had promised him faithfully that he would protect those who refused to sign the Presbyterian covenant. Antrim wrote again the following day to say that the situation in Scotland had worsened and that his allies were under threat: 'For the love of God, my lord, let us not sleep any longer, and give me leave to revenge my friends, and especially the king's quarrel, and you shall shortly see or hear a great alteration.'[32] No doubt Wentworth agreed, but it was the nature of this alteration that he was less than happy about.

Although by the middle of April 1639 the Scottish conflict had not yet resolved itself, it was clear that a position of stalemate had been arrived at as far as help from Ireland was concerned. The reason for this was related to the king's own failure in dealing with the Scots: Charles would not insist on one course of action and then commit himself to its success. At the same time he would not fall back and take Wentworth's advice and let matters lie. Thus he had many policies in operation all at the same time. On 13 April Secretary Windebank wrote to Wentworth informing him that the king had approved of his treatment of Antrim 'by which the vanity of his vast undertaking, and the impossibility of his performing anything of consideration, were handsomely discovered even to himself'. Nevertheless, he added that Antrim must not be discouraged, and as Wentworth had suggested that the earl wait until the following year, perhaps this was the best course 'but that such use be made of him as may be for the advantage of His Majesty's service'.[33] Antrim received an almost identical letter written by Windebank on the same day informing him of the king's continued goodwill and conveying his thanks for his zealous service, although it was understood that the earl's plans would take some little time to complete.

> Besides [Windebank continued], the fire in Scotland is not likely to be so soon extinguished but that your lordship's services may be as useful to His Majesty another year as now, and therefore His Majesty expects that your lordship shall, against the next spring, make all the preparations you can, for a vigorous and powerful assistance, to be employed according to such directions as you shall receive from His Majesty or the Lord Deputy.[34]

In the meantime Antrim was instructed to consult with Wentworth and was assured that the state would provide what it could. The king intended to feign an invasion of Argyll and hoped that Antrim would co-operate.

At the end of April the king wrote to Wentworth to inform him that he was sending over Sir Henry Bruce 'to conduct' Antrim's design', of which he need say no more, having already made his wishes known at length in another dispatch. The appointment of Bruce was the critical turning-point which left the Lord Deputy no choice whatsoever. If he was unwilling to follow orders, he would soon have to relinquish control. Wentworth's position in Ireland would be undermined completely if he lost local power in addition to his loss of the king's support. The appointment of Bruce was typical of the style of intrigue which Charles was adopting in his efforts to use his three kingdoms each against the other. This new development, far from easing Wentworth's predicament, could only exacerbate it. As the king's absolutist deputy he could, of course, do what he liked; but as the governor whose policy had been based on the even-handed intimidation of the whole country he would have to do a considerable turnabout if he was to favour, of all people, Antrim and his friends among the Gaelic Irish. Moreover, on a personal level Antrim's behaviour denigrated the very style which Wentworth had used to carry himself successfully through many an attack, both in Ireland and from his opponents in England.

Nevertheless, the appointment of Bruce left Wentworth no option but to support Antrim. It presented him, in addition, with the public difficulty of how this could be done. He solved the problem in a less than ideal way, and one which had very grave consequences for the future: he would call the earl's bluff (which he knew was no bluff) at the council table. Thus his personal treatment of Antrim would be seen to be consistent, but this time he would involve the New English in the game, so that if he had to concede, he would bring the council with him. There was nothing politically courageous about this, and, what was far more important, it gave the council a role in the king's secret dealings with Ulster. In effect Wentworth was buying his way out with a solution that could be very temporary indeed in the event of the king's position in England being weakened. The king's position was to be considerably weakened all too soon, and most of the responsibility for that can be laid on Wentworth's trust in parliaments.

The Lord Deputy's politics were anything but subtle. It was his politics, however, and not his religion, which lay at the root of his loyalty. For Charles the position was the perfect opposite: the king's politics were informed consistently throughout his life by his Anglicanism and by his affinity for Roman Catholicism. In view of what was soon to be Wentworth's fatal reliance on the calling of parliament, both in Ireland and England, as a solution to the king's problems, it is not surprising to find that he himself was brought up as a Calvinist. An account of his upbringing written, it would seem, by his tutor and chaplain, Charles Greenwood, records:

> He was bred up in Calvin's opinions wherein he was afterwards more moderate, preferring piety before contention, labouring to be well grounded in fundamental truths rather than to trouble himself with disputes, and he chose rather to be devout than to make show of it.[35]

This picture is consistent with Wentworth's reluctance to betray the spirit of the Irish government by favouring the Gaelic Irish. Of course, he had no sympathy for the grafting New English and the use they made of their religion of the elect, but his own upbringing meant that in the final analysis he could not understand what he judged to be the king's groundless fear of parliament. What Wentworth failed to comprehend was that the king was not at all afraid of parliament; it was the use made of the House of Commons by the Calvinists that he was determined to end. For Charles the Scottish General Assembly and the Scottish Commons were the same because their religious sympathies were the same. He regarded the religion of the English Commons as the factor that would determine their response, and if he was to bring true political catholicism to his kingdoms, it was this religious opposition that he would have to break. Wentworth not only believed the opposite to be the case (that the opposition was political and could thus be dealt with within a parliament), but he committed the king to a disastrous test of his theory that parliaments could be managed. Likewise, his treatment of the Scots Presbyterians in Ulster was in the main political in its emphasis, and the famous 'black oath' which was forced upon them required them to affirm their loyalty to the king but not to his religion. From this it would follow that Charles had plucked Wentworth from his position as a leading parliamentary opponent and set him to work not as a spiritual royalist but as an aggressive civil servant who did not even warrant elevation to the peerage. To allow such a man to take the royalist reins in England, however, was courting disaster. By the time Charles did this he had so bungled his plans that there seemed little option.

On 10 May 1639 Wentworth reported to Laud that with regard to the king's order that Antrim should have a commission under the great seal, he had summoned the council at Dublin: 'I held fit in a business of that nature to crave the advice of some six of the ablest of this council, in whose presence all was debated.'[36] It was more than clear from the king's own hand at this stage that this was not the royal wish. Charles had not ruled through the Dublin government, nor had he appointed a man of Wentworth's temperament to do so. By calling in the council Wentworth was protecting himself on the one hand but opening the Ulster question to the official scrutiny of the New English (and indeed the Old English) on the other.

At the council meeting Wentworth made sure that Antrim stuck to his original nonsensical scheme to invade Argyll because it would be on this basis that he would bring the council with him in falsely calling the earl's bluff. The Lord Deputy, who was by this time famous for his policy of 'thorough', did not, however, have the political nerve to examine the earl about the names he had submitted on paper of those Gaelic chiefs with whom he fraternised. His report of the meeting to Laud had the tone but not the content of a comfortable solution:

> The sum of all in a word is, that there is nothing to my poor understanding, as to all that heard it, more clear than that the Earl of Antrim in his first proposal intended it merely as a handsome compliment, whereby to put himself into the favour and good opinion of His Majesty, without any thought that ever he should have been called upon to the performance of his undertaking.[37]

It is not an overstatement to say that Wentworth was playing the first scene of the final act not merely of his career but of his life. He was giving the Dublin government and the whole New English community in Ireland official proof that the king was dealing behind their backs in Ulster. The first great outbreak of the 1640s took place in Ulster, and it will be shown that the response of the Dublin government was to use it to drive the Old English into the rising. That it could not do this without subverting the course of justice did not deter the government; it had enough proof by October 1641 that the New English possessions in Ireland could not be protected by the king but only by his opponents in the English parliament. Indeed, there could be no doubt on the part of the New English after Wentworth's exposure of Antrim that the king himself was against them.

Wentworth was playing with fire when he treated Antrim to his by now well-developed ploy of making a fool of him. He reported to Laud:

> His lordship's main drift was to have put the defect off himself either upon his Majesty's non-performance on his part, or upon the failing or advice of us his ministers on this side; which he began and prosecuted with as much art as his lordship is capable of. But the plain truth is, his lordship could not so easily make a fool of the cobbler that was resolved to preserve both himself and master from blemish.[38]

Wentworth would have been more than pleased if Antrim had blamed the king for his lack of support, but this is not what can be seen even from Wentworth's description. Antrim was as much putting the abeyance of his plans down to the lack of action in Scotland as to the lack of Wentworth's support. Nor did he have to invent this view: he had it from the king himself. Thus he was not suggesting for one moment that the king had let him down. Antrim then proceeded to follow the remainder of the king's instructions. According to the Lord Deputy, he then put himself 'under the counsel and direction of this state; but that would not take: for all of us protested, our counsels should not lead in a business only understood by himself'.[39] If Wentworth imagined that his own detailed knowledge, which he had himself received by the king's hand, could be dismissed as if he were merely a council member who knew nothing, he was gravely mistaken. This was one time when he could not play off one group in Ireland against another. While it had been his most successful (and perhaps his only) mode to date, it had been based not on his own wit or mastery of Irish politics but simply on the fact that the king had supported him unconditionally. This was patently not the case here as he tried to play Antrim off against the council.

When Wentworth had toyed with Antrim in private he had drawn attention to his own official status and had said that what was put before him as a man was not what might be put before him as a public servant. He was now a public servant leading what must have been a very worried council as he encouraged Antrim to put forward his demands. What followed was to prove to be Wentworth's greatest mishandling in Ireland and must also feature in any collection of vital historical moments in the country's history. Wentworth was about to push the council into support for the Gaelic Irish of Ulster on the basis that it would come to nothing. He reported to Laud:

> Next his lordship made most vast and unreasonable demands, promising [i.e. believing] unto himself without question [that] they would have been denied and so have covered himself and broken up upon a refusal. But this also failed; the difficulties he put on [were] as fast wiped away and his way made smooth for his lordship to walk in, and nothing could be asked or thought on for the king to do but it was as soon granted by us as mentioned by him.[40]

Wentworth then explained the reasoning behind this trick, but did not tell Laud who it was who was being tricked; 'for indeed we were full well assured that there would be found in the last period of the case a *Dominus opus habet*, which would set a *ne ultra* to his career and place the saddle on the beast that ought to carry it'.[41] This was a great change from his earlier position that arming Antrim was the same as arming the traitorous Irish of Ulster. Because he had no choice, he would have to ignore the fact that Antrim did indeed represent what Wentworth himself would have seen as the beast of Ulster, the 'wild Irish' who were only too willing to take the saddle.

This must represent the low point in Wentworth's career and is a clear indication that he had lost touch where the king's personal dealings were concerned. Although there were only two and a half years to go before the great conflagration in Ulster which he was now directly contributing towards, Wentworth would not be alive to see it. Abandoned by all sides and by the king himself, he was tried, convicted and executed by the English parliament a full six months before 'Antrim's friends' went to war in the king's name. The ultimate irony was that Wentworth was condemned for his Irish policies by the English parliament he had insisted on reviving; he was condemned not for his Ulster dealings, however, but for those general policies which he had personally implemented. His trial was indeed to be the first great example of the English parliament's bewilderment when faced with Ireland's affairs and its reliance on a straightforward and rigid solution to the Irish question. It was impossible for the English Puritans to comprehend, let alone represent to the public, the complexities of Ireland. They rid themselves of the newly created Earl of Strafford (at last elevated for his final task of representing the king) on a very general and unsubstantiated charge of treason because they could not possibly have unravelled the king's dealings with the Gaelic Irish. Yet it was this accusation that the king had been involved in the Ulster rising which the Puritans returned to again and again, although they could never prove it. When the rising took place Sir Phelim O'Neill had published what he claimed was the king's commission authorising the action. When captured and tried he was pressed very hard to uphold this claim, but by then what had been a valued instrument had become a danger to the whole royalist cause, and he denied it to his death.

———————

These were events which had yet to play themselves out, however, although it was here in Wentworth's failure to handle Ulster that the crux of the king's problems lay. Having got the government to concede everything thus far, Antrim went the whole way and declared that he had no money, 'which so stifled us in our replication that we had no more to say' other than that the king expected Antrim to pay for his plans.[42] Not content with this, the earl went on to abuse Wentworth in front of the council. The Lord Deputy complained to Laud:

> Only admit me to say his lordship was in differing tempers as ever I saw; sometimes the grandchild of great Tyrone, using me so roughly indeed, as if I had durst for my lord of Canterbury, I should have been more sensible than I was, and yet was not heard without offence to the rest of the company; sometimes again he descended and became more merciful and gracious, indeed, even to make himself like one of ourselves, such was his gentleness and civility.[43]

Antrim continued his condescending treatment of the government by admitting freely that he had no money and that he had not intended things to go so badly in Scotland, 'and this was so expressed and in so downright words as if it had been an art not only to be allowed but very commendable in his lordship, which I assure you some of us wondered and some smiled to hear'.[44] Antrim's position with the king was such that he could refer to what everyone knew but which was not a topic for polite conversation, namely that they were all looking to the main chance in order to secure their own personal fortune. It was precisely because Charles knew from the beginning, and made no secret of it, that Antrim's interests in Scotland were personal that the earl could flaunt himself thus. War was rapidly approaching, and it was a conflict which the king himself was bringing on by his determination to override all opposition to his personal rule. The time for niceties was passing, and this must have been made more than clear to the Irish council even if the Lord Deputy feigned ignorance of it.

As Antrim's meeting with the government drew to a close Wentworth made his false bid in front of the council in order to maintain the pressure on his adversary. The earl said that his last contact with the king was a letter dated 13 April in which Charles desired him to postpone his plans until the following spring. This was indeed the case, but Wentworth and the council smartly insisted that Antrim be held to the king's instructions of 11 April signifying action in the coming summer. This set piece was completed when Antrim replied that he was of the same opinion, and moreover that he felt he was the only man for the job.

Wentworth was finally about to do what the king had been urging him to do all along, and it is in this context that the Ulster rising can be understood. The Dublin government claimed to be surprised when the rising occurred, but it would have been far more surprising had the Gaelic Irish not used the king's support in their own interests.

Wentworth wrote to Vane that after Antrim had agreed that action should be undertaken sooner rather than later 'I the deputy then offered to the earl that he should instantly have a commission under the great seal, for raising 4,800, according to the king's direction: whereupon we took into considerations his pro-positions.'[45] The total cost of the design was estimated at a little under £30,000. Wentworth reminded Vane that this could not be borne by Ireland, but this was not mentioned to Antrim. Instead the government 'made show to him as if all these things were in readiness which were on His Majesty's part to be provided'.[46] Antrim said that he could not proceed without money and agreed with the council that the king should be informed of this. Wentworth concluded from this that if the plan was to go forward, then it would be at the king's expense, but he was obliged to point out again that the Irish revenue could not sustain the cost. Wentworth's concern about who should pay, the Irish or the English government, was an indication that he had accepted the inevitable.

Agreement was safely arrived at with Antrim because he admitted that he could not have acted at that time. What the agreement amounted to in effect, however, was a complete capitulation on the part of the Dublin government because Antrim had not backed down when bluffed. The council would now be obliged to keep matters alive 'as they may not be cast too far backward in case hereafter His Majesty in his high wisdom may resolve on such an attempt'.[47] Wentworth then grasped the nettle and at last conformed to the required logistics of Antrim's design:

> Wherefore the better to effect that and (in conformity to His Majesty's directions in the dispatches from London) to make a show as if there were a present design from hence upon the Earl of Argyll's country ... I the deputy have issued patents for half the army to march immediately into the north parts of this

kingdom, as if there were such a design to be forthwith undertaken. And we have now at this board commanded the Earl of
Antrim, not only to report and give out that he intends this
summer to invade the Earl of Argyll's country, but also
immediately to go on busily in preparing longboats that may be
of use for such a service, as if he really meant it with all speed.
We have resolved also that one of His Majesty's ships be forthwith sent to the north-west parts of Scotland, with instructions
to give all the help and furthermore that may be to the friends
of the Earl of Antrim there; and to signify to them, if they have
any places of strength near adjoining to the sea, that by countenance of that ship there may be put into those strengths some
victuals and ammunition and, if they desire it, some men and
arms; so to preserve the Earl of Antrim's friends there, or at
least the principal of them, until a further occasion; and in the
meantime to countenance and encourage them.[48]

From this point onwards it would be reasonable to say that the
rising in Ulster was one of the very few really predictable events of the
period.

On the Eve
of Revolution, 1639-41

IT can be seen from the preceding chapter that time and time again Wentworth had been confounded by the king's support for Antrim and the Ulster Irish. The king's chief minister in Ireland was forced to fall back on the support of his council when he could not accept that the king himself was cultivating the infamous rebels of Gaelic Ireland who were, to a man, notorious for their Spanish-style brand of Catholicism. Perhaps it began to occur to Wentworth at this stage that Charles's failed attempt to marry himself into the Spanish royal family and his success with the almost equally unacceptable Catholic royalty of France had more to do with the king's sympathy for Roman Catholicism than the Lord Deputy had ever bargained for.

Antrim continued to make his presence felt by Wentworth. He wrote in May 1639 informing the Lord Deputy that 300 of his followers had arrived in Ulster from Scotland, and he asked if they could have the estates of those Scots who had fled. Wentworth refused the request, 'for that would amount to a public scandal and affright the whole kingdom', but he promised Antrim ships and masts for his longboats, 'so as your lordship sees, nothing is neglected on our part that is possible to be done'.[1] By the end of the month the king's commissioner Sir Henry Bruce had conferred with Wentworth at Dublin and gone north to meet the earl to discuss the logistics of his situation. Wentworth warned the king that Bruce would find that Antrim did not have the wherewithal to go into action, and that as far as he was concerned Bruce had intimated that he was of the same opinion.

By early June, however, the danger in Scotland was past, and with it Antrim's hold over the Dublin government. Both sides were now obliged to return to the more official version of Antrim's activities, or rather lack of them. Thanks to Wentworth, however, the Dublin council had had more than a peep into the king's business by this time.

To maintain the momentum Antrim, either through Bruce or directly to the king, blamed the Dublin government for the failure of his schemes. In a lengthy reply to Sir Henry Vane, Wentworth and the council justified themselves on the basis of both Antrim's insolvency and his incompetence. Wentworth's contribution can be seen in the doubt cast on the earl's integrity through the claim that he had deliberately misguided them about the best time to launch his invasion and, more importantly, that they had themselves checked the position in the Isles (because they could not trust him). They found that the situation was not what he had claimed it to be, nor did they see any justification for the massive design Antrim had asked for. Besides all that, they simply did not have the arms or munitions to satisfy the earl, let alone to do so and protect the rest of the country.

The now awakened council made its own presence felt in the appeal to Vane to represent them to the king on the vital issue of Ulster and the state's security:

> We also humbly beseech you seriously to mention what ill consequences it might beget to His Majesty's affairs here in a time thus conditioned abroad, and wherein at home the great body of Scottish amongst us is to be secured, and the intended plantations are to be settled, to arm so many of the natives mere Irish, whereof the Earl of Antrim's whole regiments were in a manner to consist, and in a great part the sons of habituated traitors, or those that in the former times of rebellion here have been rebels themselves, and had their hands in the innocent blood of many good subjects, and who once so united, might perchance prove not so well natured as to lay down their arms, where they might espy us to be naked without weapons either to hurt them or defend ourselves.[2]

They added that Antrim had now claimed to have organised two months' victualling, but the council did not believe him. He had also requested them to cancel a debt of £700 to the Court of Wards, something they were not willing to do as a bad example. Finally, Wentworth's position was again covered by the now half-hearted claim that the whole scheme was impossible, but that if it was indeed to go on, then the cost must be borne in England.

Wentworth himself wrote to the king on 6 June in support of the Dublin council's report. The story was the same one: Antrim had behaved strangely, and the government could not deal with him when they were not privy to his real aims. For his part, the Lord Deputy could not see any possible good that might accrue to the crown, nor could he see how Antrim was capable of undertaking any mission of the kind he had suggested. The earl had requested that Wentworth order certain ships to go as far north as the Isle of Skye, but Wentworth told the king that he could not do this without express orders. 'Hence it is, that being both doubtful and fearful in myself what to do, I most humbly crave Your Majesty's direction.'[3] When the king replied in a short letter on 22 June the Scottish truce had been concluded, but his message to Wentworth could hardly have allayed the Lord Deputy's fears:

> There is a Scottish proverb, that bids you put two locks on your door when you have made friends with a foe; so now upon this pacification I bid you to have a most careful eye upon the north of Ireland. Not that I think this caution is needful in respect of you, but to let you see I have a care of that kingdom, though I have too much trouble with these.[4]

The nonchalence of the king's attitude must have startled his deputy, who now had to deal with a council alerted by his own panic. What is more, the king's cryptic message might be interpreted in several very different ways, none of which were at all comforting to the Irish government. No interpretation, however, could avoid the simple fact that the king had ordered Wentworth to grant Antrim a commission to arm Ulster and that the king was now warning the Lord Deputy casually to keep an eye on that province. Clearly Charles did not share Wentworth's, or indeed the Dublin council's, fear of the Gaelic Irish and their long traitorous traditions.

   The immediate threat had been diffused, however, and this gave Wentworth a chance to consolidate his position and re-establish contact with the king. To do this he would need to concede that Antrim's schemes were indeed mere representations of other, unspeakable matters. Sir Henry Bruce returned from Antrim and consulted with the Lord Deputy early in July. Wentworth wrote to the king recommending a personal interview with Bruce, who was 'a gentleman able to represent unto Your Majesty the outward state of these affairs'.[5] There is a suggestion here that Wentowrth had at last learned to speak the king's English. In the meantime word reached him through Sir Henry Vane that Charles had accepted his Irish government's views on Antrim and the Ulster crisis. Wentworth rejoiced that the mistaken trust in Antrim could not now damage the king, whose treaty with the Scots had taken the danger away.

> It is true [he observed] that on this side we must softly fall back
> upon those services begun for the crown, which received no
> small prejudice through those apprehensions taken upon those
> late troubles, especially in the plantations, wherein we found a
> great coldness; but now I trust all set quietly upon the right
> foot again, we shall go on with the former courage and warmth.[6]

This new-found optimism, however, was still at odds with the king's
complex involvement in Ulster and the unlikelihood that it would in
any way diminish simply because he had reached what was, as far as he
was concerned, merely a temporary truce with the Scots. (Disagree-
ment broke out almost immediately as to what had been agreed upon
and by whom.) Nor was there much comfort to be had from the
king's report of his interview with Sir Henry Bruce after he had met
him on 23 July: 'I esteem him a better soldier than a statesman, yet he
has made me some propositions in the politic way, somewhat mixed
with the martial, not to be despised yet not to be hastily embraced
without such a good commentaire as you are able to make on them.'[7]
He instructed Wentworth to come to England, but to do so on the
pretext of other business. Clearly the Ulster question had little to do
with Antrim's family problems and everything to do with the king's
forward plans. Wentworth had expressed a willingness to countenance this reality, but in some respects it was too late. He had made
public what was very obviously the king's secret business, and in
doing so he had alerted the Irish government not just to the danger in
Ulster (of which they had been vociferously aware since 1607), but to
the crucial fact that the king was involved.

―――――――――

It is clear from Wentworth's handling of the Ulster situation that he
was not at one with his master. Moreover, his difference of opinion
was strong and committed, and it is hard to see how he can be
depicted as one of the king's chief English ministers, invited back to
head off the parliamentary attack. Wentworth was groomed for
Ireland, and his job was to make money there, something he did
better than any of his predecessors. That he, together with Archbishop Laud, was the man behind the king is simply not the case as far
as the Irish evidence goes. Nor, in fairness to Wentworth himself,
could he have claimed such an exalted place. On the contrary, the

Ulster question would seem to have taught him little or nothing about the king's politics, and it was Wentworth the civil servant, not Wentworth the master of 'thorough', who wrote to Vane on 24 July when the immediate crisis had passed:

> As for my lord of Antrim, all is quiet and still there; all so fast asleep as his lordship neither pays licences of alienation, subsidies or rents. I desire to know His Majesty's pleasure whether we must awaken him or no, lest otherwise he fall into the cave of those seven sleepers we read of in the legend. In the meantime his MacDonnells are awake, they pray for the king, but will obey no warrant of deputy and council. . . . But I see this clan hath this peculiar to do no more but what and as they list themselves; and perchance it may pass well with them in the Isles, but shall not here if I can help it.[8]

As head of the Irish government Wentworth refused to allow the law to be waived where Ulster was concerned. Such obedience to the ideal of the king's government in Ireland was fundamentally out of step with the king himself. The Lord Deputy did not make his true feelings known, but if he was not willing outwardly to obey the king on the crucial question of Ulster, it seems unlikely that his recall was entirely glorious. He himself was happy that he had left Ireland greatly in his debt, but the king can hardly have shared the Lord Deputy's high estimation of his own performance.

Perhaps the greatest consequence of Wentworth's inability to handle the Ulster crisis was his falling back on the authority of the council in Dublin. It is hard to avoid the conclusion that he was afraid of giving this august body ammunition against himself in view of the gathering storm in England. Ulster was indeed in a delicate and dangerous condition by 1639, but the Lord Deputy undoubtedly compounded the king's difficulties by inviting the council into the inner sanctum of state government. It will be shown below how the attempt to seize Dublin Castle, that alleged crime which allowed the council to put the whole country under martial law, did not take place. It was indeed a dramatic plot; however, it was perpetrated not by the Ulster Irish, but by Lord Justice Sir William Parsons as part of a greater design to push the Old English over to the Gaelic side and bring the English parliament directly into Irish affairs to protect their Puritan kinsmen, the New English. Wentworth's complete mishandling of Antrim and his 'friends' played a large part in justifying to the New English any measures whatsoever which they might deem necessary to protect themselves from the Catholics. This is not to say that without the Lord Deputy's inability to see beyond Antrim's swagger, the New English Puritans could have supported the king; they could not. It is to say, however, that when he crumbled under pressure and appealed to the council to witness the righteousness of his position, he confirmed what they had known all along: that Ireland could be governed for a short time by an English deputy, but it was the people on the ground, those New English who had committed their fortunes and safety to the proper government of the country, who were the natural Protestant rulers of Ireland.

If Wentworth's behaviour caused him to be demoted in the ranks of those who enjoyed the king's confidence, it is important to remember that his actions were faultless and valid. His dilemma is a dramatic illustration of how a small matter could be one of great consequence where Charles was concerned. As far as the rest of his dealings in Ireland went, he had an easier time of it. The reason for this was the converse of his problems with the Ulster Irish. Both the Old English and the New English played by the same rules as the Lord Deputy, and when the king dealt with them, whether together or separately, he did so within the agreed constitution. This was why Wentworth could achieve so much both in his Irish parliamentary efforts and in the other areas of his administration. When that agreed constitution began to collapse, as it did after the king's failure to dominate the Scots, Wentworth was far from successful, and indeed seemed often completely unaware of what was really going on around him.

The nature of the king's failure in Scotland was subtle, but it was also crucial. Charles conceded to Scottish demands to revert to the religious settlement under James, and in doing so he relinquished some of his hold over the Scottish parliament, allowed the power of the bishops to be curtailed, and withdrew the Book of Common Prayer. None of these issues were vital matters of state, but the king's failure was. Charles had demanded obedience and it had been refused; he had then threatened violence and his challenge had been accepted. Too late the king discovered that he could not follow through because he could not physically coerce the Scots army. The reason for this was that he did not have sufficient support in England to do so—a lack which was only revealed by the attempt itself. It was with a considerable degree of bewilderment that many of Charles's English ministers looked on as he put his authority on the line. They knew that his financial position would not withstand much strain, and they wondered how this vital fact could be kept from the Scots. The Scots did not need to know it, however, because they were acting defensively. It was not the Presbyterians who were forcing their religion on the king, and if the king chose to fight a war which he could not sustain, then they had no choice but to win it.

The English Calvinists had no great love for their fellows in Scotland, but they were far nearer sharing their religion than they were the king's. The essential difference between the two countries as far as Calvinism was concerned was that it was all but established in Scotland as the state religion, while in England the tradition was one of fragmentation and independence of worship. This meant in effect that the king's English subjects watched his dealings with the Scots with a double concern. If the king won, it would spell trouble for all English Calvinists; there could be little doubt about that after 1637. If, on the other hand, the Scots were victorious, it would mean that Presbyterianism had been successfully tried and tested where it mattered most, in the field. This would give the Scots a tremendous power in the English constitutional crisis, that is to say in affairs which were not their own.

That there was a crisis was clear by 1640. Charles had ruled without a parliament since the late 1620s, and to some extent he had managed successfully. The king's finances were sound enough, but they were based upon credit, so that while he may not have been in debt to the House of Commons, he was in debt to many of the people who would otherwise have been there, and in particular he was in debt to the city of London. The king had attempted to 'live of his own', to be free to pursue his own royal policy, but he was obliged to do this through forced loans and taxes. In other words, the king could not survive without money; and it was a question of where that money was to come from. It so happened that many of his subjects did not share the assumptions upon which his government was based, and the net result of this was that, whether the money was raised by taxation or by parliamentary subsidy, the question of finance was inextricably bound up with the question of sovereignty. The problem, however, was that the question was being raised by the king himself. The onus was therefore on him to answer it successfully, and this was what he was clearly not doing in his Scottish policy.

By 1640 Ireland had proved to be a most profitable source of vital revenue. Wentworth's ability to rule Ireland according to the king's principles was by then known throughout England and Scotland. What the king lacked in these kingdoms, however, was a minister capable of doing the same. The question here was whether the singular nature of Wentworth's success was due to the peculiarity of Ireland or to the lack of ability among the king's other ministers. The real answer was, of course, that Ireland was a most peculiar political entity, not remotely similar to Scotland or England. However, this was not the impression which the king's opponents gave out. Wentworth was seen as the rather thick end of an even thicker wedge—which in fact his government was not. The proof of this came all too quickly for the Lord Deputy when he was wheeled on in England and proceeded to make one blunder after another.

The great majority of the king's English subjects were not religious outlaws as were the Old English and Gaelic Irish. They could not be dictated to by the threat of dispossession which might follow the enforcement of the Oath of Supremacy. The king was not a Roman Catholic and owed no allegiance to the pope, nor did the vast majority of his subjects. Thus, although the English constitutional crisis had to do as much with the king's sympathies as his style of government, it did not revolve around his allegiance to a foreign power. Yet this was the Irish problem in a nutshell. One ironic consequence was that the Old English (and now the Gaelic Irish) were more loyal to Charles as their king precisely because they owed their spiritual allegiance to Rome. In other words, faced with the New English eagerness to dispossess them for any reason at all, the Catholics of Ireland were forced to be as loyal as they could be within reason; and here the bounds of reason were defined best by the Old English. They had survived since the Reformation by using reason not only to demonstrate their loyalty but to justify it in abstract political terms. It seemed that they were now to be joined by the Gaelic Irish—a development which could have done nothing but trouble their very refined consciences.

The return of the Gaelic Irish to a position of prominence was less political than militaristic. It would seem that Charles had developed a very sophisticated view of his Roman Catholic subjects in the period before the Ulster rising. This view allowed him to look to one group for financial and to the other group for armed support. Apart from the matter of the king's sympathy for the Roman faith (and the ever-increasing activities of Vatican emissaries at court, supervised by the queen), Charles knew that his credit with the city of London would not last much longer. The reason for this was that the city was not sympathetic to the spirit in which the king ruled. London money was based on trade, and the merchant community had a natural affinity for the egalitarian and self-justifying principles of the low Protestant churches. The connection between the Protestant ethic and the rise of capitalism has been debated since it was first made, and it has never been possible to establish it beyond a generality. As far as London was concerned, however, the connection is important enough because the moneyed merchants were more vital to the expansion of England's economy than were the landed (and often bankrupt) aristocracy. Before Charles lost to the Scots the city had little option but to facilitate their ruler. The king's humiliation, however, did nothing for his credit among those to whom he was not willing to grant a parliament. It must be borne in mind that in less dramatic times a parliament facilitated trade by adapting legislation to new conditions and framing new laws where necessary. In this respect the king's 'eleven years' tyranny' was as much an economic liability as a constitutional challenge. Furthermore, Charles's treatment of the city's Londonderry holdings illustrated his lack of affinity for the merchant class upon whom he was relying for loans. The city had been fined the very considerable sum of £70,000 by the king's Court of Star Chamber in 1635 for the alleged mismanagement of its Ulster territories. This has been an all too obvious attempt on the king's part to squeeze money from the city, but the placing of Londonderry in the hands of a commission was a further insult and did nothing to salvage the king's relationship with his capital.

In this environment of great tension the various loyalist groups of Ireland stood out like beacons, or at least so it seemed to Wentworth. The Lord Deputy had managed to alienate everyone, but he had tried to do so without discrimination, and of this he was proud. In many respects he was even more naïve than Charles, and when he left Ireland on 12 September 1639 he believed he was leaving a country which was firmly behind the king. At a superficial level this was indeed the case, but it was only so because the disparate groups had no other choice but to conform. The New English were looking to the possibility of an alliance with a Puritan opposition once the English parliament was re-established and an end put to the personal rule of the king. The Gaelic Irish were looking to the king's physical conflict with the Scots and the benefits that would accrue to them in

Ulster. It was only the Old English who were truly loyal, and this was because they had no other future in this rapidly developing confront-ation. If blows were struck either in Scotland or England, it might redound to the benefit of either the Gaelic Irish or the New English, but it would not bode well for the Old English. The possibility of a war to end all wars in Ireland had been present since the Reformation, and it was the Old English achievement that it had not taken place. The Gaelic Irish viewed this as a lack of achievement which had cost them dearly. Equally, the New English had almost welcomed this type of conflict so long as the army was continually supplied and rein-forced from England. When the Ulster rising did eventually take place there was, amidst all the great fear occasioned by the event, some New English relief in the fact that at last the conspiracies and threats had been turned into actions which might now be dealt with by the forces of law and order. A great deal of this anxiety was shared by the Old English, but for the opposite reason. If forced to take arms against the Dublin government, they would put themselves beyond the Pale for the first time since they themselves had coined that definition of an outlaw.

When the Irish parliament was summoned by the king on Wentworth's advice there was only marginally less riding on its success than on that which was summoned in England almost simul-taneously. The Irish parliament was to assemble in March 1640, its English counterpart in the following month. On the face of it, the stakes would seem to have been considerably higher in England, but this was not the case. Wentworth, now Earl of Strafford and Lord Lieutenant of Ireland, planned to display his great Irish achieve-ments, and therefore the achievements of the king's policies, before the English public. He judged that the best way to do this was to get the Irish parliament to lead by its example. This was the mistake which cost Strafford his life. In Ireland a king's deputy could more or less do what he wished, whether it be with the consent of parliament or without it. No one had illustrated this better than Strafford himself. To take this tactic in England was not only a dire misjudgment, it was to insult the English parliamentary tradition profoundly and to confirm the worst fears of the king's critics. The English parliament had always viewed its Irish cousin not as a poor relation but as a downright bastardisation of a quintessentially English insitution. Scotland might develop a parliament, as it had always had a king (although the function of the Scottish General Assembly illustrated that there was no real love of the pure tradition as there was in England). Ireland had never had a king, however, and could never claim the monarchical constitution within which the institution of parliament was the great watchdog. Anglo-Norman Ireland (which had always been the only Ireland the English could acknowledge, let alone comprehend) was a ragbag of colonists defined only by the preservation of their original civility. When those colonists remained Roman Catholic while the English accepted the Reformation, Ireland forfeited whatever right it had to be considered English. Henceforth it was viewed by the public in England as a strange no-man's land which swallowed up armies and resources. What it was not, and could never be, was an example of loyalty and good government which might be paraded in front of an ignorant English public for its edification. Strafford could not see this, and neither, it would seem, could the king. The Lord Deputy's success in managing the Irish parliament of 1634 should not have been taken as an example of what could be done in England, considering that the king had refused to summon parliament throughout the 1630s for the very reason that it could not be properly managed.

Parliament opened in Dublin on 16 March 1640. There was a Protestant majority of 89 members and a Catholic representation of 68 Old English and six Gaelic Irish members. The returns themselves illustrated a good deal about the state of the country. The Old English had been reduced by approximately one-third since the parliament of 1634, while the New English majority had trebled. This was not as bad as it looked for the Old English, however, for it was still possible that the king would prevail over his opponents. At another time these losses could not have been conceded, but there were hopes that things would improve in the future. Indeed, it was the very weakness of the Old English representation that caused them to sing all the sweeter when asked to vote the subsidy. This was the only real response they had ever made, and within the Irish political framework there was nothing else they could do. Four subsidies were granted immediately amidst joyful delcarations of support for the king which extended to a request that His Majesty's loyal subjects be given the privilege of taking on the Scots.

This enthusiasm for the king was not as contagious as Strafford had hoped it might be. When the English parliament met in April after eleven years of obstruction its members were not interested in

Ireland or its raptures. Before it would grant any supplies the House of Commons decided to give its priorities to the many grievances which it would be the king's responsibility to redress.

It may seem to be the benefit of hindsight that allows the historian to suggest that in April 1640 Charles was one short step from the collapse of his monarchy, but hindsight is not necessary. The king's army had not been strong enough to coerce the Scots, and he was now obliged, on Strafford's advice, to solicit help from parliament. If parliament refused, the king would be in dire straits indeed. This would partly be due to the nature of the request itself. The Scottish army was massed on the English border where Charles had left it. The Scots looked on as the king asked for money to defeat them. His failure would mean the endorsement of Presbyterianism by the English parliament on a matter of the highest trust—national security.

The king supported his request for subsidies with a letter taken from a Scots commissioner arrested in London which exposed the Scots as potential allies of the French. By his actions the king was exposing himself, not the Scots. The Scottish-French alliance was no longer perceived in England as a threat, and if this was the king's highest card (which surely it was at this time of crisis), then he was indeed exposing his own weakness or at best his naïvety. (Nor did the arrest of a Scottish leader stationed in London after the Treaty of Berwick say much for the king's adherence to treaties.)

As it turned out, however, Charles had not played his best card, and faced with intransigence he was willing to try another. Sir Henry Vane appealed to the house that if the full twelve subsidies were voted, the king would abolish the collection of ship money. The abolition of ship money was not related to a parliamentary subsidy, however, and the offer to exchange one for the other revealed that what was on the surface a bargain was in fact a concession by the king on a fundamental issue of his reign. This was the first time that pressure was to cause the king to buy an initiative for the present at the expense of it in the future, and the opposition scented victory. Unfortunately for Charles, he could not make even a straight bargain look like anything other than a defeat. Under the leadership of John Pym, committees were appointed to examine the many petitions which had been submitted to parliament complaining about almost all aspects of the royal government. It became clear to the king and his ministers that the subsidies would not be voted upon before great embarrassment was caused to the government. Far from the

Commons supporting the king against the Scots, it now seemed likely that the king's policy would be criticised severely and support given to his enemies. On 5 May the council met to discuss the dissolution of the parliament. It is interesting to note that Strafford, who was to argue against dissolution, came late to the meeting, apparently because of some mistake, and so was unable to sway the government.

There are two views of the king's dissolution of this, the Short Parliament. The first is that it was greatly miscalculated because the parliament could have been managed with a little patience and skill. (This was Strafford's view, but then he could hardly have had any other, it being his idea in the first place.) The parliament which followed (the Long Parliament) was determined not only to break the king, but to take over the government of the country as well. The view that Charles had made yet another mistake is grounded in the belief that the king was a failed logician and that he had no other interest than in provoking conflicts which he could not win. The second view is less immediately discernible. The tradition within which the king was operating has not survived down to the present, whereas the parliamentary tradition has. It is difficult for the modern student to appreciate what Charles thought might happen if he had a free hand. By its very function, parliament was a vociferous and representative body given to decisions made through argument and counter-argument. When Charles rejected the constitutional right of parliament to participate in affairs of state, he did so through the power of that institution (the monarchy) of which he was the sole representative. Similarly, the difference between the various Calvinist denominations and the royalist Anglican religion in this respect was that Charles was a member of a church of which he was also the head. These two functions of headship were linked for Charles in one belief. He might have bargained with the Short Parliament and traded some of his prerogatives for a few concessions, but to do so would have been to concede that which had put him in the position in the first place. While it was at least conceivable that he might concede some political issue, he could never do so in matters of faith. For this reason the king was not accustomed to bargaining; it was not part of his political panoply, nor was it consistent with his spiritual status. Thus the bargain he had struck with the Scots was one he had no intention of keeping. Although he did not say so publicly, he made no secret of the fact that the Treaty of Berwick was a temporary respite. He would return to coercion as soon as he had consolidated his forces. The Scots were more than aware of this, not

least because the treaty itself became the subject of further irre-
concilable dispute.

When the Short Parliament rejected the king's demands they did
not do so lightly. It must be remembered that the king controlled the
only army in England at this time. Parliament's refusal to supply that
army would be a grave declaration that the Scottish threat was
preferable to that posed by Charles himself. It would also create a
military vacuum which could be filled only by the Scots or by the
king's English opponents. The reason why so much hinged on the
king's position in April was because an integral and vital part of the
English and Scottish constitutions was the king's power to wage war.
The term 'war' implied an external enemy, however, and this raised
the very basic question. Was it as the King of England or as the King
of Scotland that Charles could demand obedience? The answer was
twofold. As King of Scotland Charles had insisted on his religious
policies being implemented. A bloodless war followed which had left
the Scottish army victorious on the English border. It was now as
King of England that Charles demanded support to deal with this
national threat which had been caused by the failure of his kingship of
Scotland. It was the king's authority which had been rejected, but the
issue was all-important. As King of Scotland Charles had tried to
impose the state religion of England upon his Scottish subjects. He
had tried to do this because as King of England he was the head of
that religion, and, according to his view, the religion of a Catholic
king must also be that of his subjects. It was the Catholicism of
Charles's kingship that gave him no choice where Calvinism was
concerned.

On the question of religion, however, Charles was on more familiar
ground with the Scots than he was with the English. Scottish
Presbyterianism had grown out of a conflict with the Roman
Catholicism of the Stuarts, and so it had developed a strong unified
structure of its own. It had long been the aim of Scottish Presbyterians to make their religion catholic (that is, to make it the uniform
faith of Scotland) as the only protection against Rome. This was not
the case where England was concerned because the Anglican religion
was, by definition, English and could always accommodate itself to
its own environment. Catholic by nature, Anglicanism was Protestant because it had broken the great universal link with Rome. It
adhered to Luther's doctrine of justification by faith, and
incorporated Calvin's doctrine of predestination. These it viewed as
supplemental to the Catholic formula of mediation through ritual.

It follows from this that there was no reason in the early seventeenth century why the Anglican church might not survive as a truly tolerant form of Catholicism. Thus the Elizabethan settlement might have produced a new framework had it not been appropriated by the King of Scotland. This left the way open for emissaries from the Vatican to implement the huge task then under way throughout Europe of rolling back the Reformation. It was in this context that the rise of Arminianism was seen by English Calvinists to have huge political implications. Arminian doctrines were not only designed to put the Anglican church firmly on the Catholic side, they were also the outpost of a Counter-Reformation which by the late 1630s made no distinction between politics and religion. Parliament was used by the Calvinists because it was a legitimate and constitutional branch of sovereign government and was thus the most powerful political weapon available. This did not make the Puritans democratic or cause them to alter the basis of their Calvinism (which was exclusive where Catholicism was inclusive). Parliament provided them with an instrument to defend themselves against the king, and by 1640 it was very clear that they were going to need it.

The Short Parliament's reply to the 'eleven years' tyranny' was to abandon the king to his fate. This was the great turning-point in the history of the seventeenth century, and it had been brought about because the king had only sought parliamentary support as he did not have the means to defeat the Scots himself. Nor indeed is it an exaggeration to say that his army did not have the spirit. Writing at the end of May about the condition of his men on the front line, the king's general, Viscount Conway, expressed what was to be a critical problem:

> I am teaching cart-horses to manage, and making men that are fit for Bedlam and Bridewell to keep the Ten Commandments, so that General Leslie [head of the Scots army] and I keep two schools: he has scholars that profess to serve God, and he is instructing them how they may safely do injury and all impiety; mine, to the utmost of their power, never kept any law either of God or of the king and they are to be made fit to make others keep them.[9]

Very significantly, this was not what Conway was telling the king; here the story was quite different. Charles was cheered by Conway's news that the Scots were fighting among themselves and that their army was badly provided for. It was, however, the moral fibre of the

Presbyterian army that the king really failed to appreciate. His own men were the aggressors, but they were not fighting for anything that related even vaguely to their existence, let alone security. Nor were they imbued with any religious convinction whatsoever. The Calvinist soldier related his behaviour directly to God in the true spirit of the Old Testament, and this made him a formidable foe. Whether or not General Leslie was indeed 'instructing them how they may safely do injury and all impiety', the observation was a relevant one. No individual responsibility devolved upon the Catholic or Anglican soldier, and no one was to appreciate the fact to greater effect than Oliver Cromwell. The king's army was not a religious army, nor was it fighting for the survival of a creed. This meant that the royalist army was led by the upper classes whose natural, rather than religious, affinities were for the king. When gathering the model army that would conquer all, Cromwell knew where the king's weakness lay:

> Best to have men patient of wants, faithful and conscientious in the employment, and such, I hope, these will approve themselves to be.... I had rather have a plain russet-coated captain that knows what he fights for, and loves what he knows, than that which you call a gentleman and is nothing else.[10]

In this conflict it was only to be expected that Charles would tap the religious oppression of Ireland's Catholics as a force against Puritan ideology. The success of the Counter-Reformation in Ireland was not merely that the religion had survived, but that its adherents had been galvanised by their exclusion from politics in much the same way as the Calvinists had been in England and Scotland. Whether it would ever have been possible for Charles's Anglicanism to have asserted itself as the only religion is an unanswerable question. Certainly it could not even exist, let alone survive, in Ireland. What passed for the established church was a thin compromise with Anglicanism by the New English Calvinists in the interests of their wealth and power. There was no room for moderation in Ireland when these New English could dispossess any Catholic on a technicality of tenure. Nor was there any possibility of moderation when Catholicism in Ireand was itself split between the Old English and Gaelic Irish.

When the Scots got word that the king was powerless they invaded the north of England on 20 August 1640. Lord Conway had written to Charles's secretary Windebank early in the month giving him a rather different picture of their intentions: 'Neither do I believe the Scots will come into England; this that they do is only to brag; however, I will look to myself as well as a man may that has no money in his purse. I would send for more of the foot from Selby, but I fear unpaid soldiers more than I do the Scots.'[11] Making Newcastle their central stronghold, the Scots imposed a tax of £200 a day on the town. Negotiations took place immediately. The Treaty of Ripon obliged Charles not only to concede to the Scots, but also to pay them £850 a day for the privilege. This was money he did not have, and he was therefore obliged to facilitate all his opponents by summoning another parliament. The king had used his prerogative right to dissolve the Short Parliament after three weeks. The parliament which met in November was determined that this would not happen again; it was to remain in existence for twenty years.

Before his defeat in the Short Parliament and before his capitulation to the Scots, Charles had instructed Wentworth to raise an army in Ireland. This the Lord Deputy had set about assiduously, and by the time he left the country for the last time in April the Old English and Gaelic Irish population alike had been informed of the king's needs and how they might satisfy him. Wentworth had made many mistakes during his term of office as Lord Deputy, but the formation of a Catholic army should not be laid at his door. Charles had done his best to arm Ulster under the nominal leadership of Antrim. Wentworth had pointed out that this policy would almost inevitably lead to a rising, but it is clear that the king was already more than aware of this. It is also clear by April 1640 that the king had committed himself to victory at any price as long as it did indeed give him victory. The raising of an army in Ireland pulled the country's landowners, of all persuasions, into a new conflict with the king's English opponents. In other words, the unwillingness of the English to support their king against the Scots meant that his subjects in Ireland would have to step into the breach, and thus incur the wrath of the English parliament if the plan was to fail. The king's Irish army might have been justified in view of the great Scottish threat to England, but it proved to be the exact opposite when the English parliament sided with the Scots and thus pointed to the king himself as the great threat. Thus the Catholics of Ireland came to be seen as a dark cloud which threatened the very precarious situation which had developed in England. Had the king been obliged to fight his corner on his own territories, either in Scotland or England, the threat of civil war would have been nowhere near as great, because the king's weakness was all too plain to see. It was the attempt to raise what could only be seen as Strafford's Catholic army that brought about a profound change in the English perception of Ireland.

More than any other group, it was the Old English who were affected by this change. There had always been an Anglo-Norman colony in Ireland which could be relied upon either to govern itself or to facilitate government from England. The Old English had done so in order to preserve their very great wealth in Ireland, and they had never as a body sided with their fellow-Catholics among the Gaelic Irish against the Protestant crown. In the context of this political allegiance, the Old English had had an easy time. Wentworth had summed up the basic attitude of his government to Old English negotiation when he wrote to Laud in 1638:

> If the recusants in composition carry themselves so as to give open and public scandal, I say it was ever intended the law should be laid unto them, and spare them not in the name of God; but if modestly and silently they exercise and keep their conscience to themselves, it was agreed they should be looked at through the fingers.[12]

It was on this basis that the Old English had maintained their loyalty in the first session of the Irish parliament of 1640.

In the middle of the gathering storm, however, was the New English government of Ireland. Deputies came and went, but the essential Puritan nature of the council remained. The Dublin government had already had a personal demonstration of what the king was up to in Ulster and of Wentworth's role in serving him. Now they were to witness the formation, upon their own orders, of a Catholic army to serve against either the Scottish or the English Puritans. This they would not do, and they would have the support of the New English majority in the Irish House of Commons. Of course, they were still obliged to obey the king's instructions; it is no surprise to find, however, that while the army was assembled and training begun, it was not pronounced fit to serve the king until he had already been defeated by the Scots.

The alliance of Old English with New English in the first parliamentary session had been an unnatural one based upon the question of the subsidy. The Old English wished to subsidise the king, while the

New English wished to subsidise the government in Ireland. It was becoming increasingly clear that these were not the same thing. Moreover, the significance of the Old English in parliament was fading proportionate to the king's increasing dependence on physical means to extricate himself from the worsening crisis. Wentworth's replacement as Lord Deputy, Christopher Wandesford, lost control and was obliged to prorogue parliament until 1 October. By the time it met again the king had suffered a defeat from which he could not recover (at least not in any way consistent with his original aims). For the first time in their history the Old English were about to be caught on the wrong foot by their own loyalty, and in order to preserve their estates it was now necessary for them to do a rapid somersault. This took the form of a further alliance with the New English Puritans who were anxious to facilitate their parliamentary friends in England.

When they had sided with the king in March the Old English had declared that they would not be content until they had gone into action against the Scots. They now wished their kinsmen in the English parliament to know that the 'loyal and dutiful people of this land of Ireland, being now for the most part derived from British ancestors, should be governed according to the municipal and fundamental laws of England' and 'that by the powerfulness of some ministers of state in this kingdom, the parliament, in its members and actions, hath not its natural freedom'.[13] In other words, what the Old English now shared with their opponents in Ireland was the parliamentary tradition itself, inherited as part and parcel of their English ancestry. This was not actually a disingenuous view to take; in another context it might be the perfect summary of the Old English position since the decline of the Kildare power in 1534. What it indicated now, however, was a very strained attempt to placate the New English, whose stock had risen enormously with the collapse of the royal initiative. The English parliament was determined that Strafford would be impeached, and it looked to Ireland for the evidence. The Old English did all they could to facilitate the proceedings and also took the opportunity to express their unadulterated Englishness in a letter signed by eighty-four members of the Irish Commons (only twenty-nine of whom were Protestant) asking the Speaker of the English Commons 'to mind the near links and great ties of blood and affinity betwixt the people of this kingdom and the famous people of England from whose loins they are descended'.[14]

The push against Strafford was headed in the English House of

Commons by a New English Puritan planter from Antrim, Sir John Clotworthy. In the course of a strongly critical review of the king's policies in Ireland he made a very pointed attack on Strafford's Catholic army, and in so doing he played on parliament's fear that it had only temporarily stopped the king against the Scots, since he still had an Irish army ready to do his bidding. Clotworthy did more than simply represent the traditional New English position to the House of Commons. His real aim was to alienate the Old English who were trying to hold the middle ground. This ground could be held by constitutional arguments, but a Catholic army could not be explained away too easily. Events were to show that Clotworthy had the confidence of the house at this vital stage, and he used it, with the help of Lord Justice Parsons, to devise a scheme which had catastrophic consequences for the Old English, and consequently all Catholics in Ireland. It was based on a threat which actually existed, namely that of the Gaelic Irish, and was fuelled by the king's own secret intrigues which left almost everyone in the dark as to his activities.

Strafford's sacrifice went ahead with the consent of all his erstwhile friends, including the king. In the meantime the appointment of Sir William Parsons to head the Irish government and the exclusion of the Old English Lord Robert Dillon (and indeed the Earl of Ormond) was made by Charles at the behest of a committee from Ireland composed of seven Old English and six New English members of parliament. Their reluctance to accept Dillon was due to his staunch support for Strafford, and they accepted in his place the old and debilitated Sir John Borlase. Although Dillon was a Protestant, he was of the Anglican rather than the Calvinist persuasion, as was Ormond. The English parliament would have taken the appointment of either man as a sign that the spirit of Strafford through Dillon, or Charles himself through Ormond, was alive. The royalist spirit was indeed alive, but the Old English feared the wrath of the English parliament so much that they missed what was a great chance to burn their bridges. Although they did not do this themselves, in a matter of months it was done for them by Clotworthy and Parsons, but by then they had lost the chance of Ormond's direct support. The problem here, of course, was religious. Ormond's Anglicanism became more and more acceptable to the Old English as they lost ground throughout the remainder of the century, but they could not see this before the Ulster rising because they believed that the New English still needed them and that there was still the middle ground which they had defended since the Reformation. Their problem was the essence of the constitutional question. Their loyalty had always been to the king, but they had been obliged to demonstrate it through the Irish parliament. Now that the constitutional sovereignty was being split down the middle, they could not decide exactly who or what they were. Their Catholicism pushed them naturally towards the king, but it equally, and crucially, prevented them from embracing his cause with total commitment. The king was being opposed in England by those who were defending the constitutional rights of parliament. These were the very rights that the Old English had clung to as the expression of their identity. They could not abandon them easily to demonstrate their loyalty to a king who had no regard for the institution itself.

The committee which met the king had also been instructed to convey the decision of both houses to reduce the value of the subsidies by 70 per cent. The New English members intended this revision to illustrate their altered allegiance and that their role in London was to further facilitate the English parliament against Strafford. The Old English had a different mission. They hoped to act under cover; outwardly they would intimidate the king, but secretly they invited Charles to win their support by granting the Graces, which would secure the Old English position and allow them to take their natural place as his allies. In theory they should have had the support of the English parliament for this limitation on the king's power, but by 1641 it was their religious and not their political identity that determined their position.

The period between January and October 1641 had an air of unreality about it as far as constitutional developments were concerned. Charles had embarked upon a policy of conciliation with his English parliament the most striking feature of which was his sacrifice of the Earl of Strafford. After parliament had succeeded in his impeachment Strafford was tried on a series of charges, most of which related to allegedly treasonable activities in Ireland. There was no case whatever against him, and parliament was obliged to find him guilty by a bill of attainder in April. The bill was passed and signed by the king on 10 May while he prepared a letter to the House of Lords appealing for clemency. This he had delivered on the following day by the Prince of Wales. In it the king did not question the justice of the bill, but confirmed it. What he appealed for was not justice, but simply mercy:

> I did yesterday satisfy the justice of the kingdom, by passing the bill of attainder against the Earl of Strafford; but mercy being as inherent and inseparable to a king as justice, I desire, at this time, in some measure, to show that likewise, by suffering that unfortunate man to fulfil the natural course of his life in a close imprisonment; yet so that if ever he make the least offer to escape, or offer directly or indirectly to meddle in any sort of public business, especially with me, by either message or letter, it shall cost him his life without further process. This, if it may be done without a discontentment to my people, would be an unspeakable contentment to me.

The appeal to mercy betrayed its own weakness, however: 'But, if no less than his life can satisfy my people, I must say *fiat justitia* [i.e. let justice be done].'[15] The Lord Lieutenant of Ireland was executed on the following day.

The view that Strafford had to be stopped because he was about to make a major assault upon the king's opponents is consistent neither with his policies before his arrest nor with the fact that the king had already been forced to capitulate to the Scots. When Charles had begun the challenge to the Scots in 1637 which had got him into this crisis, the Lord Deputy had advised him against it. He had opposed the king's intrigues in Ulster and had sided with the Dublin council against Antrim. During that period he had made several attempts on his own initiative to keep the Earl of Argyll neutral. He had advocated the summoning of a parliament in both Dublin and London because he believed that mutual interests could be established. He had not favoured one group over another in Ireland, but had pursued the king's aims with a single-mindedness which was respected, although not appreciated, by all sides. Strafford's achievement at his trial was to show that the successful government of Ireland was in the general, rather than the king's, interest and that, far from being the king's demonic creature in Dublin Castle, he had a real and sympathetic understanding of his opponents' fears. It was a little over a decade since he himself had led the English parliament against the king; he could not be found guilty of treason because he had not forgotten his roots. It was ironic in the end that Strafford's moral victory was to demonstrate to parliament that what mattered most in Ireland was a strong hand. In other words, the best rule for Ireland was dictatorial, whether it be in the name of the English king or the English parliament. This could be done through the New English, but not through the Old English, bent as they were upon perpetual compromise.

The extent of the Old English compromise was apparent throughout the third and fourth sessions of the Irish parliament which met from January to March and from May until November 1641. Apart from the provision of evidence against Strafford, there was a great deal of discussion concerning the constitutional independence of the parliament itself and on the necessity for reducing the subsidy. For the moment the Old English position was having the desired affect on the king. On 3 April Charles agreed to the enactment of a statute of limitations and the cancellation of Wentworth's plantation of Connacht in favour of the earlier settlement under James. He agreed also to a wider concession of the Graces upon the preparation of the necessary bills. The political climate in which these issues were agreed upon was far more important than the agreement itself, however. In England a triennial act for the regular meeting of parliament, with or without the king's summons, was passed; a statute was enacted forbidding the dissolution of the present parliament without its own consent; prerogative taxes were declared illegal, and the prerogative courts were abolished. In short, the king's rule was dismantled piecemeal, and there were now for the first time two entirely separate views of where sovereignty lay: with the king or with parliament, but not both equally.

———————

On the evening of Friday 22 October 1641 the Ulster rising began. That it was Friday evening and not Saturday morning was the first odd fact about the news of the rising put out by Sir William Parsons as head of the council in Dublin. Parsons claimed immediately that an attempt was to be made on Dublin Castle on Saturday morning in conjunction with the major rising that did indeed take place in Ulster on Saturday. No one at the time questioned the fact that Sir Phelim O'Neill, who took the fort of Charlemont on Friday evening, appeared to have started some twelve hours before his allies were due to take Dublin. Friday night also saw the seizure of Dungannon and Mountjoy Castle in County Tyrone, while forts were taken at Tandragee in County Armagh, Newry in County Down, Castleblayney and Carrickmacross in County Monaghan. It was on the basis of the alleged Castle attempt that the council of Dublin declared martial law and made an immediate appeal to the English parliament for men and money to suppress what was claimed to be an all-Ireland Catholic rising. The consequences of Parsons's actions

were of the greatest significance in relation to the events which
followed the outbreak. The first was that the English parliament had
had its worst fears confirmed about the king and his Catholic
loyalists; the second was that the Old English were driven into the
rising by the Dublin government, which at last rid itself of its Old
English allies. When the Old English were obliged to join the rising
officially, some five weeks after its outbreak, their fate was sealed first
with the Gaelic Irish and soon with the king himself. This was the
position they had done everything to avoid in the hope that they
might hold the middle ground. As the king's rule in England
collapsed, so did the middle ground in Ireland.

1641: The Plot That
Never Was

ACCORDING to Lord Justice Parsons, the Dublin government
received a letter from Sir William Cole, Provost of Enniskillen,
the week before the Ulster rising. In it he informed the council that
Conor Lord Maguire had been observed making journeys into the
Pale, into Tyrone to the house of Sir Phelim O'Neill, and to Dublin.
He had also been writing many letters of late and issuing orders
locally for the raising of troops. Cole added: 'These matters seem the
more strange unto me for that they are so privately carried.'[1]
Strangely, the government made no attempt whatsoever to question
Lord Maguire, who was at that time sitting in the Irish House of
Lords. Nor did they make any attempt to verify Cole's warning. In
fact the government claimed to have taken no action whatsoever
until it was alerted on the night of 22 October 1641, that is to say
while Sir Phelim was in the act of taking Charlemont. The incon-
gruity of the alleged attempt on Dublin Castle can be seen from the
simple fact that no other move of any kind whatsoever was made
outside Ulster either by the Old English or the Gaelic Irish. Yet this
was precisely the impression which the government would need to
make upon its allies in the English parliament if they were to secure
their position with arms and money.

A state of emergency would need to be declared if martial law was
to be justified and the parliament suspended, and in order to do this a
tolerably coherent scenario had to be constructed, as the Old English
had so far proved scrupulously peaceful. According to the
government itself, Lord Justice Parsons was alerted on the night of the
22nd by one Owen Connolly, who claimed that Dublin Castle
was to be attacked at nine o'clock the following morning. Connolly
was supposed to have gleaned this information while drinking with
one of the plotters, Hugh MacMahon, an ex-colonel in the Spanish
army and a grandson of the great Earl of Tyrone. It was claimed that
the two men were foster-brothers and hence that they shared

intimate confidences. What made the disclosure by MacMahon of a countrywide and hitherto top-secret plot more than unlikely, however, was that Connolly, a Protestant married to an English-woman, was the servant of Sir John Clotworthy, a well-known anti-Catholic Puritan.

It might be imagined that with this horrendous news, and with the fact that he had to escape from MacMahon's company and rush to Parsons's house, there might have been some witnesses to Connolly's initial statement, but Parsons pointedly referred to the great secrecy in which Connolly supposedly told his tale. Moreover, MacMahon would seem to have told Connolly not only of the planned Dublin seizure but also of a rising throughout the country, the most important exaggeration as far as Parsons was concerned. According to the Lord Justice, the Castle was immediately fortified and guards posted throughout the city. Although the council sat throughout the night, no attempt was made at any arrests until the following morning, when MacMahon was the first to be taken prisoner. Parsons was at least frank in his admission of torture in order to extract a statement from MacMahon: 'His Majesty's power and regal authority, being still at the stake, we must vary from ordinary proceedings not only in executing martial law, as we see cause, but also in putting some to rack, to find out the bottom of this treason, and all the contrivers thereof, which we foresee will not otherwise be done.'[2]

Parsons claimed that MacMahon implicated Lord Maguire, which only then recalled to the Lord Justice's mind the letter of Sir William Cole predicting this same fact. Sheriffs were dispatched to Maguire's lodging, but he appears to have escaped in disguise before sunrise. Eventually he was found 'hidden in a cock-loft in an obscure house'.[3] His failure to flee the city, it was claimed, was the result of guards having been posted on all the gates—a fact which did not take into account that before the outbreak of the rebellion there were many breaches and unofficial gaps in the city's walls which any schemer would have known about. Indeed, even as late as April of the following year the citizens complained to the corporation that 'the city walls are very ruinous and much defective and out of repair', while twelve months later parts of the wall were still described as having 'many gaps left open for people to look into the fields'.[4]

Parsons's description of Lord Maguire's arrest was in keeping with the strict secrecy of Connolly's initial statement. That is to say that the action would appear to have taken place beyond the observation of any witnesses (other than the sheriff, whose testimony is examined below). Similarly, Maguire would seem to have left behind him the simple but vitally incriminating evidence of the hatchets, knives and hammers which were supposedly found at his lodging. In the account which he sent to England, Parsons took the trouble to emphasise that the hatchets had had their handles shortened; this was held to be indisputable evidence of intention to conceal. By nine o'clock on the morning of the 23rd, that is to say at the appointed time for the seizure, Lord Maguire had admitted his knowledge of a plot, although he denied any involvement and was under lock and key along with MacMahon 'and others' of whom Parsons gave no details whatever.

Many arrests were made of those who had entered the city the previous night, and according to Parsons this was all done before nine o'clock, so that when the allotted time came for the seizure the government were in a comfortable position to observe large groups outside the impregnable walls turn back when they found the gates closed. A proclamation was issued immediately expelling, upon pain of death, all non-residents both within the city and suburbs which, Parsons claimed, rather lamely, 'being accompanied with the example and terror of the committal of those two eminent men and others, occasioned the departure of those multitudes'.[5] A proclamation was then prepared informing the entire country of the rebellion which even then was only under way by a matter of hours. Having satisfied themselves that the Castle and city were now secure against what was supposedly a countrywide rebellion, the council dispersed. It was not until midnight that the first news of the Ulster rising began to come in.

For his part in the affair Connolly could expect to be rewarded, and this indeed would be necessary to prevent him revealing anything which might embarrass the government. The council requested that Connolly 'may have a mark of His Majesty's most royal bounty, which may largely extend to him and his posterity'.[6] The English parliament's estimation of Connolly's importance can be seen in the fact that one month after the Dublin government's request the House of Commons voted him an immediate lump sum of £500 plus a pension of £200 per annum 'until provision be made of inheritance of a greater value' (the pension was later converted to a grant of land worth £1,200).[7] (Connolly was doing well for a mere servant: a child could be educated in Dublin in the late 1630s for a fee of 6s per year; four houses in Castle Street could be had for a total yearly rent of £10.)

A committee was established in London to interrogate Connolly, one of whose members was his master and spokesman on Irish affairs Sir John Clotworthy. The leading questions put to Connolly were carefully chosen and illustrate the type of answers the English parliament was seeking:

> What ground have you to suspect that the papists had any design upon the state of Ireland? What have you heard any priests, or others, say concerning the promoting of the Romish religion? What discourse have you had with Hugh Oge MacMahon concerning any such design in Ireland? Declare the whole matter. Have you heard of any design on the like nature in England or Scotland? What is it you heard? Declare your whole knowledge.[8]

Connolly's statement before the committee was his second statement concerning the events which led up to the exposure of the plot. It is noteworthy that his first statement, taken on the night of 22 October, was not signed by Sir John Borlase, in whose house it was supposedly taken, although it was signed by Parsons. In his second statement Connolly described himself as MacMahon's near kinsman and intimate friend. He said that MacMahon was snubbed by a Mr Aldridge, a justice of the peace 'and but a vintner but a few years before'.[9] Connolly said: 'I wished him [MacMahon] that he would not think of that and that he would consider that the Irish were subordinate unto the English, in regard they were conquered by them.'[10] The comment has a hollow ring to it, not just because MacMahon was unlikely to attempt a countrywide uprising because of an insult, or indeed because it was the type of response which the committee might knowingly have expected from a dispossessed chief, but more because it casts doubt on the intimacy between Connolly and MacMahon upon which the disclosure was supposedly based in the first place. Consistent with Connolly's real loyalties was his next statement that he then, about May 1641, disclosed his knowledge of the plot to several magistrates in the north who conveniently felt that there were no grounds for believing it. This was a suitable version which ignored the fact that almost all the inhabitants of Ulster must have been discussing plots and counter-plots ever since the king's support had been given to Antrim over the preceding years. What Connolly was trying to explain was why he did nothing until events really got under way.

Things began to happen, according to Connolly, when he received a letter from MacMahon while he was on his way to Dublin. The letter reached him at Draperstown, County Londonderry. In his statement of 22 October, however, he had said that the letter reached him at Moneymore, County Londonderry. In the same statement he claimed that the seizure of Dublin Castle and the general country-wide rising was to take place by ten o'clock on Saturday morning. But in the statement subsequently made before the committee he quoted MacMahon as saying 'that this night [Friday 22nd] between eight and nine of the clock all the English towns in the whole kingdom will be surprised by our party'.[11] This significant change was made to include events as they were now known in England but had not been known when Parsons got the scheme under way on the Friday night. No mention was made in the first statement about the amount of arms which the insurgents hoped to seize in the Castle, but in his statement before the committee Connolly stated that MacMahon knew that there were arms enought for 30,000 men and where these had come from. Similarly in his second statement Connolly asserted that he had begged MacMahon for permission to go to his wife, but that MacMahon had said that it was too late for such things now. This pointed cruelty on MacMahon's behalf does not appear in the first statement despite the distress it would have caused Connolly at the time if his wife's life was in great danger. Like the details concerning MacMahon's injured pride and the amount of arms in the Castle, it would seem to have been added for the consumption of the English committee.

In his second statement Connolly said that after the plot had been revealed to him on the Firday night he adjourned with MacMahon to a tavern in Winetavern Street to meet MacMahon's comrades-in-arms. These did not turn up, and so Connolly, MacMahon and eight others stayed drinking until Connolly himself was obliged to suggest they retire 'that we might be better fitted to go about our occasions the next morning, which motion he [MacMahon] very well liked of'.[12] No preparation whatsoever appears to have been made for the supposed seizure the following day, but it was necessary to portray MacMahon and his friends as drunk in order to give credence to Connolly's story of his escape. As they left the tavern he told the others to go on, as he wished to answer a call of nature. When the plotters obliged, Connolly made a run for it to Parsons's house and divulged the whole story. Although not immediately obvious, this story has bypassed the subtle problem of how Connolly could be let in on the plot and at the same time escape comfortably. In his first version, the version taken on the Friday night by Parsons, Connolly's story is not as smooth:

> That when he was with the said Hugh in his lodging the second time [they had been looking for Maguire], the said Hugh swore that he should not go out of his lodging that night, but told him that he should go with him the next morning to the Castle, and said if this matter were discovered somebody should die for it, whereupon this examinant feigned some necessity for his easement, went down out of the chamber and left his sword in pawn; and the said Hugh sent his man down with him, and when this examinant came down into the yard, finding an opportunity, he, this examinant, leaped over a wall and two pales, and so came to Lord Justice Parsons.[13]

There were two fundamental problems with this original story. The first is that in it Connolly obviously did not share MacMahon's confidence, so that the likelihood of the latter revealing the plot and then having to guard Connolly was not great, to say the least. The second is that, having been warned and with a guard placed upon him, Connolly somehow found an opportunity to jump his way to freedom without alarming MacMahon, who waited quietly to be arrested. In other words, the original statement takes MacMahon's seriousness into account, but falls down on the unlikely escape. The second statement before the committee takes care of this by incorporating MacMahon's now impaired faculties. Alcohol could be used to sharpen the portrait of MacMahon as reasonably intelligent, predictably Irish and drunk. Thus Connolly could escape, and we may presume the committee imagined the rest: MacMahon and his friends staggering off to their beds and falling into heavy slumber and dreams of treason, unaware that their friend, Sir John Clotworthy's servant, was in conference with the government.

In Lord Maguire's narrative of the origins of the rebellion, supposedly written in the Tower of London in June 1642, he put the whole plan down to the work of Rory O'More, an Armagh land-holder from the family of the O'Mores of Kildare. According to this account, it was resolved first that nothing would be done until the Irish on the continent had been fully briefed on the plan. Then O'More is reported to have said that it was to no purpose to spend much time in speaking to the gentry. For there was no doubt to be made of the Irish, that they would be ready at any time; and that all the doubt was in the gentry of the Pale, but he said that for his own part he was really assured, when they had risen out, the Pale gentry would not stay long after, at least that they would not oppose them in any thing, but be neuters, and if in case they did, that they had men enough in the kingdom without them.[14]

There are two points of interest here. The first is the close relationship of the narrative to the events as they did indeed happen; the second is that the reluctance of the Old English would make nonsense of any story of an attempt to seize the Castle. Everyone knew by 1642 that the Old English had been forced to take up arms but had not been part of the Ulster rising. The narrative is correct, but does not explain the unlikelihood of a successful Gaelic attempt to take Dublin in the heart of the Pale. In an earlier statement made in March 1642 the version was more logical, but exposed the same weakness from another angle. Maguire stated that in May 1641 he, O'More and others sent word of the planned rebellion to Owen Roe O'Neill in Flanders by way of a priest. The priest returned about a month before the planned outbreak to say that Owen Roe

would (within 15 days after the people were up) be with him, with his best assistance and arms; and it being demanded why the said Owen should being arms, considering that the Castle of Dublin was to be taken with the arms therein, this examinant answered that they so provided for arms that they might not want any, in case they could not take the said Castle, whereof they doubted.[15]

There is an internal inconsistency here which is only properly understood by the charge against Maguire himself of the attempt on the Castle. When Parsons arrested Maguire he did so on the basis of the Castle plot as part of a countrywide rising. When Maguire was put on trial the Castle attempt was not only central to parliament's justification of its support for the New English council, it was the very foundation of its Irish policy since the rising. At about the time that Maguire's lengthy statement on the origins of the rising was being composed the king had asked permission of parliament in April 1642 to go personally to Ireland and deal with the situation at first hand. Parliament refused outright, and Charles wrote a long reply all of which hinged on the question of who exactly in Ireland was in arms against whom and for what reasons. It was vital in this context to uphold the Castle plot and the martial law which followed it even if the whole country did not immediately rise. The Gaelic Irish had already proclaimed their support for the king, and the Old English were his traditional supporters; this left Charles in a strong position if it was the New English who were acting unlawfully against their king, and if he could prove it by going to Ireland and ending the war.

Thus in the statement attributed to Maguire, Owen Roe was to bring arms, but those arms were unnecessary because it had been intended to take the Castle stores; however, this could not be relied upon (nor did it even make sense to rise first and then distribute the arms), so it was necessary to have Maguire say that they had arms enough in the first place; yet if this was the case, there was no point in risking an attempt on the Castle and thereby spoiling the element of surprise at the very centre of the enemy's control. Nevertheless, the Castle plot had to remain the pivot of the rising if all Catholic Ireland was to be outlawed and removed from any help the king might be able to give. Charles's frustration and his threat to his opponents is clear some four months before the English civil war finally broke out:

> We shall be very glad to find the work of Ireland so easy as you seem to think it; which did not so appear by anything known to us when we sent our message. And though we will never refuse or be unwilling to venture our person, we are not so weary of our life as to hazard it impertinently; and therefore since you seem to have received advertisements of some late and great successes in that kingdom, we will stay some time, to see the event of those, and not pursue this resolution till we have given you a second notice: but if we find the miserable condition of our poor subjects of that kingdom be not speedily relieved we will (with God's assistance) visit them with succours, as our particular credit and interest can supply us with, if you refuse to join us. And we doubt not but the levies we shall make (in which we will observe punctually the former and all other cautions, as may best prevent all fears and jealousies, and to use no power but what is legal) will be so much to the satisfaction of our subjects, as no person will dare presume to resist our commands; and if they should, at their peril. In the meantime, we hope our forwardness so remarkable to that service shall be notorious to all the world, and that all scandals laid on us in that business shall be clearly wiped away.[16]

Here, in the king's desire to come to Ireland and take command, is the connection between the crown and the Ulster rising. What might have been a reasonable hope (although it never proved to be at any other time in Ireland's history) was dashed by the sovereign challenge of the English parliament—Strafford's legacy to a king who had done everything since the late 1620s to avoid that very challenge.

In the period leading up to the final outbreak of war in England the question of Ireland was central to events there. In March the English parliament passed an 'adventurers' act' offering land yet to be forfeited in Ireland in return for money to suppress the rising there. For his part, the king wished to deprive his opponents of control in Ireland by calling upon the allegiance of his Irish, Old English and even his New English subjects. From the time of the Norman conquest England had wished Ireland to be safely occupied against the incursions of a foreign power; now two separate English powers contended both to occupy and to prevent the other from occupying Ireland. The king's confidence that Ireland belonged to him is clear; parliament's only defence against his authority was to continue to exclude all Catholics in Ireland from the possibility of a legal settlement. Any kind of political settlement might be achieved, but because it would be done so with Catholics the threat would not be alleviated. It was clear by the summer of 1642 that Ireland was going to go to the victor and there would be little ground for compromise.

In the statement attributed to Lord Maguire the tale of the Castle plot continued with as little sense or logic as any of its component parts had shown so far. Maguire had apparently been told by his fellow-conspirators

> that those Colonels that lately came over did proffer their service and industry in that act, and so would raise their men under colour to convey them into Spain and then seize on the Castle of Dublin, and with their arms there to arm the soldiers and have them ready for any occasion that should be commanded them; but that they had not concluded anything because they were not assured how the gentlemen of the remote parts of the kingdom (and especially of Ulster) would stand affected to that act, and that assurance of that doubt was all their impediment.[17]

The Colonels are here offering an Old English rising, but doubt the willingness of the Gaelic Irish of Ulster to participate. This only makes sense as a logical support for an illogical plot. It there really was a plot to take the Castle, then it must have the support of the Old English in the centre of whose territory it was. For this to be feasible the army which Strafford had brought into existence could be used by the Old English who had played a large part in its formation. If, however, the Old English and Ulster Irish were not united—which events had shown they were not—then an Old English attempt on the Castle would have to be made without any real support from Ulster. There is no sense to this attempt to square the circle other than to maintain the essential illusion of the Castle attempt.

According to the narrative attributed to Maguire, he was then given the job of mediating between the Old English of the Pale and the Gaelic Irish in order to convince the latter of the need to rise. Before he could do that, however, he was to start immediately for Dublin to meet the Colonels who were recruiting for Spain: 'and so (without as much as to return home to furnish myself for such a journey, *volens nolens*) they prevailed, or rather forced me to come to Dublin to confer with these Colonels'.[18] As soon as he arrived in Dublin he met one of the Colonels, Sir James Dillon, by accident in the street. Dillon said he would consult with him the next day, which he did and proceeded immediately to acquaint Maguire with his intention to seize the Castle, on the assumption, without Maguire saying anything apparently, that it was safe, 'knowing you are well affected thereunto, and I hope (said he) ready to put your helping hand to it upon occasion'.[19] Dillon supposedly went on to tell Maguire how the Castle would be taken and the arms distributed to his men. According to the statement, Maguire then declares 'this was the first motion that ever I heard of taking the Castle; for it never came into our thoughts formerly, nor am I persuaded ever would, if it had not proceeded from those Colonels'.[20] This was to say that the Colonels formulated the plot, got Maguire to sell it to the Ulster Irish and incorporate it into a rising there, but when the Colonels pulled out of the scheme the Ulster Irish carried on and sent a handful of men down to fulfil the mission. Moreover, the statement adds on Maguire's behalf: 'I began according to the directions that were sent with me to approve of their resolution, and also to let him know how sure he might be of the assistance of those of Ulster.'[21] It seems to have escaped the writer's attention that he had already made a point of saying that he had come to Dublin immediately and had had no time to even prepare for the journey, let alone consult the Ulster leaders and be in a position to reassure Dillon that he could deliver their support. Something else which seems to have escaped the author of this story is the fact that although Dillon was indeed one of the recruiting Colonels, his opposition to the rising of 1641 was such that he, together with the Earl of Westmeath and the Bishop of Meath, Thomas Dease, stood out against the Old English leaders after they had committed themselves to the rising. Rather than help, Colonel Dillon actually did his best to hinder—against opposition from his own people.

The question of who should undertake to surprise the Castle and how it should be done—although it was, according to the statement, to be the pivot of the rising—was left until all matters relating to the general outbreak had been discussed, which took several meetings; 'and so on the last meeting, it was resolved to the last doubt, touching seizing the Castle, that Colonel Plunket and Colonel Byrne should undertake that task, because they were nearer to it than any other'.[22] There is no mention whatsoever of Connolly's version about MacMahon's involvement in the picture which is then given. The last meeting was supposedly held in late August or early September and the date for the rising was fixed at 5 October:

> and everyone should make provision to rise out that day; and they were named that should first succour them that would take the Castle with men presently; namely, Sir James Dillon, who did undertake to be with them within three (or at the most four) days with 1,000 men, and so much more should come to them out of the north. For these two Colonels did not intend to use above 100 men in the surprisal, whereof they were to have twenty good able gentlemen; for they made account, that having the Castle they, with the artillery, would master all the town until they were relieved by men from the country.

A further meeting fixed for 20 September to consider the plan, 'because there was a doubt made how all this should be done in so short a time'.[23] There was a doubt indeed because this version of events does not provide anything like enough time for Ulster to be converted to a Colonels' plot centred around a simplistic tactical error.

The acknowledged leader of the Ulster rising was Sir Phelim O'Neill. He had been one of the Earl of Antrim's friends listed as worthy of Wentworth's help in arming Ulster against the Scots.

Antrim himself had brought O'Neill to Dublin to meet Wentworth and have the Lord Deputy knight him as a sign of the king's confidence in 1639. Wentworth had obliged reluctantly and had conferred the royal honour upon the leading Gaelic Irish conspirator only because Antrim, and indirectly the king, had wished it. Yet according to the statement attributed to Lord Maguire, no contact had been made with Sir Phelim O'Neill by Maguire or the Colonels as late as early September 1641. On his way home from the last meeting Maguire supposedly received a letter from Sir Phelim inviting him to his wife's funeral. Philip O'Reilly, with whom Maguire was staying, persuaded him to go 'to confer with Sir Phelim touching all those proceedings (for neither he nor I spoke to Sir Phelim concerning the matters before) but to his brother Turlough O'Neill'.[24] The only way to explain this is to say that although the list which Antrim presented to the Dublin government of his supporters named Maguire and Phelim O'Neill as being among those who were backing him, Antrim must somehow have kept both men from discussing with each other the rising which was being planned. This crazy picture was necessary, however, if the rising was to be attributed to the Colonels' attempt on the Castle and Ulster's role in the plot reduced to a very poor second place.

The Colonels' plot had never existed, but had been used up to this point as the supposedly cohesive force behind the rising because it was vital to keep the Castle attempt at the centre of the outbreak. If events were to be explained as they had come to be known by 1642, it would be necessary for the Colonels and all the Old English represented by them to pull out while Sir Phelim took over in Ulster. Not surprisingly, this is what the statement goes on to suggest, but to be able to do so it had to have some reason behind it. After the funeral of his wife Sir Phelim and the others set about discussing how Derry could be taken, but they could not agree. It was possible only if the date was postponed, and Maguire was instructed to go to Dublin to inform the Colonels of this. This was the first step. On Maguire's arrival in Dublin, Rory O'More came to him with the news that Owen Roe O'Neill had urged them not to delay and had assured them of his support within fourteen days of the rising, 'also desiring us by any means to seize the Castle of Dublin, if we could, for he heard that there was great provision in it for war; and Mr O'More morevoer said that time was not to be overslipped, and desired me to be very pressing with the Colonels to go on in their resolution'. This was the second step. Now followed the third step:

But on meeting the Colonels with them, they were fallen from their resolution, because those of the Pale would do nothing therein first, but when it was done they would not fail to assist us. Colonel Plunket did affirm, and by several meetings it was resolved on by them to desist from that enterprise for that time, and to expect a more convenient time.[25]

So Sir Phelim had pulled out temporarily, Owen Roe had urged all speed, the Colonels had followed Sir Phelim and pulled out (because it now appeared that they had no backing, although this was supposed to be their idea); but now it was necessary for Sir Phelim to be suddenly worked back in. This was the fourth step. This would be the point at which Sir Phelim would take over and the attempt on the Castle would go on without any local support or impetus.

According to Maguire's statement, he was followed to Dublin by Sir Phelim and Captain Brian O'Neill to assist him in encouraging the Colonels. It should cause no surprise to find that there were no witnesses to this link between the Colonels and Sir Phelim, because neither he nor Rory O'More

> would be seen there in themselves to those gentlemen, but would meet me privately and know what was done at every meeting; alleging for excuse, that I being first employed in that matter, it would not be expedient that they should be seen in it. And moreover, that they would not be known to be in the town but by a few of their friends, until they were in a manner ready to depart the town, at least as long as I was in town.[26]

What seems to have been overlooked in this presentation is that Sir Phelim was a leading member of the Irish House of Commons, and Maguire an equally leading member of the Irish House of Lords, in the parliament which spanned these events. It was strange indeed for Sir Phelim to avoid making any direct contact with the Colonels when he himself had been appointed by the Irish parliament in July 1640 to a committee, together with Old English leaders, to investigate ways of keeping Strafford's disbanded army in Ireland—the very centre of the Colonels' activities. That Maguire would be needed as a secret go-between, who himself could only meet Sir Phelim in secret, is ridiculous. It is only feasible at all if the Ulster leaders are accepted as the 'wild Irish', dispossessed Catholics lurking in Ulster and secretly slipping into Dublin to connive furtively at the destruction of Protestant Ireland and then slipping back to their northern lairs and fastnesses. Such a picture has all the characteristics of the Puritan need to portray Ireland as endlessly complicated and infinitely treacherous, where the only solution was to wipe out all Catholic resistance.

Maguire's statement then goes on to relate that he informed Sir Phelim that the Colonels were determined to stay out of the plot. This was the final step in a scenario in which Sir Phelim was to take command of the Castle seizure when everyone south of Ulster had abandoned the plan. A meeting was called which now only featured the Ulster Irish with two representatives from Owen Roe O'Neill's continental army: Sir Phelim O'Neill, Rory O'More and Lord Maguire for the landed Ulster Irish, and Captain Brian O'Neill and Colonel Hugh Byrne for Owen Roe. The Maguire account records:

> After long debate it was resolved, that we with all those that were of our faction should go on with that determination that was formerly made, concluded to rise out. Moreover, to seize on the Castle as the Colonels were purposed, for if it were not for their project, and the advice sent by Colonel [Owen Roe] O'Neill, we would never venture to surprise it, neither was it ever thought on in all the meetings and resolutions between us, before those Colonels did resolve on it.[27]

Perhaps the most illogical step of all now followed: 'But by reason that those other gentlemen that were privy to those proceedings were not present, the certainty of the time and the manner how to execute it was put off to a further meeting in the country.' They agreed to meet one week later at a house in Farney, County Monaghan, but 'by reason that at that meeting the gentry of Leinster could not be, considering the remoteness of the place from them, it was thought fit that Mr O'More should there meet to receive the final resolution and should acquaint them therewith'.[28] Thus the Old English were included and excluded simultaneously by arranging a meeting for their convenience which they could not attend because of the inconvenience of the location. Not surprisingly, they did not turn up, and the supposed meeting in Farney was attended only by Phelim O'Neill, Rory O'More, Brian O'Neill, Ever MacMahon and Lord Maguire ('assuring ourselves that those gentlemen absent should both allow and join to what we should determine').[29] What they determined was: 'grounding all or most part of our hope and confidence on the succours from Colonel [Owen Roe] O'Neill, to seize on the Castle and rise out all in one day'.[30] The rising was fixed for 23 October, which was then one week away; Saturday was chosen because it was a market day and there would be many non-residents in the town. This attention to local detail was not matched by the attention given to the question of who would actually take the Castle. O'More offered himself and Colonel Byrne 'and what other gentlemen of Leinster they could procure to join with them', regardless of the fact that the Colonels had pulled out and the Old English were not taking part. Maguire himself had now to be placed at the centre of the action because he was, after all, arrested in Dublin on Saturday morning. O'More said that one gate of the Castle should be taken by the men of Leinster, while the Ulstermen should take the other, ' and (said he) of necessity one of you both (meaning Sir Phelim and me) must be there, for the mere countenance of the matter, it being the glory of all our proceedings'.[31] According to Maguire, everyone liked the sound of this, including Sir Phelim, although he declined the signal honour:

> and so would I; but then all of them set on me, desiring me to be one, alleging for reason that their proceedings and resolutions were very honourable and glorious, it being for religion and to procure more liberty for their country, as did (said they) of late Scotland, and that in taking the Castle consisted all the honour and glory of the said act.[32]

Sir Phelim settled for the lesser honour of taking Derry, which he said would not be done if he did not attend personally, and so Maguire relates that 'with these and many other persuasions they obtained my consent'.[33]

The number of men to be deployed was then decided upon, and 200 (one-half from Ulster and the other half from Leinster) was agreed. These would be moved into Dublin under the pretence of enlisting for service abroad, and blank patents were to be drawn up and issued to facilitate this. Also, 'for the more colour, they bethought of what was to be done in the country that day, and it was resolved that everyone privy to that matter in every part of the kingdom should rise up that day'.[34] In other words, the countrywide rising was to be a diversion from the main event in Dublin. It was also agreed that as soon as the Castle had been taken Sir Phelim O'Neill, Philip O'Reilly, Coll MacMahon and Lord Maguire's brother would descend on Dublin with all the forces they could muster after the big event, while Rory O'More would get similar help from Leinster.

According to Maguire's alleged statement, he arrived in Dublin on the evening of Friday 22 October and met Owen Roe's officer, Captain Con O'Neill, who assured him of Owen Roe's support. A meeting was arranged immediately of all the plotters in town, and it would seem that Rory O'More had done well in enlisting Old English support. At the meeting were Rory O'More, Colonel Byrne, Colonel Plunket, Captain Fox 'and other Leinster gentlemen, a captain (I think of the Byrnes, but I am not sure whether a Byrne or O'Toole) and Captain Brian O'Neill'.[35] What none of the plotters at this meeting on Friday evening seemed to know was that the Ulster rising had by then broken out under the leadership of Sir Phelim O'Neill. What they did notice, however, was that Sir Phelim had not sent the men he had promised, nor had Coll MacMahon, 'and Colonel Byrne did miss Sir Morgan Cavenagh, that had promised him to be there, but he said he was sure he would not fail to be that night or the next morning in town'.[36] Undaunted by this and by the fact that they could account for only eighty of the expected 200 men, they pressed on with their plan, 'and all the difference was: at what time of the day they would set on the Castle, and after some debate it was resolved in the afternoon . . . and so parted that night, but to meet in the morning to see further what was to be done'.[37] This somewhat farcical account then ends quickly and neatly:

> And immediately thereon I came to my chamber, and about nine of the clock [on Saturday morning] Mr O'More and Captain Fox came to me and told me all was discovered and that the city was in arms and the gates were shut up, and so departed from me; and what became of them and of the rest, I know not, nor think that they escaped, but how and at what time I do not know, because I myself was taken that morning.[38]

The details of the June 1642 statement (upon which the above is based) which were attributed to Lord Maguire while in the Tower were not used at his trial because their central weakness lay in the attempt to explain rationally what had not happened. The statement was also useless to the prosecution because MacMahon is not mentioned once, and the oversight throws considerable doubt on Connolly's version and thus on why MacMahon was standing trial at all. The trial of the two men, and particularly of Maguire as 'leader', was of great significance to the Englsih parliament so long as it proved what should have been proved about the rising and the correctness of the Dublin government's response. The importance of the story to Irish history can be seen in the fact that Dublin Protestants who believed the council's version of events celebrated Maguire's arrest with an annual religious service for two hundred years.

Since there had been no attempt on the Castle, and since, therefore, Maguire and MacMahon were innocent, the English parliament took a long time to start the case. When they did, however, they took lengthy legal advice from several judges and appointed the best prosecution to be had. It had been judged better to keep the conspirators in prison until the story had been accepted simply because it had not been disproved. This was indeed what happened, and even the Old English themselves believed that an attempt had been made on the Castle. Arrested on 23 October 1641 as the only two conspirators (no one else surfaced as part of the plot, despite Parsons's claim that many others had been arrested), Maguire and MacMahon were not tried in London until November 1644, when both were found guilty and executed.

The escape and recapture of Maguire and MacMahon is a curious interlude in the events which followed their arrest and which no doubt hastened their trial. They were committed to the Tower of London in July 1642, where they remained until 17 August 1644, when they both escaped with the use of a small steel saw and some rope. Parliament offered a reward of £100 for each of them dead or alive. According to a contemporary historian,

> No news was heard of them till 19 September, and then they having got lodgings in a constable's house in Drury Lane, and one of them looking out of the window or balcony to call a woman that cried oysters, it happened at that instant a servant of Sir John Clotworthy's espied him, and instantly gave notice to his master and the Lieutenant of the Tower, who came and seized them and carried them back to the Tower.[39]

According to this account, their escape had been effected by two Spanish priests and a Mrs Laviston. The latter's house was searched after the pair had been captured, but because Mrs Laviston was the landlady of a French government minister the matter was politely dropped. There was a notable neatness about the escape and recapture, which would suggest the possibility of a deal being done with the insurgents which had then fallen through. Mrs Laviston could not be charged for diplomatic reasons; the Spanish embassy denied all knowledge; the pair had somehow felt secure in the house of a constable (who, by the very nature of his office, was unlikely to contradict any official version of events) and were eventually, and once again, turned in by a servant of Sir John Clotworthy. Nor would it strain credulity any further to find that the servant was the ubiquitous Owen Connolly himself; although the English House of Lords approved a payment of £200 in March 1645 to Clotworthy's servant, the individual was not named.

———————

The trial of Conor Lord Maguire opened in the Court of King's Bench in London on 11 November 1644. The first remarkable fact was that Owen Connolly was not included among the witnesses to be called; nor was he indeed even mentioned once during the trial itself. It was also notable that MacMahon had already been convicted and executed earlier in the same month. This is of interest because before his brief escape MacMahon had made a rambling appeal to the English parliament for better prison conditions. In the appeal he denied any involvement in illegal activities and 'only by chance meeting my lord Maguire once going to his father-in-law with his wife and children that he said he would likely go to Dublin for the taking of the Castle'.[40] It would seem to have been a mistake of the highest order on the prosecution's part to have had MacMahon convicted and executed after such an admission rather than use him as an incontrovertible witness against Maguire. It would not be a mistake, however, if MacMahon was actually innocent. In other words, the danger of using MacMahon against Maguire was that it could backfire completely and show that there was no evidence whatsoever of either of them being involved in an attempt on Dublin Castle. It would have to follow from this that Parsons had invented the whole thing (undoubtedly aided and abetted by Clotworthy). Thus it was wiser to get MacMahon out of the way first, even though he had allegedly given evidence against Maguire. In relation to any evidence which MacMahon might have given, it must be remembered that he was racked by Parsons from the beginning. Arrested and tortured, the best he could hope for was time, during which a deal with his allies might be struck. At Maguire's trial the same piece of evidence regarding the accidental meeting would be heard, only this time it was Maguire who allegedly implicated MacMahon.

———————

Sir Arthur Chichester

Giovanni Battista Rinuccini   (*National Gallery of Ireland*)

Owen Roe O'Neill

Cromwell at Drogheda

Petty's Down Survey map of County Sligo in the mid 1650s

A mantelpiece dated 1635 from Old Bawn House, Tallaght, Co. Dublin
(*National Museum of Ireland*)

A Cromwellian roll of account of money delivered, received and paid for public use in Ireland in the 1650s

James Butler, Earl (later first Duke) of Ormond

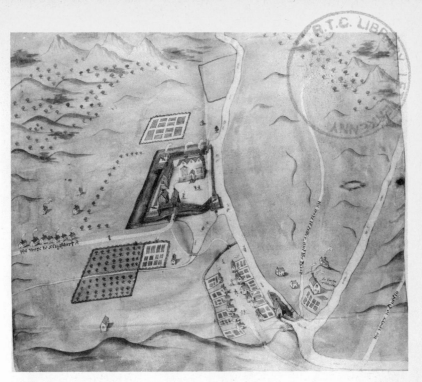

A view of the plantation town of Omagh, Co. Tyrone in the mid seventeenth century

Reverend George Walker
(*National Gallery of Ireland*)

Richard Talbot, Earl of Tyrconnell   (*National Gallery of Ireland*)

Maguire was tried both for high treason (the Castle attempt) and for his part in the massacre of Protestants, which had by the time of the trial become the great generating force for anti-Catholic propaganda in England. In other words, Maguire's trial would not only show proof that an attempt on the Castle had been made, but would also demonstrate that had it succeeded, the Irish government itself would have met the fate of what the prosecution described as 'the persons of above 200,000 men, women and children murdered, many of them with exquisite and unheard of tortures, within the space of one month'.[41] Although Maguire could not possibly win his case, owing to his long involvement with preparations for a rising in Ulster, the prosecution was nevertheless faced with a daunting task when it came to proving Maguire guilty of something which had not actually taken place. In other words, the attempt on the Castle must be proved beyond doubt, as it was the only means by which Maguire could be found guilty, even if only of intent. Nevertheless, it must be done if the image of Ireland as a hellish threat was to be sustained.

To all charges Maguire pleaded not guilty and requested that he be tried by his peers. This request raised a point of law which Justice Bacon could not ignore. Was Maguire's peerage valid in England? If so, then he could not be tried by a common jury. The prosecution presented a lengthy case to show that an Irish peer was a commoner in England. Based upon precedent and compiled in a most learned fashion, the argument was a polished example of the legal foundations upon which the court relied to come to a foregone conclusion. Predictably, Justice Bacon decided in favour of the prosecution, and his decision was endorsed by the English House of Commons, who added that 'the judge is hereby required to proceed speedily thereupon, according to law and justice';[42] this order was then endorsed by the House of Lords. Maguire had pleaded the statute of Magna Carta and a statute of Henry VII to no avail. Had his defence been at all organised, it could have been demonstrated clearly that only three years earlier the Earl of Cork had been summoned to sit in the English House of Lords (at Strafford's trial) on the sole basis of his Irish peerage.

When the trial commenced, Maguire employed delaying tactics by availing of his right to object to some jurors, but he could not delay what was by now only a matter of course. He asked for time to send for witnesses, but it was pointed out to him that he had had ample time to prepare a case and also that he had submitted no list of witnesses who might be called in his defence. It was hardly likely, however, that any witness would travel from Ireland after 1641 to speak in Maguire's defence. Maguire had no other tactics than those of delay and the hope that a deal might yet be struck for his freedom. His continued plea to call witnesses, however, inadvertently caused Justice Bacon to reveal not only his partiality but the essential weakness of the case based on the Castle seizure:

> What can your witnesses say for you? Can they say this much, that you did not conspire, as this indictment charges you? That there was no taking of these castles? Can they swear in the negative? The proof lies in the affirmation on the king's part.[43]

At this point Serjeant Whitfield, acting for the prosecution, reminded the judge that 'If we were not tied to that, to nothing but his own confession, there is enough to condemn him.'[44] This is significant; Justice Bacon revealed that the taking of castles in Ulster (because no castles were taken anywhere else) was a fact which would convict Maguire of the Dublin attempt, while Serjeant Whitfield was of the opinion that a confession—which Maguire was to deny making—was already enough proof of that attempt. In other words, half of the case would rest on the reality of the Ulster rising, although it had no bearing whatsoever, while the other half would depend on a single confession which Maguire could only have made to buy time (if, indeed, he made it at all). Because Maguire was to deny the confession outright, the bulk of the case would have to deal with the connections between the Ulster rising and the so-called Castle plot.

When the jury was called, Maguire exercised his right to challenge each member. The court was adjourned until a new jury was summoned. Maguire made another appeal to the House of Lords, to be told that 'When one is come here, to appeal to the Lords, that was never known; now you have put yourself upon the country.'[45] Maguire was already being tried by a court of commoners, and the logic was inescapable, as Justice Bacon pointed out to him: 'We have no such course in the common law; if a man will appeal from me I cannot let him appeal to any man.'[46] A new jury was appointed, but Maguire challenged it on the basis that the members might have a vested interest in his lands, now forfeited. Serjeant Whitfield replied that 'To desire that a whole jury may be demanded such a question upon their oath is that that hath not been known.'[47] Maguire responded by suggesting that any of the jury 'that have given money for Ireland for my destruction' should not be allowed.[48] This was indeed a fair point in view of the parliamentary drive to raise money for the suppression of Ireland's Catholics in return for forfeited land. It was pointed out in response that this was a matter for the king, and that if Maguire's lands were forfeit, it was within the power of the king to regrant those lands. This was a pointed reminder that although Maguire was to be accused of rising for the king, his accusers could still claim the king's law to convict him. Nevertheless, the jury was asked to declare upon oath any personal interest in Irish land; Maguire wished that the question might include their relatives, but it was disallowed and the jury was sworn.

The trial got off to an ominous start for Lord Maguire. The first witness called was Sir William Cole, the man who had written to Parsons from Enniskillen warning him of the Ulster rising and of Maguire's activities in the north. It was odd that Parsons had only recalled this letter after Connolly had supposedly betrayed the Castle plot, but nevertheless it prompted him to have Maguire arrested. Sir William Cole was, therefore, one of the strongest witnesses the prosecution could have brought against Maguire: first, because he could testify to Maguire's treacherous nature, and secondly—and of far greater historical interest—he could confirm that Parsons had indeed received a letter about a possible rising and that on the strength of this he was justified in arresting Maguire. If, on the other hand, Maguire was innocent of anything other than the general preparations that were undoubtedly going on all over Ulster in the late summer of 1641, Cole would have to perjure himself to the hilt. This he was clearly not willing to do. He was asked what the religion was of those conspirators whose names he knew. He replied that they were all papists. When asked to name them, he named Maguire, Sir Phelim O'Neill and Rory O'More (and possibly others not included in the transcript). That was all the evidence he was required to give at that stage of the trial. When he was called later it was to confirm the evidence of a witness who had actually told Cole's own story, and the clerk of the court felt there was insufficient need to record Cole's evidence other than to note that it confirmed what had been said already. As will be shown, the evidence in question had nothing to do with the Castle plot, but only with the Ulster ferment. Thus the prosecution led with Cole, but allowed someone else to give his evidence; this way he did not have to perjure himself about the precise details of his letter to Parsons and to what extent it involved Maguire in an attempt on the Castle. Once again it was a twofold problem: first it would have to be demonstrated that there was a Castle plot, and secondly that Maguire was guilty of leading it. If the first was not true, it followed that all evidence bearing on the charge would necessitate a great deal of inventive perjury.

Three witnesses were then called who testified that there had been a parliamentary committee set up in May 1641 to investigate the rumour of a plot to blow up the Irish Houses of Parliament. Lord Maguire was accused of using his membership of this committee as a means of gaining access to the store of arms at Dublin Castle to discover their quantity and precise location. The lack of certainty of Maguire's involvement in this committee in the first place was to be seen in the hesitation of the witnesses, speaking as they were under oath. Sir Francis Hamilton gave evidence that 'There was search made [of the parliament building] and (as I remember) the Lord Maguire was one of the committee.'[49] Sir William Stewart supported the claim, but could not actually say that the state of the armoury had been examined: 'Then they inquired for the king's magazine, and I believe my lord Maguire now here was one of the committee that went to search for the House of Lords, and he did search very narrowly, and they were desirous to know where the store was.'[50] Henry Lord Blayney then tried to connect the alleged plot to blow up parliament with the alleged attempt on the Castle and then to unite these with the reality of the Ulster rising. This was the effect aimed at by the prosecution, but there was no factual proof that these events had actually taken place. Blayney's deposition was an honest attempt (if such was possible) to convict Maguire without perjuring himself:

> So near as I can I will give you the business, it is so long ago. This I remember, that there was one of the Lords' house, whether it were my lord Fingal or my lord Macary moved it, I cannot certainly depose, but I am sure it was one of them. This occasion was: one of the Earl of Strafford's coachmen said he hoped to see some of the Lords blown up for it [i.e. Strafford's death]; it was about a fortnight after the Earl of Strafford was beheaded here. Thereupon they got an order for it and so they went down and they did not find the powder, but they made as narrow a search [of the parliament building] as ever any was. I asked what the meaning was of this, for we had strange censures of it ourselves. Says one of them, the Lord Clanmorris: 'They are afraid of a powder plot of the Protestants.' I answered that I

had heard of a powder plot of the papists, but never of the Protestants in my life. But if you ask the reason for it, it was to assure themselves of their strength, for we found by woeful experience of it afterwards it was their end.[51]

None of this evidence proved that the committee gained access to the government's armoury; nor could it even be shown that Maguire had been a member. Blayney was then asked what religion Fingal and Clanmorris were; he replied that Fingal was a papist and Clanmorris 'a pestiferous papist'. Serjeant Whitfield made the point succinctly and moved on: 'All papists. We shall now read the examination of [Maguire's] taking and then his own examination.'[52] Thus the three witnesses could offer no evidence whatsoever for an attempt on the Castle, and the prosecution had confined itself to a general portrayal of Catholics blowing up parliament buildings. Nor was this done idly, or simply to impress the jury with the fact that Catholics were traitors. The point being made in the middle of the English civil war was that Catholics had no affinity with parliaments. The term 'papist' implied allegiance to Rome rather than the sovereign government, which was founded on the institution of parliament.

Evidence was then read on behalf of the former Sheriff of Dublin, John Woodcock, relating to the events leading up to Maguire's arrest. Notice having been given to Woodcock on the night of Friday 22 October 1641 'of some great design intended', he 'did by virtue of his office walk up and down the city that night'.[53] It is important to note that the sheriff had been alerted, but not instructed to arrest anyone at all. In both statements made by Connolly, and particularly in the one made on that Friday night to Parsons, Maguire is specifically named as one of the leaders of the proposed attempt. The sheriff had not been aware of this on his patrol, however, as his evidence clearly showed:

> And coming to the house of one Nevil, a surgeon, in Castle Street, he understood by the said Nevil that the Lord Maguire with some ten or twelve others were there; this examinate [i.e. Sheriff Woodcock] told him it was fit for his guests to be in bed at that time of night, but the said Nevil did bring this examinate word that the Lord Maguire and his company were then going to bed.[54]

Perhaps in the simplicity of both the sheriff's and Maguire's behaviour is to be seen the most glaring proof that the plot to seize the Castle was a fabrication. Connolly is on record as having named Maguire to Parsons, who then alerted the city's chief law officer, who, when he accidentally came upon the man he was supposed to be looking for, informed him that it was time he was in bed! Without explaining any of this, Sheriff Woodcock went on in his evidence (which, being a written submission, was presumably the best he could do) to tell the court that a watch was put on the house where Maguire was now known to be. Apparently this guard later came to Woodcock to tell him that Maguire had removed himself (now that he had been warned) to the house in Dublin where the actual arms were kept for the Castle seizure. Strangely enough, Maguire and his company were not at this house when the sheriff arrived and found the arms mentioned by Parsons; the cache included the incriminating hatchets with shortened handles, as well as 'other arms of the Lord Maguire's'.[55] Sheriff Woodcock did not deem it necessary to explain how the arms had been identified as belonging to Maguire, and so passed over a very vital and incriminating piece of evidence. His deposition continues by stating that he brought the arms to Parsons, and that the council then ordered the arrest of Maguire. In other words, after the city had been put on full alert and the named leader of the plot ordered straight to bed, no attempt whatsoever had been made to arrest him until he had left his room and gone straight to his cache of arms; then, having drawn the forces of the law there, he had managed somehow to escape; and it was only at this stage that the Dublin government issued an order for his arrest. 'Upon which, the said examinate [Woodcock] searching narrowly for him, at last found him in a cock-loft with a cloak wrapt about him, there being no key to be found; as also, the master of the house flying away and making an escape to the enemy.'[56] It would seem from this that Lord Maguire made no attempt to leave the city, despite the fact that even the owner of the cock-loft could not only foresee the inevitable arrest but had the presence of mind to make good his escape, carefully locking up his house before he left, and leaving Lord Maguire to shiver in the loft.

The farcical evidence presented by the Sheriff of Dublin could only pass unquestioned before a court that was more concerned with vindicating the action taken by the Dublin government in October 1641 than with any notion of justice. It is more than likely that the gist of Woodcock's evidence is true. He probably was on alert that night and did indeed order Maguire to retire. Maguire was a noted government opponent in the House of Lords and a close associate of the Earl of Antrim. He may have been under surveillance all the time, but Woodcock was not straying far from the possible truth when he said that a watch was put on the house. If Woodcock was not part of the plot (which it is very unlikely he was, as a mere one-year corporation official), what happened then was that Parsons's man came to him and told him they had followed Maguire to a house in which were the required arms. Of course Maguire was not there when the sheriff arrived, because he had not gone there. If there had been such a house, it is surely the one place in the entire city that Maguire, the leader of a coup only hours away, would have avoided after receiving a warning by the sheriff and having a watch being put directly on him.

Maguire's alleged statement of March 1642 was then read to the jury, who were told that it had been made five months after his arrest, as 'they could get nothing out of him' in the meantime.[57] His far longer 'relation' which had been apparently 'written with his own hand in the Tower' some months later was not used as evidence. It was replaced by another statement, a short examination taken by magistrates just one month before the trial. In view of the fact that Maguire was to deny that the signature on the short examination was his, the handwritten account might prove even less resilient to a claim of forgery and was undoubtedly omitted for this reason. Moreover, the March statement was straightforward and did not make the mistake of omitting Hugh MacMahon. Rory O'More, it asserted, had proposed a rising which would have the support of Leinster and Connacht, whereupon, without any further ado, Maguire joined the movement. Word was sent to Owen Roe O'Neill, who promised support within two weeks of the outbreak, and the appointments were made of those who would take the Castle. Shortly afterwards a Franciscan, John Barnewall, told Maguire that the Pale gentry were in on the general rising. 'And lastly saith, that of those persons who came to attend him [Maguire] for the surprise of the said Castle of Dublin, only Cuchonnacht Maguire [his brother] was privy unto the business in hand.' In this account, the last meeting before the rising was attended by 'Ever MacMahon, vicar-general of the diocese of Clogher, Thomas MacKearnan, a friar of Dundalk, Sir Phelim O'Neill, Rory O'More and Brian O'Neill'. A postscript to the examination was added, although it is not known if it was read to the court, in which Maguire agreed with the contents except the fact that he was told by the Franciscan that the Pale gentry were privy to the plot (without specifying which plot); likewise he denied his brother's involvement.

Both of these denials lessened considerably the implications of the statement and suggested that Maguire himself was, in the end, the only leader of the Castle attempt.

The statement which Serjeant Whitfield had referred to at the opening of the trial, the statement which required no other evidence, was that which was attributed to Maguire on 1 October 1644. It was short and to the point. He said he was but a mean instrument in the design in Ireland, but that he had nevertheless intended to take Dublin Castle 'and keep it till they had redress of some grievances, which they purposed to propound to the parliament there; one whereof was to have a toleration of the Roman Catholic religion'.[58] This was the first time such an explanation of a Castle plot was put forward. The conclusion that it was written not by Maguire but by an English parliamentarian completely ignorant of the Irish constitution is hard to avoid. As a member of the Irish House of Lords which he was about to hold to ransom, Maguire would have been the first to know that Poynings' Law of 1495 required all matters put before an Irish parliament to have the approval of both the Irish and the English governments. Constitutionally, the action ascribed to Maguire was nonsensical; in the context of a simultaneous country-wide rising, or even just an Ulster one, it made even less sense. The statement goes on to say that on his way up to Dublin Maguire came accidentally to Philip O'Reilly's house, where he met Hugh MacMahon, 'and that his [Maguire's] intention of coming up to Dublin was to put the aforesaid design in execution and that then and there they had speech about that design, but he remembereth not the particulars'.[59] It was surprising that he did not remember the particulars in view of the role MacMahon obviously took upon himself after this encounter. The statement itself, read before the court, is also a direct contradiction of the statement which had been read out just a few minutes before, which Maguire had allegedly made in March 1642. In that statement Maguire named MacMahon as being among those appointed to take the Castle at a meeting in May 1641. The March statement of general conspiracy made some sense and would have appealed to the jury. Why it should be added to, at the expense of contradicting it, was simple. Before his escape from the Tower in August 1644 (only three months before his conviction) MacMahon would appear to have accused Maguire of plotting to take the Castle. He said he had discovered this when he came upon Maguire accidentally and the latter had said that he would probably go to Dublin for the seizure. It is not known if, or under what conditions, MacMahon had made the claim, but it was public and it was too good not to work into the prosecution's case—even at the expense of contradicting the only other statement of Maguire's which was offered to the jury.

Evidence of one John Carmick, an inhabitant of Enniskillen, was then presented to the court. In what would appear to have been a written statement, Carmick said that all the details of the Castle plot and general rising were revealed to him by a follower of Brian Maguire, cousin of Lord Maguire, on 21 October 1641. This was done despite the fact that while the informer insisted in advance that it be kept from Sir William Cole and all other Englishmen, Carmick replied that he would keep the secret 'so far as it went with his allegiance and conscience'.[60] The request for secrecy was not only unreasonable, in view of the danger being revealed, it was also inconsistent, because a letter (written in Irish) was later produced in court to show that Brian Maguire was considered by the defendant to be 'abundantly inclined to the English, which did very much trouble' Lord Maguire.[61] The most important fact as far as the jury was concerned, however, was that the informer named Lord Maguire and Hugh MacMahon as leaders in the proposed Castle attempt. It was indicated that there were others, but they were not named (although this would have strengthened the claim). When the informer left, Carmick acquainted Sir William Cole with the details he had learned. Later that same day Brian Maguire sent a local freeholder directly to Cole to confirm that the plot was one of taking 'the city and Castle of Dublin, the castle of Enniskillen and all the castles and strengths in Ireland' and 'was to be put in full execution by the papists, October 22nd and 23rd 1641 throughout the said kingdom'.[62] He too named Lord Maguire and MacMahon specifically as leaders of the Castle plot; 'of all which Sir William advertised the Lords Justices and council of Ireland the same day'.[63]

This last piece of evidence is very significant. In his own version of the events of 22-23 October, prepared for the English government on the 25th, Lord Justice Parsons wrote:

> Upon conference with [MacMahon] and others, and calling to mind a letter we received the week before from Sir William Cole (a copy whereof we send your lordship here enclosed), we gathered that the Lord Maguire was to be an actor in surprising

the Castle of Dublin. Wherefore we held it necessary to secure him immediately, thereby also to startle and deter the rest when they found him laid fast.[64]

If there was indeed a letter about conspiratorial movements around Enniskillen, it is more than likely that Maguire's name was mentioned in it. Parsons would have forwarded a copy of this letter as proof of the crisis he was facing if this traitor Maguire was now in Dublin. The whole point, as far as Parsons was concerned, was to link the Ulster rising with a coup in Dublin which would justify martial law and allow a strong plea for arms and money. However, the prosecution at Maguire's trial had to cover what was a glaring deficiency in Parsons's reaction—because if it was not Parsons's reaction that was deficient, then it was Cole's letter regarding the plot. In other words, Parsons could not have received 'the week before' the type of warning which had been given to Cole and ignored it. Obviously Cole's warning had been general and did not contain details of a coup to be staged by Maguire and MacMahon. It is only a small point, but nevertheless a significant one, that Parsons said he received the letter 'the week before'. He was warned by Connolly on a Friday, so 'the week before' meant at least a week.

The only way out of this for those who wished to frame Maguire properly was to have it specified clearly at the outset of Carmick's statement that the warnings which prompted Cole to write to Parsons were given on 21 October. It was therefore necessary to alter Parsons's own official record of events in order to make sense of the attempted coup. Again it is only a small point, but there is hardly another specific date given by a witness in the whole trial apart from this vital one. The jury could not have known that the date given by Parsons had been changed, since it was one of the many incongruous facts of this trial that Parsons's account was not used, just as Connolly was not called as the principal witness. There can be no doubt, however, that the committee appointed by the English House of Commons to oversee the trial, and indeed to commission the best legal advice in London, were more than aware of where the weakness lay in matching Parsons's account with Cole's letter. Carmick closed his evidence by outlining the activities, after the outbreak, of one Captain Rory Maguire whose relationship to the accused was not specified—a deficiency which the jury themselves might make good. Carmick put the death toll in his area at 794 (at least eighteen of whom had been incinerated after taking refuge in their church), 'and I did hear there was about 152,000 that they had destroyed in that province of Ulster in the first four months of the rebellion'.[65]

The testimony of Sir William Cole himself, which followed Carmick's, was reduced by the clerk of the court to the briefest comment: 'Then Sir William Cole (being present in court) gave in his evidence, much to the same effect as in Carmick's testimony.'[66] Cole had actually been the first witness called in the case against Maguire, but only to be asked to name the conspirators he knew of and to give their religion. It is notable that the question did not specify any particular plot: 'You know a great many of their names, which you have heard that were conspirators with this lord; what religion were they of?'[67] Thus nothing in Cole's evidence which was pertinent to the case was recorded. It is possible that Carmick's account was used—despite the fact that he was giving crucial evidence on behalf of a principal witness present in court—because he may have believed that Brian Maguire had included a Castle coup in his warning. If Brian Maguire did indeed send a warning to Carmick, it is likely that Carmick could now be persuaded that the Castle plot was part of it, without truly perjuring himself. This would not be true of Cole, however, since it was he who had committed the details to paper and sent them to Parsons. Perhaps for this reason his evidence was equivocal on some important points and was omitted from the record because publication of the proceedings was intended (they were in fact published in London in the following year, 1645). The question of perjury is important, because those who gave evidence could not have perjured themselves lightly. For this reason the evidence relating to the plot to blow up the Irish parliament is realistically vague about the important details, and Lord Blayney pointed out that it was so long ago that he might not remember accurately. Similarly, the evidence of the Sheriff of Dublin does not actually indicate that he perjured himself. In each case a careful line can be drawn between what is being said and what is implied, and indeed, in the sheriff's case, what followed from his actions. None of the evidence, however, indicates any blatant perjury, and this may have been the case also with Sir William Cole.

Testimony was then given by Sir William Stewart about the landing of arms and men by Owen Roe O'Neill after the rising had begun. Lady Caulfield, mother of the late Sir Toby, governor of the fort of Charlemont, was then called. Lady Caulfield was asked to tell what she knew of the taking of Charlemont, which had in fact been captured by Sir Phelim O'Neill on the evening of 22 October 1641 on the pretext of an invitation to dinner. That was not, however, what the court was about to hear; Lady Caulfield's evidence ran as follows:

> The 23rd of October 1641, Sir Phelim O'Neill and others came into the castle, they seized upon all, murdered [Sir Toby's] servants; and those that were alive they bound them, and put them in prison; and at that time Sir Phelim O'Neill himself, and other of his companions, told her that Dublin Castle and city, and most other forts of Ireland were surprised by their confederates the papists; and that he was sorry for his cousin the Lord Maguire, and that he was afraid he was taken.

Serjeant Whitfield asked 'What was done with my lord Caulfield?' Lady Caulfield replied: 'He was murdered; he begged for his life and they durst not but do it.'[68] The picture is not a true one for several reasons, not least of which is the fact that Sir Toby Caulfield lived for several months after the taking of Charlemont. More significant, however, are the words which were put into Sir Phelim's mouth. It was necessary once again to change the date so that Sir Phelim could have said what otherwise he could not have said. Charlemont was actually taken on Friday evening, before Lord Maguire had been tracked down to the cock-loft. Quite apart from this, the prosecution were held to a time of nine or ten o'clock on Saturday morning as the time of Maguire's arrest, so that Sir Phelim's action had to be post-dated to Saturday if he was to incriminate Maguire and regret his capture at the same time as he took Charlemont. This post-dating could not be extended beyond Saturday, however, because that was the day upon which the whole province of Ulster rose, and so the best that could be done was that the jury be asked to believe that news of Maguire's arrest got through to Sir Phelim on the day of its occurrence. One way or the other, nothing Lady Caulfield said conformed to the events as they are known.

As if the evidence was not inconsistent enough, Serjeant Whitfield further added of his own accord:

> When Sir Phelim O'Neill had taken my lord Caulfield, then they got this lady to write to the Lords Justices, that my lord Maguire might be exchanged for her son, but that would not be; and thereupon they murdered my lord Caulfield, Francis Davis and others.[69]

It would seem from this interjection that Lady Caulfield had forgotten her lines. The intention was still, however, to fit Maguire firmly into the Ulster rising and its consequences. Caulfield had been a prisoner at Charlemont before his death some fifteen weeks after the outbreak, and the prosecution would appear to have wanted Lady Caulfield to commit herself to the prisoner-exchange story so long as the impression was maintained that the murder took place very quickly after the rising. There was probably more fact here than fiction, and many attempts must have been made to save Maguire during the period when he was a prisoner in Dublin and London. There is reasonable evidence (although not particularly reliable) to suggest that Sir Phelim attempted to use his power in the early stages of the rising in an effort to secure the release of Maguire and MacMahon. The government refused because the propaganda value of their prisoners and the necessity of seeing them executed prevented negotiation. Either way, Sir Toby Caulfield was of little value to the government by comparison; and whatever deals were attempted, they hardly hinged on the unfortunate Sir Toby or the letter-writing of his mother.

The circumstances surrounding Caulfield's death are not clear; it would seem that he was indeed shot in captivity, but while he was being transferred from one fort to another. Whether this is true or not is impossible to say, but the implication would be that he was shot by someone not privy to the terms of his imprisonment. It seems unlikely that Sir Phelim O'Neill had a hand in the murder, although he was the commander of all forces in the area and the responsibility for the deed was undoubtedly his. Sir Phelim had only gained access to Charlemont in the first place because he had been invited to dinner by Sir Toby. If Sir Phelim had his erstwhile friend murdered, it would indicate a good deal of desperation and unnecessary cruelty at a time when there was the least reason for it. Whitfield's interjection was pointed, however. If accepted, it meant that Lady Caulfield had written immediately to Parsons and offered an exchange. Lady Caulfield's presence in court was itself an emotional testimony to the hideous consequences of Maguire's schemes, and that she personally should have had to write the letter heightened this shocking effect.

The most effective part of Lady Caulfield's evidence was its revelation of the simple declaration by Sir Phelim, in the act of taking Charlemont, that Dublin had been seized but that he was sorry Maguire had been captured. In view of the bitterness she undoubtedly felt over her son's death, and the likelihood that she was informed officially that her version was true, Lady Caulfield was

probably not aware of the great inconsistencies of her evidence. As far
as she was concerned, Lord Maguire was on trial for the Ulster rising.
Her evidence was supported by another woman present when Sir
Phelim took Charlemont. Like all the evidence so far marshalled
against Maguire, however, that given by Mrs Mary Wordrose contradicted what had just been said. She deposed:

> That he [Sir Phelim] came on Friday night about ten or eleven a
> clock, to break into the castle; I, hearing the noise, asked what
> was the matter. I went to call up some of our gentlemen; when I
> came in again they had taken some of our gentlemen and
> bound them.[70]

The remainder of her evidence in the published account was
reduced to a single comment: 'She also testified the murdering of
Lord Caulfield, Francis Davis and others; and the former words
concerning the Lord Maguire.'[71] This certainly adds to the picture
being presented that Sir Toby Caulfield was killed almost as soon as
was possible. As far as her recorded words go, however, Mrs
Wordrose did not actually perjure herself. Sir Phelim did indeed
come on Friday evening; this fact contradicts Lady Caulfield's
specified date of the 23rd, but Lady Caulfield had not added that the
23rd was a Saturday. Thus the jury would not have noticed the
gread difference in Mrs Wordrose's version, or that Maguire could
not have been mentioned by Sir Phelim because he had not been
arrested at that time. Serjeant Whitfield drew the simple but incongruous conclusion on behalf of the jury before moving on: 'These
two witnesses prove that of Charlemont, how far the rebels owed to
the Lord Maguire.'[72]

The published account of the trial was undoubtedly the best edited
version possible, and in it Mrs Wordrose was the last witness to have
a direct bearing on Maguire's case. Other witnesses were listed, but
do not seem to have been called. The prosecution concluded with
testimony related to the general rising and papal involvement. A copy
of the papal bull of May 1643 was appended, but it is not clear if it had
been read to the court. Serjeant Whitfield then addressed the jury,
but while doing so turned his attack on Maguire himself. His address
shows clearly the weakness of the Castle story, and also demonstrates
how Maguire was being tried for the general rising in Ireland,
including that of the Old English. Whitfield told the jury:

We have troubled you with a long relation of the actions of the Confederates with the Lord Maguire, though not done in his own person, and his own particular act. But [as] for this that was done by the generality, I heard my lord say at the bar 'What's that to me?' Yes, my lord, this is to you: you were one of the conspirators in the first plot, and you contrived the business. And that had been treason alone to send the priest to fetch Owen [Roe] O'Neill into Ireland with arms and soldiers. But you contrived this and conspired it, and you are as guilty in law of all these cruel murders and burnings in every place. For the law of England is: in treason you are all principals—no accessories. Your son was there, your lady is rewarded; [as] for the Supreme Council, they have taken care of you. Why? Because you were one of the first complotters of it, and this will light upon you and fall very heavy. And [as] for your exchange: it was propounded for the Lord Caulfield, but when they could not have that agreed upon, then what becomes of the poor Lord Caulfield? Murdered too. And you see what encouragement you have from the complotters and from the devil too—for they were both together in it. And now you have seen the indictment fully made.[73]

In his own defence Maguire denied the statements attributed to him in court. He said that he had been in Dublin on personal business connected with his estate, and that he had been arrested simply because he was there. He said he did not lodge within the city, but outside, although he used to lodge with Mr Nevil. He was certain that some of the places in which he was supposed to have been in connection with the conspiracy had not been visited by him for a year before his arrest. As to the number of Protestants slain in the early stage of the rising, he did not think there were that many Protestants in the whole kingdom. He had spent his time between his own house and Dublin and had only heard of the plot by hearsay. (We may presume he meant the general plot—to have acknowledged the Castle plot would have been to concede a great deal to the prosecution.) One of the judges put it to him that he had confessed his part in the Dublin attempt in his signed confession. Maguire replied that he was in the cock-loft at the relevant time and knew nothing about any army. Serjeant Whitfield pointed out that Maguire was forgetting what he had acknowledged with his own hand. The examination was shown to Maguire, who on seeing it remarked: 'There's my name, but not my hand.'[74] One of the judges pointed out that this examination had been witnessed by at least one of the judges present (Sir John Bramstone, Lord Chief Justice of the King's Bench). The signature was then verified by Lord Blayney, who said that Maguire had written him lots of letters, though Maguire maintained that he was not aware of having written many letters to Blayney. One of the judges then intervened and addressed the jury. If Maguire's confession was true, then there was more than enough evidence to convict him, because in it there was no doubt of his deep involvement in the general rising or of his leadership in an attempt on the Castle. Maguire then intervened to say that he did not confess it and that he referred himself to the jury.

Just before the jury retired, one of the judges extracted what he presumably thought was the most damning piece of evidence, apart from the confession which Maguire was now denying:

> Gentlemen, you are to know, that to conspire to raise a war, if any of the conspiracy do act it, as you here see Sir Phelim O'Neill did, if you observe the testimony of my lady Caulfield, he came and surprised the castle of Charlemont; and then it was given out that my lord Maguire had taken Dublin; so that though it did not take effect, that which is done by any is testimony enough. Go together and consider of it.[75]

This particular judge, who is not named in the transcript, had thereby taken a very great liberty with the evidence of Lady Caulfield, evidence which itself was riddled with fabrications. What Lady Caulfield had said was that at the time Charlemont was taken

> Sir Phelim O'Neill himself, and other of his companions, told her that Dublin Castle and city, and most other forts of Ireland were surprised by their confederates the papists; and that he was sorry for his cousin the Lord Maguire, and that he was afraid he was taken.[76]

As has been shown, Lady Caulfield's evidence could not have been true, but even as it stands it does not incriminate Maguire. In Lady Caulfield's testimony Sir Phelim is under the impression that not just the city but the whole country had risen successfully, but that somehow Lord Maguire had been arrested. This is incongruous in itself, but, more to the point as far as the jury was concerned, it was not what the judge was now attributing to Lady Caulfield. He misquoted her blatantly when he said: 'then it was given out [by Sir

Phelim] that my lord Maguire had taken Dublin'. To this he added the final cut: 'so that it did not take effect, that which is done by any is testimony enough'.[77] Lady Caulfield had not said that Maguire had taken Dublin, only that he had been arrested. No one in the whole contrived case had yet dared to suggest that Maguire had actually taken Dublin. This even contradicted the original Parsons version which was the basis of all other versions. Nevertheless, it was the last thing the jury heard before they retired 'and, staying a short space, returned their verdict, which was that they found him guilty of all the treasons according to the indictment'.[78]

Before sentence was passed Maguire again objected that he had not been tried by his peers. A judge replied that this was a general objection which had already been made; if Maguire could make a particular objection, he would be heard. Maguire asked for counsel to advise him, to which the judge replied that he had already had counsel on that question: 'Now your time is past for counsel, you must have none assigned to pick holes in the indictment.'[79] Maguire again asked the court to consider his peerage, to which the reply was brief: 'You offer nothing to the court that is of any difficulty.'[80] Maguire's self-defence throughout the trial had been non-existent, but it would seem that the judges were aware that if he could delay sentence, he might engage counsel 'to pick holes in the indictment'. That is to say the prosecution had shown its hand and revealed its case to be composed of evidence which was not only weak and circumstantial but mostly falsified. The judge who passed sentence reminded Maguire that he had had a fair trial and that all his objections had been carefully considered before they were overruled. He added: 'It is fitter for you now to bethink yourself, what your offences are and prepare yourself for death, rather than seek to mask or put colours upon those things which are so manifestly proved to all the world.'[81] Sentence was then handed down by the same judge:

> The judgment that I am by law to pronounce against you is this: Conor Maguire, Esquire, you being found guilty of the treasons whereof you are indicted, your judgment is, that you shall be carried from hence to the place from whence you came, that is, the Tower, and from thence to Tyburn, the place of execution; and there you shall be hanged by the neck, and cut down alive, your bowels taken out and burnt before your face, your head to be cut off, your body to be divided into four quarters, and the head of your body to be set up and disposed of as the state shall appoint. And the Lord have mercy upon your soul.[82]

Insurrection
and Confederation, 1641-4

WITH the defeat of the royalist cause and the advent of government by the English parliament, the Earl of Antrim was
obliged, in 1650, to look to his own interests. In so doing he let it be
known that there had been a plan on the late king's part to stage a
coup in Ireland using Strafford's army; as part of this coup Dublin
Castle was to have been taken, along with the government itself.
Asked how exactly it was to be done, he answered:

> That the Castle of Dublin then to be surprised if the Lords
> Justices should oppose the design; the parliament then sitting
> should declare for the king against the parliament of England,
> and that the whole kingdom should be raised for the king's
> service; and that if the Lords Justices would not join in the
> work, they should be secured and all others who would or
> might oppose them should also be secured.[1]

When asked to confirm this statement, however, Antrim added an
important qualification:

> And whereas it is said [in my statement] that the said late king
> appointed that the army with us to be continued and raised in
> Ireland should be employed against the parliament—it [was] to
> be intended if occasion should be for so doing.[2]

Antrim's testimony at the end of the war in Ireland and in the face
of total defeat by the English parliamentary forces has a good deal of
venom in it, but as a plan in the wider context of the king's position in
1641 it makes some sense. It is important to remember, however, that
the vital phrase 'if occasion should be for so doing' means in effect
that the plan, if it ever existed, was nothing more than a plan. The
Dublin government made certain that Strafford's army was not used
and consequently botched any designs based on that army. It also
made certain that as soon as the rising took place in Ulster the entire

Old English community would be implicated as quickly as possible and a *de facto* war declared. This was followed immediately in March 1642 by an act passed in the English parliament called the 'adventurers' act'. The act was an attempt to raise £1 million by selling shares in what would be a forfeited country; to this end 2½ million acres of Ireland were laid aside as early as March 1642 for plantation as soon as the war was won. What was even more significant than the declaration of open season on Catholics was the curtailment of the king's powers as part of the act. Hitherto it had been within the king's prerogative to dispose of forfeited land as he wished; this right was now taken away. The king was no longer allowed to pardon rebels, and, perhaps of greatest significance, the English parliament reserved for itself the right to decide when the war was over. Thus it was a war and not a rebellion; the king could have ended a rebellion by pardoning those involved and allowing them to return to his fold. By abolishing this right the English parliament took upon itself sole responsibility in this central question of sovereignty.

In other words, the English parliament was determined from the beginning that the king's best card could not be played. Charles was in a position to deplore the rebellion of his subjects in Ireland but at the same time encourage their undoubted loyalty to him against the English parliament. This middle position which the king occupied—a king tolerant of his Roman Catholic subjects, but as a Protestant monarch—was turned against Charles by the simple demand of his opponents in England that he outlaw his so-called supporters in Ireland. Great confusion was created by the fact that Charles could not come out openly in support of the rising in Ireland without alienating the basis of his support in England—a basis which he would need to expand, not contract, if he was to triumph in the win-or-lose battle that was now inevitable.

Immediately following the Ulster rising, the Irish parliament was suspended and a proclamation issued by the government informing the country that the rising had taken place. This was qualified by an additional proclamation exonerating the Old English from a direct role, although at the same time the government refused to arm the loyal lords of the Pale. Dundalk fell to the insurgents by the beginning of November, an event which signalled the invasion of the Pale by the Gaelic Irish army. On 4 November Sir Phelim O'Neill published a commission which appeared to carry the king's seal and which gave the insurgents authority for their actions. A great deal of controversy surrounded the authenticity of this document, and many scholars have addressed the problems raised by it. No certain answer can be given other than the short one: Charles would not have served his immediate interests by lending his name to the rising. On the contrary, he would have alienated almost all of England on the question of his already shady leanings towards Roman Catholicism. It was far more in the New English interest to see the commission legitimised, since this would galvanise support in England for the Irish government's position. The less ambiguity about the Catholic threat in Ireland, the more troops and money could be raised. In this sense it was a mistake on Sir Phelim's part to make the claim, but from another point of view his action was justified.

The propaganda value of the royal commission outweighed the risks taken in publishing it. The reason for this was that early in November 1641 the Old English leaders were earnestly trying to accommodate themselves to both sides and to use their parliamentary expertise to do so. These leaders did not actually represent the ordinary inhabitants, who had since been alerted by the government's proclamation of the rising. The 'common sort', as they were referred to, had a stake in events because they shared the religion which would be suppressed should the rising fail. If this was indeed a defence of the Roman faith in the guise of a fight for the king, then there was not one Catholic in Ireland who would escape the effect of the battle's outcome. To publish what appeared to be a royal commission was, therefore, a bold move designed to reach the lower strata over the heads of the Old English gentry. Nor should the simplicity of the move be overlooked. After the government's loud declaration that the rising was countrywide, rumours and counter-rumours circulated at great speed throughout the provinces. The very lack of hard news would have created a climate most receptive to the simple declaration that the rising was in support of the king who was being attacked by his Protestant enemies. The king was indeed being attacked by the Puritans, and he did indeed give a great deal of indirect support to the insurgents, and he had proved himself far more tolerant of Roman Catholicism than of Presbyterianism. Sir Phelim's commission took advantage of this position in the full knowledge that the government would equally do all in its power to enlist the complete support of the English parliament; the invention of a Castle coup had already shown the extent to which it would now go to achieve this. In the meantime almost the entire standing army in Ireland had been called into Dublin. In addition to this, commissions were issued for the raising of additional troops as the rising itself spread to Londonderry, Roscommon, Sligo and many other counties where organisation was under way.

Pressure was now brought to bear upon the government to lift the suspension on parliament and allow the Old English to play their part in bringing the crisis under control. The government flatly refused and made little attempt to enlist what it had by now come to see as Catholic support. It agreed, however, to a parliamentary meeting of one day's duration so that the Old English could have their say. The declaration passed by the House of Commons did not satisfy the Lords because it did not properly condemn the rising or describe the insurgents as traitors, or even rebels. A statement was eventually agreed upon which described the action—though not the actors—as traitorous and rebellious. This was neither here nor there; more to the point was the establishment of a committee to deal with the insurgents and discover the causes that lay behind their actions. Of even greater significance was a petition addressed to the king which was drawn up while the one-day session went into extra time. The Old English appealed to Charles to deal with the rising by granting the concessions which he had already promised, and they also requested that the king refrain from sending either a Scottish or an English army to Ireland to restore order. The government countered this petition with its own account of the situation, which it sent to the Lord Lieutenant in England. This was done in secret, however, and those in the government who were partly sympathetic to the Old English position (Ormond being the principal) were not informed of it.

As the rising spread rapidly throughout the country the Ulster leaders dismissed any attempts by the parliamentary committee to negotiate a settlement. For its part, the government settled for a defensive line from Drogheda through Dublin to Wicklow. An attempt to reinforce Drogheda failed when it was intercepted by the insurgents, but Sir Charles Coote succeeded in reinforcing Wicklow without difficulty. In his progress he did nothing to endear the government to the inhabitants when he hanged several men and women for receiving stolen goods. Meanwhile the Gaelic Irish, under the leadership of Rory O'More, had made great inroads into the Pale and were now attempting to persuade their fellow-Catholics to join them. After some secret negotiations a public meeting was announced to be held at the Hill of Crofty (or Knockcrofty) near Drogheda. The meeting, which took place on 3 December, was attended by the Old English leaders of the Pale (led by Viscount

Gormanston), while the Gaelic Irish were represented by Rory O'More, Philip O'Reilly and Colonel Hugh Byrne. The case put forward by O'More was simple and twofold: first, the rising was in support of the king, who was now under serious threat; secondly, the New English government was about to sweep the country with a Scottish army that would make no distinction between Irish and Old English. The only hope for Catholicism in Ireland, he argued, lay in joining the rising in support of the king. Agreement was arrived at immediately, and the Old English of the Pale declared for the insurgents in what was indeed a turning-point in their long history in Ireland. For its part, the government was happy to take the view which it had been the first to propagate. The Old English were doing what it had been assumed they would do all along, and if the government's claim of a Castle coup had been inaccurate, it had merely declared the true position too soon. Now all was clear and there need be no question of who stood where. All Catholics were now traitors, and not even the king could deny it.

The year 1642 was the year in which the real position of the entire Catholic community in Ireland was established. This was because it was the first time that the various groups involved in the conflict were obliged to declare themselves openly. This, of course, was not the traditional mode of operation for the Old English, and they began to suffer the consequences of their weakness almost immediately. In January the king was forced to call for a surrender of his supporters in Ireland, thus putting them in a very peculiar constitutional position. By the end of March the Old Irish had been pushed back out of the Pale, while April saw the arrival of a Scottish army under Major-General Robert Monro which was about to overturn most of the Irish gains and establish Presbyterianism for the first time on an official basis (the first presbytery met at Carrickfergus in June). In March the English parliament passed an act which Charles was obliged to sign whereby Ireland was declared forfeit and shares might be bought which would be made good as soon as the country's landowners could be dispossessed. Also in March a provincial synod met at Kells under the auspices of the Catholic Archbishop of Armagh, Hugh O'Reilly. The synod called for the establishment of an official body of laymen and clerics who would run the war and those parts of the country in Catholic hands. As Monro rallied the Presbyterians and recaptured Newry, Mountjoy and Dungannon, the Irish cause received a long-awaited boost by the arrival of Owen Roe O'Neill in County Donegal with a small number of men and arms. O'Neill was immediately appointed commander-in-chief of the Ulster forces. His continental rival from the Old English camp, Thomas Preston, arrived in September and was similarly appointed as head of the Leinster army.

The first meeting between the clergy and the insurgents took place on 10 May at Kilkenny. The structure of a confederation was agreed upon and an oath of association drawn up for all the Catholics of Ireland. The Confederation of Kilkenny must be understood in two ways in order that the divisions within it can be related to the events as they unfolded. There were two groups, the Gaelic Irish and the Old English, but the Gaelic Irish were actually further divided into those landed Irish who had risen in 1641 and those Irish who looked to the Confederation to restore the land their ancestors had lost as a result of the Nine Years' War and the Ulster plantation. The two most obvious representatives of these groups were Sir Phelim O'Neill for the landed Irish and Owen Roe O'Neill for the dispossessed. There was a division here within the Irish camp simply because many of the Gaelic leaders themselves held land which had belonged to the returned exiles and which they had no intention of handing back. The land had only been granted to these Gaelic Irish in the first place because of their allegiance to the crown at the time of the war, and this was not forgotten by their new allies. The division itself was a straightforward one, but it is rarely taken into account.

The Gaelic Irish have been seen as many things: oppressed nationalists, Catholic martyrs, the last bearers of racial and cultural purity, or simply the victims of circumstance. Perhaps in the most misunderstood and misapplied appellation they have been called republican. They were none of these things, for the simple reason that in the final analysis they split down the middle over the possession of land; before the war was over Phelim O'Neill had sided with Ormond, while Owen Roe O'Neill had sided with the Cromwellians (before then siding with Ormond). In order to arrive at this position, both sides had to dispense with a great deal of rhetoric, and in the end even Archbishop Rinuccini had to pull back from supporting Owen Roe because, as he wrote to the Vatican, papal support would end up 'being shared with the heretics'.[3] The fact of the matter is that the Gaelic Irish had been obliged since the sixteenth century to compete against each other for the benediction of the English crown. The great Hugh O'Neill was also the English Earl of Tyrone who, although he had stood out against the crown, moved faster even than his persecutors in positioning himself and his heirs firmly within the English law; his Gaelic enemies were loyalists desperate to replace him and to do better. Both wished to hold land under the crown, not to declare a new state, and in this both sides were ministered to by the Catholic Church, whose position had always been sympathetic to sovereign authority. There was nothing romantic about this picture, but there was equally nothing romantic about the cynical grasp of the Protestant Church of Ireland upon the legalities of land tenure, or indeed about the pained conscience of the Old English Catholics who accepted lands taken from the monasteries by Henry VIII.

The Gaelic cause has always been associated with disunity in the face of solid opposition. It is too much of a coincidence that the Irish always seemed to fall at the last fence, and usually as a result of turning on each other. For the situation to make any sense, however, the analysis must be reversed. That is to say that the reason why the Gaelic Irish did not unite was that it was not within their culture to do so. The central problem for the Gaelic Irish since the arrival of the Normans had been the problem of sovereign kingship. At any given time in pre-Norman Gaelic Ireland there had been up to two hundred 'kings' in a country with a tiny population. These 'kings' had been forced by the Vikings into partial unity in the face of an external threat, but this unity had nothing to do with a 'high kingship' which might have competed against the European concept of kingship which the Normans later brought with them. An Irish 'king' had been a strong man who could hold a territory for a group of people. He did not make law, his power was not based in any governmental institution, and his rule was not hereditary. Brian Boru may indeed have been a high king who defeated the Viking invasion and who died while doing so, but he was not succeeded by either of his two surviving sons. At the same time as the Normans came to Ireland the Vatican was reforming Catholicism along the new lines of a papal monarchy. This entailed close co-operation, not with societies such as Gaelic Ireland, but with the remnants of the Roman Empire, among which the Normans were prominent. Whether the pope 'gave' Ireland to Henry II or not, the king behaved as if he had, and Pope Adrian did nothing to contradict him. A papal monarch had handed sovereignty to a political monarch over the heads of the Gaelic 'kings', who were now obliged, because of their Catholicism, somehow to reconcile their own culture with the new Catholic king who had the full support of the pope. Events were to show that this was a tall order indeed, but no consistent analysis of post-Norman Gaelic Ireland is possible if the notion that the Irish were waiting for the return of their high king—whether it be the English-educated Earl of Tyrone or the European soldier Owen Roe O'Neill—is an essential patriotic ingredient. The turning-point for the Gaelic Irish was 1541, when Henry VIII became the first King of Ireland. When asked to sign away their Gaelic power base in return for a state guarantee of private ownership, not one of the great Gaelic chiefs preserved his people's land at the expense of his own aggrandisement. In doing so they abandoned the very essence of the Gaelic culture which had put them there in the first place. Hugh O'Neill may have ruled in the Gaelic manner, but his authority was identical with that of the best English aristocrat, and it was his authority—that is to say his own personal wealth and power—which he wished to preserve.

All of this is to say that the Gaelic Irish of the 1640s were faced with the same constitutional crisis posed by Charles's kingship as were their fellow-Catholics, the Old English. While the Gaelic Irish had no need of theories to substantiate what was for them an open-and-shut case, this was not true of the Old English, since they were already in possession of their estates. Their problem was not how to obtain or consolidate them, but how to keep them. The Old English were the natural leaders of the new Confederate government because it was firmly fixed within their own tradition of parliamentary representation. They were at an advantage as far as the manipulation of the executive and indeed the assembly were concerned, but their success only highlighted their alienation from that other constitutional government in Dublin which had the sanction of the king himself. The theories which they propounded in support of their actions and the ease with which the Confederation was established did not take from the fact that they could not, within the terms of their own definition, claim legality, let alone sovereignty, for their decisions. The Confederation might be seen as the foundation of a new government in Ireland, but this would be to miss a point which the Old English themselves were more than aware of. The measures they took were interim, and their purpose was to find a way, as quickly as possible, to relieve the king of his Irish problem and to unite behind him against the English parliament. Matters were complicated, however, by the fact that the king's lieutenant was head of a government which was most unsympathetic to this aim. In addition to this, the king's own hands were tied by the fact that he could not acknowledge Catholic support without jeopardising his domestic position. Nor could the Old English call themselves anything other than Catholics, and as such they were obliged to obey the dictates of their clergy.

The Catholic Church was not simply an institution that spanned both Gaelic Irish and Old English, it was the only authority which, of its own accord, could lay claim to sovereignty. The claim was a religious or spiritual one, but the circumstances of mid-seventeenth-century Ireland meant that there was little or no difference between politics and religion. This gave the hierarchy a unique power which lay outside the political constitution but which could be used at any time within the bounds of the quasi-legal Confederation. Apart from the general willingness of the Vatican to influence governments and their politics, the breakdown in Ireland particularly obliged the church to play a full role. The problem, however, was as simple as the church's authority was unquestioned: what policy to adopt when a divergence of interests arose? It was the hierarchy who might prove to be the great unifying agent and who might bridge the civil division of sovereignty until such time as the Dublin government itself could be incorporated into a new confederation which would eventually receive full royal recognition. There was one difficulty, however, and it proved to be the rock upon which all groups foundered in the end. When Henry VIII dissolved the monasteries as part of his break with Rome a large proportion of the land was granted to the Old English as the price of their support for the government. This is not to say that the Old English Catholics betrayed their religion; they did not. What they did do, however, was facilitate the birth of the Church of Ireland as far as the letter of the law was concerned. As part of this agreement a *modus operandi* had evolved whereby the religious loyalty of the Old English would not be scrutinised and in return the new Established Church would not be impeded so long as it remained unobtrusive. None of this could suit the Roman Catholic Church, however, as its mission was bound up with both diocesan and, more importantly for the 1640s, monastic land. If the Confederate war was to produce a true restoration of the church, it would be necessary also to restore its land in full—even that which was in the possession of its own Old English flock.

There is another dimension to this question of Catholic land which must be added to any treatment of the Confederation. From the conversion of the Dublin Vikings to Christianity and throughout the period of Norman settlement the Pale was connected through the capital to England and to the English bishoprics. In short, Norman Catholicism was bound up with the administrative divisions taken over from the old Roman Empire by the Catholic Church. The natural church organisation for the new colonists was thus diocesan and episcopal. The Old English were, of course, served by the regular orders, but after the suppression of the monasteries their religion took on an even greater English dimension. What had characterised the Anglicanism of Henry VIII and what now characterised the Roman Catholicism of the Old English (and in particular the families of the Pale) was the diocesan and episcopal structure within which the religious ministry was carried out.

The converse of this position was that of the Gaelic Irish. The Roman Empire had never extended to Ireland, and the Irish had never been obliged to organise themselves into any kind of political unit with a law-making king. Much of the function of government in this respect was performed by the Catholic Church, but in that form which suited Irish conditions best—that of the monastic and regular orders. The net result of this had been that Gaelic Irish Christianity had developed outside the mainstream of Europe in many respects, but the most important effect as far as the Confederation was concerned was that the regular orders, in particular the Franciscan Friars Minor, felt that the Old English, along with their clergy, had done well out of the Reformation at their expense and had caused them a great deal of hardship.

By the mid-seventeenth century the divisions within the Catholic Church in Ireland had assumed very large proportions and were consistent with an international debate on the future of Catholicism itself. The regulars looked to Spain, and the Old English secular clergy looked to the Anglican and Gallican churches for their lead. Both sides were committed to papal obedience, but even in the Vatican the struggle went on between the constitutionalists who favoured some concessions to temporal power and the purists who saw disintegration as a consequence of negotiation in matters spiritual. This division might not have been so important (and in one way or another it had existed for centuries) had the Reformation not forced the Vatican to decide on whether it could have separate missions in countries of differing political persuasions. In Ireland's case there were two distinct missions with two cultures, two different political aspirations (if indeed there could be said to have been a truly Gaelic political dimension) and two quite separate modes of Catholicism. Old English worship was clearly consistent with the new theology of the Counter-Reformation; the Gaelic Irish could not easily have adopted this when they did not have the administrative structure, the tradition, the opportunity or even the incentive to do so. In view of these divisions, the motto on the Confederation's new seal was a bold one: *Pro Deo, rege et patria Hiberni unanimes*: for God, king and country, the Irish united.

In England the months between March and August 1642 saw the conflict between Charles and his parliament move inexorably towards open war. It had occurred to the king's opponents by this time that neither they nor their non-Arminian beliefs and practices would be safe unless the king's powers were greatly curtailed. No one believed that Charles would accede to this willingly, and war seemed the only way to solve an otherwise intractable problem. One thing was clear, however, regardless of the point of view taken. Once open war had been declared, the only solution that could have been found, sooner or later, would be a constitutional one. The reason for this was simply that neither side could have ruled without the other. The king had the uniformity of his political and religious position, but he had no representative support of any kind. Parliament, on the other hand, had almost too much representation and not enough unity; and this position was exacerbated by the religious inclination towards complete freedom of worship. Whether the essence of the nation's sovereignty was founded on the law of kingship or on the common law, there was not yet a country in western Europe which did not have to spread its constitutional authority over more than one political institution, even if the only representation of this was a 'house of lords' independent of the commons.

Ironically, the new Confederation of Kilkenny lay outside these more pressing constitutional questions, and in some respects the first general assembly which met on 24 October 1642 was the English parliament's opposite. It wanted to be recognised by the king as a true body of support, but one which wished to dissolve itself under his command as soon as was feasible. After the constitution of the Confederation had been agreed upon and an official oath approved, an address to the king was drawn up. The address and the constitution itself may be taken together because they amounted to the same thing. The Confederation bound itself to a recognition of English common law and to the crown as the arbiter of all disputes in

Ireland. Catholicism would be restored, but in the context of loyalty to the king. That is to say a bargain of toleration in return for loyalty would be struck. Although even these general aspirations veiled some deep divisions in the Confederate ranks, the position was a totally unreal one. The bargaining point which allowed the aspiration itself arose out of Charles's English dilemma, which made outright concessions impossible. Political loyalty to a Protestant king, qualified by loyalty to the pope, was by now a constitutional question of some refinement when the king himself was fighting an all-out war against those who hardly recognised him as a king, let alone a Protestant one.

Thus as early as 1642 the position amounted to a constitutional deadlock because those who supported the king were opposed by the king's own government who themselves did not support the king. It was no secret that Parsons and his fellows on the council were parliamentarians. Ormond was the only one in Ireland with the authority to manoeuvre on both sides, and he did this with considerable skill. His problem, however, was that he could only come to terms with the Confederation as would a governor accepting the submission of rebels who had laid down their arms. For the Old English to concede this point could well have had dire consequences for them in the future. Charles had been forced to sign an act which would open Ireland up to his parliamentary enemies. In the meantime the king's opponents in the Dublin government would do all in their considerable power to block Ormond and simultaneously to keep the war going until the English parliament was in a position to take it on and finish it.

Despite these complications, however, Ormond's mission was clear. First, he must obtain a truce in Ireland so that the king could draw on his Irish support against the English parliament. This would also free the considerable forces employed by Ormond and his command which might then also be employed in England. Secondly, he must establish a loyal government in Dublin and summon a parliament to unite the country behind Charles. A good deal of progress would have to have been made for this to happen, but it was not beyond the bounds of possibility. If it could be brought about, then the third objective might be achieved. When asked by parliament to endorse its plan for the confiscation of Ireland, Charles had said that he would be willing instead to go there personally and appeal to his subjects to lay down their arms. Events were to show that when Charles's position weakened in England his own person became a liability to the royalist cause. Conversely, possession of the king's person proved to be of immense value to his opponents. If the possibility had been open to him to come to Ireland as a means of regrouping his forces, or even of holding court, a great deal of manoeuvring time might have been bought. The idea seems somehow unlikely, but Charles's kingship of Ireland was technically no different to that of England or Scotland, and should Ireland have been pacified in his favour, there was no reason why he could not have been more successful than his son James II was to be. Thus the logic of Ormond's policies was to make Ireland safe for the king. This would mean that Charles would take command of a nation of rebels, but this would have been infinitely preferable to what he was obliged to do in the end, namely surrender to the Scots on the promise of establishing Presbyterianism. In this context it must be remembered that the first stage of the Restoration took place almost before the English republican Commonwealth got under way, when the Scots crowned Charles II in 1651, just two years after his father's execution. What might have been is an almost futile matter of conjecture, but it is nevertheless significant that until Ormond's final departure he worked to place Ireland at the centre of royalist support.

His policies in this respect should not be viewed as English, but as a variation of Old English. The only qualification of this was that the Lord Lieutenant was a Protestant, and even this was mediated by his High Church beliefs, despite the fact that he was often obliged, by virtue of his pivotal position, to make Puritan-like pronouncements. Ormond himself was the head of one of the earliest Old English families in the country. His uncle, Lord Mountgarrett, was president of the Confederation's Supreme Council. He was, in his own official capacity, fighting to preserve his own tradition as much as those with whom he sought to make peace. There was a great desire on the part of the Old English in particular to come to terms as quickly as possible, and Ormond took full advantage of this.

On 6 December 1642 the Franciscan Luke Wadding was appointed as Vatican agent to the Supreme Council. He was instructed to obtain indulgences for the insurgents and to establish diplomatic relations between the Vatican and states sympathetic to the Confederation. He was also asked to request a papal declaration admitting of no appeal for those who did not support the war, such as the Catholic

Bishop of Meath, Thomas Dease (who would not sign the declaration justifying the conflict). The most important of Wadding's instructions, however, was that which sought the excommunication of all 'direct or indirect opponents, as well as against neutrals in Ireland'.[4] At this early stage such a power was still welcome to the Old English, who needed to consolidate the Confederation, but they would not have countenanced its extended use. In supporting the request, however, they were opening a door which proved impossible to close. The power of excommunication was quite contrary to the spirit of the Confederation itself because it was not in any sense of the word constitutional. Furthermore, it would be difficult for the Vatican not to regard the request as an invitation to take a direct role. This was because the power of excommunication could best be wielded on the spot; but whether this was in the true interests of all the Catholics concerned was yet to be seen.

In the meantime a peculiar amalgam of negotiation and confrontation took place between the Confederation and the Dublin government. Charles issued Ormond with a personal commission to negotiate with the insurgents in January 1643. This was to circumvent the presence in Dublin of the parliamentarian Parsons, but it was also a clear indication that the king was about to entrust his government to Ormond alone.

On 17 March a meeting took place at Trim between representatives of Kilkenny and Dublin. As if to remind the insurgents of their precarious position, Ormond defeated Preston near Old Ross on the following day, after he had failed to take the town of New Ross. Nevertheless, the meeting at Trim served the purpose of allowing the Confederates to express their support as well as their grievances. First, however, both support and grievances were related in one respect, namely that the Dublin negotiators had denigrated Confederate loyalty by describing the insurgents as rebels. It was pointed out to them, however, that this was the term that had been used by the king himself when calling for the talks. Obliged to accept this answer, the Confederates called for a repeal of discriminatory laws against Roman Catholics and requested that the acts of the English parliament should not be binding on Ireland. This, of course, it was not in the king's power to grant when it was parliament he was fighting. On a more practical note, a complaint was made about Sir William Parsons and his parliamentarian adherents on the council; this was an issue close to the king's own heart.

On 16 March 1643 the Lords Justices and council had reported to

Charles that by the end of March 1642 154,000 Protestants had been killed by the insurgents, while many thousands more had been killed since then. This was a gross exaggeration which, since it came from his own Irish government, was designed to embarrass the king as much as possible. Nor surprisingly, in April Parsons was removed from office; he was arrested and imprisoned along with three other parliamentary supporters in August. By this time the king was under no illusion about the necessity to clear Ormond's path and to find a way of incorporating the Confederation directly into his Englsih affairs. Nor, for that matter, were his opponents; on 14 July the English parliament offered double portions of land in Ireland in order to raise more money for the war.

Ormond's commission was made specific on 23 April (in keeping with the dismissal of Parsons), and he was instructed to treat with the Confederates. Between 20 May and 19 June the second general assembly of the Confederation took place at Kilkenny. The meeting at Trim had concluded with an offer of a temporary truce on the king's part. Initially the assembly could consider the offer on its merits. The Old English were anxious to express their loyalty as quickly as possible, but the Irish party (still united), backed by the bulk of the clergy, had hoped to be more demanding. On 13 June, however, news came in that Owen Roe O'Neill had been badly beaten by Sir Robert Stewart at Clones. The net effect of this blow was that negotiations began between Ormond and the Confederation on 24 June.

This was as the Old English wished it, but it had been a matter of chance that O'Neill was defeated at the appropriate time. Had the battle gone the other way, the clerical–Irish alliance might have proved more than hard to handle. The point was taken and acted upon while the initiative was still with the Old English. On 28 June the Supreme Council wrote to Wadding in Rome thanking him for the appointment of Pier Francesco Scarampi as papal envoy to the Confederation (Scarampi arrived at Kilkenny in July). The opportunity was also taken to remind Wadding of two standing requests which were of great importance. The first was that the Vatican should defer all new episcopal appointments until after the war. The second was

> that you procure such a bull as Cardinal Pole had in Queen
> Mary's days for settling the estates devolved to the crown by
> the Suppression. The giving way to the first would be a great

inconvenience to our affairs, and the obtaining of the other would quiet the minds of many who, without assurance of this kind will, of all likelihood, be won to adhere to them with whom their possessions will be unquestionable.[5]

What the Supreme Council was trying to do was to contain the situation as it now existed, but the very arrival of Scarampi was not conducive to that end. If they anticipated problems from new Vatican episcopal appointments, they could hardly expect a great deal of support from its envoy. The second point, however, was the crux of the matter. Whether or not the Vatican could be persuaded to allow the Old English to keep their monastic possessions would depend on the course of Charles's war in England. The return of church lands was not an issue confined to the Pale; Rome watched events in England closely with a view to taking advantage either of the king's strength or his weakness. Either way, the Vatican would be unlikely to pronounce so early on an issue of such vital importance as the recognition of the Henrician monastic dissolution.

If the Supreme Council were under any illusions about Vatican policy, they were soon to be disabused of them by the new envoy. Scarampi led the argument against a truce on the basis that the Confederation should wait until it was in a better bargaining position. This, for Scarampi, amounted to waiting for Owen Roe to re-establish himself. For the Old English to do so would be to miss the opportunity created by his setback; Scarampi was overruled, and a one-year truce was signed on 15 September at Sigginstown, County Kildare.

Meanwhile in England the king's fortunes were about to take a turn for the worse. Five days after the Confederate truce the king's army was forced to retreat at the Battle of Newbury. Five days after this, on 25 September, the Solemn League and Covenant was signed between the English parliament and the Scots. This was an important step in unifying the king's opponents, who by this time had less in common than might have appeared. The English opposition to the king was composed of two quite different 'Puritan' groups who are best described under their general names. The 'Presbyterians' were a loose alliance of those who believed in some formal establishment of Calvinist worship. The 'Independents' were those who believed that the same worship was best served if communities were allowed to determine their own form of worship. It was with the first group that the Scots hoped to work in order to determine the eventual religious settlement that would follow a peace treaty. The two groups of Presbyterians were, however, quite different in many respects, not least because the Scottish form had long been unified in its aims and had evolved in direct opposition to the Stuarts, while their English counterparts had developed within a much broader political settlement. Needless to say, both groups were distrusted and opposed by the Independents, but for the moment all were obliged to work together to defeat their common enemy. The Solemn League and Covenant improved the strength of the English parliament considerably, but at the cost of raising very large questions among its own members about the type of religious settlement that could be obtained through unity with the Scots. In short, the Scottish Presbyterians knew exactly what they wanted—and they were well aware that it could be obtained even from the king himself—while the English were not even united on the aims of the war. As a general political grouping, the Presbyterians on both sides of the border were conservative and would wish to include the monarchy in a settlement; the Independents contained many very radical sects, some of whom had no use for any government which was not democratic to its roots. It was the latter group, and particularly the radical army, which more and more determined the pace.

Between 7 November and 1 December 1643 the third general assembly of the Confederation was held at Kilkenny. Seven delegates were appointed to meet the king. The effect of the truce was to make Charles's involvement with the Catholics of Ireland more visible to the English public, but it is unlikely that anyone involved in the conflict was surprised by the agreement. While it did mean that many of the king's Protestant supporters in Ireland—and the Ulster Presbyterians in particular—would now view Ormond as the enemy together with the Confederation, this had been the *de facto* position from the start. Indeed, Ormond was now in a less precarious position, if only because he could not be obliged to trust those whom he knew to be unsympathetic to the king. Raised to a marquisate, Ormond was appointed Lord Lieutenant of Ireland on 13 November (he was sworn in by Charles in January) and was now in sole command of the king's government in Ireland. His appointment as Lord Lieutenant and the Confederate truce were condemned by the English parliament, who now viewed the Irish government and most of the country as wholly royalist. The Ulster Scots rejected the truce and naturally adhered to the Solemn League and Covenant and put themselves wholly under the command of Monro. The truce was likewise ignored by Lord Inchiquin, who had taken over Sir William St Leger's forces in Munster on the latter's death in May 1642. At first Inchiquin had observed the truce, but when he was passed over for appointment to St Leger's former post of President of Munster he declared for parliament on 17 July 1644. One positive effect of the truce, however, was that Charles was now free to send to Ireland for reinforcements. In November he had ordered the dispatch of 2,500 government troops from Dublin to England, although their addition to the king's army did not prevent it from being defeated at Nantwich in January 1644.

On 24 March 1644 the Confederate delegation arrived at Oxford to meet the king; they were followed on 17 April by a delegation of Protestants from Ireland. The Old English were very careful to stay within their own self-defined limitations. In return for an army of 10,000 men they sought concessions which were not merely modest (in view of what they were offering) but actually disregarded entirely the position of their landless Gaelic Irish allies. They asked for the cancellation of whatever acts had been passed by the Irish parliament since the summer of 1641, together with a pardon for all possible offences committed by the insurgents since that date and the reversal of some of Strafford's policies which had cost them forfeitures. As far as they were concerned, however, this was the best that could be got from the king at this time, and they were proved more right than they would have liked when he informed them that he would have to give the matter more lengthy consideration and referred them back to Ormond. One reason for the king's tardiness was the presence at court of the Protestant delegation from Dublin, who did their best to force him to denounce the Irish 'rebels' and break off the truce. Another reason was not just his public image in England but the need to anticipate the future and manoeuvre with a view to the strongest settlement once the war ended. A Catholic army under the royal banner would not be the best advertisement of Charles's benevolent intentions.

While Charles instructed Ormond to take over the negotiations in June, Owen Roe O'Neill was forced south into Louth by Monro. The Supreme Council reinforced him with a large army under the Earl of Castlehaven, but nothing came of this except further division in the Confederate ranks caused by Owen Roe himself. His career in Ireland was neither glorious nor happy, and the reason was straightforward: O'Neill was not fighting the same war as either the landed Gaelic Irish or the Old English. His only real ally—and it was a considerable ally to have—was the Catholic Church because almost until the end of the war their interests were identical—the restoration of expropriated land. His great weakness in the field lay not in his command and not in his officers, but in his rank and file, who were less impressed with his Gaelic lineage than they might have been had he been a resident chief. As if all of this was not enough, Owen Roe's task was to defeat one of the most gifted generals in the whole of the civil war conflict, Robert Monro. Unlike O'Neill's men, Monro's Presbyterians had a great deal to lose, and apart from everything else they were committed to their religion in a way that the Gaelic Irish under O'Neill would have considered fanatical. Success went to the Presbyterians when Monro took Belfast on 14 May 1644.

As the war ground on in England the king's fortunes were mixed, but what he could not do to improve them was capitalise on his support in Ireland. Some attempt was made, but with no great effect. On 27 June a force which had been raised by the Earl of Antrim left Waterford to join Montrose in Scotland. On 1 September the earl's forces (commanded by Alasdair MacDonnell) in conjunction with Montrose defeated the Scots near Perth. The English parliament's response was to order on 24 October that any Irishman taken in arms in England or Wales was to be executed.

On 2 July Charles suffered a major military defeat at the Battle of Marston Moor at the hands of a combined Scottish and English army. The effect of this as far as Ireland was concerned was that the king was under greater pressure and consequently might be forced into making concessions which he had not hitherto felt capable of. Between 20 July and 31 August the fourth general assembly of the Confederation took place at Kilkenny. A delegation was appointed to continue the peace talks with Ormond. These got under way, but the only agreement arrived at was for a temporary truce. This was really a face-saving exercise while both sides waited for the king's position to become clear after Marston Moor. In the meantime, however, another event had taken place which was to have enormous consequences for all sides. On 29 July Pope Urban VIII died, and a new pope, Innocent X, was elected on 15 September.

The difference between the two men can be summed up quite simply: Urban had been pro-French, while the new pope was pro-Spanish. Moreover, Urban's pontificate had spanned over twenty crucial years of Old English survival and had witnessed a considerable development in understanding between Charles's Anglicanism and the Vatican's Gallican sympathies. This was the climate in which the Old English had been able to hold their ground. Whether they could do so under a pro-Spanish pontiff would remain to be seen. Shortly after Innocent's election the secretary of the Confederation, Richard Bellings, was sent to Rome to solicit help. The new pope informed him personally that he had appointed a nuncio to Ireland, Archbishop Giovanni Battista Rinuccini. Whether or not Bellings, or indeed the Old English in the Confederation, realised it, things were about to change.

In Search of a Settlement: Ormond, Rinuccini and Cromwell, 1645-53

A MOMENTOUS change took place which was to have pro-found consequences on the whole history of Ireland when Pope Innocent X came to the papal throne on 15 September 1644. Thus far Charles's religious politics had been greatly facilitated by the presence in the Vatican of a pro-Gallican pope who had reigned since 1623. The concept of Catholic constitutionalism, which centred on the king's right to appoint bishops, had been fully expressed by the French Catholic Church, and it had been in this context that Charles had pursued his own attempt at an Anglican Catholic settlement through what is known as Arminianism. Now, when he needed it most in Ireland, that support had gone with the election of Innocent X.

The Royal court was fully aware that it would lose the vast potential of Catholic Ireland if it did not grasp the nettle immediately—that is the say before the pope did so. The Spanish party in the Vatican were not renowned for compromise, and the only way to break a deadlock would be to anticipate it by granting as many concessions as possible and by doing so as quickly as possible. The king's French Catholic wife was in some position to treat with the pope from her exile in Paris, and Charles gave her full power to negotiate major concessions on his behalf. As far as Ireland was concerned, he commissioned his close friend the Catholic Earl of Glamorgan to go to Kilkenny and do likewise. Glamorgan's mission was more immediately vital because the new pope would do what the last one had judiciously refrained from doing: he would appoint a nuncio with the full papal power of excommunication. What the king needed desperately from Ireland was an army, and this single power of excommunication could prevent his getting it. The question of sovereignty was about to be tested to its limits.

Glamorgan received his final commission to treat with the Confederation on 12 March 1645. Ormond had facilitated the required public perception by offering his resignation previously in November. Charles had, of course, declined it, but the point had been made for all to see that the Protestant Ormond might yet be replaced by a Catholic. As far as direct negotiations were concerned, this was actually to be the case. Ormond could only represent the king's official position, and if the Confederation could not respond to that, then a more Catholic approach was called for. This would allow the king two separate modes of negotiation, each of which would seem to be opposed to the other, which of course they were not. The only difference between the two was that Glamorgan's mission would have to be secret.

It did not take long for the Irish hierarchy in the Confederation to take full advantage of the great change in Vatican policy. Between 15 May and 31 August its fifth general assembly met at Kilkenny. Of far more importance, however, was the Convocation of regular as well as secular clergy which also met in Kilkenny and which issued a decree on 1 June which was to alter the course of events even before the arrival of the new nuncio. Convocation declared that in any treaty with the crown

> [the] Confederate Catholics be bound in conscience by virtue of their oath of association, or other tie, to make an express article with the Protestant party for keeping in our hands such churches, abbeys, monasteries and chapels now in our possession and recovered by us for the true worship of God.[1]

Convocation declared itself to be fully aware of the fact that if it insisted upon this demand, the king would break off negotiations. They were equally aware, they said, that if they did not insist, the king would grant religious toleration. Charles's view of toleration was no longer what the church felt it had to put up with, however. The decree continued:

> We therefore, after invoking the assistance of the Holy Ghost, and after mature deliberation of the said question and all circumstances thereof, do answer, declare and resolve with a unanimous assent and consent of us sitting together in the said House of Convocation, that conformably to the tenor and true meaning of the said oath of association, the principles of laws and disunity, the said Confederate Catholics are bound in con-

science absolutely, expressly and clearly to set down in the said treaty of peace a special article to the effect meant in the oath; and in case the said article be not consented unto, and that the said Confederate Catholics proceed to agreement for other temporal points without such article as above, we do declare them to be violators of the oath of association and transgressors of the divine law.[2]

Backed by the new pro-Spanish pope, the regular clergy were now coming to the fore and employing a tactic to which the Old English might have no real answer. The Old English Confederates were not going to be dictated to so easily, however, and their reply would be made by reference to the wording of the oath itself which they had drawn up. Not for nothing had the Old English specialised in constitutional history and law. It is worth pausing to make the point that here—right in the centre of seventeenth-century Ireland—the question which had plagued the country for centuries was now being raised and would have to be answered once and for all. The question was: where did sovereignty lie—with the political constitution or with the pope? There was no time now to defer an answer, and whichever course was taken would have the greatest influence on the remainder of Ireland's history. The simple fact was that the alternative to Charles was the English parliament, with its backers already signed up for their estates in Ireland. The Old English were now standing at the frontier of the great European split in Roman Catholicism, the split between those who looked to constitutional dialogue with the temporal power and those who emphasised faith and obedience above political and constitutional rights.

The question had now to be answered as to whether the Old English were indeed breaking the divine law as Convocation (in the name of the Holy Ghost) had said they were. Were they in fact breaking the letter or even the spirit of the oath of association? Their answer was that they were not and they could prove that they were not. The point at issue was the fourth article of the oath of association, and it is worth comparing it with Convocation's description of its contents. The article states:

> That the primates, archbishops, bishops, ordinaries, deans, deans and chapters, archdeacons, chancellors, treasurers, chanters, provosts, wardens of collegiate churches, prebendaries and other dignitaries, parsons, vicars and other pastors of the Roman Catholic secular clergy and their respective suc-

cessors, shall have, hold and enjoy all the churches and church
livings, in as large and ample manner as the late Protestant
clergy respectively enjoyed the same on the first day of
October, in the year of our Lord 1641, together with all the
profits, emoluments, perquisites, liberties and the rights to
their respective sees and churches belonging, as well in all places
now in the possession of the Confederate Catholics, as also in
all other places that shall be recovered by the said Confederate
Catholics from the adverse party within this kingdom, saving
to the Roman Catholic laity their rights, according to the laws
of the land.[3]

It should be pointed out that there were only three other articles in
the oath of association: the first concerned itself with the free and
open practice of Roman Catholicism; the second with the religious
jurisdiction which would be restored to the secular clergy; and the
third with the abolition of fines for the practice of Roman
Catholicism which had been on the statute book since the reign of
Henry VIII. The fourth article was the only one to address itself to
the question of a restoration of church property, and it is more than
clear from the above quotation that the restoration of abbeys and
monasteries which was now called for by Convocation was not in the
oath of association. On the contrary, the wording illustrates the
extent to which the Confederation had gone to spell out that the restoration would be a diocesan one and would not cover the regular
orders. Although it is a point within the realms of theology rather
than history, it is worth pointing out that the Old English were thus
not in any sense contravening any law, divine or otherwise, and that
opposition to the decree of the entire Catholic hierarchy could be
maintained with a free conscience. The invocation of the Holy Ghost
was indeed a serious matter for faithful Catholics, but not at all so
serious if it had been done to support an untruth—as indeed it had.
The conflict was now an open one in which the Old English could
expect the full weight of canon law to be employed against them.
Their only hope was that the law upon which their own identity was
based, the temporal law of the Irish constitution, could be upheld in
the struggle.

This was indeed more of a hope than an expectation. While the
Earl of Glamorgan prepared for his visit to Kilkenny the king was
defeated on 14 June at Naseby by Oliver Cromwell's New Model
Army. This very decisive defeat was significant for two reasons. The

first was that Cromwell had come to the fore as an army leader who could unite military success with singular Puritan zeal at a time when the unity of these qualities was greatly needed. Secondly, Naseby was no less significant because documents were found which indicated the king's involvement with papists and his intended use of an army of Catholics from Ireland. This came as a surprise to no one on the parliamentarian side, but it was the first time that real proof could be used to sway those members of the public who still believed that Charles was essentially a Protestant and not a crypto-Catholic.

Glamorgan's mission to Ireland could only succeed if he could make a successful agreement before Rinuccini, the newly appointed papal nuncio, arrived. In order to do this, he insisted on dealing only with the committee who were negotiating with Ormond. That is to say he avoided a general assembly that could easily be controlled by the hierarchy. For his part, Scarampi did what he could to hold out for Rinuccini by questioning Glamorgan's authority to negotiate and by casting doubt on the king's offers. Speed was of the utmost importance, however, and an agreement was arrived at on 25 August 1645. The king guaranteed complete toleration for Roman Catholics; all churches acquired since October 1641 were to remain with the Confederation 'other than such as are now actually enjoyed by His Majesty's Protestant subjects',[4] that is, those of the Established Church which still remained in operation. Roman Catholics were to be exempted from Protestant clerical jurisdiction, with no obstructions to their own; public office was to be open to Roman Catholics; and the treaty was to be ratified by an Irish parliament. The articles were to be binding even on Ormond, and the king was to give his word that he would honour all these concessions. In return he was to receive 10,000 men under Glamorgan for service in England, Scotland or Wales.

Scarampi pointed out that the treaty would result in the dissolution of the Confederation just at the very moment when the nuncio was expected to arrive with full papal recognition. Ormond could not have agreed more and accordingly urged Glamorgan on. His letter of 22 November to the earl is of the greatest significance because it shows clearly that both men were in full agreement with the king's policy. Ormond acknowledged the role he had been required to play, as one crossing a flooded river:

> Having told your lordship that I am at the highest I will venture on in this great affair, I should beseech your lordship for accom-

plishment of these noble ends that induced you through so great and apparent dangers to undertake this journey, now to set all your strength upon bringing it to a good, that is a speedy conclusion. But my experience of your judgment and indefatigable industry informs me that such a request is needless. We have here reports (made I believe without ground of truth) of the manner of the Italian bishop's reception at Kilkenny, but though I believe not all he said of his errand, yet I conceive your lordship may observe something, the knowledge whereof might direct me how to govern myself in the account I take myself obliged to give His Majesty of the coming of so unbidden a guest into his kingdom.[5]

Archbishop Rinuccini had arrived at Kilkenny with money and arms ten days previously, and on doing so had made clear where the new pope stood as far as the Confederation was concerned. Glamorgan had succeeded in getting his treaty, but he was now faced with an obstacle which his own Catholicism would prevent him from surmounting. This was the essence of Rinuccini's power, and he was to use it relentlessly as soon as he arrived in Ireland.

On 28 November 1645 Glamorgan replied to Ormond: 'Before Sunday night I am morally certain a total assent from the nuncio shall be declared to the proposition for peace.'[6] In a further letter he added a comment which threw some light on the interesting use of the word 'moral': 'When my heart is full I am on fire till I find way to express myself, it being love with reality that is the predominate passion in me.'[7] More than anything else, Glamorgan's mission was rooted in reality, but the question was whether Rinuccini would acknowledge this. Glamorgan clearly felt that Rinuccini was morally obliged to do so because the fate of Catholic Ireland now hinged on the king's position. For his own part, Rinuccini was careful to avoid any direct criticism until he was called upon officially. This is important because it had the crucial effect of setting Glamorgan up for a fall, as is clear from the hope expressed to Ormond by the Catholic earl:

And what I wrote to your excellency, that before Sunday night I expected to gain the nuncio his consent to the ways now in agitation [i.e. under discussion] and, as it were, prescribed by

> you, truly my lord I think I have obtained it fully but yet impli-
> citly, for until today the articles will not be showed him, but I
> undertake to the council here to get his consent unto them,
> which, though with some pains and industry, I am confident of,
> but it will be Thursday morning before I shall wait upon your
> excellency, but then at the furthest, and then I hope to your
> contentment or else I am sure it cannot be to mine.[8]

What followed this patient optimism, however, was fast and to the
point. Rinuccini revoked the treaty and dictated a new one to
Glamorgan on 20 December. The new agreement struck at the heart
of the Confederate weakness. The nuncio demanded that the next
Lord Lieutenant be a Catholic, that Catholic bishops sit in the next
parliament, and that the Supreme Council should not be dissolved
until the king had formally ratified his religious concessions. Where
Glamorgan's Catholicism had been a central support to his mission,
it now became a weight of unbearable proportions, and the mission
collapsed overnight. Glamorgan agreed lamely to incorporate the
nuncio's demands, but this ignored the fact that the treaty had been
agreed with the Confederate representatives, not with the papacy.

The game was over as far as Glamorgan's mission was concerned.
The Vatican had taken direct control, and the king had no choice but
to repudiate his own very crucial embassy. The job was now left to
Ormond to put some public face on the king's great embarrassment.
Ormond had Glamorgan arrested on 26 December on a charge of
high treason (i.e. for conspiracy with a foreign power). He was
released almost immediately. The point had been made, the king's
face was very roughly saved, and the treaty was dead. Whatever
chance the Confederation had had to come to terms, both for their
posessions and for their own Catholicism, very quickly evaporated
after the papal nuncio took control.

The king's forces had been holding out in Chester in the expectation of the imminent arrival of the Confederate army of 10,000
men. This hoped-for relief was now no longer forthcoming. On 3
February 1646 Chester fell to the parliamentary forces. On 5 May the
king surrendered himself to the Scots near Newark.

From about this time onwards—that is to say from the king's surrender to the Presbyterians—it was not the nature of the king's
victory which was being fought for, but rather the nature of his restoration. All was by no means lost, but Ormond would be obliged to
take on Glamorgan's role and to make great concessions to

Catholicism in order to save the Confederation. So far Charles had lost the war (if not all his battles) after he had been obliged to stand down against the Scots in 1637. He had attempted to assert his Anglican kingship in the field, and he had failed there too. His surrender to the Scots was an ironic watershed, but within the logic of his defeat it made perfect sense. Presbyterianism had fought for its official establishment in Scotland almost from its arrival there. A state church would be best established under a sovereign monarch—for the simple reason that the whole seventeenth-century problem would have been solved rather than shelved. It would actually be the only solution possible, and indeed the only solution that did eventually come about, first by the recognition of Charles II by the Scots almost immediately after the death of Charles I; later by the English Restoration; and finally by the invitation to the Dutch Calvinist William of Orange to take the English throne. The Scots had understood this position better than any other group. They offered their allegiance to Charles II straightaway on condition that he denounce what his parents had stood for and that he recognise the kirk. By that time, however, Scotland had to face what Ireland too had to come to terms with, namely Oliver Cromwell. The point is a simple one, however. From the moment that Charles I had been broken, his value as the first potential constitutional monarch became established. This was the point where the English parliament itself began to split: the English Presbyterians began to preserve the king's interest for the same reason as the Scots, but they were opposed by the Puritan groups who believed in true nonconformism or Independency. It followed from this that just as the king's value for the Presbyterians rose, so did the chances of his own execution at the hands of the Independents increase proportionately. The great difference between the Presbyterians, both English and Scottish, and the other Puritan parliamentarians was that the Independents were, by definition, not theologically united. Thus the only way they could keep power was not through any religious settlement with the king but through control of the army. Cromwell's religious commitment would have been useless without his ability to inspire his soldiers with that same commitment. Unlike the Scots, he could have no use for an ex-Anglican king who was willing to compromise. His true match in this sense was Charles I himself, who proved consistently that he would put himself on the line rather than concede his religion. The great irony was that Charles should die at Cromwell's hands because he put his monarchy before all else, after which Cromwell's rule was to suffer continual constitutional collapse until he himself was offered the crown. The highest had not worked, nor could the lowest, but the problem remained.

———————

At the time the king surrendered himself to the Scots, events in Ireland were also beginning to take on the same quick pace. The king's surrender removed a linch-pin in his political armoury, and the coming of Rinuccini similarly altered the political balance greatly in Ireland. The constitution which the king had tried to maintain but could not even establish was about to come apart because Rinuccini now represented a greater authority.

Faced with the power of the newly arrived nuncio and the collapse of the Glamorgan mission, Ormond and the Supreme Council were obliged to come to terms as quickly as they could. They finally agreed on a peace treaty on 28 March 1646 which was proclaimed in Dublin on 30 July and four days later by the Supreme Council at Kilkenny. In response, an ecclesiastical synod to be presided over by Rinuccini was convened away from Kilkenny at Waterford early in August. The question the clergy had set themselves was: 'whether they were to be declared perjured who would accept the peace contained in thirty articles'.[9] The crucial question, for all Catholics in Ireland, of what was to be done if the peace was rejected, was neither asked nor acknowledged. Since March 1642 the country had been literally sold by the English parliament. If the king was abandoned to the mercy of the English parliament, so too would be his subjects in Ireland.

The clergy's ruling, however, was unequivocal:

> Each man's opinion and reasons being first heard, and the writings of some doctors of divinity read: it is decreed by the unanimous consent and votes of all (none contradicting) that all and singular the Confederate Catholics who shall adhere or consent to such peace, or to the fautors thereof, or otherwise embrace the same, be held absolutely perjured; especially for this cause, that in these articles there is no mention made of the Catholic religion, and the security thereof, nor any care had for the conservation of the privileges of the country, as is found promised in the oath.[10]

This was indeed a remarkable view to take of the articles of peace. For example, the first five articles may be compressed as follows. The

Oath of Supremacy was to be abolished; all fines and penalties against the practice of Roman Catholicism were to be removed 'and the said Catholics to be allowed the freedom of the Roman Catholic religion'.[11] A parliament was to be called to confirm these and other religious freedoms, and it was to sit before the following December; its task would be to confirm all the articles of the treaty. All parliamentary acts prejudicial to Catholics since 7 August 1641 were to be repealed, and all indictments, attainders, etc., since that date were to be nullified immediately in order to clear Catholics for membership of the new parliament. All grants of land made on the attainder of Catholics since 1641 were to be made void.

The remaining twenty-five articles equally warrant mentioning. Part of the Graces of 1628 were to be conceded; Catholic free schools and a Gaelic Irish inn of court were to be established; the rights of Catholics to bear arms and to join the army and the civil government were granted, with particular recognition of the Gaelic Irish, 'that in the distribution of ministerial offices or places which now are, or hereafter shall be void in this kingdom, equally shall be used to the Roman Catholic natives of this kingdom as to other His Majesty's subjects'.[12] Catholics were to be free to command forts, garrisons, castles, etc. The Court of Wards was to be abolished (for a rent of £12,000), and only those with estates in Ireland could vote in parliament (where the proxy votes were to be reduced to two). Of great significance was Article XI, which stated that the independence of the Irish parliament from its English counterpart was to be declared and defined by itself when it met. On matters of plantation, the Dublin government was to be forbidden to interfere with the course of law; export prohibitions were to be lifted and Confederate commissioners appointed to set new customs rates. The Lord Deputy or other governors were to be removed if not found suitable; an act of oblivion was to wipe out all offences, capital, criminal and personal, committed since October 1641 by those living or dead; the dues on all forfeited rents, goods, etc., taken since 1641 were to be cancelled; Confederate commissioners would be appointed to judge outstanding crimes committed before the rising. No chief government ministers could now be customs farmers; an act against monopolies would be passed; the Court of Castle Chamber was to be regulated by Confederate commissioners; the forbidden Gaelic practices of ploughing by the tail and burning oats in the straw were to be legalised; grievances against the Court of Wards were to be investigated; maritime causes were to be heard in Ireland; Strafford's rent increases were to be abolished; interest on all debts since 1641 was to be cancelled and a three-year ceiling of 5 per cent imposed; Confederate commissioners were to have power to raise money for the king's army; they were also to appoint their own magistrates, justices of the peace, etc., throughout the country. All lawsuits etc. were to be suspended pending a parliament; the Confederation was to continue in its possession of all cities, towns, territories, etc., until the new parliament met; customs would henceforth be paid directly into the royal exchequer; and commissioners were to be appointed to hear all criminal cases from 15 September 1643 (the date of the one-year truce) until the next parliament.

To say, as the clergy did, 'that in these articles there is no mention made of the Catholic religion, and the security thereof, nor any care had for the conservation of the privileges of the country' was quite a claim.[13] To use that claim to excommunicate all who adhered to the peace because it was contrary to the oath of association almost defies comprehension, but this was nevertheless what happened. As far as the Confederate Catholics were concerned, they had not contravened their oath. That they had not contravened the four appended articles to the oath has already been demonstrated; that they could not now have been in contravention of the oath itself is best seen by quoting its words:

> I A.B. do promise, swear and protest before God, and his saints and angels, during my life to bear true faith and allegiance to my sovereign lord Charles by the grace of God, King of Great Britain, France and Ireland, and to his heirs and lawful successors; and that I will to my power, during life, defend, uphold and maintain all his and their just prerogatives, estates and rights, the power and privilege of the parliament of this realm, the fundamental laws of Ireland, the free exercise of the Roman Catholic faith and religion throughout this land, and the lives, just liberties, estates and rights of all those that have taken, or shall take this oath and perform the contents thereof; and that I will obey and ratify all the orders and decrees made, or to be made, by the Supreme Council of the Confederate Catholics of this kingdom, concerning the public cause, and that I will not seek, or receive, directly or indirectly, any pardon or protection, for any act done, or to be done touching this general cause, without the consent for the major part of the said council; and that I will not, directly or indirectly, do any act or

acts that shall prejudice the said cause, but will, to the hazard of my life and estate, assist and prosecute and maintain the same. So help me God and his holy gospel.[14]

The wording of the oath speaks for itself, and there can be no doubt that the Supreme Council had neither perjured itself nor contravened the oath by the articles of peace signed with Ormond. Much worse was to follow for the Confederates, however, when the clergy further decided not to stop with a public denunciation. Five days later an interdict was laid on all territories adhering to the peace. This was followed on 1 September by the use of the ultimate power: the excommunication of all those observing the peace.

This was still only the beginning, however, albeit the beginning of the end. On 5 June Monro had been defeated by Owen Roe O'Neill at Benburb, County Tyrone. Instead of consolidating his position after Benburb, O'Neill marshalled his forces behind Rinuccini. The nuncio entered Kilkenny at the head of this army on 18 September and imprisoned his opponents on the Supreme Council. The council itself was disbanded, and a week later a new council was nominated under the presidency of the nuncio. The first decision taken was to make a direct military attack on Ormond in Dublin. On pain of excommunication, Preston, the head of the Confederates' Leinster army, was forced to declare for Rinuccini, and together with O'Neill they set about taking Dublin.

The new clergy-dominated general assembly of the Confederation met between 10 January and 4 April 1647 at Kilkenny. (Rinuccini's power may be seen in his appointment of ten new bishops in 1647 alone.) A declaration against the Ormond peace was made on 2 February. Moreover, an addition to the oath of association was passed, under duress, repudiating any peace not approved of by the general assembly. The very necessity for this change in the oath belied the claim that the original oath had been contravened as it was.

Heavily under pressure from Rinuccini's all-out attack, Ormond now had his back to the wall, with no choice but to open negotiations with his enemies in the English parliament. What he hoped for was some agreement that would see Dublin reinforced against the effects of the Confederate self-destruction which the clergy had now fully committed themselves to. If this was possible, he might gain time on behalf of the king, but he had little or nothing to offer an English parliament that had declared Ireland forfeit as early as 1642. The English parliament saw no need to give Ormond a job which a Puritan army could do without any compromise whatsoever. Indeed, they took full advantage of Ormond's dilemma by turning it against him. The point of no return in Ireland's history was approaching with the advance of Rinuccini's army under the divided command of Preston and O'Neill. By early November the nuncio's army was within a few miles of Dublin. Clanricard was delegated by Ormond to open negotiations with Rinuccini. The latter had not brought his army to Dublin to negotiate, however, and he demanded full recognition of Catholicism from a king who was all but powerless and for whom such recognition would be his immediate ruination in England. If Rinuccini and Owen Roe O'Neill could not or would not see this, it was at least clear to Preston that the Confederates were about to destroy themselves. If they broke with the king now, they would be excluded from whatever Charles could yet salvage from the war in England (and some form of constitutional settlement seemed a real possibility in England at this stage). If the Confederates turned their back on the king—for whom their loyalty had been the one thing they were able to agree on—they would face the wrath of a Cromwellian army without any possibility of sympathy from the king's supporters.

O'Neill dismissed the overtures made by Clanricard on Ormond's behalf, but Preston gave them serious consideration. When it looked as if he might agree on peace terms and indeed help Ormond, he was ordered, on pain of excommunication, to withdraw his army. The Confederate cause collapsed under the weight of Rinuccini's papal authority, and it was never to recover. Ormond was now the only leader in Ireland who, because he could not be threatened with excommunication by Rinuccini, had not thus far compromised his loyalty to the king. As far as support in Ireland was concerned, Charles had been officially abandoned when Preston and the Old English buckled under the nuncio's power.

The Lord Lieutenant was obliged to negotiate with the king's parliamentary enemies in England about their proposed occupation of Dublin. He did this in the slender hope that the king might still retain a foothold in Ireland; but there was no need for the English parliament to negotiate what was now theirs by default. On 7 June an English parliamentary army landed near Dublin under the command of Colonel Michael Jones. Two weeks later, on 19 June, Ormond surrendered Dublin to commissioners for the English parliament and shortly afterwards left for England.

———————

By the time Dublin was surrendered to the English parliament the king was in the hands of the New Model Army. Matters looked bleak for the Catholics in Ireland, now without any point of reference for their allegiance other than their clergy. Ormond's departure had left a vacuum. The only option open to the Old English was to negotiate with the Irish Protestant Inchiquin, who was in control of almost all of Munster, in an effort to unite against the coming English parliamentary threat. Desperation had likewise given them the incentive to wrest control of the Confederation from the clergy, but there was still nothing they could do against the power of excommunication. A truce was agreed between the Confederates and Inchiquin in May 1648, but Rinuccini immediately declared all supporters of this peace excommunicated. The Supreme Council appealed to Rome against the sentence (a hearing was postponed) and at the same time relieved O'Neill of his command for his support of the nuncio. O'Neill responded by attacking Kilkenny itself, but he soon retreated and found himself obliged to make a treaty with Inchiquin. By this time Owen Roe O'Neill was almost literally going round in circles. He had been used by the clergy as the military arm of papal power, but this had not been his original aim. He had come to Ireland in the belief that the Catholics were true supporters of the king and that if he served either him or them, he would be restored to at least some of his family estates. A good deal of his problems had stemmed from the fact that unlike the landed Gaelic Irish he could not command personal support on the basis of anything other than his name; he had not brought an army with him. Consequently he suffered a lack of discipline in his troops which was actually rooted in their lack of allegiance to his own interests. His officers increasingly dissociated these interests from their own when time began to run out. Against him was ranged the landed Gaelic Irish, who had as much stake in the Confederation as had the Old English—and it must be remembered that some of them held land which might otherwise have been the inheritance of Owen Roe himself. In the end he lost large numbers of troops and officers through desertion.

O'Neill was proclaimed a traitor by the Supreme Council on 30 September. Six months later he was fighting on the side of the

English parliament in Ulster; six months later again he was on Ormond's side just before his death in November 1649. His principal mistake had been not a military but rather a tactical one. The Gaelic Irish who rose in 1641 and their Old English allies were all landed. O'Neill was the great landless outsider whose name had been used to invoke the spirit of Tyrone, but he had little or no knowledge of the complexities of Irish politics and he had little or no real power in Ireland. His way around this had been to stand behind Rinuccini when the latter used his almighty clerical sanction. This proved to be a grave mistake on the nuncio's part, but it also cost O'Neill his position in Ireland because Rinuccini's failure was consequently his own.

The Gaelic Irish were as pragmatic about their identity as any other group in the seventeenth century who pursued their own personal interests in whatever way they could. They can, of course, be defined or identified by their language and culture as a group, and this is how they often—but not by any means always—defined themselves. The romantic nineteenth-century notion that the Gaelic Irish after 1607 were landless revolutionaries who gave their country a foundation for its future struggles is not borne out by the evidence. The facts are a good deal less heroic, but they also place the Gaelic Irish within the ordinary realm of human affairs and not as torchbearers across the centuries. The great Hugh O'Neill was no different from any other Irish or English or Scottish aristocrat. As the Great Tyrone (rather than the Great O'Neill) he was a Gaelic-English earl who succeeded all too quickly after 1603 in illustrating his deep grasp of how to survive under English law; Sir Phelim O'Neill refused to betray a deceased Protestant King of England even to save his own life; Owen Roe O'Neill fought for and against every combination of his fellow Gaelic Irish and his fellow Roman Catholics and on the side of anyone who could keep him in any position to win back his estates.

To couple the name of O'Neill with the survival of Gaelic purity in Ulster can only be done emotionally, and it cannot be done with reference to the facts. Indeed, it would be as permissable and as comfortable as any other misreading of history were if not for the fact that the problem of Ulster itself lay at the heart of the Irish question. Ulster's rich Gaelic heritage has often been used as a vehicle to illustrate the failure of the whole of Gaelic Ireland. Romantic apologists grouped their views around the dynamic pharse 'if only'. If only Hugh O'Neill had not fought on the side of the queen against his

Gaelic Irish neighbours; if only he had declared his true claim to lead all Ireland sooner; if only the Irish had united behind him; if only between 1603 and 1607 he had not concentrated on consolidating his private possessions within English law; if only he had refused to leave in 1607; if only he had come back. The list of Irish historical 'if onlys' is endless, and to it may be added the elusive 'help from abroad': if only the help which came from abroad had been the right amount of the right sort at the right time in the right place, Ireland could have thrown off the yoke of its foreign oppressor. Rinuccini's mission to Ireland demonstrated as clearly and as quickly as could be that there was more than one 'foreign' power operating in Ireland.

After the Confederate collapse and just before Rinuccini's departure the Catholic Church in Ireland split down the middle on this question of power and the use of it. In the final analysis, the divisions were the same as those which had characterised the church in Ireland since the twelfth century. It has been said that these divisions were racial, but they were far more cultural in their per-petuation of identity. In the main, the Old English kept to their diocesan Counter-Reformation structure, while the Gaelic Irish sup-ported their regular, unreformed clergy, best represented by the Franciscan Friars Minor. Between the late 1640s and the late 1670s the Old English clergy ostracised their erstwhile allies by attempting to reform what had by then become the only Gaelic identity left in Ulster. The Old English clergy continued their support for the English monarchy, but in doing so they pushed the Gaelic Irish into fierce resistance. The most dramatic example of this was the use made by the English government of Gaelic-Franciscan opposition based in south Armagh to the Old English Primate, the now canonised Oliver Plunkett.

Ireland was to become part of England's continuing constitutional crisis until the end of the century. The last Stuart kings present a crisis of containment followed by the disruption of that very contain-ment. James I was extraordinarily successful in his ability to keep the religious peace. Charles I pushed this ability into disruption. Charles II presided over a solution of containment which James II insisted on pushing into disruption. The problem had started with the Roman Catholicism of the Stuarts, and so it was to end. What they managed to ignore was that in the meantime they had embraced Anglicanism, a

monarchical religion which had embraced the Reformation before
Calvin had sanctioned the deposition of monarchs.

Ireland's sorry history before the Confederate collapse belongs to
the realm of what might have been. The king's great governor of
Ireland, the Earl of Ormond, was an Anglican-type Protestant, but
he belonged to the political community of Ireland. He was a bridge
between the Anglican king and his Roman Catholic subjects. The
religious split in sovereignty was so great, however, that even
Ormond had needed his own bridge to deal with the Confederation.
This role had been well filled by the Catholic Earl of Clanricard, but
when these bridges had proved too narrow the king had appointed
the Catholic Earl of Glamorgan with almost full sovereign powers.

The possibilities for constitutional Catholic self-government in
Ireland collapsed along with the Confederation of Kilkenny. Henceforth all parties would have to decide clearly and unequivocally which
sovereign power they adhered to, the temporal or the spiritual. What
was now clear was that the dual option which the Confederation had
represented was gone. The Cromwellian settlement drove the
erstwhile landed Catholics west of the Shannon, but Cromwell could
never address matters which properly belonged within the ambit of
the other great sovereign power, the Vatican. What the Cromwellians
achieved was indeed remarkable, and it was done by the rapid introduction of new structures of administration and government—in
effect a new constitution—but the ease with which this was done was
in marked contrast to the very same problem of the settlement of
England, where no constitution short of a restoration proved
durable.

By the end of January 1649 Ormond had concluded a new peace treaty
with the Confederation, but the exercise was pointless as the king
was tried and executed by the end of the month. In February Archbishop Rinuccini left the country, and a month later Cromwell was
appointed commander-in-chief in Ireland. Cromwell viewed Ireland
from outside the complicated framework in which its inhabitants
dwelt and within which there was nothing but disunity. He brought
the country to peace much as Mountjoy had done when called in to
deal with Tyrone. Cromwell's massacre of the inhabitants of

Drogheda and Wexford was done officially (that is to say for English public consumption) to revenge the massacres of 1641, but in fact to demonstrate his determination to stamp out resistance in Ireland as quickly as possible. (A total of about 4,600 people were put to death in the two towns.) His motive was a pressing one. Ireland had been a major source of income during the civil war on the basis of land shares which had been sold. It would be necessary to make good the English claims; confiscation was also necessary to compensate the army for lack of pay. Furthermore, the proper manipulation of these claims would allow Cromwell to siphon off many of the elements from a growing band of discontents in England and induce them to settle in Ireland. In addition to these more particular reasons there was a pressing need to return to England quickly without the fear that Ireland would have to be dealt with again, or indeed that it might be used by the enemies of the Commonwealth. All of this is to say that Cromwell understood the Irish problem from a purely self-orientated point of view, and in this he was no different from Mountjoy or Strafford or, for that matter, Rinuccini. By the time of his departure in May 1650 he had broken the main resistance and was in a position to hand over the campaign and the governorship to Henry Ireton. The last formal surrender of the war was made by Philip MacHugh O'Reilly at Cloughoughter in April 1653.

By August 1650 Charles II had joined the Scots against his father's English enemies. Although he was defeated by Cromwell at Worcester over a year later, he managed in the meantime to wreck whatever chance Ormond had of maintaining any policy in Ireland. As part of his agreement with the Scots, Charles disowned the Ormond peace treaty of 1649 and in so doing brought all initiative to an end. In December 1650 Ormond appointed Clanricard to the deputyship and left for France. Thus by the beginning of the 1650s the inhabitants of Ireland had been abandoned to the Cromwellians by the sovereign powers of the king and the pope and left to shift for themselves while their estates were transferred to English ownership.

The union of Charles II with his father's erstwhile Scottish opponents was the beginning of the end of England's new Commonwealth. What the Scots wanted was an established Presbyterian church, and they had no problem of conscience in converting a king to that position. There was no 'dissent' in Scotland, and so the country was immune to the perpetual convulsions which the English were to suffer for the next decade. The execution of the king had opened a Pandora's box of near anarchy in which the force of ideology and the force of arms were the only two components of any action. The most extreme ideologists were the radical democrats who wished to extend the franchise to all men, propertied or not. In the wake of the king's execution the emotional tide of revolution was with them. The other force was simply the army, the only institution were 'order' was still maintained. In addition to these there was a third group composed of 'Presbyterians', who wished for both an established church settlement and the conservation of their wealth. This group did not determine the pace, but they did in the end determine the solution. This was because in the final analysis the problem for the revolution was the same problem of democracy faced by all revolutions. To give the non-propertied, or, as they were called, those with no 'interest', a say in the government could quickly result in the removal of the government itself. Those with an 'interest' in the country were only a tiny proportion compared with the landless wage-labourers, and it had to be pointed out to this group as quickly as possible that the revolution had not been brought about in their name. Thus it has been in the constitutional crises of the 1650s that historians have seen the confrontation of the revolution with its own unpalatable and chaotic reality.

How radical were the radicals and how conservative the conservatives are questions that will continue to be asked, perhaps endlessly, unless English history is divided into a pre-revolutionary period in which the Stuarts, and Charles I in particular, are seen to be doing all the pushing—and a second period when the 'revolutionaries' were obliged to remove the king because of what he was doing and replace him with something else. The 'something else' was the essence of the constitutional problem of the 1650s, but if the first half of the seventeenth century could be explained in terms of a 'Puritan revolution', one would have thought that fifty years was long enough to answer the vital question of what form the new government would take. The fact of the matter is, however, that the Commonwealth itself bore witness to the lack of anything other than day-to-day thinking about government. History came full circle when Cromwell was offered the crown of England. He rejected it very reluctantly, and it may be argued that he should not have done so—that what he should have done was to anticipate the constitutional monarchy of the Calvinist William III and save England the bother of clearing out the last of the Stuarts. This is to miss the point of Cromwell's great weakness, however. Neither Cromwell nor any of the governments of the 1650s could claim sovereignty in any name other than the revolution, or the people, or non-conformism, or however one wishes to express the various forms of cohesive ideologies and sects that gave the Commonwealth its identity. What Cromwell or the Commonwealth could not do, however, was claim sovereignty on behalf of the royalists, whether king, aristocracy, merchant, farmer or labourer. He could not do this because the religion of the Commonwealth was Puritan and the royalists (by and large) were not. Charles I did not embrace a uniform settlement, but he had tried to impose one and had lost. Cromwell could not do so for the very reason that Charles and the royalists had come to represent religious persecution for the Puritans. What was needed, therefore, was a king with the necessary credentials to rule, and one who was willing to settle with all sides. Between 1650 and 1660 almost every combination and permutation of rule was tried until it became clear that only the agreed sovereignty of a king could give the necessary ballast to a new constitution. This is in effect what Charles II had come to represent as the Commonwealth wound down into chaos, but the solution he offered could only be temporary. The new king's credentials did not agree with the concept of 'settlement'. He was a Stuart son of Charles I, as he proved himself to be when he signed a secret treaty with Louis XIV whereby he would become a Roman Catholic in return for French support. The 'settlement' side of Charles II was to be seen more in Ireland than in England itself.

The English civil war had in effect begun as a result of Charles I's attempt to enforce Anglicanism on the Scots. He had done this as a Scottish king and in the context of the Scottish religious conflict, which was a black-and-white one. The Scottish Presbyterians were unified in their religion and so played a major role in what was to follow when English Protestantism divided into ever-increasing 'churches'. When Charles II was proclaimed by the Scots in 1650 it was done on the understanding that he would establish Presbyterianism in Scotland. This was the effective end of the conflict begun by Charles I in 1637, but it was also the beginning of the end for the Commonwealth because Charles II was now putting himself forward as a monarch willing to rule within a new and non-Anglican constitution. The most significant aspect of this for Ireland was that in August 1650 Charles repudiated Ormond and his treaty with the Old English. He was forced to do this by the Presbyterians, who had no desire to see unity between the Catholics and the established Church of Ireland, even if that new Protestant establishment was Cromwellian in its Independency. The Scots clearly had an eye to the later and full restoration and wished to preserve their own non-episcopal establishment. As far as the Catholics were concerned, the Cromwellian settlement made them all outlaws, and there could have been little point throughout the 1650s in discussing the type of restoration they desired. While the clergy were officially banished from the country, thousands of men were deported to the West Indies. It was clear from 1650 that not even Charles II was going to attempt to rectify the Catholic position.

Two major developments took place as a result of the Cromwellian settlement and persecution. The first was that the Old English Catholic clergy set about coming to terms with what, one way or another, was going to be Protestant rule. The problem was not the pre-1649 one of how to preserve estates and integrity—it was simply the theological difficulty of ministering within a Protestant administration. In other words, the great irony is that the Old English Catholics were obliged to solve a question which, should they find the answer, would not restore them to their earlier position when the same answer might have also saved their estates. The problem then and the problem now was the Gaelic Irish and their earlier adherence to dictatorial attitudes and policies for which the Old English had no use whatsoever. Moreover, if was within the Gaelic church that the second significant development took place, for it was here, during the decades following 1649, that modern Catholic nationalism was born.

Rinuccini's handling of the constitutional question had banished it altogether from the political horizon. It was not replaceable by any other concept, and the net effect was that the Catholics were for the first time united in their political loss. After Rinuccini's departure there was a great division of opinion among the Catholics as to whether they had failed or succeeded. Did they fail to preserve their estates and their religion? Or was this an impossibility under a heretical monarch, and was it merely a matter of time before they would be obliged to forfeit their possessions for their faith? The majority of the Old English viewed the 1649 failure as the end not just of their estates but of the opportunity for Catholics to govern themselves. In this they were supported by a sizeable number of Old English clergy, but the view was not shared by the majority.

9

Theology and the Politics of Sovereignty: Jansenist, Jesuit and Franciscan

ON 27 January 1622 Cornelius Jansen requested the support of his follower, the Abbot of St Cyran, for the foundation of a college for Irish Franciscans in Paris. Jansen had been asked to lend his own support by the Archbishop of Tuam, Florence Conry, a Franciscan and a Jansenist, who wished to organise the small group of his confrères then residing in Paris. This was the beginning of a link between the Franciscans and the Jansenists which was to have profound effects on the history of the second half of the seventeenth century and which was to cause the greatest split in Catholicism which Ireland was ever to see.

Jansen was a theologian at the University of Louvain in the Spanish Netherlands; he later became Archbishop of Ypres and died in 1638. He became famous (after his death) for his study of St Augustine and for the central conclusion which this study had led him to. The conclusion lay at the heart of the great controversy which had plagued Catholicism: whether God's grace was resistible or not. The question is best put in its simplest terms, because otherwise the divisions which it caused would defy understanding. Does God confer his divine grace on all, or does he select certain people? Is it possible to choose to undergo a conversion of utter personal conviction, or, to reverse the question, can one resist a surge of grace which would otherwise sweep one into heaven? The answer to the question has always been experiential. In other words, those who had undergone a great rebirth or who had lived within such a theology had always argued that God's grace was a thunderbolt of enlightenment which could not be resisted. It followed from this that there were people who lived and died who clearly had not been struck by this thunderbolt, and it was concluded that these were not of the same spiritual status as the 'elect', i.e. those who had been specially selected. This was the theory of predestination, namely that God had chosen his elect from among the mass of humanity.

The opposite view was that God's grace was conferred on all equally, and that it was used, or cultivated, or expressed through the actions of one's life. It followed from this that a man was free to use his own will either to accept or reject God's grace. This was the theory of free-will, namely that all might be saved by their own actions.

On the face of it, the implications of each view would seem not to have any great or profound consequences, but on closer examination this is found not to be the case. Because the Roman Catholic Church was above all catholic, or universal, it held that there was such a thing as free-will, and that it was the church's role to channel a man's will towards God, and that no one should be excluded from salvation for the want of mediation. The two components of this mediation were ritual and good works. By observing certain ritualistic actions a man could purify his soul, and he might enhance the effect by doing good works as well. It was above all an external manifestation of faith—or justification by action.

St Peter was foremost among the Apostles, and it was to him that Jesus had pointed when he spoke of the foundation of a church in his name. St Peter brought Christianity to Rome and has been termed its first bishop and in that sense was the first great Roman Catholic. St Paul, on the other hand, never knew Jesus personally. He came to Christianity through a great thunderbolt conversion. Consequently he based his teaching on justification by faith alone because this was his experience. That is to say it is not by good works that a man is saved, but by his faith, which will result in a great rebirth of the man himself. Paul thus emphasised the teaching that a man may not enter the kingdom of heaven unless he is born again of water and the Holy Spirit. In this case the Holy Spirit may be taken as a manifestation of grace, or vice versa. Hence the notion that God's grace is that which cannot be resisted.

St Augustine was the first and in many respects the greatest of Christian theologians, but what is of the utmost significance is that he came to Christianity after a momentous conversion. He had led a life of pleasure until the day he heard a voice directing his attention to the teachings of St Paul (and in particular Romans 13:13). The conversion which Augustine subsequently underwent, when added to Paul's teaching, caused him to conclude that God's grace was indeed irresistible.

Thus St Paul came to represent a different type of Christian experience to that of St Peter 'the rock'. Peter came to represent the lawful practice of ritual (through the mass), while Paul came to represent the spiritual nature of salvation (through baptism). Augustine's writings may be used to support both sides, but the notion that God chooses those whom he would save appears to be the more pronounced view. In this respect Augustine was truly a Platonist. Plato held that man is drawn towards invisible ideals, and indeed that everything has its own ideal somewhere beyond the known world. In a Christian context this is strongly predestinarian because a man cannot aspire to being something which he is not. The works of Plato disappeared from western civilisation for the period of the Catholic Church's development, and only Augustine remained to pose the Platonic possibilities. The great exponent of Paul and Augustine was Martin Luther after he had undergone the very same rebirth conversion. As with Augustine, it came to him through the words of Paul, but he also had real Platonic foundations after the rediscovery of Plato's works during the Renaissance. Thus Luther came to oppose free-will and to uphold predestination, and it followed from this that he would have to break with Rome.

The sovereignty of St Peter as the first bishop was at stake on the question of conversion, and because of this it was the pope in Rome who came to represent the catholic and all-embracing nature of Christianity. Any view which stressed personal and subjective conversion would be opposed to the institution of the papacy.

Seventeenth-century France witnessed a great divide on the question of the pope's power to depose a king. The Catholic Church in France had for a long time been semi-independent of Rome. As Spain declined towards the end of the sixteenth century, so France grew in power. Unlike the rigorous Spanish Catholicism or the breakaway Anglican church, the Gallican church retained its religious allegiance to Rome but gave its political support to the French king. Spain had had to contend with Islam and so looked to the papacy for the strength of unity. The position of France was the opposite. It had not been overrun by the infidel, and it was also geographically open to all influences, namely from Spain, Germany, Holland and England.

As Spain declined, the seventeenth century saw a great upsurge in French power. This was not due only to the natural balance of forces in Europe; it was also due to the significance of France for the Counter-Reformation. If the Catholic Church was to fight Protestantism, it would not find the answer within Spain or within the states of Italy itself. The Reformation was a northern phenomenon, and battle would have to be done in a great northern Catholic country. The Jesuits were founded by a Spaniard devoted to papal power and determined to undo the Reformation, but Loyola founded the order in Paris rather than in Madrid. France had become the battleground of the Counter-Reformation, and purely by accident it produced a king worthy of the fray in Louis XIV, who came to the throne in 1643 and died in 1715. If the accident of geography was crucial to France's history, so also was the Sun King's health and longevity.

The question of sovereignty between king and pope lay at the core of the Gallican problem. In the seventeenth century it was taken up in the theological field by a Dutch theologian, but it quickly became a French problem. Cornelius Jansen argued for St Augustine and against the supremacy of the papacy. Against him were ranged the Jesuits, the great order of missionaries set up as an instrument of absolute obedience to the pope. Jansen's greatest apologist and anti-Jesuit intellectual was Blaise Pascal after the latter had undergone his thunderbolt conversion. Pascal's conversion experience was well within the Pauline and Augustinian mode; he turned from the great pleasure he obtained from mathematics and devoted himself to the rigours of Jansenism. Pascal almost singlehandedly undermined the Jesuit theological foundations by exposing them as casuists devoted only to the papal monarchy.

The Jesuits were often mistrusted without any appreciation of what their particular religious mission was. In France this mission was quite simply to retain the allegiance of the king to Rome. In order to do this, they were obliged to put forward several rather qualified and equivocal views on certain rigid theological propositions, but where fundamentals were concerned they were as unwavering as any order. Most importantly, they upheld the notion of free-will.

In the controversy between Jesuit and Jansenist can be seen the great catholicity of Roman Catholicism. The Jesuits wished to retain the allegiance of the king, while the Jansenists criticised the 'laxity' which was necessary to do this and advocated a far more exclusive and rigorous approach to religion. Almost all theological views of the seventeenth century could be divided into the two great camps of free-will *versus* predestination, and even where regular orders were not immediately concerned with either view they were obliged to take sides. The Jesuits used reason above emotion, and consequently they gained the general support of the Dominicans, the order of friars whose greatest writer was the Aristotelian philosopher St Thomas Aquinas. (Theological bridges had already been built, for example by the Jesuit Francesco Suarez, who based his theology on Aquinas.)

The Franciscan order had two great teachers among its members: Duns Scotus and William of Occam. The essential difference between Scotism and the philosophy of Aquinas was that Scotus put love and will before reason and knowledge. Aquinas absorbed the mechanistic Aristotle whole; the great Franciscans could not consult Plato, but this division between law and spirit is a division of human nature itself, and the Franciscans discovered their own branch of Platonism, even without Plato, through the elevation of love over reason. At the heart of the Franciscan philosophy, therefore, was the notion that nature is subject to God's will rather than dependent on his law. The essence of the true religious experience, it held, is to be found in the love of God. The way to this experience is, of course, through Jesus, but it is almost equally to be found through the Virgin Mary, as she who physically carried the divine love and who must therefore be directly of that love. That is to say that Jesus and Mary are both of God and are therefore of each other in a special way not extended to other mortals. To give precise theological expression to this view, Scotus gave the clearest, and indeed the final, definition of the Immaculate Conception. For Mary to have been free from that original sin from which all of humanity suffered and from which it was to be redeemed, she was pre-ordained by God to be without sin before her own birth. Thus, according to Scotus, Mary was pre-destined to salvation. Occam gave shape to the implications of this view in what is called 'nominalism': the notion that ideas and intellectual concepts may indeed exist in the mind, but they do not do so in the real world which exists outside the mind. Science, therefore, deals in words and concepts, but true knowledge can only come through intuition. It is intuition that connects man's will to the will of God, not logic or science. Thus the Franciscans would have put Plato before Aristotle if they had had the opportunity, while the Dominicans would have retained their rigorous logic. (It was mainly the Dominicans who administered the 'logic' of Catholicism throughout the Inquisition.)

Not surprisingly, Martin Luther described Occam as his teacher because Luther shared with the great Franciscan theologians the reliance of inner intuitive and emotional revelation as the means of true salvation. Thus when Cornelius Jansen put forward a view of man as predestined to salvation (or not, as the case may be) he was

looking in one direction towards the Protestants (and especially to
Calvin who, after his own sudden conversion, extended Luther's
view to its fullest) while in another direction towards the Franciscans.
That is not to say that the Franciscan order *per se* was Jansenist, for it
was not; it is to say, however, that there was a great deal of natural
sympathy for Jansen from the Franciscans in his battle against the
Jesuits.

All this might seem to be far removed from questions of papal
sovereignty, but it is not. The Jansenists had declared that the spirit
of their teaching was contravened by the mass inclusion of all other
teachings and doctrines by the papacy. In other words, the Jansenists
were exclusive, while the papacy was inclusive. As far as the pope was
concerned, Jansenism was fundamentally opposed to the universal
nature of Catholicism—which universality was one of the marks of
the true church. As far as the French monarchy was concerned,
however, things were not so simple. On the one hand, Louis XIV
sided with the Jesuits because in upholding the sovereignty of papal
rule as an absolute principle they also upheld his own royal
absolutism—albeit only in the temporal sphere. On the other hand,
however, because Jansenism denied the absolute spiritual authority
of the pope, it quickly tended towards the general Gallican position
of independence from Rome—and Louis could hardly have frowned
upon such a new and vital theological support for his national
church.

As far as Ireland was concerned, it was this notion of a 'national
church' which caught on among some Franciscans and gave rise to a
movement within Ireland towards religious independence. It must be
pointed out that the nature of this independence was not to be in any
way anti-Catholic, but rather that local conditions would play a
much greater role in determining the Catholic mission. Just as the
Franciscans would be the order most sympathetic to this, the
Counter-Reformation church would be its greatest opponent. The
context in which such a confrontation could take place was that of
post-Rinuccini Ireland. The nuncio had employed papal powers not
simply to silence his opponents or to achieve toleration for
Catholicism, but also in his attempt to carry out his mission of
bringing Ireland within the clear boundaries of the Tridentine
decrees. Not only had he failed in this, but in splitting the church in
Ireland he opened the way for a movement sympathetic to Jansenism
and which would have the support of at least some Franciscans—and
therefore could bridge the great gap between Gaelic Irish and Old

English. It must be remembered that while the Franciscans had many Old English members, they were deeply rooted also in Gaelic Ireland. The great strength of the order throughout Irish history was to give credence to those very conditions which were uniquely Irish, and consequently they had appeal for all sides. It is true that the Old English would tend towards the French Jesuit position or even towards the Dominicans, but the Franciscans were not one-sided and could be as lawful and particular as any Dominican or Jesuit. Gaelic Irish identity was cultural and emotional, while that of the Old English was constitutional and intellectual. The Jesuits were not concerned with the Gaelic Irish because the latter were not in the front line of battle, while the Dominicans could have received merely token support from a people who were only organised around their culture and certainly not around Roman or English law.

It may be clear from all of this that after Rinuccini's sabotage of the Confederation, Ireland might become part of a much wider international dimension than it had been. It would be a dimension which contained the conflict between the French state and the papacy; between Louis XIV's Jesuits and his Jansenists; indeed, between the great Catholic and Protestant powers of Europe. The area of overlap would be England and its internal conflict between Anglicanism and nonconformism. What Rinuccini did was to remove any form of representative political power which the Catholics had enjoyed under the Anglican crown. As Anglicanism had been under threat from the Puritans, so too were the constitutional Catholics of Ireland from the papacy. The delicate and subtle relations which had been established between the Confederate Catholics and the Anglican royalists were shattered from two directions: on one side by the supremacy of Rinuccini, and on the other by Cromwell, both men with little time for niceties.

The net effect of Rinuccini's policy was to remove from Ireland any question of political independence and raise all issues to a level of high religion. In other words, the struggle within Ireland became a Catholic one which saw Cromwell or Charles II only in terms of theological ideologies. The real Old English political dimension left the scene as quickly as did the nuncio himself in 1649. The Old English would attempt a comeback under James II, but this would be a new landless response unlike their old traditional power; success would be on an all-or-nothing basis, and there would be no room for negotiation. All this can be put down to the Ulster rising of 1641 and the forcible inclusion of the Old English in it—on one side by the Gaelic

Irish and on the other by the Calvinist Parsons and his colleagues in the Dublin government.

———————————

In August 1652 the English queen-mother, Henrietta Maria (the French Catholic wife of Charles I), recommended to Cardinal Barberini in Rome two Irish Franciscans, both Jansenists (George Dillon and Raymond Caron), who wished to found what had been mooted since the early 1620s and had been backed by Jansen himself: an Irish Franciscan college in Paris. This link between the Anglican monarchy and Jansenism was not new. For example, Antonio de Dominis, the Catholic Archbishop of Spalato, attacked papal supremacy in his work *De Republica Ecclesiastica* and was as a result obliged to resign his see, although he received the support of a strong minority at the theological faculty of Paris University. James I of England gave him refuge and made him Dean of Windsor, where, in 1617, he assisted in the consecration of the Bishop of Lincoln and was one of the consecrators of Archbishop Laud. (De Dominis returned to the Roman faith after he left England in 1622, but died in the prison of the Inquisition at Rome, after which his body was publicly burnt.)

———————————

After a period of over thirty years attempting to found an Irish Franciscan college in Paris it was finally established by a mandate from Louis XIV in July 1653. As soon as Charles II had made a pact with the Scots, and at the same time as Cromwell was overrunning Ireland, a great contest began among the clergy in the wake of Rinuccini's departure. There were those who looked to a restoration of the Stuarts for a renewal of constitutional toleration, and there were those who accepted Cromwellian rule in temporal affairs in return for simple religious toleration without any reference to politics. In terms of modern Irish nationalism and republicanism (whose traditions are in many respects polar opposites), it may be surprising to learn that the Catholic Church in Ireland competed against itself for English Protestant toleration, and that this included negotiations with the Cromwellian slaughterers of Drogheda and Wexford, but the fact must be borne in mind that the church had never perceived its mission as political in either nationalist or republican terms. Naturally it favoured certain types of government, but if it had no option but to deal with Cromwellians, then so be it. If the Catholic Church was to be either nationalistic or republican, it would contravene the very essence of its catholicity which was neither racial nor political. The question at issue was whether the church had actually brought about the necessity to deal with Cromwell by its papal appointment of Rinuccini. That the nuncio was conscious of what he did to the Confederation can be seen in his counter-policy, the main practitioner of which was Edmund O'Reilly, Archbishop of Armagh from 1657 to 1669.

In his negotiations with the Cromwellian commander Michael Jones, Owen Roe O'Neill was represented by Edmund O'Reilly, the Vicar-General of Dublin. O'Reilly's principal opponent was the Jansenist Franciscan Peter Walsh. Walsh sent Archbishop Fleming of Dublin a letter which proved that O'Reilly was dealing with the Cromwellians, and the archbishop was obliged to remove him. O'Reilly continued, however, to solicit support for Owen Roe from Jones. Before Owen Roe changed sides again and came to terms with Ormond, O'Reilly had been accused of betraying the royalists at the crucial Battle of Rathmines in August 1649 and indeed of leading a relief force astray. Ormond had tried to take Dublin from the Cromwellians, but as he marched on the city he was surprised by Jones, who seems to have had vital information on the Lord Lieutenant's movements. The defeat was so total that Ormond could only escape to Kilkenny with a few men, leaving behind all stores and arms. Two weeks later Cromwell himself arrived in Dublin with 3,000 of his Ironsides.

O'Reilly was restored to the vicar-generalship of Dublin after Cromwell's arrival. He participated in several meetings initiated by Rinuccini's auditor while in Ireland, Dionisio Massari, to invite Louis XIV's opponent the Duke of Lorraine to assume the protectorate of Ireland. The idea was more symbolic than practical, but even as a symbol it had little use in the new Cromwellian Ireland. Indeed, there was no real need for an outside protectorate in that O'Reilly himself enjoyed Cromwellian support and acknowledged this. On a visit to England in 1658, for example, he wrote to the secretary of Propaganda in Rome that English Catholics under Cromwell had not enjoyed such freedom of worship since the days of the Catholic Queen Mary, and that although conditions were less favourable in Ireland, they were improving.

The freedom which O'Reilly enjoyed under Cromwell was compromised in a rather embarrassing courtroom encounter in Dublin in 1653. O'Reilly was giving evidence against the O'Tooles when one of the defendants recognised him as the Vicar-General of Dublin and the court was obliged to order his arrest. He was tried on a series of capital crimes and found guilty, but was released after a short stay in captivity. His name was put forward for the see of Dublin in 1654, but no appointment was made. Three years later at the behest of Massari (who had assumed Rinuccini's position in Irish affairs on the latter's death in 1653) he was made Archbishop of Armagh.

O'Reilly received a bad press from many quarters for his actions. These actions were not duplicitous, however, and criticism tended to be based on a political notion of what the church's mission in Ireland actually was. If O'Reilly's activities were considered purely as those of a priest, or indeed Vicar-General of Dublin, the hostile reaction to them might not have extended beyond the bounds of personal invective. His elevation to the headship of the whole Catholic Church in Ireland could not, however, be explained or understood in terms of political sectarianism or betrayal. O'Reilly represented the papal supremacy of Rinuccini, which was increasingly coming under threat from Jansenism.

The nuncio, it will be remembered, had been sent to Ireland by the pro-Spanish Pope Innocent X. Innocent appointed a commission (in which he himself took part) in April 1651 to examine the 'Five Propositions' which were supposedly to be found in Jansen's *magnum opus*, the *Augustinus*. The result was the papal bull *Cum occasione* of May 1653, which condemned the Five Propositions out of hand. The Jansenists replied that the pope could so act as a matter of right, and as such they were obliged to obey him; but—and this was the point—he could not condemn the *Augustinus* as a matter of fact because the Five Propositions were not to be found therein. Nevertheless, the Five Propositions, whether they existed or not, were judged to be heretical.

Innocent died in January 1655 and was succeeded by Alexander VII. Pope Alexander soon showed his colours by indulging the Jesuits on the question of the rites of indigenous peoples. He issued a decree in March 1656 supporting their tolerance in China of non-Christian ceremonies, and he waived the rule which would have obliged the Chinese clergy to read the office in Latin. This was in fact an example of what the Jansenists pointed to as the doctrinal dangers of papal power. For his own part, Alexander went further than

Innocent and ruled specifically that the Five Propositions were as a matter of fact to be found in the *Augustinus* (thus making the book itself a heretical work). Furthermore, in February 1665, in accordance with the French king's wishes, he ruled that all clergy were to subscribe to a formulary denouncing the Five Propositions and giving unequivocal support to papal sovereignty.

This was the climate in which Edmund O'Reilly became head of the church in Ireland in 1657. His mission was to maintain the Roman faith among his flock, and his opponents were Irish Jansenists in general and certain Franciscans in particular. The architect of concordance among the Jansenist party was the Franciscan Peter Walsh. Walsh had been a thorn in Rinuccini's side, and in the face of the nuncio's threat of excommunication the Franciscans themselves had split into supporters for and against the legality of the censure. Needless to say, the split expressed itself in racial terms, Walsh's followers being almost entirely Old English while the nuncio retained some Old English support and almost all that of the Gaelic Irish. This question of the legality of the censure was tailor-made to fit the great theological-political debates then raging in Paris. An appeal had been made to the theological faculty by the Supreme Council in the person of a Carmelite friar, John Rowe, who was on his way to Rome for the same purpose. Significantly, the faculty refused to make a decision. Rowe had the support in Paris of a prominent Jansenist priest from Cork, John Callaghan (who had been the Supreme Council's nominee for the see of Cork in 1646). The nuncio himself was not without support in Paris, his main spokesman being the Franciscan Paul King. In May 1649 King had published a pamphlet in Paris which was severely critical of all those who had opposed Rinuccini. Callaghan brought Jansenism directly into the debate when he wrote a powerful reply which stood throughout the 1650s as the definitive attack on the entire policy of the nuncio. Rinuccini's supporters had the book put on the Index in 1654, but the ban may not have been effective because the work was wrongly ascribed to Richard Bellings (who had written a similar defence of the Confederation published in Paris). Callaghan claimed that the Supreme Council's dealings with a Protestant monarchy were nothing new in history, and indeed the future Pope Alexander VII had not employed the great censure when he represented the Vatican at the negotiation of the Peace of Westphalia in 1648. Rinuccini was accused of subverting his spiritual power for political ends, and it was maintained that the proof of this was to be seen in his final criticisms of the Supreme Council, which were, according to Callaghan, purely political because religious toleration had already been secured. Thus the censures were illegal precisely because the nuncio used them to achieve ends which lay outside his spiritual mission. Moreover, the Supreme Council, far from wishing to abjure papal authority, had prepared a detailed appeal to the pope indicating the grounds upon which the censures were clearly illegal. If this appeal had not automatically suspended the censures until judgment was made, there would be no point in having the right of appeal at all; thus the appeal (which had not yet been answered) of itself suspended the censures, if only temporarily. This last point was a reasonable one, but it ignored the turbulence and extreme conflicts which had animated the divisions in Ireland. The fact of the matter was that while the appeal had not been heard, the validity of Rinuccini's authority would be maintained, and this, in effect, was a diplomatic rejection by the Vatican in what was, after all, a very acrimonious conflict between Catholics.

While the debate was clearly central to the political dimensions which were beginning to take shape around Jansenism, the whole question might never have got any nearer to a solution as far as Ireland was concerned if the Cromwellian regime in England had been erected on concrete foundations. The Puritan settlement of Ireland was remarkably successful, but this had everything to do with the unique disunity of the inhabitants rather than the constitutional integrity of the Cromwellian government in England. The Commonwealth did not last because it had no sovereignty other than a collective government ostensibly acting in the name of 'the people' but unwilling and unable to define precisely what that meant. The Commonwealth collapsed when it could neither justify its claim to sovereignty nor adequately answer the growing view that only Charles II could provide the necessary headship. Cromwell's death in 1658 signified the removal of a truly vital linch-pin from a wheel of the runaway Puritan bandwagon.

It may seem to have been one of the great injustices of Irish history that the Restoration did not result in the Catholic supporters of the Stuart cause being rewarded with the return of their lands, but that would be to presume that the restoration of the monarchy was a total one, which it was not. Charles I had attempted an Anglican settlement which was as religious as it was political. His failure left his sons disinclined to sacrifice their lives and kingdoms for the Book of Common Prayer. Instead Charles II and James II were to be noted for their reliance on Louis XIV for support against their non-Anglican opponents. This was the beginning of what was to become essentially a political division between Whig (as Nonconformist) and Tory (as Anglican), but its significance for Ireland was quite straightforward. Louis XIV's political catholicism had use for the Stuarts, and indeed would have had use for the Confederation had it survived. The Confederation had collapsed in the face of its own Catholic disunity, and it was the very success of papal supremacy that removed any real opportunity for a recovery. Louis was not wrong in thinking that papal supremacy and Spanish supremacy were closely connected, and he did not lose sight of the fact that his favourite order, the Jesuits, were a Spanish conception. Nevertheless, he managed to ride two horses simultaneously in Jesuit absolutism and Jansenist independence because his own aims embraced these. In his royal person Louis was the meeting-point of rigorous Gallican–Jansenist independence and Jesuit absolutist rationale. If there was a competition for the king's religion, he was clearly in a position to use one side against the other as no one else in Europe was in a position to do.

The offer by Rinuccini's supporters of a protectorate of Ireland to the Duke of Lorraine was symbolic of the competition for the political control of Catholicism which began in the 1650s. Naturally if the French king ever did decide to use Ireland and his fellow-Catholics there, he would not look to that branch which had supported Rinuccini. However, as the entire political base of the other branch had been thoroughly removed, Ireland might only be used as a source for troops or, as was also to happen, as a battlefield. Thus the difference between the interest which Louis XIV might take in Ireland was a very far cry from that which had been shown by Charles I. It followed also from this that any political initiatives taken from within Ireland would be thin and of no immediate importance. When the Kings of England were on the French payroll such questions as the Irish parliament's relation to the crown would be matters that seemed to belong to another century.

While such an overview was not possible for the principal actors in Ireland after the Restoration, one or two things were indisputable.

The Catholic Church had taken a logical and coherent decision to preserve the faith whatever the political climate. Equally, if ever progress was to be made by the old Confederate Catholics, it would have to be done in defiance of the papacy and done brazenly. Archbishop O'Reilly's report penned in July 1660 to the Vatican of his first diocesan inspection was a portent of things to come:

> While I was acting thus in the month of March a storm from hell suddenly arose and a trumpet sounded, proclaiming that I was an incendiary, inciting the people to rebellion, that I came therefore to this land to seduce the people from due obedience to the government (God is my witness that nothing was further from my thoughts). But the schismatic and motley crowd, according as it was influenced and changed, pronounced at one time that I was acting against the Anabaptists, at another against the Protestants, at another for the Anabaptists against the Presbyterians. Finally they cried that I was working against his most serene majesty the king. *Sed testis est mihi Deus quia non mentior!* It is the crowd which changed, not I, who only put before myself the glory of God, the increase of religion and obedience to the authority ordained by God (whosoever it might be) at least in those things which do not offend God.[1]

The reference in the letter to the Protestant sects related to charges made against O'Reilly at the Stuart court that he had rallied the Nonconformists and tried to get them to resist the Restoration; that he had promised them Gaelic Irish support; and that he was freeing his flock from their oath of allegiance to the Stuarts.

Before Charles II left the Netherlands for England he asked the Spanish ambassador to indicate to the Vatican that O'Reilly should be withdrawn because otherwise he would have to sign his death warrant. It took some time for word to reach the archbishop of his recall, and it was undoubtedly of no comfort to him that it came through the Jansenist Peter Walsh. He wrote to Walsh defending himself and asking for the latter's support. Walsh suggested to O'Reilly that he should live for two or three years in Rome, during which time he (Walsh) would see what he could do. Before his departure the Primate was obliged to nominate Walsh as his agent at court when the latter asked for a gesture of support for the king's restoration. This was actually the new state of affairs. Walsh and his followers became the acceptable face of Catholicism although they did not themselves enjoy papal support, whereas those who did would not have been recognised by Charles.

It must be remembered, however, that it was not Charles himself who wished to turn his back on the kind of staunch obedience that O'Reilly would undoubtedly have advocated. The problem was simply that the Stuart King of England was not now, nor was he ever again to be, master in his own house. After 1649 the monarchy came to represent not an end in itself but merely a means to an end. Unlike Charles I, the new king had never been in a position to act except under duress. Charles II was seven years of age when his father forced the Book of Common Prayer on the Scots, and from that time onwards his experience of politics was bound up with buying and selling. In many respects he was the personal antithesis of his father, just as his development had taken place under equally opposite conditions. The new king was under no illusions whatsoever about his position, and as the constitutional crisis of his reign progressed he declared himself certain that he would not be killed as long as his Catholic brother was next in line.

————————

The king's new government in Ireland was characterised throughout the 1660s by Ormond's attempts to retain control for the king against his opponents at court, and his recall in 1669 was due to this, rather than maladministration or disloyalty. The rise of faction and later of parties in England meant that the nature of office-holding had changed because the whole constitutional balance had begun to shift in favour of the subject rather than the crown. Many characteristics of eighteenth-century Ireland (including Dublin's façade) have their origin in the 1660s, although the pattern was to be interrupted by the short and impossible reign of Louis's puppet, the Catholic James. To call James a French puppet may seem to exaggerate the case, but the facts speak for themselves. When he championed Catholicism James did not receive the support of the pope, and at the famous Battle of the Boyne it was William of Orange who had Vatican support precisely because French and Anglican Catholicism was not Roman. James did not under any guise represent Rome rule, and indeed owed his position to the opposite view that Catholicism should be independent. Nor is it incomprehensible that the Vatican should give tacit (if not actual) support to William of Orange. Like Cromwell, William stood for religious toleration, and there was great potential and scope for precisely that if the political conflict could be averted.

It was Louis's political intolerance and his overt use of clerical office that was the problem.

If Ulster Presbyterians ever believed that it was 'popery' that laid siege to Derry in 1689, they would themselves become the victims of history (as must all who believe that emotional slogans are superior to facts). 'Popery' was the only convenient rallying-cry of all who feared James II, but it missed the vital French content of the king's policy. It was an eighteenth-century French environment that produced the very republicanism which saw the United Irishmen founded by Belfast Protestants. Republicanism grew within French Catholicism precisely because the latter was not Roman. In 1689 the inhabitants of Derry were indeed under threat from a great Catholic force, and they may well have felt that Cromwell's revenge of the 1641 massacres was now about to be revenged upon them; but this was not Rome rule. This was a small Anglo-Catholic king acting on behalf of a great French-Catholic king in the hope that he could rule Ireland for France because he certainly could not rule England. If James had won the Battle of the Boyne, he would have had to hold Ireland in a perpetual war against England, something which had never been done and could never have been done. At any time England's Irish problem was a problem of security; once this was taken care of, Ireland's Irish problem could go its own way. The last two Stuart kings, however, were bent upon using the great Irish religious force for other than religious ends.

The powers that restored Charles II to England in 1660 had a great stake in the continuation of stability in Ireland, and this was expressed by a growing tendency to rule the country from London. Although the Irish parliament was now in Protestant hands, those hands were largely Cromwellian. The new owners would be allowed to keep Ireland (so long as they kept it secure), but they could not be allowed to aspire to being a sovereign government. Here was the beginning of the exclusion of the Irish Protestants from the English settlement precisely because they represented only a fragment of what aspired to be the new English constitution. This was the very problem which the Old English had had to face, but the rewards were considerable. Those who would rule Ireland for England—without raising impossible constitutional questions—could keep it for as long as they could hold it. This was, of course, an anomalous situation, but Ireland had always been an anomaly after Henry VIII became both King of Ireland and an enemy of the pope. The Old English had been Roman Catholics who were obliged to make a theological sacrifice to the crown, but in this they were no different to the New English, before and after Cromwell. The history of the Established Church in Ireland was also the history of compromise as Calvinist bent before episcopacy in order to gain and retain possession. The consequences for Ireland of either compromise were profound. Roman Catholicism was to preserve its religious identity at the expense of a secular culture, while the Protestant ascendancy was to sacrifice its religious integrity and settle for public cultural display. Both, of course, took place simultaneously and produced the criss-cross image of rural stagnation and Dublin sophistication which characterised the eighteenth century. The façade was indeed brilliant, and the hidden Ireland was indeed devoted, but the twain were never destined to meet. It must be said, however, that the world did benefit greatly from this cultural schizophrenia. The Protestant Anglo-Irish were to become a marvel of creative brilliance until the Catholics eventually came into possession, while on the other hand Ireland became one of the great bulwarks of Catholicism and an unending source of supply for the religious mission abroad.

The only group in Ireland who did not compromise and thus did not have either their identity or their energies divided were the Ulster Presbyterians. The Presbyterians in both Scotland and Ulster had an incalculable effect on the seventeenth-century crisis because they themselves were quite sure of what they wanted and what they might have to do to achieve it. They had a great advantage over the vacillating English Nonconformists and the equally compromised Confederate Catholics. While they could never have achieved complete success, they were not slow to take whatever advantage was offered in this direction, and the Scots' agreement with Charles II was the first great step. To some extent they succeeded in Scotland, where Presbyterianism eventually became the established church, but this could not have happened in Ireland, although as a group they were to be characterised by unshakable unity of purpose and great industry. It was this industry which was to give the Presbyterians a stake in Irish parliamentary independence and unite them economically with the established post-Cromwellian ascendancy and the Old English themselves. If any unity other than economic interest was possible, it was to be found in the religious exclusivity and predestinarianism of Jansenism and Calvinism.

The first moves towards Irish political independence were made in the 1660s when the English government began to view Ireland as a dependent rather than a satellite state. Just as Charles II could not be an old-style King of England (or Ireland), it followed that Ireland's constitutional claims would need to be equally compromised. For example, Irish exports of cattle to England were prohibited by an act of the English parliament in 1663 (and extended in 1667) which also set a limit on Irish trade with the colonies (which was further restricted in 1671). It was this particular approach to Ireland that gave rise to a movement for Irish parliamentary independence—first by the new Protestant ascendancy and later by the descendants of the old Confederate Catholics who wished to regain their constitutional position (and later again by the Protestant ascendancy when it regained control). On the continent Jansenism and Calvinism were to have much in common as both became the focus of anti-papal and anti-monarchical philosophies, so that the eighteenth century was witness to an otherwise impossible marriage between American Calvinist and French Catholic revolutionary doctrines. The king who stood out against all claims to independence, papal or otherwise, and who dominated the late seventeenth-century conflict was Louis XIV. Like Charles I, however, he could not be content while surrounded by those who did not recognise the essence of his authority. If Louis survived and succeeded politically, his success would inevitably draw the whole of western Europe into his great battle for monarchical and religous unity. As on so many other occasions, Ireland was to be the last outpost of Europe to be directly involved; and as on many other occasions also, it was to bear the brunt of European development without sharing the circumstances which gave rise to that development.

10

Ideologies
in Conflict, 1660-91

AFTER Archbishop O'Reilly's departure from Ireland his opponents lost no time in drawing up a full declaration of loyalty to the king which did not baulk at the question of papal supremacy. While Peter Walsh solicited support from Irish bishops living on the continent, so too did O'Reilly in an effort to oppose this loyal formulary. Now exiled in Rome and faced with a grave split in his Irish church, the archbishop's prescription for Ireland was pointed. All clergy loyal to the Vatican should be ordered to return to Ireland to serve the church. Furthermore, and in anticipation of his own replacement (who was to be Oliver Plunkett), O'Reilly advocated a new type of hierarchy:

> It is necessary that in our larger provinces, namely Armagh and Cashel, an archbishop and two bishops should be appointed in each; in the smaller provinces, Dublin and Tuam, an archbishop and at least one bishop. In the remaining juris-dictions let vicars apostolic be appointed, all of them men who are learned, proven, saintly, of good family, zealous for the Apostolic See and obedient to the royal majesty, not schis-matics, parasites or gnathons.[1]

Nor was the Primate blind to the personal consequences of such a renewal and struck a prophetic note for his successor:

> But some more timid men, who have never experienced per-secution, may say [that] if the number of bishops is increased, a storm of persecution will commence. But this is not likely; and even if persecution arises, who shall suffer except the person only who is bishop? Those are the fears of children. The blood of martyrs is the seed of Christians. The church is not lessened by persecutions but increased.[2]

As far as the royal supremacy was concerned, O'Reilly was equally under no illusions:

> Either the king honours and loves the Catholic faith or he does not. If he honours and loves it, he will give it connivance, and hence it cannot be argued by the Puritans that what is done is done without his knowledge and consent. If he does not love it, it is not proper to await his consent: we must obey God rather than men.[3]

This was a clear resolution of the question of sovereignty as far as the Catholic Church in Ireland was concerned. It followed, however, that those who disagreed would not do so half-heartedly. In early anticipation of the charges that would be made against Oliver Plunkett, O'Reilly was accused in 1663 of planning to bring an army of 25,000 men to Ireland.

Despite these groundless accusations, O'Reilly managed to establish a new foundation for Catholicism in Ireland for the very reason that his fellow-Catholic opponents were busy trying to reconcile their political with their religious allegiance. The restoration of the Stuarts raised as yet unanswered constitutional questions, but the remedy sought both in England and Ireland was the *modus vivendi* of party and faction. This meant that those Catholics in Ireland who supported the Stuarts would undoubtedly enjoy greater toleration than those who remained loyal to the papacy, but it also meant that they were pinning their religious hopes on the fate of a now purely political monarchy (and one which was increasingly dependent upon Louis XIV for support). Thus factional control in England can be related directly to the government of Ireland: Ormond served as Lord Lieutenant from 1662 to 1669, but was replaced by the Presbyterian Lord Robartes from 1669 to 1670; Robartes was replaced by the pro-Catholic Lord Berkeley, who in turn was replaced in 1672 by the Earl of Essex; Essex lasted until 1677, when Ormond again took over and remained in office until the end of the reign.

Archbishop O'Reilly represented what Oliver Plunkett was not to be. Plunkett was to be an instrument of an essentially European Counter-Reformation. As such he was fully in accord with O'Reilly's dedication to Rome, but Plunkett's appointment in 1669 occurred after another great Vatican shift towards France. Popes who took the name of Clement were generally open to French rather than Spanish influence and the period 1667-76 saw the reigns of Clement IX and Clement X. Where O'Reilly looked to the lowest common denominator to define the new church, Plunkett represented the view that the Counter-Reformation would have to iron out all differences but at the same time keep the sympathy of the king. What this meant in effect was that O'Reilly looked to the vitality of the Gaelic Irish church, while Plunkett favoured the fully reformed European model. The appointment of bishops is one example of the difference between the two men: O'Reilly favoured vigorous maintenance of the episcopal sees regardless of local difficulties; Plunkett, on the other hand, urged the Vatican to restrain its policy of appointing bishops, since conditions were such that they would have to live beneath their dignity and would thus discredit their status.

O'Reilly must rank as one of the great archbishops of Ireland, if only because he was one of the very few people who truly understood that the Irish church could neither be Jansenist, as Walsh would have had it, or European, as Plunkett would have wished. This meant that a great deal of flexibility would have to be employed, but this had always been the only successful policy in Ireland. The Catholics and their clergy were being divided in a great European debate in which they had no direct interest. O'Reilly returned to Ireland in 1666 to oppose Walsh's Loyal Remonstrance, but he permitted his clergy to sign a qualified document which also included three (out of six) Jansenist propositions which had been declared valid in Paris. This was not what he personally wished to do, but it was a compromise which freed the church from the internal threat posed by Ormond in the guise of Walsh. This was a considerable achievement for a man who had only been allowed to return on condition that he did what he was told, and the Lord Lieutenant was not pleased:

> The meeting of the Romish clergy is now dissolved, but without their having subscribed to the Remonstrance or to anything of like force. The titular Primate is a juggler and seems to deny that he knew of any condition whereupon he was permitted to come over. My purpose is to send him back again, after some time in which it may be discerned whether he had not some worse purpose in his coming.[4]

The archbishop returned to the continent, where he died two years later. His realistic compromise did not please his critics, nor indeed was his general policy continued by Oliver Plunkett. It was not until the entire Catholic political cause had collapsed that the Vatican allowed the Irish church of the eighteenth century to base itself on local Irish conditions.

Throughout the 1660s and 1670s English politics were dominated by a conflict between the Cavaliers and a combination of Presbyterians and old Cromwellians; between the Anglicans and the Nonconformists, the pro-French and the pro-Dutch. It was only on his deathbed in February 1685 that Charles II declared himself a Roman Catholic. He was succeeded by his brother James II, who had converted in 1673. The religious sympathies of both kings were extraneous to the factions which surrounded them, but they were at the same time an intrinsic part of the constitutional question which the Stuarts had posed since early in the century. A great deal had changed as a result of the civil war, and a great deal had also been settled as far as the government of the country was concerned. The problem was no longer that Charles or James were Anglican, it was that they were pro-French Catholic. In 1670 Charles signed two treaties with Louis. The first was secret; Charles agreed to do all he could to restore Roman Catholicism in return for financial support. The second treaty committed England to an alliance against the Dutch. This was a French rather than an English policy. There had, it is true, been great rivalry between the Dutch and the English throughout the century, and a war with the Dutch was nothing new. It was France's vast ambitions, however, that made the Treaties of Dover a grave threat to English national security, since it was the intention of France to destroy more than Dutch economic superiority. A victory for Louis against the Dutch would not be a matter of a treaty; it would be the French occupation of Holland and the end of a great Protestant bulwark in Europe. In March 1672 England went to war against the Dutch, not for economic interest but as part of Charles's bargain with Louis. In the same month Charles announced a Declaration of Indulgence in favour of Nonconformists and Roman Catholics, while a few months later Presbyterian ministers in Ireland received a royal stipend. Charles was playing for the support of Dissenters against the Anglicans and simultaneously slipping in religious toleration for Catholics. This was the formula employed more openly by James in the late 1680s, and it raised the vital question of what the Stuarts thought they would do with the Anglicans they were so assiduously alienating.

They had an answer, but it could never have been a solution: it was hoped that the Anglicans could be drawn into a Catholic alliance with France—in other words, that Gallicanism and Anglicanism would fuse into a new non-Roman-dominated monarchical religion. Three considerations were omitted from this unreal hope: first, that the Nonconformists who had fought and won a civil war would accept the imposition; secondly, that Anglicanism was nothing other than a fragment of Roman Catholicism waiting to be brought back into the light; and thirdly, that the entire English political nation would willingly agree to be a dependent state in a new French empire. There was yet another, wholly untested, assumption: that English Catholics would automatically declare their allegiance to the king and not to Rome.

England was not behind Charles, but that did not stop him signing another secret treaty with Louis in 1676 whereby in return for a subsidy he agreed not to negotiate with any power without French approval. The king's policy brought about the collapse of his ministerial government and caused him to revoke the Declaration of Indulgence. The problem was not just one of policy, however. Charles had supervised the establishment of a standing army which by the mid-1670s was several thousand strong, and he had done this in the teeth of opposition from both Nonconformists and Anglicans. Furthermore, he had no legitimate son, and the next in line was James, whose religion was by then publicly known. A crisis was approaching unless Charles would agree to facilitate the country by compromising his own and his brother's legitimate position, and this he was remarkably unwilling to do.

Developments in Ireland kept pace with the precarious rise of Stuart Catholicism. Richard Talbot, James's personal friend, became the official spokesman of the Old English Catholics when he presented a petition to Charles on their behalf in January 1671. Both houses of the English parliament responded with an address to the king which warned of the dangers of popery and of Irish popery in particular. The advent of the pro-French popes Clement IX and Clement X which spanned the years 1667-76 saw some significant Old English episcopal appointments. The most notable of these were Oliver Plunkett to Armagh, Peter Talbot (Richard's brother) to Dublin, and Patrick Tyrrell to Clogher. Plunkett and Tyrrell came up against fierce Gaelic opposition. Although Old English, Oliver Plunkett as the new head of the church in Ireland was successor to Edmund O'Reilly in one important respect. O'Reilly had proved himself capable of working under almost any political regime in order to maintain the essentially Roman and anti-Jansenist nature of

Catholicism in Ireland. Plunkett's mission was undertaken by different, more sophisticated, means, but towards the same end. O'Reilly's solution would have been to revitalise the church from the bottom upwards, and in doing so cognisance would have been taken of the Gaelic position. Plunkett favoured an approach from the top downwards, and it was not long before he suffered the fate of all who believed that any such approach had ever worked in any area of life in Ireland.

As Bishop of Clogher, Patrick Tyrrell came up against the problem raised by his own appointment over that of Gaelic Irish candidates, the most notable being Phelim O'Neill, the Franciscan son of the late Gaelic leader. By the 1670s the church in Ireland had split three ways: pro-Jansenist, pro-Jesuit, and Gaelic Irish. The Gaelic Irish group were to be found in the Ulster province in general and in south Armagh in particular. This was no accident, for Armagh was the seat of religious sovereignty in Ireland, so that if and when outside reform was instituted, it would be done by and through the Primate, and his first target would have to be his own immediate diocese.

Oliver Plunkett was tireless in the cause of the Counter-Reformation. The problem was contained in his proposed solution, however. Not content to effect religious change, he made great personal efforts to encourage Gaelic Irish dissidents (known loosely as tories) to leave the country in large numbers. In this he was blind to the significance which his Gaelic flock attached to survival 'on the run'. In one respect or another the Ulster Irish had been 'on the run' since Chichester and Davies introduced the king's writ into the province in the first decade of the century. In another respect Gaelic Irish culture was fluid in its concepts and lifestyle, and as such had always been well served by the Franciscans. Plunkett was a man of order and demonstrated this when he decided a major dispute between the Franciscans and Dominicans in favour of the latter. Whether he was aware of the fire he was feeding, or whether he was simply naïve is a matter of conjecture. No one could have doubted his patent sincerity and courage, but by the 1670s the Ulster Irish had nothing left but their personal religion. In 1677 Bishop Tyrrell wrote to Rome: 'Two of my priests, Ardle Matthews and Bernard Connolly, were recently sentenced to a year's imprisonment for exercising papal jurisdiction. The case occasioned great scandal among Catholics, for another priest was mainly responsible for it.'[5]

Just before Edmund O'Reilly died in March 1669 four new bishops were nominated to Ireland: Peter Talbot to be Archbishop of Dublin, and William Burgat, James Lynch and James O'Phelan to Cashel, Tuam and Ossory respectively. They chose as their representative in Rome Oliver Plunkett. O'Reilly's ability to work with the Cromwellians and then later with Ormond himself had prompted the Lord Lieutenant to describe him as a juggler. The appointment of the new bishops was not to be an exercise in balance, but rather a process of ironing out the question of sovereignty still left unanswered among the clergy since the time of Rinuccini. That is to say that Jansenist Catholicism had been using loyalty to the English as a rallying-point, and now it was time for Roman Catholicism to answer by itself declaring its loyalty to the king. O'Reilly had been the first to face the problem, but in trying to embrace more than one side he weakened the authority of Rome itself. What would have to be done now would be to reassert Roman authority while at the same time stressing temporal loyalty to the English crown. The great turning-point was when Charles II agreed to concede the validity of the censures, and thus a union took place between the Catholic Church and the King of England. The two Catholic groups who could be expected to oppose this new union would be the Jansenists themselves and the Ulster Irish clergy particularly served by the Franciscans, because this latter group would have to be reformed as a matter of course. On the one hand the new policy would have to outdo the Jansenists in loyalty, while on the other it would have to insist on the decrees of the Council of Trent. This was quite an undertaking, as events were to prove.

The new Archbishop of Dublin wrote to Oliver Plunkett in May 1669:

> I was consecrated in Antwerp on Sunday last and I now return in haste to London to meet Peter Walsh and oppose his infamous efforts against God, the king and his country; although he pretends nothing but allegiance to the king, I know that this is only a mantle with which such plotters ever seek to mask their evil designs.[6]

By this time the problem was acute in that opposition to the validity of the Rinuccini censures had grown so great among the Catholic clergy that the Vatican was finding it hard to cope because the king himself had agreed to uphold the censures. Talbot went on:

> I have heard that a memorial was presented to the Sacred Con-

gregation, or to the Holy Father, soliciting the power to absolve those who incurred the censures of Rinuccini; this would occasion great disorder, as there is a rigorous edict of the king against all who ask for such an absolution; and I believe it is not the desire of the Sacred Congregation that any noise should be made in this matter. It is well that we should have the power of absolving *in coro conscientiae* all such as have any scruples on this head, but it would be unwise to send any public document to that effect. In the province of Armagh there is such confusion that I suppose an archbishop will soon be appointed.[7]

Clearly the archbishop was against lifting the censures. He had a problem, however, when, before his views were made known by Oliver Plunkett to the Sacred Congregation, the power was granted to the Irish bishops to absolve those censured. Talbot had not wanted the Vatican to acknowledge officially that there was a problem at all, but now that they had done so he would have to change his tactic quickly:

I have received letters of Your Eminence dated 27 April, by which faculty is granted to absolve all who solicit absolution from the censures fulminated by Rinuccini. I embrace with due obedience and humility the paternal goodness of His Holiness; but it seems to me that the publication of such a faculty would be attended with great danger, as it was enacted by a law of the king and parliament of Ireland, that anyone asking to be absolved from the censures of Rinuccini should be incapable of aquiring property or receiving any inheritance, and by far the greater number of Catholics applaud this law; nor do I remember anyone having had recourse for absolution from these censures to those who formerly received a like faculty; for all, with one accord, attribute the ruin of our country to the divisions occasioned by these censures. Nor are they the ignorant alone who say this, but even the greater part of the clergy, secular and regular, warmly contend that the censures were invalid. Wherefore it surprises me how a petition to absolve from them could be presented to His Holiness in the name of the Catholic bishops of Ireland. I indeed deem it very proper that we should have power to absolve in the tribunal of penance all such as recur to us; but should this become known, the whole hierarchy of Ireland would be exposed to great risk and the Irish laity would be compelled to declare by public document that they never gave any commission to have such a request forwarded to His Holiness. Whereof I think it expedient, and I stated so to His Excellency the internuncio, that this faculty should be given by word of mouth to the arch-bishops, but that the letters of Your Eminence should in no wise be transmitted to Ireland, till such time as an answer may be received to this difficulty, which with due submission I propose.[8]

This was a twofold approach: the validity of the censures would be denied, and so the bishops would not need the power of absolution; while at the same time that very power would be granted verbally, but only to the archbishops. In other words, the only way to solve the problem was from the top downwards, and this was to be the new keynote. Talbot got his way shortly afterwards when the written faculty of absolution went unpublished. In the meantime Archbishop Talbot worked with his agent Oliver Plunkett in Rome to remove at every turn the influence enjoyed by Peter Walsh. At the same time Talbot held out to Walsh the open invitation to rejoin the orthodoxy. For his part, Walsh expressed a willingness, but never seemed to act on it. The willingness itself would seem only to have been due to the fact that as the Restoration proceeded and as the Vatican extended O'Reilly's policy of complete loyalty to England, Walsh and the Irish Jansenists began to lose ground. By 1670 they had lost the protection of the English queen-mother, Ormond had left office, and they were faced with a formidable opponent when Oliver Plunkett was appointed to Armagh on 14 July 1669.

The commitment of the new Archbishop of Armagh was clear within weeks of his arrival in Ireland in March 1670. Within six weeks he had held two synods, performed two ordinations and administered confirmation to over ten thousand people (and estimated that in his province alone there were more than five times that amount as yet unconfirmed). On his way to Ireland through London he noted the sympathetic climate at court and its effect on the government of Ireland:

I found that four of the principal persons in court were secretly Catholics, and these maintain the viceroy in his favourable sentiments and esteem for the Catholics; so much so that not long since he wrote a long letter to the king in favour of the Irish clergy, declaring that they were good subjects and worthy of the favours of His Majesty.[9]

While this general sympathy at court could be relied upon as far as it went, it did not extend to the factional changes in the English government which came to be represented in Dublin. Ormond, who had been a supporter of Walsh, was replaced by Robartes. who favoured the new hierarchy but who was himself replaced almost immediately by Berkeley, whose instructions were clear:

> Several popish clergy, since the return of the Duke of Ormond hither, have exercised their jurisdiction, to the great grief of the Remonstrants. If so, execute the laws against the titular archbishops, bishops and vicars-general that have threatened or excommunicated the Remonstrants; and see that you protect such Remonstrants as have not withdrawn their subscriptions.[10]

This concentration on the hierarchy was as Edmund O'Reilly had predicted, but by its nature the policy was not concerned with the ordinary practice of religion but with the question of loyalty. Thus court faction in the early period of the Restoration did not produce persecution, and Berkeley's brief was not intended to curtail the new Primate if the latter maintained his loyalties to England. It was clear that what the Remonstrants under Walsh offered could also be offered by the orthodox hierarchy and be equally, or even more, acceptable for the simple reason that the greater the temporal loyalty of Roman Catholicism the easier Ireland would be to rule. Thus Plunkett could write of Berkeley:

> The viceroy himself privately treats some members of the clergy with great courtesy, exhorting them to live peaceably, without tumult and without meddling in state matters, attending solely to their ecclesiastical functions, on which condition he promises them every protection; and indeed it seems that this protection will be afforded should that condition be fulfilled.[11]

To the pope he wrote: 'We experience in this kingdom, Holy Father, the benign influence of the King of England in favour of the Catholics, so that all enjoy great liberty and ease.'[12]

A declaration of loyalty to the king was drawn up at the synod of bishops called by the new Primate in June 1670. In shifting the emphasis away from the question of the pope's jurisdiction, which the Jansenists concentrated upon, the new loyalty had a clear Jesuit bias:

We, Your Majesty's subjects, the clergy of the Roman Catholic Church, do hereby declare and solemnly protest before God and his angels, that we own and acknowledge Your Majesty to be our lawful king and the undoubted monarch, as well of this realm of Ireland as of all other Your Majesty's dominions; and consequently we confess ourselves bound in conscience to be obedient to Your Majesty in all civil and temporal affairs as far as any other subjects can or ought to be to their princes, as the laws of God and nature require from us; and therefore we promise that we, during life, will inviolably bear true allegiance to Your Majesty, your lawful heirs and successors, and that no power on earth shall be able to withdraw us from our duty herein; and that we will, even to the loss of life and property, if occasion requires, assert and defend Your Majesty's rights against all that shall invade the same, or attempt to deprive Your Majesty, your lawful heirs and successors, of any part thereof. And in order that this, our sincere protestation may more clearly appear, we further declare the doctrine to be false and intolerable which teaches that any private subject may lawfully kill his prince, the anointed of God. Wherefore, deeply persuaded of the abominable and sad consequences which ensue from its practice, we oblige ourselves to discover unto Your Majesty or some of your ministers any attempts of that kind or rebellions against Your Majesty's person, crown or royal authority, which may come to our knowledge, that thus such horrid evils may be prevented. In fine, as we hold the aforesaid things to be just and agreeable to good consciences, so we will preach them, and seek to inculcate them on our respective flocks, ready to confirm them with our oaths.[13]

In this declaration can be seen the seeds of the Titus Oates plot as it related to Ireland. As far as the new Roman hierarchy was concerned, there was a great deal in common between the predestinarian Catholic Jansenists and the predestinarian Calvinist Protestants, both of whom could look upon the king himself as already beyond salvation and thus a legitimate target. This worked both ways, however, and a plot could easily be concocted in London which showed that the Jesuit-supporting Oliver Plunkett was planning a French invasion of Ireland for the Stuarts, helped by the Jesuits both in London and Paris.

It should not need to be mentioned, but may be stated nevertheless: there was no attempt whatsoever on the part of Oliver Plunkett to bring French soldiers to Ireland. The whole basis of his mission was to demonstrate just how loyal the Catholics could be. For example, Berkeley only retained office for two years and was replaced by the Earl of Essex, who, although he did not have Berkeley's sympathies, joined the latter in seeking a pardon for the Primate after Plunkett's trial; the reason for seeking the pardon being that the Primate could not possibly have betrayed England as was alleged.

The conflicts which were to make Oliver Plunkett a martyr had far more to do with the internal Catholic struggles of Ireland than with English or French politics. Although the archbishop's problems centred around the Franciscans, the latter were by no means the only ones affected by the conflict bequeathed to Ireland by Archbishop Rinuccini. In April 1671 Plunkett wrote that 'The good Archbishop of Tuam was imprisoned anew during the past Lent, on the accusations of [the Augustinian] Martin French, and was found guilty of *praemunire*—that is, of exercising foreign jurisdiction.'[14] The way in which the Primate dealt with this was significant of his general policy and his total personal commitment. The Archbishop of Tuam, freed from prison, himself wrote:

> [French] had recourse to the most illustrious Lord Primate, who freed him from censures, and more than once notified the same to us by letters, praying also and beseeching us that we would admit to our communion this man, no longer subject to censures or irregularities, and that we would cast every fault, if there were any, upon his own [i.e. the Primate's] shoulders; and to this testimony we have given every credence.[15]

This was a good example of the way in which Oliver Plunkett took personal responsibility for solving the religious conflict. The obvious danger, however, was that a feeling might take hold among the opposition that if the Primate was somehow to be removed, things would return to normal. Unlike O'Reilly, however, the new Primate was single-minded and continually made certain that his actions had the backing of Rome; this made his removal by ordinary means far more difficult.

The official climate of toleration in which the Primate worked in the early 1670s was precarious. By the end of 1673 it was becoming more directly related to English politics than previously, as the House of Commons unsuccessfully tried to prevent the future James II from contracting a Catholic marriage. In February and March the house overruled the Declaration of Indulgence and passed a test act specifying the taking of the Anglican sacrament by all office-holders. Moreover, the fear of Catholicism among the English public was becoming irrational in that it was perceived as being a visible threat at the head of the government, but one which somehow had no body. This was the natural environment for plots and conspiracies based on the great unknown. Commenting on this in a report to his superiors, the Primate noted that the Commons had desired 'that no Catholic should reside within five miles of London, and that all Catholics should have some distinctive mark, as the Jews in Rome'. This comparison of the treatment of the Jews in Rome with what might be done to Catholics in London was an ominous one for Archbishop Plunkett himself in that it suggested the development of real hysteria which might easily be turned to effect.

This did not daunt him in his reforms, however, and in particular in tackling the problem, as he saw it, of the Franciscan mission in Ireland. Franciscans with Jansenist leanings such as Walsh had a great deal of influence among the Old English community in general and with the government in particular. The order also spanned the entire Gaelic culture, however, so that the Franciscans posed a considerable obstacle to a man who had personally introduced the Jesuits into Armagh. The first obstacle to reform was the government of the order itself. The Primate's solution was that the Irish Franciscan province should be divided into two, with Ulster and Connacht being a separate province from Leinster and Munster. In this he was attempting to isolate the Gaelic element in order to encourage its reform and to increase his own chances of doing so by splitting the opposition. In a report to Rome in September 1672 he spelt out the problem:

> It is ambition that prevents their consenting to a division of the province, although they are sure, as many of them declared to myself, that it would be a source of perpetual peace to themselves and to others. The constant dissensions of the Franciscans have for many years disturbed the spiritual tranquillity of this kingdom, and they still disturb it, and occasion great scandal to our flock, and to our adversaries. They sometimes even bring their trials before the secular tribunals. They make such a medley of novices, without education or virtue and without any selection, that it is no wonder that scandals arise. They should send their novices to be trained at Louvain or

Prague or Rome. They have here about seventy convents, which in a kingdom with only one provincial, cannot easily be governed. The Commissaries, Father James Darcy and Father John Brady, get up factions here lest any division be made. They have now the rod of government in their hands, and they hope to always have a finger in the management of matters, and they would sooner have it extend to the whole kingdom than to half. In three years it will fall to Armagh to have the provincial, and this Brady is morally certain that he shall be elected; and hence, he now does all in his power to prevent a division, for he wishes to govern all and not a part. It was once commanded in their provincial chapter that the province should be divided, but the war and other events prevented the decree from being carried into effect. Monsignore, I pray you not to attend to the complaints or threats of difficulties which some will propose against this division. Let a brief be published ordering the division to be made, so that Ulster and Connacht form one province, and Leinster and Munster another, and all difficulties will at once disappear.[16]

In the meantime rumours began to abound that the Primate was actually preaching against the friars and that he had ruled that the four lesser orders in Ireland should take precedence over the Franciscans, both of which rumours he denied; nevertheless, he made it clear that he had no intention of altering his course:

The Franciscans alone have twelve or thirteen novitiates in the one province of Armagh; imagine then, how many there are in the other provinces.... I write continually on this matter because I see the great necessity there is for it, and I fear that a great tempest will one day arise, unless a remedy be soon applied to this root of many future disorders.[17]

The great tempest did indeed arise, but the problem was whether the Franciscans, as one of the greatest orders within the church, and one which in Ireland spanned both communities and had served since the beginning of the thirteenth century, could simply be overruled because the new Primate had the power to do so. The quality which characterised the Irish Franciscans above all else was passion, and while this was not one which the Primate would have put higher than reason, he himself was driven by his beliefs: 'Nothing stands in such need of reformation. I tire Your Excelellency and Their Eminences with so many letters but "the zeal of the house of God hath eaten me up".[18] Writing from prison in 1680 after his arrest for high treason, the Primate described the extent of the conflict as it had existed in 1674:

> I am consoled by hearing of the calumnies of an apostate friar, Anthony Daly, *dimidium animae* of Father Phelim O'Neill. This Father Anthony sought to take away my life here, instigating the tories to kill me. They came at midnight about six years ago to the house of my vicar-general, where I then was. They broke open the doors and took away all the money from myself and my vicar-general, and my secretary, Michael Plunket, who is now in Rome, and they held a sword to my throat. The chief of this band was afterwards taken, and before death declared in prison to the parish priest of Armagh and to his curate, that Father Anthony told him to kill me and that afterwards he would give him absolution. The curate, Patrick O'Donnelly, is now in Paris and before embarking swore this in the presence of the Bishop of Clogher. I have in my possession a letter written by the same Anthony, in which he says: 'If God tried to injure the Franciscan order, I would rise up against God.'... I suspended him from preaching and hearing the confessions of the laity.... He nevertheless continued to preach and to hear confessions sacrilegiously.[19]

The Primate not only sought to reform the Franciscan order and to divide it in two; he also advocated the appointment as its minister provincial the Old English Franciscan Bishop of Clogher, Patrick Tyrrell. Tyrrell had already encountered great opposition among the local Gaelic clergy to his appointment to Clogher; what opposition he might have encountered on a wider scale could only have been even greater again. The point at issue was not that Tyrrell, as a Franciscan, could not become head of the Irish order; it was the conflict of authority and the thrust behind the possible appointment. Similarly, Plunkett sought preferment for Cornelius Daly on being satisfied that the Franciscan was no longer a Jansenist. The Primate was fully aware of what was at stake, but so too were the Irish Franciscans, as was explained to him clearly by one of their leaders, Phelim (or Felix) O'Neill: 'Father Felix O'Neill explains the propositions that he made use of, that, forsooth, the flock is not bound to support the parish priest and that His Holiness could not suppress the order of St Francis.'[20] In its simplest form, this was where Jansenism united with the uniqueness, in European terms, of Gaelic culture; and this marriage had naturally taken place within the Irish Franciscan order.

The Primate wished to eradicate all but Roman influences among the educated clergy as the best defence against Jansenism. He wrote: 'It is worthy of remark that no priest educated in Rome adhered to Peter Walsh of the Remonstrance, but only those from France and Belgium; and hence out of the 150 boys I have here at school I would wish to select half a dozen of the best and send them to Rome.'[21] Meanwhile the educational emphasis within Ireland would be a Jesuit one. Thus Plunkett wrote to his superiors:

> I have received your most welcome letter of 2 September [1672] and this whole kingdom is indebted to you for the stipend procured for the Jesuits. They do a great deal of good; they have in Drogheda, in my diocese, 160 students. Oh what toils had I to undergo, what efforts had I to make, to sustain them! How many memorials were forwarded to the viceroy and supreme council against me and against them; and they give the more annoyance to our adversaries because they are in Drogheda (i.e. Pòntana) only four hours' journey from Dublin, where no Catholic school is allowed. And then to have there the Jesuits, whom they hate above all others, was the greatest eyesore possible; but now the very adversaries caress both me and them, in order to have permission for their children to come to them; and in reality, many Protestant boys come to them belonging to the principal families, who afterwards assist us in defending them.[22]

Here was the problem as far as laxity was concerned. The Jesuits were criticised precisely because they could attract Protestant children and be supported by the Protestants. It was the very Jesuit ability to survive among the heretics which gave rise to doubts as to their true nature. Throughout the 1670s the English public came increasingly to associate Rome rule with the Jesuits. The great irony was that the Jesuits looked to French conflicts for their grounding, and in so doing they were loyal in politics not to Rome but to Louis XIV. The problem was not their religious devotion to Rome; it was their ability to reconcile this with one of Rome's great opponents, the Catholic Louis.

Time was running out for the Primate, however, because the accession of one of the seventeenth century's greatest popes, Innocent XI, in September 1676 (he reigned until August 1689) brought to an end the pro-French policies of the Vatican and consequently any official support for the pro-Louis Jesuits. This meant in effect that the Vatican tide would turn for the Irish Franciscans, though they would still be faced on the ground with their great reforming opponent. When the opportunity presented itself in 1679 to remove the Primate as part of a great anti-Jesuit plot in England, the temptation was too much for certain Franciscans from south Armagh, who walked to London to testify against him. This was not in any way indicative of personal hatred; on the contrary, it was a testimony of the passion which the Gaelic Irish had for their cultural and religious identity. Since the arrival of the Normans they had been defined not in terms of what they were, but in terms of what they were not. This had never proved to be a successful way of eradicating an identity.

The provincial synod convened by Archbishop Plunkett at Ard-patrick in August 1678 was the high point of the reform movement; it took place only a month before the Titus Oates storm broke in London. Its first ruling was against the tories who, 'under the pre-tence of defending the national rights', brought dishonour on their faith. The second decree was that the doctrine that allowed the clergy to have a say in the appointment of their bishops was erroneous and that oaths taken against acknowledging the officially appointed clergy were damnable. Thirdly, those who would make presentments to the Vatican in order to solicit support for their own candidates were to be subjected to censures reserved to the pontiff. The fourth decree condemned 'as perverse and erroneous, the ravings of those who affirm that it belongs to the people to choose their own pastors and to fix for them, independent of the ordinary, the stipend to be given to them'.[23] Any doctrine which declared that the laity were not obliged to contribute towards their clergy was declared to be con-trary to scripture. (This was a move against the Franciscans, who were only maintained by begging and consequently were, unlike the seculars, free from greater administrative dependence.) It was for-bidden to take the goods of any Protestant or any others. The clergy were prohibited from teaching pupils who had been fostered by the Franciscans; priests were forbidden to drink whiskey in public or to attend public markets without permission. The decrees continued in a vein which was clearly intended to tackle the problem posed by the irregularities of Gaelic society: the clergy must fast strictly before saying mass; no marriages could take place without the presence of the parish priest and two witnesses. Finally, all clergy were asked to pray perpetually for the king, queen and royal family, and especially for the viceroy in Dublin, for the tranquillity of the nation, and for peace among Christian princes. They were also instructed to command their flocks to do likewise.

The pope, however, had taken a stand against Louis XIV and it only took a little over five years before the Archbishop of Cashel, Plunkett's great friend, was singing the praises of the Franciscan mission to Ireland:

> I confess there are some amongst them of scandalous life, but these are very few, compared with the great number of fathers who are here of exemplary life and of great zeal and learning, who labour incessantly and with abundant fruit for the glory of God and the salvation of souls. I may even add confidentially that the Franciscan fathers of strict observance in this kingdom do more good than any other religious order.[24]

By this time, however, Oliver Plunkett had taken his place among the great martyrs for the Catholic faith.

————————

When the political storm broke in England during 1678-9 the rallying-cry against the Stuarts was 'no popery'; and as the greatest collection of dispossessed and seething papists was to be found in Ireland, it was necessary to single out the head of the Irish church as a grave threat to England's security. English Protestant fears were indeed well grounded, but they were equally misplaced. The king's acceptance of financial aid from Louis was exposed, while a horrific 'popish plot' was disclosed by one Titus Oates in which Jesuits were to be found lurking under every bed. The fear of the Jesuits had actually little to do with religion; it was fuelled by a very understandable fear of the great Jesuit patron Louis XIV. The French question of sovereignty as it now impinged upon England, and thus upon Ireland, was clear: was Louis master of his Jesuits, or were they master of him?

The fear of the vast majority of Englishmen was understandable because of all the Catholic orders the Jesuits were the least easy to recognise or to define. When this characteristic was combined with the Jesuit mission to the French monarchy (with whom it was now known that Charles had had questionable dealings) a popish panic was inevitable. The great tragedy for the Catholic Church in Ireland was that Gaelic Irish Franciscans and their supporters were used to vent their frustration with Archbishop Plunkett by acting as chief witnesses against him at his staged trial in London. The Primate had opposed Jansenism and had favoured the Jesuits. The latter, however, were now taken to be a spiritual representation of the absolutist monster that the English had been trying to fight off since James I brought his theory of divine right down from Scotland. Now Jesuit absolutism seemed to be embodied in Louis XIV and, through him, in the Stuarts, who were clearly in his pay.

Plunkett's trial and execution in July 1681 (without a shred of concrete evidence against him) was hugely significant for the Catholics of Ireland. The vast majority had lost their lands, but very few had abandoned their faith. Whether they were Jansenist or Jesuit was going to make no difference to English fears of an invasion and to a growing feeling that the Stuarts were committed to an almighty confrontation. The problem for the Catholics of Ireland, however, was precisely the fact the James II did not look to Rome but to France. James concluded his brief reign by running away from England to France, by then claiming Catholic support in Ireland, but by running back to France as soon as he realised he was out of his depth. In his wake he left thousands of Irish dead who could hardly have known what exactly they were fighting for. The great irony is that if James had won the Battle of the Boyne, his enemy would have been the Catholic Church, and we may assume that the Old English would once again have split on the question of sovereign allegiance. No such split among the Gaelic Irish would have been likely, since they would not have been needed to rule the country and so would not have been reinstated on their lands. Had James won, it would have been a purely Old English victory.

Throughout the period which led up to the outbreak of war in Ireland the pope was ardently anti-French. Innocent XI defended assiduously his religious prerogatives against Louis. The extent of the clash can be seen in the adoption by the French clergy (under pressure from the king) of four definitively Gallican articles in 1682. Innocent rejected the articles and refused to recognise any bishops who adhered to them; the result was that by the beginning of 1688 there were thirty-five vacant bishoprics in France, and Innocent had informed Louis confidentially that he was now excommunicated. In using Gallicanism as he had used the Jesuits, Louis was planting the seeds of French monarchical destruction; this was because the spirit of Gallicanism was conciliar and independent and as such had a good deal in common with revolutionary Calvinism.

By the time James II came to the throne in 1685 France was undoubtedly the most powerful country in western Europe, and there appeared to be no reason for the Catholics of Ireland to be anything other than optimistic. Unfortunately the Irish question was not a French but an English one, and the English had no choice but to reject James as their king. This was because as the months passed no one could have been under any illusion as to what the king's plans were and there was no more visible example of this than in Ireland. The king's loyal servant Richard Talbot (created Earl of Tyrconnell in June 1685) dominated the Irish government, although he was not appointed Lord Deputy until early in 1687. In the meantime he disbanded the Protestant militia and secured commissions for a number of Catholic officers. Catholics were appointed to the judiciary, to the municipal corporations, and to the government itself in Dublin. By a royal warrant of March 1686 Catholic archbishops and bishops were to receive payments from the Exchequer. After Tyrconnell's official appointment as head of the Irish government the army was greatly increased and made up almost entirely of Catholics. Preparations were made for a parliament, while all municipal corporations were reformed in the Catholic interest.

The high point of the crisis in England came when on 10 June 1688 the queen gave birth to an heir. Twelve days later Whigs and Tories came together to invite William of Orange (who was married to James's daughter Mary) to come to England and take the throne. On James's orders, troops were sent over from Ireland in October, but shortly after William's landing in November James fled the country for France. Events were overtaking even James's rapid pace, however. By the time he reached France Louis had declared war on the Dutch (which was now tantamount to war on England), so that as soon as James arrived in France he was packed off with a small French entourage to Ireland, where he was told to make war and distract the English.

William and Mary were proclaimed monarchs of England (after their acceptance of a Bill of Rights) in February 1689. In March James arrived in Ireland, and a major European war on Irish soil was inevitable. Magnanimously James acceded to a call from his supporters for a parliament, which met from 7 May to 18 July and which became known as the 'Patriot Parliament', though it might just as easily have been called the paradoxical parliament. In the meantime he took himself up to Derry in the hope that his royal Catholic presence would melt Protestant resistance in this central Ulster stronghold (which was by now full of refugees). When the Protestants proved less than overjoyed to admit James to the city, the siege of Derry began.

With regard to the Dublin parliament, James confounded his supporters by denying the repeal of Poynings' Law, which the Old English had naturally expected in view of the fact that they were about to take up arms for James precisely because his own link with England had been broken. James was determined to persevere in his view that he was still King of England and so did not wish to alienate his loyal subjects there by granting independence to the Irish parliament. No doubt if Poynings' Law could have been explained to Louis, he would have agreed to its abolition and James would have followed suit (he was pressed by his French assistants to realise the nature of his situation, but he held firm). He refused to establish full Roman Catholicism and would agree only to liberty of conscience; he was equally reluctant to repeal the Cromwellian and Restoration land settlements, and although he agreed under duress, his attitude did nothing to instil confidence among the Old English. An act of repeal paved the way for a pre-1641 settlement, but James hindered the establishment of a court of claims lest it distract the country from its duty to fight his coming battle. In return for all his help James was voted £20,000 a month for thirteen months. Although this was, relatively speaking, a lot of money, James was fearful that it might not be enough; and as there was no more of the real stuff to be had, he ordered a new coinage of melted down brass, copper and gun-metal which he urged the country to pretend was silver until he was restored to his English kingdom. The immediate consequence of the new 'brass money', not surprisingly, was inflation.

Clearly James had not come to Ireland as a Catholic king coming among his oppressed Catholic subjects, but the Old English were in no position to do other than make the best of it. In one respect, however, they made too much of it when parliament passed an act of attainder which undermined the position of thousands of Protestants throughout the country. Times had changed greatly since 1649 and the Old English had suffered catastrophic dispossession, but the very fact that their lands had not been returned to them throughout the Restoration (or at least nothing more than a tiny fraction) might have caused them to reflect on the fact that they were not sought out any more as the natural rulers of Ireland—even by the Stuarts. They might therefore have looked to a policy of greater conciliation with what would seem to have been the new reality of Protestantism in

Ireland. By taking a win-or-lose approach without particular reference to the unique Irish context, they ran the risk of equally stringent legislation against themselves should they lose the war.

James arrived in Ireland at Kinsale on 12 March 1689 and took flight from the same harbour a little over a year later on 4 July 1690. The war did not finally come to an end until the Treaty of Limerick in October 1691. During this time the Catholics of Ireland sided with France in a war which Louis had undertaken simultaneously against England, Spain, the Holy Roman Empire, the Netherlands, Sweden, Denmark, Bavaria, Brandenburg and Savoy and which was the first war of its kind to be fought both in the Americas and in Asia on the same terms as in Europe. Louis's war with most of the western world did not finally end until the Peace of Utrecht was concluded in 1713, and at any given time he had over 400,000 men in the field.

To call the war 'the war of the two kings' is apt if the kings are William and Louis, since it was they who represented the vast European conflict between constitutional settlement and the absolutist power of monarchy. James did not represent Catholic Ireland, and even if he did, the conflict of sovereignty posed by Rinuccini would have had to be fought yet again. Ireland had failed that political test because its own sovereignty had always been divided, although it never failed the test of religious faith. The Gaelic Irish and the Old English had kept separate faiths, but only the Old English had political conceptions to match. These, however, went down with Charles I and his Anglicanism. They could not have been resurrected by the Restoration, because the sons of Charles I neither looked to Anglicanism or even to England itself, as their father had done, but to French Catholicism. The great turning-point was 1649 because Charles II was quickly acknowledged by the Scots Presbyterians, who understood sooner than others that any religious settlement must be constitutional if it was to survive, and that the best settlement was a static one under a monarchy. This was what William of Orange had been to the Dutch, and was now to be to the English.

Charles II and James II would not have been in a position even to contemplate the establishment of Roman Catholicism in England without it being part of a vast French design. In this respect they invested heavily in Louis, but in so doing they could not point to any political settlement which might have induced the English to accept French puppet status. The problem for England (or Ireland) was not at all a problem for Louis, as he had no designs other than continental ones. What he wanted from the Stuarts was support and security, but he did not ever envisage taking England and holding it as he had hoped to do with the Netherlands. Louis sought to extend the French monarchy into as many parts of Europe as was feasible; but if the seventeenth century was the century of France, it was also the century of the Dutch. Louis once described the Dutch as nothing but businessmen and cheese merchants, but time was to show that the greatest country in Europe ruled by one of the greatest kings in European history could not actually defeat its neighbouring handful of cheese merchants. When Louis was making his preparations to invade the Netherlands it was from the Dutch themselves that he bought arms and ammunition. The Dutch had moved rapidly from their own revolution against the Spanish to leading the world in trade. They did this through a process of political decision-making which had no absolutist inclinations of any kind. Louis's dynamic was similar to that of Charles I in that both had to grow and go on growing if they were to stand still. To stand still was the ambition of the divine-right kings because this was the ultimate reflection of the unity of God's power. Thus Louis's famous expression that he was the state was an aim which would continually be botched by cheese merchants because not even the state could control supply and demand.

—————————

Ireland could only play a walk-on part in the drama of autocracy *versus* democracy which was begun with the wars of religion that followed the Reformation and which was not to end for centuries. Ireland had nothing to offer either William or Louis that was positive, because Protestant Ireland was as great a compromise as its Catholic counterpart. William found it hard to understand the Church of Ireland clergy who presented themselves to him during his brief stay. How had they managed to preserve their Calvinist sympathies and be bishops simultaneously? How had they managed to hold clerical office under Charles II and, worse, under James II? Likewise, the French in Ireland could not understand how a small group of the Old English seemed determined to exclude all but themselves from a political future which seemed quite unrealistic.

The key to an understanding of the great military conflicts which took place between 1689 and 1691 is to be found on the Catholic side: there was no temporal or spiritual sovereign power. The king was not a ruler, and the Catholics were not catholic; neither possessed the sovereign power of Charles I or of Rinuccini. By contrast, William was truly King of England by consent of Anglican and Nonconformist alike in both political and religious contexts. There were two famous sieges during this war, and they illustrate the difference between unity and disunity more clearly than anything else. The apprentice boys of Derry shut its gates against James, and although the citizens were starved into eating vermin they did not surrender and were relieved by William's forces. The other great siege was the siege of Limerick, where the town similarly closed its gates. Inside it, however, were upwards of 20,000 soldiers waiting for their leaders to organise some sort of treaty whereby they would be allowed to leave the country. By comparison with a few apprentice boys, the number of troops idling in Limerick was almost equal to the number dissipated by James at the Boyne (where his army was the largest ever assembled from Ireland's inhabitants). Perhaps the greatest misreading of seventeenth-century Ireland has been the view that Derry did not surrender to popery and that Limerick was betrayed. Derry was besieged by a ragbag of diverse interests which symbolised the very opposite of popery and which was in the service of a French king who had been excommunicated by the pope himself. On the other hand, Limerick was a dramatic example of the Irish solution of exporting its human resources to succeed famously elsewhere. The century had begun with a defeat for Gaelic Ireland at Kinsale in which the Irish were hardly engaged in battle and which defeat was followed by the mass exodus of Gaelic leadership. The century was to end with an equally final defeat for the Old English at the Boyne in which their troops were hardly engaged in battle and which defeat was followed by their own mass exodus. In both cases it was hoped that foreign help would win Ireland, and in both cases the hope proved disastrous because 'Ireland' was more of a mythical concept than a concrete reality. Ireland's history and mythology were the only things that mixed well in a country that had to make do with the 'flight of the earls' and the 'flight of the wild geese' as a frame for its seventeenth-century historical folklore. What the country had not done was come face to face with the potential and then inevitable collapse, at the very centre of the seventeenth century, in 1649. Not so with the 'outsiders', however. The plantation of Ulster was a great success after the flight of the earls, and the Protestant ascendancy was an even greater success after the wild geese had flown. This cultural dichotomy between failure and success was the great legacy which seventeenth-century Ireland bequeathed to its inhabitants.

Louis XIV did not discard James until the Treaty of Ryswick in 1697, when he recognised William as King of England and agreed not to support the Stuart cause any longer. Even this treaty, however, was merely a pause as Louis prepared for the War of the Spanish Succession. All of Louis's battles which were not fought on the European continent were means to an end, but they were not ends in themselves. This was to become all too plain in Ireland. Throughout the Irish war of 1689-91 it became clear that Louis was only interested in holding Williamite troops in Ireland, and therefore the French were as willing to retreat as they were to advance so long as this objective was fulfilled. Although upwards of 25,000 men were slaughtered in battle (or fleeing from battle) and many thousands of Ireland's inhabitants died of famine and disease, the diversion was a happy one for Louis.

Derry was relieved by sea on 28 July 1689, and the Jacobite army decamped three days later. The Williamite Duke of Schomberg landed in Bangor Bay, County Down, with an English army of 14,000 men, and the Jacobites retreated from Ulster altogether. The French actually wanted to abandon the whole country east of the Shannon. These were not generals desperate for victory. However, the Jacobite army was also led by the Old English, who now had nothing to lose. Thus Tyrconnell persuaded the French to hold the line in Leinster. This was all that was done, however. The Jacobite army was numerically superior, and although the ensuing months saw over one-third of the Williamite army wiped out by an epidemic (which ravaged Ulster), no great encounter took place.

The French were content to let disease do their work because replacements would have to be sent for from the Williamite allies, both to replenish the army and to bring it up to, or beyond, the number of Jacobites. Thus while between 6,000 and 10,000 additional Williamite troops arrived from Denmark, Holland and England, the French simply exchanged their Irish soldiers for French ones who might not be so willing to fight as the Irish—or, to put it another way, who might better appreciate the strategic nature of a tactical retreat. All of this was a straightforward invitation to William to commit himself fully to an Irish victory which was in the offing if he would pay the cost; and this was what he did.

On 14 June 1690 William appeared off the coast at Carrickfergus with 500 ships laden with supplies, arms, money, almost 10,000 horses and 15,000 men. By the end of the month a combined army of 36,000 men had been drawn up to do battle against a Jacobite force of 25,000. Louis had achieved his immediate objective, and retreat was now the order of the day. The Jacobite army turned back from Dundalk, but was followed as far as the Boyne by William's army. Tyrconnell and Sarsfield did their best to rally the Old English cause, but their French allies were not of like mind. Before the battle had even begun most of the Jacobite artillery was heading back along the open road to Dublin.

The greatest battle in Irish history, when it came on 1 July, was a somewhat less than glorious event. William moved a decoy detachment upstream, where it stopped. The French regiments and James himself followed suit, pretending that they were going to fight, only to find that the armies were separated by a marsh and sadly could not come to blows. Tyrconnell had refused to participate in this set piece and stayed behind with a third of the Jacobite force to face the great bulk of the Williamite army which now descended upon the Old English. Thus while James and the main force of the Jacobites looked across the marsh at a Williamite detachment, the Jacobite detachment under Tyrconnell did battle with the main force of the Williamite army. By all accounts, Tyrconnell's men fought until retreat was the only course left. Word was then sent upstream to the French that the battle was over, and the entire Jacobite army united once again in retreat. James II distinguished himself in the race back to Dublin. He was first to arrive, but only spent the night there before setting out for Kinsale, from where he went back to report to Louis three days after his confrontation with William. The losses at the Boyne were not great, as it had been French policy to lose the battle, not men. The victory over Louis was celebrated in all the countries at war with him, but the French dismissed it as a brief encounter rather than a battle. The Williamites likewise suffered no great losses, as they had fought with 25,000 men against about 9,000 men under Tyrconnell. Not surprisingly, therefore, most of the dead were on the Old English side.

As the Jacobites still held all of Connacht and most of Munster, their natural retreat was to Limerick. William followed them there in August, but he was content to see the Jacobites holed up in the city, and he had no great need to commit himself to a long siege. He returned to England with his European army on 5 September. This should have been a time of great resurgence among the Jacobites, but the French had achieved as much as they could have done. Now that William had come and gone, it was time for them to depart. Tyrconnell left for France with the French army a week after William and his army had departed. That Louis had never intended to win Ireland for anyone should now have been clear. With the removal of the great European powers from the field of action, the remainder of the war had a more traditional Irish conclusion. The Earl of Marlborough arrived near Cork on 23 September with 5,000 English soldiers to return the south to a state of quietude. Kinsale fell immediately as the old divisions of the 1640s began to take their toll again. While the Protestant New English Earl of Orrery was holding out against Marlborough, the Catholic Old English burned his stronghold at Charleville. The country succumbed quickly, however, and the Jacobites were now confined to Kerry, Limerick and most of Connacht; a militia was set up to hold Cork (it proudly boasted of killing 3,000 stragglers caught on the wrong side of a countywide restoration of law and order).

An appeal was made to the Old English weakness when a tentative offer of security of tenure to all officers who held or purchased property between 1660 and 1685 was circulated. Tyrconnell's return in January 1691, followed by the French general St Ruth in May, stymied this initiative, but the terms of a peace became a principal concern as much to the Protestants as to the Catholics of Ireland. The Williamite army under Ginkel took the stronghold of Athlone at the end of June, after which he issued a proclamation offering security of tenure to all Jacobite officers surrendering with their troops and to the citizens of Galway and Limerick who would do likewise.

Dissension was by now rife in all quarters behind the Jacobite lines. As his only means of retaining control of a rapidly degenerating situation, St Ruth decided on a pitched battle against Ginkel. Both sides were evenly drawn up outside the town of Aughrim on 12 July and were evenly matched when the fighting took place. That St Ruth was by then the only acknowledged authority on the Jacobite side became clear when, in full dramatic irony, he was decapitated by a cannon-ball. The result was chaos. The Jacobite cavalry escaped quickly and safely, but in so doing they left their foot-soldiers to the mercy of the enemy horsemen. The Williamite cavalry managed to kill over 7,000 of these foot-soldiers as they ran defenceless from the field. Who these men were and what they thought they were being killed for will never be known. They were not dying for Louis XIV or James II, both of whom had now lost interest. Nor were they dying as property-owning Old English, for these had fled with the cavalry. They were not dying as Catholics, because the papacy had not supported the war. They were not 'dying for Ireland', because there was as yet no romantic myth to die for. It is hard to avoid the conclusion that they died for nothing at all. Had they been spared, it would have made no difference to the general surrender, which was now a foregone conclusion.

As 20,000 Jacobites retreated to Limerick city, Galway surrendered to Ginkel on 21 July on even more favourable terms than he had offered earlier, although these only applied to those in the town at the time of its surrender. Sligo followed suit, which left Limerick as the last stronghold. Tyrconnell's death on 14 August facilitated those who wished for peace. The French argued in favour of holding out until help came, because their brief was to tie Ireland up for as long as was possible. Tyrconnell's loyalties would have been divided between his foreign masters and his own men, who had by now lost whatever hope they had and wished for a settlement. His death simplified the divisions and allowed for negotiation. Ginkel laid siege to Limerick on 25 August, and a truce was agreed by 24 September, followed by a treaty signed on 3 October.

The Treaty of Limerick was generous in its intention because its intention was to get rid of 20,000 soldiers as quickly as possible. The military provisions of the treaty allowed all who wished to leave for France to do so unhindered, although they would forfeit any property in Ireland by so doing. On the face of it, this appeared incongruous while the Williamite army was still at war with France, but it was not. The whole campaign in Ireland had been a huge diversion of resources from the main Protestant forces in Europe. A few thousand Irish soldiers would quickly disappear in the hundreds of thousands then serving in the European war. The government of Ireland could then re-commence in a civil rather than military environment. The civil terms of the treaty must be seen as the natural corollary of the military provisions. They promised religious toleration as it had existed under Charles II and the security of property rights, with an undertaking that a future parliament would be asked to recognise these, although it could not, of course, be obliged to do so. The success of the military treaty was immediate. By the end of December the main body of the Jacobite army had left for France, and Ireland was secure for the new English crown. The problems posed by the civil articles of the treaty became symbolic for the new Ireland of the eighteenth century.

ABBREVIATIONS

Amer. Phil. Soc. Trans.	American Philosophical Society Transactions
Anal. Hib.	Analecta Hibernica
Anc. rec. Dublin	Calendar of Ancient Records of Dublin
Archiv. Hib.	Archivium Hibernicum
Belfast Natur. Hist. Soc. Proc.	Proceedings and Reports of the Belfast Natural History and Philosophical Society
Cal. S.P. Ire.	Calendar of the State Papers relating to Ireland
Clogher Rec.	Clogher Record
Collect. Hib.	Collectanea Hibernica
Cork Hist. Soc. Jn.	Journal of the Cork Historical and Archaeological Society
Desid. cur. Hib.	Desiderata Curiosa Hibernica
E.H.R.	English Historical Review
Econ. Hist.	Economic History
Econ. Hist. Rev.	Economic History Review
Galway Arch. Soc. Jn.	Journal of the Galway Archaeological and Historical Society
Gent. Mag	The Gentleman's Magazine
H.M.C.	Historical Manuscripts Commission First
H.M.C. rep. 1 [etc.]	[etc.] report
Hist. Studies	Historical Studies
I.E.R.	Irish Ecclesiastical Record
I.H.S.	Irish Historical Studies
I.M.C.	Irish Manuscripts Commission
Ir. Cath. Hist. Comm. Proc.	Proceedings of the Irish Catholic Historical Committee
Ir. Geog.	Irish Geography
Ir. Jurist	Irish Jurist
Ir. Sword	Irish Sword
Ir. Theol. Quart.	Irish Theological Quarterly
Jn. Ecc. Hist.	Journal of Ecclesiastical History
Lords' Jn. Ire.	Journal of the House of Lords [of Ireland], 1634-1800 (8 vols, Dublin 1779-1800)
Louth Arch. Soc. Jn.	Journal of the County Louth Archaeological Society
N. Munster Antiq. Jn.	North Munster Antiquarian Journal
P.R.I. rep. 1 [etc.]	First [etc.] report of the Deputy Keeper of the Public Records in Ireland
R.I.A.	Royal Irish Academy
R.I.A. Proc.	Proceedings of the Royal Irish Academy
R.I.A. Trans.	Transactions of the Royal Irish Academy
R.S.A.I. Jn.	Journal of the Royal Society of Antiquaries of Ireland
Studia Hib.	Studia Hibernica
U.J.A.	Ulster Journal of Archeology

References

Chapter 1: Identities and Allegiances, 1603-25 (pp. 5-35)
1. *Cal. S.P. Ire., 1599-1600,* 208-9.
2. Quoted in C. P. Meehan, *The Fate and Fortunes of Hugh O'Neill, Earl of Tyrone* (Dublin 1886), 21-2.
3. Quoted in Richard Bagwell, *Ireland under the Stuarts,* repr. (London 1963), 10.
4. *Cal. S.P. Ire., 1603-6,* 67.
5. Ibid., 60.   6. Ibid., 212.
7. Quoted in J. P. Kenyon, *The Stuart Constitution* (Cambridge 1966), 41-2.
8. *Cal. S.P. Ire., 1603-6,* 358.
9. Ibid., 372.   10. Ibid., 401-2, 445ff.   11. Ibid., 584.
12. *Cal. S.P. Ire., 1606-8,* 222.
13. Ibid., 246.   14. Ibid., 74.   15. Ibid.
16. Ibid., 76.   17. Ibid., 330.   18. Ibid., 362.
19. Ibid., 498-9
20. *Anc. rec. Dublin,* iii, 546.
21. P.R.O., S.P., 63/217/17.
22. Quoted in Bagwell, op. cit., 37.
23. *Cal. S.P. Ire., 1606-8,* 259.
24. Ibid., 19.
25. Quoted in Bagwell, op. cit., 41.
26. *Cal. S.P. Ire., 1606-8,* 270.   27. Ibid.
28. Quoted in Bagwell, op. cit., 85.
29. Quoted in T. W. Moody, 'The Irish Parliament under Elizabeth and James I', *R.I.A. Proc.,* xlv, sect. C, no. 6 (1939), 41-81.
30. Quoted in Bagwell, op. cit., 152.

Chapter 2: The Crown and the Catholics: Royal Government and Policy, 1625-37 (pp. 36-58)
1. Brendan Jennings (ed.), *Wadding Papers, 1614-38* (Dublin 1953), 331.
2. *Cal. S.P. Ire., 1625-32,* 498.   3. Ibid., 504.
4. *Cal. S.P. Ire., 1647-60,* 140.
5. *Cal. S.P. Ire., 1625-32,* 522.
6. William Knowler (ed.), *The Earl of Strafforde's Letters and Dispatches* (London 1739), i, 199.

7. H. F. Kearney, *Strafford in Ireland*, repr. (Manchester 1961), 66.

8. Knowler, op. cit., i, 270.

9. *Anc. rec. Dublin*, iii, 305-8.

10. *H.M.C. rep. in var. coll.*, viii (1913), 44.

11. Kearney, op. cit., 99.

Chapter 3: Fateful Ideologies: The Stuart Inheritance (pp. 59-76)

1. Quoted in Caroline Bingham, *The Stewart Kingdom of Scotland, 1371-1603* (London 1974), 251.

Chapter 4: Wentworth and the Ulster Crisis, 1638-9 (pp. 77-108)

1. William Knowler (ed.), *The Earl of Strafforde's Letters and Dispatches* (London 1739), ii, 187-8.

2. Ibid.   3. Ibid., 191-2.   4. Ibid., 195.

5. Ibid., 203-4.   6. Ibid., 211.   7. Ibid., 225-6, 232.

8. Ibid., 228.   9. Ibid., 233.   10. Ibid.

11. Ibid., 235.   12. Ibid., 235-6.   13. Ibid. 250.

14. Ibid., 269.   15. Ibid.   16. Ibid., 275.

17. Ibid., 278.   18. Ibid.   19. Ibid., 287.

20. Ibid., 289.   21. Ibid.   22. Ibid., 296-7.

23. Ibid., 297.   24. Ibid., 300.   25. Ibid.

26. Ibid.   27. Ibid.   28. Ibid., 303.

29. Ibid., 312-13.   30. Ibid., 318.   31. Ibid., 318-19.

32. Ibid., 321.   33. Ibid., 322.   34. Ibid., 323.

35. Quoted in C. V. Wedgwood, *The King's Peace* (London 1966), 458.

36. Knowler, op. cit., ii, 334.

37. Ibid.   38. Ibid.   39. Ibid.

40. Ibid.   41. Ibid.   42. Ibid.

43. Ibid.   44. Ibid.   45. Ibid., 419-20.

46. Ibid.   47. Ibid.   48. Ibid.

Chapter 5: On the Eve of Revolution, 1639-41 (pp. 109-132)

1. William Knowler (ed.), *The Earl of Strafforde's Letters and Dispatches* (London 1739), ii, 353-4.

2. Ibid., 355-6.   3. Ibid., 359-60.   4. Ibid.

5. Ibid., 363.   6. Ibid., 422.   7. Ibid., 372-3.

8. Ibid., 426.

9. Quoted in David Mathew, *Scotland under Charles I* (London 1955), 292.

10. W. C. Abbot (ed.), *The Writings and Speeches of Oliver Cromwell* (Cambridge, Mass. 1937-47), i, 256.

11. Quoted in Mathew, op. cit., 292-3.

12. Knowler, op. cit., ii, 194.

13. Quoted in Aidan Clarke, *The Old English in Ireland* (London 1966), 134, 135.

14. Ibid., 136.

14. Charles Petrie (ed.), *The Letters of Charles I* (London 1935), 116.

Chapter 6: 1641: The Plot That Never Was (pp. 133–167)

1. *Lords' Jn. Ire.*, iv, 415.
2. *Ormonde MSS,* new series, ii (1903), 3.
3. Ibid., 2.
4. *Anc. rec. Dublin*, iii, 390, 402.
5. *Ormonde MSS,* new series, ii, 3.
6. Ibid., 6.
7. J. T. Gilbert (ed.), *A Contemporary History of Affairs in Ireland from A.D. 1641 to 1652* (Dublin 1879), i, pt 1, 355.
8. Ibid., 356.   9. Ibid., 357.   10. Ibid.
11. Ibid., 359.   12. Ibid.   13. Ibid., 354.
14. Ibid., i, pt 2, 50.   15. Ibid., 498.
16. Charles Petrie (ed.), *The Letters of Charles I* (London 1935), 120–1.
17. Gilbert, op. cit., i, pt 2, 504.
18. Ibid.   19. Ibid., 505.   20. Ibid.
21. Ibid.   22. Ibid., 506.   23. Ibid.
24. Ibid.   25. Ibid., 507–8.   26. Ibid., 507.
27. Ibid., 507–8.   28. Ibid., 508.   29. Ibid., 509.
30. Ibid.   31. Ibid.   32. Ibid.
33. Ibid.   34. Ibid., 509–10.   35. Ibid., 511.
36. Ibid.   37. Ibid.   38. Ibid.
39. Rushworth quoted in *Cobbett's State Trials*, iv (London 1809), 654.
40. Gilbert, op. cit., i, pt 2, 562.
41. Cobbett, op. cit., iv, 654.
42. Ibid., 665–6.   43. Ibid., 667.   44. Ibid.
45. Ibid., 669.   46. Ibid., 670.   47. Ibid.
48. Ibid.   49. Ibid., 672.   50. Ibid.
51. Ibid.   52. Ibid.   53. Ibid., 674.
54. Ibid.   55. Ibid.   56. Ibid.
57. Ibid.
58. Gilbert, op. cit., i, pt 2, 628.
59. Ibid., 628–9.   60. Ibid., 629.   61. Ibid., 630.
62. Cobbett, op. cit., iv, 677.
63. Ibid.
64. *Ormonde MSS*, new series, ii, 2.
65. Gilbert, op. cit., i, pt 2, 630.
66. Ibid.   67. Ibid., 626.
68. Cobbett, op. cit., iv, 678.
69. Ibid.
70. Gilbert, op. cit., i, pt 2, 631.
71. Ibid.   72. Ibid., 631.   73. Ibid., 634.
74. Ibid., 635.   75. Ibid., 636.   76. Ibid., 631.
77. Ibid., 636.   78. Ibid.   79. Ibid.
80. Ibid.   81. Ibid., 637.   82. Ibid.

Chapter 7: Insurrection and Confederation, 1641–4 (pp. 168–187)

1. Richard Cox, *Hibernia Anglicana* (London 1689), appx xlix, 208.
2. Ibid., 209.
3. Quoted in J. I. Casway, *Owen Roe O'Neill and the Struggle for Catholic Ireland* (Philadelphia 1984), 236.
4. J. T. Gilbert (ed.), *History of the Irish Confederation and the War in Ireland, 1641–9* (Dublin 1882–91), ii, 118.
5. Ibid., 277.

Chapter 8: In Search of a Settlement: Ormond, Rinuccini and Cromwell, 1645–53 (pp. 188–208)

1. Gilbert, *Ir. Confed.*, iv, 270.
2. Ibid., 271.   3. Ibid., ii, 212.   4. Ibid., v, 72.
5. Ibid., 199.   6. Ibid., 200.   7. Ibid., 209.
8. Ibid., 210.   9. Ibid., vi, 71.   10. Ibid.
11. Ibid., v, 288.   12. Ibid., 292.   13. Ibid., vi, 71.
14. Quoted in T. W. Moody, F. X. Martin and F. J. Byrne (ed.), *A New History of Ireland*, iii (Oxford 1976), 298.

Chapter 9: Theology and the Politics of Sovereignty: Jansenist, Jesuit and Franciscan (pp. 209–226)

1. Quoted in Tomás Ó Fiaich, *Luke Wadding* (Dublin 1957), 193.

Chapter 10: Ideologies in Conflict, 1660–91 (pp. 227–255)

1. Quoted in Tomás Ó Fiaich, *Luke Wadding* (Dublin 1957), 204.
2. Ibid.   3. Ibid.   4. Ibid., 217.
5. Quoted in Tomás Ó Fiaich, 'The Appointment of Bishop Tyrrell and its Consequences', *Clogher Rec.*, i, no. 3 (1955), 10–11.
6. Quoted in P. F. Moran, *A Memoir of Oliver Plunkett*, 2nd ed. (Dublin 1895), 25.
7. Ibid.   8. Ibid., 26.   9. Ibid., 50.
10. Ibid., 54.   11. Ibid., 58.   12. Ibid., 59.
13. Ibid., 135–6.   14. Ibid., 101.   15. Ibid., 101–2.
16. Ibid., 95.   17. Ibid., 100.   18. Ibid., 97.
19. Quoted in Alice Curtayne, *The Trial of Oliver Plunkett*, repr. (Dublin 1975), 140–1.
20. Quoted in Moran, op. cit., 104.
21. Ibid., 124.   22. Ibid., 117–18.   23. Ibid., 150.
24. Ibid., 107.

Bibliography

This bibliography of printed sources is based on J. G. Simms's bibliography to T. W. Moody, F. X. Martin and F. J. Byrne (ed.), *A New History of Ireland*, iii (Oxford 1976; repr. 1978).

RECORDS

1. Records of Central Administration

'Book of Survey and Distribution, Cork', *Cork Hist. Soc. Jn.*, xxxvii (1932), 83–9; xxxviii (1933), 39–45, 72–9; xxxix (1934), 33–7, 79–84; xl (1935), 43–8, 91–4; xli (1936), 37–41, 97–104

'Book of Survey and Distribution, Kilkenny' in William Healy, *History and Antiquities of Kilkenny* (Dublin 1893), i, app. i

The Book of Survey and Distribution of the Estates in the County of Westmeath forfeited in the year MDCLII, ed. J. C. Lyons (Ledestown 1852)

Books of Survey and Distribution, ed. R. C. Simington, 4 vols (I.M.C., Dublin 1944–67)

[Carew] *Calendar of the Carew Manuscripts preserved in the Archiepiscopal Library at Lambeth, 1515–1624*, 6 vols (London 1867–73)

[Castle Chamber] 'Court of Castle Chamber Records' in Egmont MSS, *H.M.C. rep. 17*, app. 1 (1905), pp 1–60.

A Census of Ireland circa 1659, with supplementary material from the Poll Money Ordinances (1660–1661), ed. Séamus Pender (I.M.C., Dublin 1939)

Chester Customs Accounts, ed. K. P. Wilson (Liverpool 1969)

[Chichester] 'Seventeen Letters from James I and Council of England to the Lord Deputy and Council of Ireland, 1605–7' in *Desid. cur. Hib.*, i, 441–513

_____'Letter-Book of Sir Arthur Chichester, 1612–14', ed. R. D. Edwards, *Anal. Hib.*, no. 8 (1938), 3–177

The Civil Survey, A.D. 1654–56, ed. R. C. Simington, 10 vols (I.M.C., Dublin 1931–61)

[Clanricard] *Letter-Book of the Earl of Clanricard*, ed W. J. Lowe (Dublin 1983)

[Clarendon] *Calendar of the Clarendon State Papers preserved in the Bodleian Library*, 5 vols (Oxford 1872–1970)

_____*The Correspondence of Henry Hyde, Earl of Clarendon, and of his brother, Laurence Hyde, Earl of Rochester, with the Diary of Lord Clarendon from 1687 to 1690*, ed. S. W. Singer, 2 vols (London 1828)

_____*The State Letters of Henry, Earl of Clarendon, Lord Lieutenant of Ireland.... and His Lordship's Diary for the years 1687, 1688, 1689, and 1690*, 2 vols (Oxford 1765)

[Clarke] 'George Clarke's Irish War Correspondence, 1690–91', ed. N. B. White, *Anal. Hib.*, no. 10 (1941), 245–9

[Commonwealth] *Ireland under the Commonwealth: being a Selection of Documents relating to the Government of Ireland, 1651–9*, ed. Robert Dunlop, 2 vols (Manchester 1913)

'Commonwealth Records', ed. James MacCaffrey, *Archiv. Hib.*, vi (1917), 175–202; vii (1918–21), 20–66.

'Commonwealth State Accounts, 1650–56' ed. Edward MacLysaght, *Anal. Hib.*, no. 15 (1944), 227–321

The Compossicion Booke of Conought, ed. A. M. Freeman (I.M.C., Dublin 1936); *Index*, by G. A. Hayes–McCoy (I.M.C., Dublin 1942)

[Cromwell] *The Writings and Speeches of Oliver Cromwell*, ed. W. C. Abbott, 4 vols (Cambridge, Mass. 1937–47)

_____*The Letters and Speeches of Oliver Cromwell, with Elucidations by Thomas Carlyle* (1845), ed. S. C. Lomas, 3 vols (London 1904)

The Desmond Survey of Courty Kerry, ed. S. M. Hussey (Tralee 1923) (privately printed); repr., *Kerryman*, Aug.–Oct. 1927

Docwra, Henry, 'A Narration of the Services done by the Army employed to Lough-Foyle' in *Miscellany of the Celtic Society*, ed. John O'Donovan (Dublin 1849)

[Hearth money] 'Seventeenth-Century Hearth-Money Rolls with full transcript relating to Co. Sligo', ed. Edward MacLysaght, *Anal. Hib.*, no. 24 (1967), 1–89

Letters and Papers relating to the Irish rebellion, 1642–6, ed. James Hogan (I.M.C., Dublin 1936)

[Patent Rolls] *A Repertory of the Inrolments on the Patent Rolls of Chancery in Ireland, commencing with the reign of James I*, ed. J. C. Erck, Vol. i, pts 1–2 (Dublin 1846–52)

_____*Irish Patent Rolls of James I: Facsimile of the Irish Record Commission's Calendar prepared prior to 1830*, foreword by M. C. Griffith (I.M.C., Dublin 1966)

[Privy Council] *Acts of the Privy Council of England, 1542–1631*, 46 vols (London 1890–1964)

_____*Privy Council Registers preserved in the Public Record Office, 1637–45, reproduced in facsimile*, 12 vols (London 1967–8)

_____*Register of the Privy Council of Scotland*, Vols viii–xiii (1607–25), ed. David Masson (Edinburgh 1887–96)

[Proclamations] *A Bibliography of Royal Proclamations of the Tudor and Stuart Sovereigns and of others published under their royal authority, 1485–1714*, ed. R. R. Steele, 2 vols (Oxford 1910)

[Salisbury] *Calendar of the Manuscripts of the... Marquess of*

Salisbury...preserved at Hatfield House, 23 vols (H.M.C., London 1883-1973)

[State Papers] *Calendar of State Papers relating to Ireland, 1509-1670*, 24 vols (London 1860-1912)

———*Calendar of State Papers preserved in the Public Record Office, Domestic Series, 1547-1695*, 81 vols (London 1856-1972)

[Strafford] *The Earl of Strafforde's Letters and Dispatches*, ed. William Knowler, 2 vols (London 1739)

Strafford Inquisition of County Mayo (R.I.A., MS 24 E 15), ed. William O'Sullivan (I.M.C., Dublin 1958)

[Talbot] 'Letter-Book of Richard Talbot', ed. Lilian Tate, *Anal. Hib.*, no. 4 (1932), 99-133.

Thurloe, John, *A Collection of State Papers of John Thurloe, Secretary first to the Council of State and afterwards to the Two Protectorates*, ed. Thomas Birch, 7 vols (London 1742)

[Treasury Books] *Calendar of Treasury Books, 1660-92*, Vols i-ix (London 1904-31)

'Ulster Plantation Papers, 1608-13', ed. T. W. Moody, *Anal. Hib.*, no. 8 (1938), 179-298

'The Ulster State Papers', ed. H. F. Hore, *U.J.A.*, 1st series, vii (1859), 45-65

[William III] *Correspondence van Willem en van Hans Willem Bentinck, eersten Graf van Portland*, ed. Nicholas Japikse, Vol. iii (The Hague 1927)

[Wine trade] 'The Irish Wine-Trade, 1614-15', ed. H. F. Kearney, *I.H.S.*, ix, no. 36 (Sept. 1955), 400-42

2. Records of Local Administration

[Belfast] *The Town Book of the Corporation of Belfast, 1613-1816*, ed. R. M. Young (Belfast/London 1892)

[Cork] *The Council Book of Cork*, ed. Richard Caulfield (Guildford 1876)
———'Original Documents relating to the County and City of Cork', ed. Richard Caulfield, *Gent. Mag.*, 1862.

[Dublin] *Calendar of Ancient Records of Dublin in the possession of the Municipal Corporation*, Vols i-vi (1172-1716), ed. J. T. Gilbert (Dublin 1889-96)

[Galway] 'Archives of the Town of Galway', ed. J. T. Gilbert, in *H.M.C. rep. 10*, app. v (1885), 380-520

Kilkenny City Records: Liber Primus Kilkenniensis, ed. Charles McNeill (Dublin 1931); trans. A. J. Otway-Ruthven (Kilkenny 1961)

[Kinsale] *The Council Book of Kinsale*, ed. Richard Caulfield (Guilford 1879)

[London] *The Bishopric of Derry and the Irish Society of London, 1602-1705*, ed. T. W. Moody and J. G. Simms, Vol. i (1602-70) (I.M.C., Dublin 1968)
———'Schedules of the Lands in Ulster allocated to the London Livery Companies, 1613', ed. T. W. Moody, *Anal. Hib.*, no. 8 (1938), 299-311

[Waterford] 'Archives of the Municipal Corporation of Waterford', ed. J. T. Gilbert, in *H.M.C. rep. 10*, app. v (1885), 265–339

――*Council Book of the Corporation of Waterford, 1662–1700*, ed. Séamus Pender (I.M.C., Dublin 1964)

――'Report by J. T. Gilbert on Corporation Records of Waterford' in *H.M.C. rep. 1*, app. (1874), 131–2

[Youghal] *The Council Book of Youghal*, ed. Richard Caulfield (Guildford 1878)

3. Parliamentary Records

(a) Statutes

The Statutes at Large passed in the Parliaments held in Ireland, Vols l–lv (Dublin 1786)

The Statutes of Ireland . . . newly perused and examined, ed. Richard Bolton (Dublin 1621)

The Statutes at Large of England and Great Britain, Vols ii–iii (1509–1708) (London 1811)

Acts and Ordinances of the Interregnum, 1642–1660, ed. C. H. Firth and R. S. Rait, 3 vols (London 1911)

(b) Journals

Journal of the House of Lords [of Ireland], Vol. i (1634–99) (Dublin 1779)

Journals of the House of Lords [of England], Vols i–xiv (1510–1691)

Journals of the House of Commons of the Kingdom of Ireland, Vol. i, 2 pts (1613–66) (Dublin 1796)

Journal of the House of Commons [of England], Vols i–x (1547–1693)

Commons Debates, 1621, ed. Wallace Notestein and others, 7 vols (New Haven 1935)

The Commons Debates for 1629, ed. Wallace Notestein and others (Minneapolis 1921)

The Journal of Sir Simonds D'Ewes, ed. Wallace Notestein (New Haven 1923)

4. Legal Records

[Courts] *His Majesties Direction for the Ordering and Settling of the Courts, and Course of Justice, within his Kingdom of Ireland* (Dublin 1622)

Davies, John, *A Report of Cases and Matters in Law* (Dublin 1762)

[Depositions] *Ireland in the Seventeenth Century, or the Irish Massacres of 1641–2*, ed. Mary Hickson, 2 vols (London 1884)

Inquisitionum in Officio Rotulorum Cancellariae Hiberniae Asservatarum Repertorium, 2 vols (Dublin 1826–9)

[Irish law] 'Ancient Irish Deeds and Writings', ed. James Hardiman, *R.I.A. Trans.*, xv (1826), pt 2, 3–95

[Outlawries] 'Oireachtas Library: List of Outlaws, 1641–7', ed. R. C. Simington and John MacLellan, *Anal. Hib.*, no. 23 (1966), 317–67

_____'Irish Jacobites: Lists from T.C.D., MS N.1.3', ed. J. G. Simms, *Anal. Hib.*, no. 22 (1960), 11–230

[Strafford] *The Trial of Thomas, Earl of Strafford*, ed. John Rushworth (London 1680)

5. Ecclesiastical Records

[Brenan, John] *A Bishop of the Penal Times*, ed. Patrick Power (Cork 1932)

[Christ Church, Dublin] 'Calendar to Christ Church Deeds', ed. M. J. McEnery, In *P.R.I. rep. D.K. 20* (1888), *23* (1891), *24* (1892), *27* (1895)

[Cistercians] 'Three Unpublished Cistercian Documents', ed. Colmcille Ó Conbhuí, *Louth Arch. Soc. Jn.*, xiii, no. 3 (1955), 252–78

[Derry] *The Bishopric of Derry and the Irish Society of London, 1602–1705*, Ed. T. W. Moody and J. G. Simms, Vol. i (1602–70) (I.M.C., Dublin 1968)

[Dublin] 'Archbishop Bulkeley's Visitation of Dublin, 1630', ed. M. V. Ronan, *Archiv. Hib.*, viii (1941), 56–98

_____'The Royal Visitation of Dublin, 1615', ed. M. V. Ronan, *Archiv. Hib.*, viii (1941), 1–55

[Flanders] 'Catalogue of Material of Irish Interest in the Collection Nunziatura di Fiandra', ed. Cathaldus Giblin, *Collect. Hib.*, i (1958), 7–134; iii (1960), 7–144; iv (1961), 7–137; v (1962), 7–130; ix (1966), 7–70; x (1967), 72–138; xi (1968), 53–90; xii (1969), 61–101; xiii (1970), 61–99

[Franciscans] *Liber Lovaniensis: A Collection of Irish Franciscan Documents, 1629–1717*, ed. Cathaldus Giblin (Dublin 1956)

[Jesuits] *Ibernia Ignatiana: seu Ibernorum Societatis Jesu Patrum Monumenta Collecta*, ed. Edmund Hogan, Vol. i (1540–1607) (Dublin 1880)

[Louvain] *Facultates Lovanienses, 1426–1797, praecipue quae Nomen Hibernicum Spectant*, ed. Timothy Corcoran (Dublin 1939)

'Miscellaneous Documents, 1588–1715', ed. Brendan Jennings, *Archiv. Hib.*, xii (1946), 70–200; xiv (1949) 1–49; xv (1950), 1–73

[Plunkett] *Memoir of the Most Rev. Oliver Plunkett, Archbishop of Armagh*, by P. F. Moran (Dublin 1861)

[Salamanca] 'Students of the Irish College, Salamanca', ed. D. J. O'Doherty, *Archiv. Hib.*, ii (1913), 1–36; iii (1914), 87–112

Spicilegium Ossoriense, being a Collection of Original Letters and Papers illustrative of the History of the Irish Church from the Reformation to the year 1800, ed. P. F. Moran, 3 vols (Dublin 1874–84)

[Vatican] 'Miscellanea Vaticano-Hibernica', ed. John Hagan, *Archiv. Hib.*, iii (1914), 227–365; iv (1915), 215–318; v (1916), 74–185; vi (1917), 94–155; vii (1918–21), 67–356

6. Family and Personal Papers

'The Arthur Manuscripts', ed. Edward MacLysaght and John Ainsworth, *N. Munster Antiq. Jn.*, vi (1949–52), 29–49; vii, no. 1 (1953), 168–82; no. 4 (1957), 4–10; viii (1958–9), 2–19, 79–87; ix (1962–3), 51–9, 113–16, 153–64

Blake Family Records, 1606-1700, ed. M. J. Blake (London 1905)

[Boyle, Richard, Earl of Cork] *Lismore Papers*, ed. A. B. Grosart, 10 vols (London 1886-8)

[Chamberlain] *The Letters of John Chamberlain*, ed. N. E. McClure, 2 vols (Philadelphia 1939)

[Cork] 'Wills and Inventories, Cork', ed. Richard Caulfield, *Gent. Mag.*, 1861

[de l'Isle and Dudley] *Report on the Manuscripts of Lord de L'Isle and Dudley*, 6 vols (H.M.C., London 1925-66)

'Doneraile Papers: Interim Report' by Edward MacLysaght, *Anal. Hib.*, no. 15 (1944), 335-62

Dowdall Deeds, ed. Charles McNeill and A. J. Otway-Ruthven (I.M.C., Dublin 1960)

[Downshire] *Report on the Manuscripts of the Marquess of Downshire preserved at Easthampstead Park, Berks*, Vols i-iv (H.M.C., London 1924-40)

'Dunsdale Papers: Interim Report' by Edward MacLysaght, *Anal. Hib.*, no. 15 (1944), 392-405

[Egmont] *Report on the Manuscripts of the Earl of Egmont*, 2 vols (H.M.C., London 1905-9)

[Gearnon] 'Papers of Anthony Gearnon, O.F.M.', ed. Anselm Faulkner, *Collect. Hib.*, vi (1964), 212-24

[Hacket] *The Letters of Sir John Hacket*, ed. E. F. Rogers (West Virginia 1971)

The Hamilton Manuscripts, ed. T. K. Lowry (Belfast 1867)

[Hastings] *Report on the Manuscripts of the late Reginald Rawdon Hastings*, ed. Francis Bickley (H.M.C., London 1930-47)

Henslowe's Diary, ed. W. W. Greg, 2 vols (London 1904-8)

Herbert Correspondence, ed. W. J. Smith (I.M.C., Dublin 1961)

[Inchiquin] 'Seven Irish Documents from the Inchiquin Archives', ed. Gearóid Mac Niocaill, *Anal. Hib.*, no. 26 (1970), 45-70

The Inchiquin Manuscripts, ed. John Ainsworth (I.M.C., Dublin 1961)

[O'Hara] *The Book of O'Hara*, ed. Lambert McKenna (Dublin 1951)

[O'Hartigan] 'The Strange Letters of Mathew O'Hartigan, S. J., 1644-5', ed. Thomas Morrissey, *Ir. Theol. Quart.*, xxxvii (1970), 159-72

[Ormond] *Calendar of the Manuscripts of the Marquess of Ormonde preserved at Kilkenny Castle*, 11 vols (H.M.C., London 1895-1920)

———*Calendar of Ormond Deeds*, Vols iii-vi (1413-1603), ed. Edmund Curtis (I.M.C., Dublin 1935-43)

[Orrery] *Calendar of the Orrery Papers*, ed. Edward MacLysaght (I.M.C., Dublin 1941)

———*A Collection of the State Letters of the First Earl of Orrery*, ed. Thomas Morrice, 2 vols (Dublin 1743)

[Oviedo] 'Some Unpublished Letters of Mateo de Oviedo, Archbishop of Dublin', ed. P. P. McBride, *Reportorium Novum*, i (1955-6), 91-116, 351-68

[Papebroch] 'Letters of Daniel Papebroch, S.J., to Francis Harold, O.F.M. (1665-90)', ed. Fergal Grannell, *Archivium Franciscanum Historicum*, lix (1966), 385-455

Petty-Southwell Correspondence, 1676-87, ed. Marquess of Lansdowne (London 1928)

[Radcliffe] *The Life and Correspondence of Sir George Radcliffe*, ed. T. D. Whitaker (London 1810)

Rawdon Papers, ed. Edward Berwick (London 1819)

[Wadding] 'Some Correspondence of Father Luke Wadding, O.F.M.', ed. Brendan Jennings, *Collect. Hib.*, ii (1959), 64-94

Wadding Papers, 1614-38, ed. Brendan Jennings (I.M.C., Dublin 1953)

7. Other Records

[Avaux] *Négociations de M. le Comte d'Avaux en Irlande, 1689-90* (I.M.C., Dublin 1934)

The Danish Force in Ireland, 1690-91, ed. Kevin Danaher and J. G. Simms (I.M.C., Dublin 1962)

[Flanders] *Wild Geese in Spanish Flanders*, ed. Brendan Jennings (I.M.C., Dublin 1964)

'Franco-Irish Correspondence, 1688-91', ed. Lilian Tate, *Anal. Hib.*, no. 21 (1959), 1-240

[Ginkel] 'Correspondence of General Ginkel (de Ros MSS)' in *H.M.C. rep. 4* (1874), app., 317-215

Macpherson, James (ed.), *Original Papers*, 2 vols (London 1775)

[Milan] *Calendar of State Papers and Manuscripts existing in the Archives and Collections of Milan, 1385-1618* (London 1913)

[O'Neill] 'The Last Years of Hugh O'Neill', ed. Micheline Walsh, *Ir. Sword*, iii (1957-8), 234-44; v (1961-2), 223-35; vii (1965-6), 5-14, 136-46, 327-37; viii (1967-8), 120-9, 230-41, 299-303; ix (1969-70), 59-68, 135-46

[Venice] *Calendar of State Papers and Manuscripts relating to English Affairs...1534-1674*, Vols v-xxxviii (London 1873-1947)

CONTEMPORARY WORKS

1. Contemporary Histories and Descriptions

Adair, Patrick, *A True Narrative of the Rise and Progress of the Presbyterian Church in Ireland (1623-70)*, ed. W. D. Killen (Belfast 1866)

Advertisements for Ireland, ed. George O'Brien (Dublin 1923)

Borlase, Edmund, *The History of the Execrable Irish Rebellion* (Dublin 1680; 2nd ed., Dublin 1743)

Clarendon, Edward Hyde, Earl of, *The History of the Rebellion and Civil Wars in Ireland* (London 1720)

Cox, Richard, *Hibernia Anglicana, or the History of Ireland from the Conquest Thereof by the English to this Present Time*, 2 pts (London 1689-90)

Davies, John, *Complete Prose Works*, ed. A. B. Grosart, 3 vols (London 1869-76)

———*A Discovery of the True Causes Why Ireland Was Never Entirely Subdued... until... His Majesty's Happy Reign* (London 1612; fascimile repr., Shannon 1969)

Dineley, Thomas, 'Extracts from the Journal of Thomas Dineley [1681]', ed. E. P. Shirley, *R.S.A.I. Jn.*, iv (1856–7), 143–6, 170–88; v (1858), 22–32, 55–6; vii (1862–3), 38–52, 103–9, 320–38; viii (1864–6), 40–8, 268–90, 425–46; ix (1867), 73–91, 176–202; ed. F. E. Ball, ibid., xliii (1913), 275–309

Gilbert, J. T. (ed.), *A Contemporary History of Affairs in Ireland from A.D. 1641 to 1652*, 3 vols (Dublin 1879)

———*The History of the Irish Confederation and the War in Ireland (1641–9)*, 7 vols (Dublin, 1882–91)

———*A Jacobite Narrative of the War in Ireland, 1688–1691* (Dublin 1892, repr., intro. J. G. Simms, Shannon 1971)

King, William, *The State of the Protestants of Ireland under the late King James's Government* (London 1691)

Mackenzie, John, *A Narrative of the Siege of Londonderry* (London 1690)

Mullenaux, Samuel, *Journal of the Three Months' Royal Campaign of His Majesty in Ireland* (London 1690)

Ó Cianáin, Tadhg, *The Flight of the Earls*, ed. Paul Walsh (Dublin 1916)

O'Ferrall, Richard, and O'Connell, Robert, *Commentarius Rinuccinianus, de Sedis Apostolicae Legatione ad Foederatos Hiberniae, Catholicos per annos 1645–9*, ed. Stanislaus Kavanagh, 6 vols (I.M.C., Dublin 1932–49)

Petty, William, *The History of the Survey of Ireland commonly called the Down Survey, A.D. 1655–6*, ed. T. A. Larcom (Dublin 1851)

———*The Political Anatomy of Ireland* [1672] (Dublin 1691)

Porter, Francis, *Compendium Annalium Ecclesiasticorum Regni Hiberniae* (Rome 1690)

Rich, Barnaby, *A New Discovery of Ireland* (London, 1610; ed. Edmund Hogan, London 1878)

Sidney, Henry, *Diary of the Times of Charles II*, ed. R. W. Blencowe, 2 vols (London 1843)

Story, George, *A True and Impartial History of the Most Material Occurrences in the Kingdom of Ireland during the Last Two Years* (London 1691)

———*A Continuation of the Impartial History of the Wars in Ireland* (London 1693)

Temple, John, *The Irish Rebellion: or the History of the Beginning and First Progress of the General Rebellion raised within the Kingdom of Ireland, upon the three and twentieth day of October, 1641* (London 1646; later eds, 1674, 1679)

Walker, George, *A True Account of the Siege of Londonderry* (London 1689)

2. Pamphlets and Newspapers

Blenerhassett, Thomas, *A Direction for the Plantation in Ulster* (London 1610)

Callaghan, John, *Vindiciarum Catholicorum Hiberniae ... libri duo* (Paris 1650)

Caron, Raymond, *Remonstria Hibernorum contra Lovanienses Ultra-montanasque Censuras* (London 1665)

Collins, John, *A Plea for the Bringing of Irish Cattel* (London 1680)

Darcy, Patrick, *An Argument delivered... by the express order of the House of Commons* (Waterford 1643; repr., Dublin 1764)

A Discourse concerning Ireland and the Different Interests Thereof in answer to the Exon and Barnstable Petitions (London 1698)

Ireland's Declaration, being a Remonstrance (Dublin 1649)

Leslie, Charles, *An Answer to the Book intituled The State of the Protestants in Ireland under the late King James's Government* (London 1692)

Milton, John, *Observations on the Articles of Peace... and a Representation of the Scots Presbytery at Belfast in Ireland* (London 1649)

Punch, John, *D. Richardi Bellingi Vindiciae Eversae* (Paris 1653)

Reily, Hugh, *Ireland's Case Briefly Stated* ([Louvain] 1695)

Walsh, Peter, *The History and Vindication of the Loyal Formulary or Irish Remonstrance* (n.p. 1674)

———*Causa Valensiana* (London 1684)

———*Queries concerning the Lawfulnesse of the Present Cessation* (Kilkenny 1648)

SOURCE COMPILATIONS

Brady, John (ed.), 'The Irish Colleges in the Low Countries', *Archiv. Hib.*, xiv (1949), 66–91

Burke, W. P. (ed.), *The Irish Priests in the Penal Times (1660–1760)* (Waterford 1914)

Carty, James (ed.), *Ireland from the Flight of the Earls to Grattan's Parliament (1607–1782): A Documentary Record* (Dublin 1949)

Desiderata Curiosa Hibernica, or a Select Collection of State Papers, ed. John Lodge, 2 vols (Dublin 1772)

English Historical Documents (general editor D. C. Douglas), Vol. viii (1660–1714), ed. Andrew Browning (London 1953)

Facsimiles of the National Manuscripts of Ireland, ed. J. T. Gilbert, 4 vols (Dublin 1874–84)

Gwynn, Aubrey (ed.), Reports on the Rawlinson Collection of Manuscripts *Anal. Hib.*, no. 4 (1932), 139–286

McNeill, Charles (ed.), 'Reports on the Rawlinson Collection of Manuscripts preserved in the Bodleian Library, Oxford', *Anal. Hib.*, no. 1 (1930), 12–178; no. 2 (1931), 1–92

Miscellany of the Celtic Society, ed. John O'Donovan (Dublin 1849)

Simington, R. C. (ed.), *The Transplantation to Connacht, 1654–58* (I.M.C., Dublin 1970)

The Tanner Letters, ed. Charles McNeill (I.M.C., Dublin 1943)

Vallancey, Charles (ed.), *Collectanea de Rebus Hibernicis*, 6 vols (Dublin 1770–1804)

Walsh, Micheline (ed.), *Spanish Knights of Irish Origin: Documents from Continental Archives*, 3 vols (I.M.C., Dublin 1960–70)

SECONDARY WORKS

Aiazzi, Giuseppe, *Nunziatura in Irlanda* (Florence 1844); trans. Annie Hutton with title *The Embassy in Ireland* (Dublin 1873)

Albion, Gordon, *Charles I and the Court of Rome* (London 1935)

Andrews, K. R., Canny, N. P., and Hair, P. E. H. (ed.), *The Westward Expansion* (Liverpool 1978)

Bagwell, Richard, *Ireland under the Stuarts and during the Interregnum*, 3 vols (London 1909-16; repr. 1963)

Barnard, T. C., 'Planters and Policies in Cromwellian Ireland', *Past & Present*, no. 61 (1973), 31-69

——*Cromwellian Ireland: English Government and Reform in Ireland, 1649-1660* (Oxford 1975)

Bartlett, Thomas, and Hayton, D. W. (ed.), *Penal Era and Golden Age* (Belfast 1979)

Beckett, J. C., *Protestant Dissent in Ireland, 1687-1784* (London 1948)

——'The Confederation of Kilkenny Reviewed', *Hist. Studies*, ii (1959), 29-41

——*The Making of Modern Ireland, 1603-1923* (London 1966; repr. 1969)

——'Irish-Scottish Relations in the Seventeenth Century' in *Confrontations: Studies in Irish History* (London 1972)

Blake, J. W., 'Transportation from Ireland to America, 1653-60', *I.H.S.*, iii, no. 11 (Mar. 1943), 267-81

Bolton, F. R., *The Caroline Tradition in the Church of Ireland* (London 1958)

Bossy, John, 'The Counter-Reformation and the People of Catholic Europe', *Past & Present*, no. 47 (1970), 51-70

——'The Counter-Reformation and the People of Catholic Ireland, 1596-1641', *Hist. Studies*, viii (1971), 155-69

Bottigheimer, Karl, *English Money and Irish Land: The 'Adventurers' in the Cromwellian Settlement of Ireland* (Oxford 1971)

——'The Restoration Land Settlement in Ireland: A Structural View', *I.H.S.*, xviii, no. 69 (Mar. 1972), 1-21

——'The Failure of the Reformation in Ireland: *une question bien posée*', *Jn. Ecc. Hist.*, xxxvi, no. 2 (1985), 196-207

Boyle, Patrick, *The Irish College in Paris, 1578-1901* (London 1901)

Brady, Ciarán, and Gillespie, Raymond (ed.), *Natives and Newcomers* (Suffolk 1986)

Brady, John, 'Oliver Plunket and the Popish Plot', *I.E.R.*, 5th series, lxxxix (Jan.-June 1958), 1-13, 340-54; xc (July-Dec. 1958), 12-27

Butel, Paul, and Cullen, L. M. (ed.), *Cities and Merchants: French and Irish Perspectives on Urban Development, 1500-1900* (Dublin 1986)

Butlin, R. A. (ed.), *The Development of the Irish Town* (London 1977)

Canny, N. P., 'The Treaty of Mellifont and the Reorganisation of Ulster, 1603', *Ir. Sword*, ix (1969-70), 249-62

_____'The Flight of the Earls, 1607', *I.H.S.*, xvii, no. 67 (Mar. 1971), 380–99

_____ 'Why the the Reformation Failed in Ireland: *une question mal posée*', *Jn. Ecc. Hist.*, xxx (1979), 423–50

_____*The Upstart Earl* (Cambridge 1982)

_____'The Formation of the Irish Mind: Religion, Politics and Gaelic Irish Literature, 1580–1750', *Past & Present*, no. 95 (May 1982), 91–116

_____and Pagden, Anthony (ed.), *Colonial Identity in the Atlantic World, 1500–1800* (Princeton 1987)

Carpenter, Andrew, 'William King and the Threats to the Church of Ireland during the Reign of James II', *I.H.S.*, xviii (1972), 22–8

Carte, Thomas, *An History of the Life of James, First Duke of Ormonde*, 3 vols (London 1735–6); 6 vols (Oxford 1851)

Casway, J. I., 'Owen Roe O'Neill's Return to Ireland in 1642: The Diplomatic Background', *Studia Hib.*, ix (1969), 48–64

_____*Owen Roe O'Neill and the Struggle for Catholic Ireland* (Philadelphia 1984)

Ceyssens, Lucien, 'François Porter, franciscan irlandais à Rome (1632–1702)' in *Miscellanea Melchor de Pobladura*, i (Rome 1964), 387–419

Clark, G. N., *The Later Stuarts, 1660–1714* (Oxford 1934; 2nd ed. 1955)

Clark, Ruth, *Strangers and Sojourners at Port-Royal* (Cambridge 1932)

Clarke, Aidan, 'The Earl of Antrim and the First Bishops' War', *Ir. Sword*, vi (1963–4), 108–15

_____'The Army and Politics in Ireland, 1625–30', *Studia Hib.*, no 4 (1964), 28–53

_____*The Graces, 1625–41* (Dundalk 1968) (Dublin Historical Association, Irish History Series, no. 8)

_____'Ireland and the General Crisis', *Past & Present*, no. 48 (1970), 79–99

_____*The Old English in Ireland, 1625–42* (London 1966)

_____'The Policies of the Old English in Parliament, 1640–41', *Hist. Studies*, v (1965) 85–102

_____'A Discourse between Two Councillors of State, the One of England and the Other of Ireland, 1642', *Anal. Hib.*, xxvi (1970), 177–233

_____'The History of Poynings' Law, 1615–41', *I.H.S.*, xviii, no. 70 (Sept. 1972), 207–22

_____and Fenlon, Dermot, 'Two Notes on the Parliament of 1634', *R.S.A.I. Jn.*, xcvii (1967), 85–90

Cleary, Gregory, *Father Luke Wadding and St Isidore's College, Rome* (Rome 1925)

Coonan, T. L., *The Irish Catholic Confederacy and the Puritan Revolution* (Dublin 1954)

Cooper, J. P., 'The Fortune of Thomas Wentworth, Earl of Strafford', *Econ. Hist. Rev.*, xi (1958), 227–48

_____'Strafford and the Byrnes' Country', *I.H.S.*, xv, no. 57 (Mar. 1966), 1–20

Corish, P. J., 'Bishop Nicholas French and the Second Ormond Peace, 1648–9', *I.H.S.*, vi, no. 22 (Sept. 1948), 83–100

——'Rinuccini's Censure of 27 May 1648', *Ir. Theol. Quart.*, xviii (1951), 322–37

——'John Callaghan and the Controversies among the Irish in Paris, 1648–54', *Ir. Theol. Quart.*, xxi (1954), 32–50

——'The Crisis in Ireland in 1648: The Nuncio and the Supreme Council: Conclusions', *Ir. Theol. Quart.*, xxii (1955), 231–57

——'The Reorganisation of the Irish Church, 1603–41', *Ir. Cath. Hist. Comm. Proc.*, iii (1957), 1–14

——'An Irish Counter-Reformation Bishop: John Roche', *Ir Theol. Quart.*, xxv (1958), 14–32, 101–23; xxvi (1959), 101–16, 313–30

——'The Origins of Catholic Nationalism' in Corish, *Ir. Catholicism*, iii, ch. 8 (1968)

——*The Catholic Community in the Seventeenth and Eighteenth Centuries* (Dublin 1981)

——(ed.), *Radicals, Rebels and Establishments* (Belfast 1985)

——*The Irish Catholic Experience* (Dublin 1985)

Cosgrave, Art, and McCartney, Donal (ed.), *Studies in Irish History presented to R. Dudley Edwards* (Dublin 1979)

Craig, Maurice, *Dublin 1660–1860: A Social and Architectural History* (London 1952)

Cregan, D. F., 'Daniel O'Neill, a Royalist Agent in Ireland, 1644–50', *I.H.S.*, ii, no. 8 (Sept. 1941), 398–414

——'Some Members of the Confederation of Kilkenny' in Sylvester O'Brien (ed.), *Measgra i gcuimhne Mhicíl Uí Chléirigh* (Dublin 1944), 34–44

—— 'An Irish Cavalier: Daniel O'Neill', *Studia Hib.*, iii (1963), 60–100; iv (1964), 104–33; v (1965), 42–77

——'Irish Recusant Lawyers in Politics in the Reign of James I', *Ir. Jurist*, new series, v (1970), 306–20

——'The Social and Cultural Background of a Counter-Reformation Episcopate, 1618–60' in Art Cosgrove and Donal McCartney (ed.), *Studies in Irish History presented to R. Dudley Edwards* (Dublin 1979), 85–117

Cullen, L. M., *Anglo-Irish Trade, 1660–1800* (Manchester 1968)

——*An Economic History of Ireland since 1660* (London 1972)

——'Population Trends in Seventeenth-Century Ireland', *Economic and Social Review*, vi, no. 2 (Jan. 1975), 149–65

——*The Emergence of Modern Ireland, 1600–1900* (London 1981)

——and Smout, T. C. (ed.), *Comparative Aspects of Scottish and Irish Economic and Social History, 1660–1900* (Edinburgh n.d.)

Cunningham, Bernadette, 'The Composition of Connacht in the Lordships of Clanricard and Thomond, 1577–1641', *I.H.S.*, xxiv, no. 93 (May 1984), 1–14

Davies, Godfrey, *The Early Stuarts, 1603–1660* (Oxford 1937; 2nd ed. 1959)

——*The Restoration of Charles II, 1658–1660* (San Marino/London 1955)

Devine, T. M., and Dickson, David (ed.), *Ireland and Scotland, 1600-1850* (Edinburgh 1983)

Dolley, Michael, 'Anglo-Irish Monetary Policies, 1172-1637', *Hist. Studies*, vii (1969), 45-64

Duffy, P. J., 'The Territorial Organisation of Gaelic Landownership and its Transformation in County Monaghan, 1591-1640', *Ir. Geog.*, xiv (1981), 1-26

Dunlop, Robert, 'The Forged Commission of 1641', *E.H.R.*, ii (1887), 527-33

———'The Plantation of Leix and Offaly, 1556-1622', *E.H.R.*, vi (1891), 61-96

———'A Note on the Export Trade of Ireland in 1641, 1665, and 1669', *E.H.R.*, xxii (1907), 755

Dwyer, J., Mason, R. A., and Murdoch, A. (ed.), *New Perspectives on the Politics and Culture of Early Modern Scotland* (Edinburgh 1982)

Edie, C. A., 'The Irish Cattle Bills: A Study in Restoration Politics', *Amer. Phil. Soc. Trans.*, new series, lx, pt 2 (1970), 5-66

Edwards, R. Dudley, 'Church and State in the Ireland of Míchél Ó Cléirigh, 1626-41' in Sylvester O'Brien (ed.), *Measgra i gcuimhne Mhicíl Uí Chléirigh* (Dublin 1944), 1-20

———and Moody, T. W., 'The History of Poynings' Law: Part I, 1494-1615', *I.H.S.*, ii, no. 8 (Sept. 1941), 415-24

Ellis, P. Berresford, *Hell or Connaught! The Cromwellian Colonization of Ireland, 1652-60* (London 1975)

Farrell, Brian (ed.), *The Irish Parliamentary Tradition* (Dublin/New York 1973)

Finegan, Francis, 'Irish Rectors at Seville, 1619-1687', *I.E.R.*, 5th series, cvi (July-Dec. 1966), 45-63

Fitzpatrick, T., *The Bloody Bridge and other papers relating to the Insurrection of 1641* (Dublin 1903)

———'Sir Phelim's Commission', *New Irish Review*, xxi (1904), 333-48

———'The Ulster Civil War, 1641', *U.J.A.*, new series, xiii (1907), 133-42

Ford, G. A., *The Protestant Reformation in Ireland, 1590-1641* (Frankfurt 1985)

Fransciscan Fathers (ed.), *Father Luke Wadding: Commemorative Volume* (Dublin 1957)

Gabrieli, V., 'La missione di Sir Kenelm Digby alla corte di Innocenze X, 1645-1648' in *English Miscellany*, v (Rome 1954), 247-88

Gardiner, S. R., *History of England from the Accession of James I to the Outbreak of the Civil War, 1603-42*, 10 vols (London 1863-81; 2nd ed., 1883-4)

———*History of the Great Civil War, 1642-9*, 3 vols (London 1886-91); revised ed., 4 vols (London 1893)

———*History of the Commonwealth and Protectorate, 1649-56*, 3 vols (London 1894-1901); 2nd ed., revised by C. H. Firth, 4 vols (London 1903)

Giblin, Cathaldus, 'The Franciscan Mission to Scotland, 1619–47', *Ir. Cath. Hist. Comm. Proc.* (1957), 15–24

――――'Hugh MacCaghwell, O.F.M., and Scotism at St Anthony's College, Louvain' in *De Doctrina Ioannis Duns Scoti*, iv (Rome 1968), 375–97

Gillespie, Raymond, 'The Origins and Development of an Ulster Urban Network, 1609–41', *I.H.S.*, xxiv (1984), 15–29

――――'Harvest Crises in Early Seventeenth-Century Ireland', *Irish Economic and Social History*, xi (1984), 5–18

――――*Colonial Ulster* (Cork 1985)

――――'Mayo and the 1641 Rising', *Cathair na Mart*, v (1985), 38–44

Grubb, Isabel, *Quakers in Ireland, 1654–1700* (London 1927)

Hamilton, C. L., 'Scotland, Ireland and the English Civil War', *Albion*, vii (Appalachian State University 1975), 120–30

Hand, G. J., 'Sir John Davies', *Gazette of the Incorporated Law Society of Ireland*, lxiv (1971), 174–7

Hand, G., J., and Treadwell, V. W., 'His Majesty's Direction for Ordering and Settling the Courts within the Kingdom of Ireland, 1622', *Anal. Hib.*, xxvi (1970), 177–223

Harkness, David, and O'Dowd, Mary (ed.), *The Town in Ireland*: Hist. *Studies*, xiii (Belfast 1981)

Hayes, Richard, *Old Irish Links with France* (Dublin 1940)

Hayes-McCoy, G. A., 'Sir John Davies in Cavan in 1606 and 1610', *Breifne*, i, no. 3 (1960), 177–91

Hazlett, Hugh, 'The Financing of the British Armies in Ireland, 1641–9', *I.H.S.*, i, no. 1 (Mar. 1938), 21–41

Hepburn, A. C. (ed.), *Minorities in History*: Hist. *Studies*, xii (London 1978)

Hill, George, *An Historical Account of the MacDonnells of Antrim* (Belfast 1873)

Hogan, James, 'Two Bishops of Killaloe and Irish Freedom', *Studies*, ix (1920), 70–93, 213–31, 421–37

Hunter, R. J., 'Towns in the Ulster Plantation', *Studia Hib.*, no. 11 (1971), 40–79

――――'The Settler Population of an Ulster Plantation County', *Donegal Annual*, x (1972), 124–8

――――'The English Undertakers in the Plantation of Ulster, 1610–41', *Breifne*, iv, no. 16 (1973–5), 471–99

――――'Carew's Survey of Ulster, 1611: The Voluntary Works', *U.J.A.*, xxxviii (1975), 81–3

――――'Sir William Cole and the Plantation of Enniskillen, 1607–41', *Clogher Rec.*, ix (1978), 336–50

Irwin, Liam, 'The Suppression of the Irish Presidency System', *I.H.S.*, xxii no. 86 (1980–81), 26–29

Jackson, Donald, *Intermarriage in Ireland, 1550–1650* (Montreal 1970)

James, F. G., *Ireland in the Empire, 1668–1770* (Cambridge, Mass. 1973)

Jennings, Brendan, *The Irish Franciscan College of St Anthony at Louvain*

(Dublin 1925)

_____ 'Hugh, son of Rory O'Donnell, Earl of Tyrconnel, 1607–42', *Studies*, xxx (1941), 219–34

_____ 'Irish Swordsmen in Flanders, 1586–1610', *Studies*, xxxvi (1947), 402–10; xxxvii (1948), 189–202

_____ 'Florence Conry, Archbishop of Tuam', *Galway Arch. Soc. Jn.*, xxvi (1948–9), 83–93

Kearney, H. F., 'Richard Boyle, Ironmaster', *R.S.A.I. Jn.*, lxxxiii (1953), 156–62

_____ 'The Court of Wards and Liveries in Ireland, 1622–1641', *R.I.A. Proc.*, lvii, sect. C, no. 2 (1955), 29–68

_____ 'Mercantilism and Ireland, 1620–40', *Hist. Studies*, i (1958), 59–68

_____ *Strafford in Ireland, 1633–41: A Study in Absolutism* (Manchester 1959; repr. 1961)

_____ 'Ecclesiastical Politics and the Counter-Reformation in Ireland, 1618–1648', *Jn. Ecc. Hist.*, ii (1960), 202–12

Knox, R. Buick, *James Ussher, Archbishop of Armagh* (Cardiff 1967)

Lennon, Colm, *Richard Stanihurst the Dubliner, 1547–1618* (Dublin 1981)

_____ 'Civic Life and Religion in Early Seventeenth-Century Dublin', *Archiv. Hib.*, xxxviii (1983), 14–25

Lowe, John, 'The Earl of Antrim and Irish Aid to Montrose in 1644', *Ir. Sword*, iv (1959–60), 191–8

_____ 'Charles I and the Confederation of Kilkenny', *I.H.S.*, xiv, no. 53 (Mar. 1954), 1–19

_____ 'The Glamorgan Mission to Ireland, 1645–6', *Studia Hib.*, iv (1964), 155–96

MacCarthy-Morrogh, Michael, *The Munster Plantation* (Oxford 1986)

MacCormack, J. R., 'The Irish Adventurers and the English Civil War', *I.H.S.*, x, no. 37 (Mar. 1956), 21–58

MacCurtain, Margaret, *Tudor and Stuart Ireland* (Dublin/London 1972)

McGuire, J. I., 'Why Was Ormond Dismissed in 1669?', *I.H.S.*, xviii, no. 71 (Mar. 1973), 295–312

MacLysaght, Edward, *Irish Life in the Seventeenth Century: After Cromwell* (Dublin/London 1939; 2nd ed. Cork 1950)

Mant, Richard, *History of the Church of Ireland*, 2 vols (London 1840)

Martin, F. X., *Friar Nugent, Agent of the Counter-Reformation* (Rome/London 1962)

Mathew, David, *Scotland under Charles I* (London 1955)

Mayers, C. R., 'The Early Stuarts and the Irish Peerage', *E.H.R.*, lxxiii (1958), 227–51

Meehan, C. P., *The Confederation of Kilkenny* (Dublin 1860)

_____ *The Rise and Fall of the Irish Franciscan Monasteries and Memoirs of the Irish Hierarchy in the Seventeenth Century* (Dublin 1869)

Melvin, Patrick, 'Irish Troop Movements and James II's Army in 1688', *Ir. Sword*, x (1971), 87–105

Mews, Stuart (ed.), *Studies in Church History*, xviii: *Religion and National Identity* (Oxford 1982)

Miller, John, 'The Earl of Tyrconnell and James II's Irish Policy, 1685–88', *Hist. Jn.*, xx, no. 4 (1977), 803–23

Millett, Benignus, *The Irish Franciscans, 1651–1665* (Rome 1964)

——'Irish Scotists at St Isidore's College, Rome, in the Seventeenth Century' in *De Doctrina Ioannis Duns Scoti*, iv (Rome 1968), 399–419

Milligan, C. D., *History of the Siege of Londonderry, 1689* (Belfast 1951)

Mitchison, Rosalind, and Roebuck, Peter (ed.), *Economy and Society in Scotland and Ireland, 1500–1939* (Edinburgh 1988)

Moody, T. W., 'Redmond O'Hanlon', *Belfast Natur. Hist. Soc. Proc.*, 2nd series, i (1937), 17–33

——'The Treatment of the Native Population under the Scheme for the Plantation in Ulster', *I.H.S.*, i, no. 1 (Mar. 1938), 59–63

——*The Londonderry Plantation, 1609–41: The City of London and the Plantation in Ulster* (Belfast 1939)

——'The Irish Parliament under Elizabeth and James I', *R.I.A. Proc.*, xlv, sect. C, no. 6 (1939), 41–81

——(ed.), *Nationality and the Pursuit of National Independence: Hist. Studies*, xi (Belfast 1978)

——, Martin, F. X., and Byrne, F. J. (ed), *A New History of Ireland*, iii (Oxford 1976; repr. 1978)

Mooney, Canice, 'The Golden Age of the Irish Franciscans, 1615–50' in Sylvester O'Brien (ed.), *Measgra i gcuimhne Mhichíl Uí Chléirigh* (Dublin 1944), 21–33

——'The Irish Sword and the Franciscan Cowl', *Ir. Sword*, i (1951), 80–7

——'Accusations against Oliver Plunkett', *Seanchas Ardmhacha*, ii (1956), 119–40

Morrissey, Thomas, *James Archer of Kilkenny* (Dublin 1979)

Murphy, J. A., 'The Politics of the Munster Protestants, 1641–9', *Cork Hist. Soc. Jn.*, lxxvi (1971), 1–20

O'Boyle, James, *The Irish Colleges on the Continent* (Dublin 1935)

O'Brien, George, *The Economic History of Ireland in the Seventeenth Century* (Dublin 1919)

——'The Irish Staple Organisation in the Reign of James I', *Econ. Hist.*, no. 1 (1926), 42–56

Ó Domhnaill, Seán, 'Sir Niall Garbh O'Donnell and the Rebellion of Sir Cahir O'Doherty', *I.H.S.*, iii, no. 9 (Mar. 1942), 34–8

O'Faolain, Seán, *The Great O'Neill* (London 1942)

Ó Fiaich, Tomás, 'The Appointment of Blessed Oliver Plunkett to Armagh', *Ir. Theol. Quart.*, xxv (1958), 144–53

——'The Fall and Return of John MacMoyer', *Seanchas Ardmhaca*, iii (1958), 51–86

——'Republicanism and Separatism in the Seventeenth Century' in *Leachtaí Cholm Cille* (Maynooth 1971), 74–87

Ogg, David, *England in the Reign of Charles II*, 2 vols (Oxford 1934)
———*England in the Reign of James II and William III* (Oxford 1955)
Ó Mordha, Séamus, 'Ever MacMahon: Soldier Bishop of the Confederation of Kilkenny', *Studies*, xli (1951), 323–33; xlii (1952), 91–8
Pawlisch, H. S., *Sir John Davies and the Conquest of Ireland* (Cambridge 1985)
Perceval-Maxwell, Michael, 'Strafford, the Ulster Scots, and the Covenanters', *I.H.S.*, xviii, no. 72 (Sept. 1973), 524–51
———*The Scottish Migration to Ulster in the Reign of James I* (London 1973)
———'The Adoption of the Solemn League and Covenant by the Scots in Ulster', *Scotia: American-Canadian Journal of Scottish Studies*, ii (1978), 3–18
———'The Ulster Rising of 1641 and the Depositions', *I.H.S.*, xxi (1978–9), 144–67
———'Protestant Faction, the Impeachment of Strafford and the Origins of the Irish Civil War', *Canadian Journal of History*, xvi (1982), 235–55
Petrie, C. A., *The Jacobite Movement* (London 1934); 2nd ed., 2 vols (London 1948–50); 3rd ed. (London 1959)
———*The Great Tyrconnell: A Chapter in Anglo-Irish Relations* (Cork/Dublin 1972)
Phillips, W. A. (ed.), *History of the Church of Ireland*, 3 vols (London 1933–4)
Prendergast, J. P., *The Cromwellian Settlement of Ireland* (London 1865; revised ed. 1870; 3rd ed., Dublin 1922)
Ranger, T. O., 'Richard Boyle and the Making of an Irish Fortune', *I.H.S.*, x, no. 40 (Sept. 1957), 257–97
———'Strafford in Ireland: A Revaluation' in Trevor Aston (ed.), *Crisis in Europe, 1560–1660* (London 1965), 271–93
Read, J. M., 'Atrocity Propaganda and the Irish Rebellion', *Public Opinion Quarterly*, ii (1938), 229–44
Reid, J. S., *History of the Presbyterian Church in Ireland*, ed. W. D. Killen, 3 vols (Belfast 1867)
Rice, Gerard, 'Attitudes to the Counter-Reformation in Meath, 1600–1630', *Ríocht na Midhe*, v (1972), 54–63
Robinson, Philip, 'British Settlement in County Tyrone, 1610–66', *Irish Economic and Social History*, v (1978), 5–26
———*The Plantation of Ulster* (Dublin 1984)
Roebuck, Peter (ed.), *Plantation to Partition* (Belfast 1981)
Ryan, Conor, 'Religion and State in Seventeenth-Century Ireland', *Archiv. Hib.*, xxxiii (1975), 122–32
Seymour, St J. D., *The Puritans in Ireland, 1647–1661* (Oxford 1921: repr. 1969)
Sheehan, A. J., 'The Recusancy Revolt of 1603: A Reinterpretation', *Archiv. Hib.*, xxxviii (1983), 3–13
Silke, J. J., 'Later Relations between Primate Peter Lombard and Hugh

O'Neill', *Ir. Theol. Quart.*, xxii (1955), 15–30

———'Primate Lombard and James I', *Ir. Theol. Quart.*, xxii (1955), 124–50

———*Ireland and Europe, 1559–1707* (Dundalk 1966)

Simington, R. C., 'A "Census" of Ireland, c. 1659', *Anal. Hib.*, no. 12 (1943), 177–8

Simms, J. G., 'The Civil Survey, 1654–6', *I.H.S.*, ix, no. 35 (Mar. 1955), 253–63

———*The Williamite Confiscation in Ireland, 1690–1703* (London 1956)

———*Jacobite Ireland, 1685–91* (London 1969)

———*William Molyneux of Dublin*, ed. P. H. Kelly (Dublin 1982)

———*War and Politics in Ireland, 1649–1730*, ed. D. W. Hayton and Gerard O'Brien (London/Ronceverte 1986)

Stephens, Nicholas, and Glasscock, R. E. (ed.), *Irish Geographical Studies in Honour of E. Estyn Evans* (Belfast 1970)

Stevenson, David, *Revolution and Counter-Revolution in Scotland* (London 1977)

———'The Irish Franciscan Mission to Scotland and the Irish Rebellion of 1641', *Innes Review*, xxx (1979), 54–61

———*Alasdair MacColla and the Highland Problem in the Seventeenth Century* (Edinburgh 1980)

———*Scottish Covenanters and Irish Confederates* (Belfast 1981)

Swords, Liam (ed.), *The Irish-French Connection, 1578–1978* (Paris 1978)

Treadwell, V. W., 'The Irish Court of Wards under James I', *I.H.S.*, xii, no. 45 (Mar. 1960), 1–27

———'The House of Lords in the Irish Parliament of 1613–1615', *E.H.R.*, lxxx (1965), 92–107

———'The Establishment of the Farm of the Irish Customs, 1603–13', *E.H.R.*, xciii (1978), 580–602

Walsh, T. J., *The Irish Contenental College Movement* (Dublin 1973)

Wedgwood, C. V., *Strafford, 1593–1641* (London 1935)

———*Thomas Wentworth, First Earl of Strafford, 1593–1641: A Revaluation* (London 1964)

Wight, Thomas, and Rutty, John, *A History of the Rise and Progress of the People called Quakers in Ireland, from the year 1653 to 1700* (Dublin 1751)

Williams, T. D. (ed.), *Hist. Studies*, viii (Dublin 1971)

Wood, Herbert, 'The Court of Castle Chamber', *R.I.A. Proc.*, xxxii, sect. C (1913–16), 152–70

Woodward, D. M., 'The Anglo-Irish Livestock Trade of the Seventeenth Century', *I.H.S.*, xviii, no. 72 (Sept. 1973), 489–523

Index

absolutism, 87, 245, 248-9
Adrian, Pope, 174
adventurers' act, 141, 169
Alexander VII, 218-20
America
  Calvinism, 73, 226
Anabaptists, 222
Anglicanism, 59, 61, 65, 211, 223
  Arminianism, form of, 66
  compulsory for office-holders, 239
  form of Catholicism, 122-3
  and Gallicanism, 231
  in Ireland, 2, 124
  new liturgy, 66-7
  and nonconformism, 215
  position of monarch under, 57, 58, 62,
    75, 121, 207
  structure of, 177
  and the Stuarts, 101, 203-4, 220-1,
    230-1
Anglo-Norman community
  see Old English
Antrim, Co, 29
Antrim, Earl of (Randal MacDonnell),
  69-70, 90, 91, 112, 113, 125, 157
  agrees to invasion, 107-8
  arms for, 77, 88, 89, 95-7
  failure of, 109-11
  joins Montrose, 186
  and Phelim O'Neill, 143-4
  before Privy Council, 103-8
  receives commission, 99-100
  support of Charles I for, 77-8, 88-9,
    97-8, 168
  and Ulster Rising, 77-83
  Wentworth's distrust of, 86, 89-98,
    100-8, 130
Aquinas, St Thomas, 213
Ardpatrick, synod of, 243-4
Argyll, Earl of, 88, 89, 92, 130
  Earl of Antrim's plan against, 95-6,
    99-100, 103, 107-8
  suspected of invasion plan, 78, 81-2,
    83, 90, 98

Aristotle, 213
Armagh, Co, 28
  diocese, 227, 232, 240
Arminianism, 44, 57, 178, 188
  rise of, 66, 123
army, in England, 184
  enlarged by Charles II, 231
  Ireland fears arrival of, 171-2
  low morale, 123-4
  New Model Army, 124, 206, 217
  weaknesses of Charles I's forces, 124
army, in Ireland
  Catholic numbers increased, 246
  Charles I's plans for, 87-8, 185, 192
  new troops raised, 170-1
  objection to billeting, 39-41
  Old English to subsidise, 37-8, 43
  raised by Wentworth, 80, 82-3, 88,
    125-6, 142, 168
  strength of, 79
army, in Scotland
  sent to Ireland, 171-2
  strength of, 123-4
Atherton, John, Bp Waterford and
  Lismore, 57
Athlone, Co Westmeath, 253
Aughrim, Battle of, 253-4
Augustine, St, 212
  and Jansen, 208-11
Augustinus (Jansen), 218-19

Bacon, Justice
  Maguire trial, 151-2
Bacon, Sir Francis, 30
Ball, Alderman Robert, 12
Ballinrobe, Co Mayo, 52
Barberini, Cardinal, 216
Barnewall, John, 157
Barnewall, Sir Patrick, 14-15
Bath, Sir John, 37, 38
Bellew, William, 40
Bellings, Richard, 187, 219
Benburb, Battle of, 199
Berkeley, Lord, 228, 236, 238

Berwick, Treaty of, 120, 121
billeting, objections to, 39-41
bishops, appointment of, 229
Black Acts, 1584, 62
black oath, 102
Blayney, Henry Lord, 154-5, 161, 166
Bolton, Richard, 20-1
Book of Common Prayer, 221, 223
  in Scotland, 63, 67, 79
  withdrawn, 114
Borlase, Sir John, 128
boroughs, creation of, 30-2, 46-8
boundary commission, 24
Boyle, Co Roscommon, 52
Boyne, Battle of the, 36, 223, 224, 245, 250, 252-3
Brady, Father John, 240
Bramhall, John, Bp Derry, 57
Bramstone, Sir John, 166
brass money, 247
Brian Boru, 174
Bristol, 34
Brouncker, Sir Henry, 16-17, 18
Bruce, Sir Henry, 101-2, 109, 111-12
Buckingham, Duchess of, 89
Buckingham, Duke of, 38, 39, 43, 56, 61
Burgat, William, Abp Cashel, 233, 244
Byrne, Colonel Hugh, 143, 146-7, 148, 172
Byron, Captain, 90

Callaghan, John, 219-20
Calvin, John, 60, 61, 73, 122, 204, 214
Calvinism, 65, 101-2, 225
  in England, 59
  influence in parliament, 102, 123
  in Ireland, 2, 74, 249-50
  and Jansenism, 226, 237
  position of monarch under, 73, 87, 121
  in Scotland, 60-1, 115
  and the Stuarts, 67, 77, 79, 122
Campbells of Argyle, 69, 77, 79, 122
capitalism, rise of, 117
Carew, Sir George, 9, 30
Carey, Sir George, 11
Carmick, John, 159-61
Caron, Raymond, 216
Carrickfergus, Co Antrim, 83, 172, 252
Carrickmacross, Co Monaghan, 131
Carroll, Sir James, 48-9
Cary, Henry *see* Falkland, Viscount
Cashel, Co Tipperary, 9

  diocese, 227
Castleblayney, Co Monaghan, 131
Castlehaven, Earl of, 186
Catelyn, 41
Caulfield, Lady, 161-4, 165, 166-7
Caulfield, Sir Toby, 161-4, 165
Cavaliers, 230
Cavan, Co, 28
Cavenagh, Sir Morgan, 148
Cecil, *see* Salisbury, Earl of
Chappell, William, Bp Cork and Ross, 57
Charlemont, 131, 133, 161-4
Charles I, 75, 122, 141, 170, 178, 200, 201, 206, 216, 250
  accession, 35
  attempts to visit Ireland, 139-40, 179-80
  looks for Irish army, 87-8, 125-6, 185, 192
  and Roman Catholicism, 75-6, 101, 109, 116-17, 170
  constitutional policy, 45, 85-7, 226, 249
  duplicity of, 98-9
  financial problems, 55-6, 115, 117
  gives commission to Ormond, 181-2
  Glamorgan treaty, 192, 194
  and the Graces, 37-9, 54, 131
  Irish parliament subsidies, 37, 118-19, 129
  and Irish Privy Council, 109-11
  marriage, 35, 36
  military defeats, 186-7, 191
  need for Irish settlement, 188-9
  petition from Irish parliament to, 171
  plantation policy, 53, 54
  relations with Old English, 36-7, 73-4, 116, 118, 185, 248
  relations with parliament, 36, 56, 129-31, 169, 172
  relations with Wentworth, 42, 46, 56-7, 78, 86-7, 89-92, 96-8, 111-12, 114, 129-30
  religious policy, 36-7, 44, 57-8, 62, 65-8, 79-80, 101, 195-6, 207, 220-1
  and Scotland, 56-7, 65-8, 85, 98, 112, 114-15, 120-2, 207-8
  Scottish coronation, 66-7
  and Short Parliament, 119-23
  supports Earl of Antrim, 77-8, 94-5, 105-7, 168
  surrenders to Scots, 194-6
  execution 204, 206
Charles II, 22, 129, 203, 215, 222-3

and Roman Catholicism, 66, 208, 230, 233, 244-5
constitutional position, 207, 220, 223, 226
crowned by Scots, 180, 195, 207
Ireland under, 223, 224-6, 228
and Louis XIV, 207, 221, 228-31, 244, 248-9
pact with Scots, 205, 216, 225
political opponents, 230
relations with parliament, 121-2
religious policy, 221
and validity of censures, 233-5
charters, 7, 10, 11, 69
enquiries into, 19-20
importance of, 15-16, 18
Chester, 20, 194
Chichester, Sir Arthur, 13, 14-15, 16, 33, 50, 71
arrests conspirators, 70
charters enquiry, 20
commission on new boroughs, 31-2
customs fight, 22
Ulster plantation, 28, 29, 31-2, 33
Ulster policy, 23-6
China, Jesuits in, 218
Church of England, 65, 74
Church of Ireland, 1, 58, 174, 176, 225
Ulster plantation, 29
and William of Orange, 249-50
Civil War, 126, 178, 183-4
course of, 185, 186-7
effects of, 205-6
movement towards, 109-32
Charles surrenders, 194-6
Clanmorris, Lord, 154-5
Clanricard, Earl of (1), 46, 51, 52-3, 204, 205
and Rinuccini, 200
death, 54
Clanricard, Earl of (2), 56
Clement VIII, Pope, 71
Clement IX, Pope, 229, 231
Clement X, Pope, 229, 231
Clones, Co Monaghan, 182
Clonmel, Co Tipperary, 9
Clotworthy, Sir John, 128, 134, 136, 138, 149-50
Cogan, Robert, 55
Coke, Sir Edward, 43, 47-8
Cole, Sir William, 133, 134
Maguire trial, 153, 159-61
Coleraine, Co, 28, 83
Colonels' plot, 141-6

Commonwealth
break-up of, 205, 207
weaknesses of, 206-7, 220
confiscations, 1, 3, 34, 205
Connacht, 31-2, 47
plantation, 46, 51-4, 55, 56, 131
Connolly, Bernard, 232
Connolly, Owen, 150
Castle conspiracy statement, 133-4, 143, 153, 155-6, 157, 160
interrogation of, 136-8
Conry, Florence, Abp Tuam, 71, 209
constitutional question, 36, 178, 208
absolutist monarchy, 248-9
after Restoration, 206, 223, 228
in Ireland, 129, 175, 190
problem of democracy, 206
roots of, 66
Convocation of clergy, 189-91
Conway, Viscount, 123, 125
Coote, Sir Charles, 171
Cork, Co Cork, 253
Catholic revolt, 9-10
Cork, Earl of, 39, 43, 151
billeting controversy, 39-42
Counter-Reformation, 68-9, 73, 85
diocesan structure, 203
in England, 123
in France, 211-12
in Ireland, 77, 124, 178
and Oliver Plunkett, 228-9, 232
opposed to 'national church' theory, 214
Court of Castle Chamber, 14, 53, 54, 197
court of claims, 247
Court of Star Chamber, 117
Court of Wards, 35, 110, 197
Cranfield, Lionel
see Middlesex, Earl of
Crofty, Hill of, 171-2
Cromwell, Oliver, 45, 195, 201, 215, 217, 223, 233
in Ireland, 204-5, 216, 217
New Model Army, 124, 191, 201, 217
offered crown, 66, 196, 206
religious commitment of, 195-6
and Scotland, 195
success of, 191-2
death, 220
see also Cromwellian settlement
Cromwellian settlement, 104, 220, 247
outlaws Catholics, 208
Cum occasione (papal bull), 218
customs farming, 17, 21-2, 197

under Wentworth, 51, 55-6
customs rates, 197
   new book, 20, 55

Daly, Anthony, 241
Daly, Cornelius, 241
Darcy, Father James, 240
Darcy, Martin, 54
Davies, Sir John, 11, 19, 71, 72
   plantation policy, 28, 29, 31
   Ulster policy, 23-6
Davis, Francis, 162, 164
de Burgo, William, Earl of Ulster, 53
de Dominis, Antonio, Abp Spalato, 216
De Republica Ecclesiastica (de Dominis),
   216
Dease, Thomas, Bp Meath, 143, 181
Declaration of Indulgence, 230-1, 239
defective titles, commission for, 47, 49
democracy, 3, 73, 206, 249
Denmark
   troops to William, 252
Derry, Co Londonderry, 27, 83
   siege of, 224, 247, 250, 251
Desmond, Earl of, 85-6
Dillon, George, 216
Dillon, Lord Robert, 128
Dillon, Sir James, 142-3
Dissenters, 74
divine right of kings, theory of, 9, 245,
   248-9
   and the Stuarts, 61-2, 85
divine service
   fines for non-attendance, 12, 13, 34
   mass disrupted, 39-41
Docwra, Sir Henry, 23-5
Dominicans, 68, 213, 215, 232
Donegal, Co, 22, 28
Dover, Treaties of, 230
Down, Co, 29
Downham, George, Bp Derry, 38, 57
Drogheda, Co Louth, 20, 21, 171
   Catholic revolt, 9
   Cromwellian massacre, 204-5, 216
Dublin, Co
   diocese, 227
Dublin, Co Dublin, 9, 20, 223
   army called to, 170
   attacked by Confederation of
      Kilkenny, 199-200
   model town, 7-8
   moves against corporation of, 10-15,
      19-20
   moves against merchant guilds of, 21-2

moves against trade of, 20, 48-9
Oath of Supremacy, 33
objections to army billeting, 39-41
Ormond defeated, 217
piracy, 50
surrendered to English parliament,
   200-1
trade increase, 18
Dublin Castle, 27
   'plot' to seize, 76, 78, 113, 131-2,
      133-67, 170
   Earl of Antrim's statement, 168
   store of arms, 154-5
Dundalk, Co Louth, 169
Dungannon, Co Tyrone, 5, 6-7, 26, 131,
   173
Duns Scotus, John, 213

Edward II, 21
Edward VI, 2, 3, 59
Elizabeth I, 2, 3, 59, 62, 64, 71, 123
   death, 5
Elphin, diocese, 57
Ely O'Carroll, 32-3
Essex, Earl of, 228, 238
Everard, Sir John, 31
excommunication, 181, 188, 245
   Rinuccini's use of, 198-9, 201, 219-20

Falkland, Viscount (Henry Cary), 35, 48
   and the Graces, 37-9
Fermanagh, Co, 28
Fingal, Lord, 154-5
FitzMaurice (FitzGerald), James, 71
Five Articles, 63, 64, 67
Five Propositions, 218-19
Fleming, Abp Dublin, 217
Flight of the Earls, 22, 25-8, 71, 250-1
Flight of the Wild Geese, 250-1, 254-5
Forster, Sir Christopher, 39, 41, 49
Fox, Captain, 148
France, 87, 226
   Franciscan Irish College, 209, 216
   invasion of England suspected, 237
   and Ireland, 6, 68, 177
   Jansenism, 214, 215, 221
   Jesuits in, 68
   peace with England, 38
   republicanism, 73, 224
   rise of, 36, 211-12, 246
   and Scotland, 59-60, 64-5, 120
   and the Stuarts, 109, 230, 230-1, 248-9
   and the Vatican, 86, 187, 188, 211,
      228-9, 242-3, 245

Wild Geese to, 254-5
see also Gallicanism; Louis XIV
Franciscans, 41, 71, 203, 232
  and Counter-Reformation, 85-6
  French Irish College, 209, 216
  in Ireland, 68-9, 177, 214-15, 244
  and Jansenism, 209, 214, 216, 217, 219, 238-42
  and Oliver Plunkett, 238-42, 243, 244-5
  and Spain, 68
  teachers, 213
  theory of 'national church', 214
  in Ulster and Scotland, 77
free trade, 17-22, 48-50
free will, theory of, 210, 211, 212-13
French, Martin, 238

Gaelic Irish, 2, 72, 125, 177, 203, 229, 232
  and Charles I, 58, 78-85, 111, 116, 117-18
  in Confederation of Kilkenny, 173-6, 219
  and Franciscans, 215, 239-40
  and Gaelic Scots, 67-8, 69
  growing importance of, 116-18, 128
  loyalty of, 140
  and New English, 3, 74
  and Old English, 68, 72-3, 113-14, 124, 208
  opposed to Owen Roe, 201-2
  opposed to Plunkett, 203
  in Pale, 169, 171-2, 172
  plantations, 33
  political disunity, 174-5
  Privy Council support for, 104-5
  Roman Catholics, 3-4, 248
  and Spain, 35
  in town liberties, 8
  Ulster plantation, 28-9, 30
  Ulster Rising, 92-3, 96-7, 142
  and Wentworth, 44, 101, 102
Gallicanism, 6, 211-12, 214, 221, 223, 245
  and Anglicanism, 231
Galway, Co
  plantation, 46, 51-4, 56
Galway, Co Galway, 21, 253, 254
Germany, 68
Ginkel, Baron von, 253-4
Glamorgan, Earl of, 204
  collapse of treaty, 196
  and Confederation of Kilkenny, 188-9, 191, 192-3
  and Rinuccini, 193-4

Gormanston, Viscount, 171-2
Graces, the, 46-7, 131
  and Connacht plantation, 53-4
  negotiations, 37, 38-9
  in Ormond treaty, 197
great customs, 20-1
great seal, 15, 77, 78
  for Earl of Antrim, 94, 99, 102, 107
Greenwood, Charles, 101
guild monopolies, 19

Hamilton, James, 29
Hamilton, Marquis of, 78
Hamilton, Sir Francis, 154
Hapsburg Empire, 85
Henrietta Maria, Queen, 36, 58, 117, 188, 216, 235
Henry II, 21, 174
Henry III, 21
Henry VII, 2
Henry VIII, 1, 59, 61, 175, 176, 177, 191, 225
Hibbots, Thomas, 17
high kingship, 174-5
Hopton, Sir Arthur, 84
House of Lords, Irish, 46
humanism, 68

Inchiquin, Lord, 185, 201
independence, Irish
  moves towards, 226
Ingram, Sir Arthur, 49, 54, 55, 56
Innocent X, Pope, 86, 187, 188, 190
  and Five Propositions, 218
Innocent XI, Pope, 242-3, 245
Inquisition, the, 6, 213, 216
Ireton, Henry, 205

James I, 36, 56, 60, 71, 203, 216
  borough creation, 31-2, 46
  Connacht landowners agreement, 53-4
  divine right of kings, 9, 61, 85, 245
  MacDonald Rising, 70
  and New English, 12
  and Presbyterians, 61-4, 67
  proclaimed king, 9-10
  proclamation to Ulster, 24
  religious policy, 8-9, 62-3, 66, 114
  death, 35
James II, 75, 180, 203, 223, 245
  and Roman Catholicism, 66, 230, 238
  and France, 230, 248-9
  Irish war, 248, 250-3
  and Old English, 215
  religious policy, 221

rule of, 246-8
James IV, 60
James V, 59, 60
Jansen, Cornelius, 209, 212, 213-14
    Augustinus, 218-19
Jansenism, 209-11, 233, 236
    and Calvinism, 226, 237
    in France, 214, 215, 221
    and Franciscans, 209, 214, 216, 217,
        219, 238-42
    in Ireland, 219-20, 225, 229, 232
    and Jesuits, 212-13
    threat of, 218
Jesuits, 32, 68-9, 215, 218, 232, 239
    accused of invasion plot, 237
    feared in England, 244-5
    influence of, 236-7
    and Jansenism, 212-13
    and Louis XIV, 221
    Plunkett on, 242
Jews, 239
John, King, 10
Jones, Colonel Michael, 200, 217

Kells, Co Meath, 172
Kilfenora bishopric, 57
Kilkenny, Co Kilkenny, 9, 201
    Convocation held in, 189-91
    see also Kilkenny, Confederation of
Kilkenny, Confederation of, 173-8, 215
    collapse of, 4, 200-2, 203, 204, 221
    delegation meets Charles I, 185
    first assembly, 178-9
    second assembly, 182
    third assembly, 184-5
    fourth assembly, 186-7
    fifth assembly, 189
    Glamorgan treaty, 192-3, 193-4
    Inchiquin truce, 201
    loyalty to king, 178-9
    military defeats, 186
    Ormond negotiations, 182-3
    Ormond treaty, 196-9
    Supreme Council, 194, 219
        appeals against excommunication,
            201
        appeals to Rome, 182-3
        excommunication of attacked,
            219-20
    and the Vatican, 180-1, 182-3, 187,
        189-91
    truce, 183, 184-5
    Belling's defence of, 219
King, Paul, 219

kingship *see* monarchy
Kinsale, Battle of, 5, 71, 250
Kinsale, Co Cork, 253
Knox, John, 60

land settlements
    after monastic dissolutions, 1, 39, 174,
        176, 182-3, 191
    after Restoration, 247
    see also plantations
Laud, William, Abp Canterbury, 57, 66,
    86, 112, 216
    correspondence with Wentworth, 78,
        80, 84, 102-5, 106, 126
Laviston, Mrs, 149-50
Leinster, 31-2, 47
    recusancy, 33
Leitrim, Co, 46, 51
Leslie, General, 123, 124
Leslie, Henry, Bp Down and Connor, 57
Ley, Sir James, 14-15
Limerick, Co Limerick, 9, 253
    charters examined, 19-20
    siege of, 250
Limerick, Treaty of, 248, 254-5
Lionel, Duke of Clarence, 53
Loftus, Lord Justice, 39, 43
    billeting controversy, 39-42
Lombard, Peter, Abp Armagh, 70-2
London, 9, 20-1, 33
    and Londonderry, 29
    relationship with Charles I, 117
Londonderry, Co, 23, 28, 117
    rising in, 171
Long, William, 17
Long Parliament, 121, 125
    attacks Wentworth, 127-8
Longford, Co
    plantation of, 32-3, 46, 51
Lord Deputy, role of, 1, 2, 8
lords of erection, 65
Lorne, Lord
    see Argyll, Earl of
Lorraine, Duke of, 217, 221
Louis XIII, 36
Louis XIV, 36, 65, 66, 215-17, 247
    absolutism, 214, 226, 245, 248-9
    and Charles II, 207, 221, 228, 230-1,
        244, 248-9
    and Ireland, 221, 251-2, 253
    and James II, 223-4, 252
    and Jesuits, 242
    opposed by Vatican, 244, 245
    treaty with William, 251

war with Dutch, 246
war with Europe, 248
Loyal Remonstrance, 229, 236, 242
loyalty, 1-3, 6-8, 11, 13-16, 18
and Old English, 74-6, 126-8
of towns, 15-16
Loyola, St Ignatius, 212
Luther, Martin, 122, 213
predestination, 211
Lutheranism, 60, 61, 85
Lynch, James, Abp Tuam, 233

Macary, Lord, 154
MacCaughwell, Hugh, Abp Armagh, 70
MacDonald, Coll, 70
MacDonalds, 69-70, 93, 96
MacDonnell, Alasdair, 186
MacDonnell, Alexander, 70
MacDonnell, Randal *see* Antrim, Earl of
MacDonnell, Sorley, 70
MacDonnells, 69-70, 78, 113
MacHenry, Turlough, 97
MacMahon, Coll, 147, 148
MacMahon, Eugene, 71
MacMahon, Ever, 146, 157
MacMahon, Hugh, 78, 97, 163
implicated by Connolly, 133-4, 136-8
in Maguire statement, 157, 158-9, 160
trial of, 148-9
executed, 150
MacSweeneys, 24
Magennis, Lord, 97
Maguire, Captain Brian, 161
Maguire, Captain Rory, 160
Maguire, Conor Lord, 97
arrested, 139
statement of, 138-40, 141-9
trial of, 148-67
Ulster Rising, 78, 133, 134-5
Maguire, Conor Roe, 24
Maguire, Cuchonnacht, 24-6, 157
mandates controversy, 71
Marlborough, Earl of, 253
Marston Moor, Battle of, 186-7
martial law, 113, 131, 133, 140
Mary I, 2, 59, 217
Mary of Orange, 246
Mary Queen of Scots, 60, 61
Massari, Dionisio, 217, 218
Matthews, Ardle, 232
Maximilian, Emperor, 85
Mayo, Co
plantation, 46, 56
Mellifont, Treaty of, 22

Melville, Andrew, 61-2
merchant guilds
attacked, 16, 17-18
monopolies abolished, 19
Middlesex, Earl of (Lionel Cranfield), 35
monarchy, 87, 174
under Anglicanism, 57, 58, 62, 75
under Calvinism, 73, 87, 121
monasteries, dissolution of
property to Old English, 1, 39, 174,
176, 182-3, 191
Moneymore, Co Londonderry, 137
monopolies, 19, 197
Monro, Major-General Robert, 172, 173,
185, 186, 199
Montgomery, Hugh, 29
Montrose, Earl of, 186
Moore, Sir Garret, 26
Mountgarrett, Lord, 180
Mountjoy, Charles Baron, 11, 45, 204,
205
destruction of Ulster, 23
and Earl of Tyrone, 4, 5, 23-4
revolt of towns, 9-10
death, 25, 26
Mountjoy, Co Tyrone, 131, 173
Mountnorris, Lord, 54-5, 56
municipal corporations, 15-16
attacked by Wentworth, 48-50
enquiries into charters, 19-20
and Oath of Supremacy, 33-4, 35
objections to army billeting, 39-41
Munster, 16-17, 31, 47
recusancy, 33

Nantwich, Battle of, 185
Naseby, Battle of, 191-2
nationalism, 4, 74
and Catholic Church, 217
Netherlands, 49-50, 230, 252
and Charles I, 87
and Spain, 73, 85, 249
war with France, 246
Nevil, Mr, 155, 165
New English, 2, 3, 4, 116, 170
attitude to Gaelic Irish, 77, 87-8
Calvinist, 74
and Charles I, 37, 114
Connacht plantation, 51-2
and Dublin Castle 'plot', 139-40
and the Graces, 37-8
in Irish parliament, 119
and James I, 12
loyalty of, 117-18

and monarchy, 225
Puritan, 57
relations with Old English, 43, 113-14,
  126-8, 129, 216
threat to all Catholics, 172
and Wentworth, 44, 54-5, 101, 102
New Ross, Co Wexford, 181
Newbury, Battle of, 183
Newry, Co Down, 131, 173
Nine Years' War, 4, 86, 173
reasons for, 5-8
'no bishop, no king', 61-2, 66
nominalism, 213
Nonconformists
Declaration of Indulgence, 230-1
  under Charles II, 230
Northumberland, Lord, 79
Nottingham, Earl of, 17
Nutt (pirate), 50

Oates, Titus, 237, 243, 244
Oath of Association, 189-91, 198-9
Oath of Supremacy, 18, 64, 116
abolition promised, 37, 197
enforced, 11-12, 32, 35
and municipal corporations, 33-4
obligatory for election, 30
test of loyalty, 74
for undertakers, 29
oblivion, act of, 197
O'Boyles, 24
O'Cahan, Donal, 23, 24, 25-7
Occam, William of, 213
O'Doherty, Sir Cahir, 4, 22, 23, 27, 29
O'Donnell, Manus, 24
O'Donnell, Rory see Tyrconnell, Earl of
O'Donnell, Sir Niall Garbh, 23-4, 27-8
O'Donnelly, Patrick, 241
O'Hara, Coll, 87
Old English, 34, 45, 181, 185, 201, 202,
  208
attitude of England to, 119
Battle of the Boyne, 252-3
Roman Catholicism of, 1-4, 68, 73,
  176-7
and Charles I, 36-7, 73-4, 116, 118
and Confederation of Kilkenny, 175-6,
  180, 203
constitutional dilemma, 3, 36-7, 71-2,
  73-6, 130-1, 172
and Counter-Reformation, 69, 77
economic divisions among, 19
and Franciscans, 215, 219
in Irish parliament, 30-2, 43, 119, 171

and James II, 245, 247, 251
Jansenism among, 239
loyalty of, 18, 125-8, 129
and monastic land, 1, 39, 174, 176, 183,
  191
Nine Years' War, 6-8
Oath of Association, 190-1
Oath of Supremacy, 12, 14
offered security of tenure, 253
petition to Charles II, 231
plantations, 46
political beliefs, 248, 250
political power removed, 215-16,
  224-5, 250
relations with Gaelic Irish, 68, 72-3,
  113-14, 124, 208
relations with New English, 43, 74,
  113-14, 126-9, 216
revolt of towns, 8-10
and Spain, 35
and the Graces, 37-8
and the Vatican, 182-3, 187
Ulster Rising involvement, 103,
  113-14, 132, 133, 140-6, 149, 169-72,
  215
and Wentworth, 43-4, 46-7, 51-4
O'More, Rory
Ulster Rising, 138-9, 144-8, 153, 157,
  171-2
O'Neill, Art Oge, 97
O'Neill, Captain Brian, 145, 146, 148,
  157
O'Neill, Captain Con, 148
O'Neill, Daniel, 90, 91
O'Neill, Father Phelim, 232, 241
O'Neill, Hugh see Tyrone, Earl of
O'Neill, Owen Roe, 173, 175, 183, 217
attacks Dublin, 199-200
changes sides, 201-2
defeats Monro, 199
military defeats, 182, 186
treaty with Inchiquin, 201
and Ulster Rising, 138, 140, 144-8, 157,
  161, 165
O'Neill, Sir Phelim, 97, 105, 131, 173,
  202
publishes commission, 169-70
takes Charlemont, 161-4, 166-7
Ulster Rising, 78, 133, 143-8, 153, 157
O'Phelan, James, Abp Ossory, 233
O'Reilly, Edmund, Abp Armagh, 217,
  219, 228-9, 238
call for new hierarchy, 227-8
and Cromwell, 217-18

and Gaelic Irish church, 231-2
goes to Rome, 227
loyalty policy, 235
obedience to papacy, 222-3
death, 233
O'Reilly, Hugh, Abp Armagh, 70, 172
O'Reilly, Philip, 144, 147, 158, 172
O'Reilly, Philip MacHugh, 205
Ormond, Earl of, 80, 128, 171, 204, 229,
235, 236
and Charles II, 205, 207, 223, 228
and Confederation of Kilkenny, 173,
179-87, 192-3
and Glamorgan, 192-4
military defeats, 217
offers resignation, 189
and O'Neill, 217
and O'Reilly, 233
attacked by Supreme Council, 199-201
treaties, 182-3, 196, 205
Orrery, Earl of, 253
O'Tooles, 218
Oviedo, Mateo de, Abp Dublin, 71

Pale
administrative divisions, 177
Gaelic Irish in, 169, 171-2
Papacy *see* Vatican
parliament, English, 113, 131, 149, 151,
178, 186
bans Irish exports, 226
Bill of Rights, 42
and Wentworth, 98, 105
Calvinists in, 123
and Charles I, 36-7, 45, 56, 102
condemns truce, 184-5
constitutional crisis, 115, 117
controls Dublin, 200-1
and Dublin Castle 'plot', 139-40
fear of Catholicism, 125-8, 231, 238-9
Ormond negotiates with, 199-200
punishment for Ulster Rising, 169-72
right to forfeited land, 169, 172
and Scotland, 88, 125, 205-6
Short Parliament, 119-21, 121-3, 125
Solemn League and Covenant, 183-4
splits after Charles I's surrender, 195
threat to monarchy, 87
see also Long Parliament
parliament, Irish, 45, 126, 131, 145, 192,
197
act of attainder against Protestants,
247-8
appeal to lift suspension, 171

Catholic seats diminished, 47-8
Cromwellian, 224-5
independence called for, 197, 226
new boroughs created, 30-2
Old English in, 126-7
'Patriot Parliament', 246-7
plot to blow up, 154
Poynings' Law, 38, 158
subsidies, 32, 129
summoned, 118-19
suspended, 169
under Wentworth, 46-8
parliament, Scottish, 102, 118
Parsons, Sir William, 128, 153, 157, 179,
181, 216
arrests Maguire, 139
Caulfield exchange, 162-3
Dublin Castle 'plot', 113, 128, 131,
133-8, 150, 156, 167
imprisoned, 182
testimony, 159-60
Pascal, Blaise, 212
'Patriot Parliament', 246-7
Paul, St, 210-11
Paul III, Pope, 59
Paul V, Pope, 71, 86
Paulet, Sir George, 27
Peter, St, 210-11
petty customs, 20-1
piracy, 50-1
plantations, 32-3, 197
planned, 169, 172
see also Ulster Plantation
Plato, 211, 213
Plunket, Colonel, 143, 148
Plunket, Michael, 241
Plunkett, Oliver, 203, 228, 233, 238-42
accused of plotting invasion, 237-8
Archbishop of Armagh, 231-2, 235
Ardpatrick synod, 243-4
and Counter-Reformation, 228-9, 232
declaration of loyalty, 236-7
and Talbot, 234-5
arrest, 241
trial and execution, 244-5
Pole, Cardinal, 182
ports
trading rights, 17-18, 21-2
Portumna, Co Galway, 52-3
poundage, 20, 21-2
Poynings' Law, 38, 158, 247
predestination, theory of, 210, 211, 212-
14, 225, 237
prerogative courts, 131

Presbyterianism, 120, 170
  covenant, 99
  in Ireland, 172
  James I opposed to, 62-4
  in Scotland, 8-9, 59, 62-3, 180, 184,
    194-5
  structure of, 122
Presbyterians, English
  and Cromwellians, 230
  support Charles II, 195
Presbyterians, Irish, 222
Presbyterians, Scottish, 67, 225
  and James I, 67
  opposed to Charles I, 115, 207-8
  opposed to English parliament, 205-6
  strength of, 123-4
Presbyterians, Ulster
  against O'Neill, 186
  and James II, 224
  no compromise, 225
  and Ulster Rising, 79, 80, 83, 84
Preston, Colonel Thomas, 90, 173, 181
  attacks Dublin, 199-200
Privy Council, English, 5, 121
  additional customs, 22
  charters enquiry, 20
  and recusancy, 34
  Ulster plantation, 28-9
  warnings to Chichester, 14, 15, 16
Privy Council, Irish, 81
  campaign against Dublin Corporation,
    10-15
  and Charles I, 109-11, 112
  and Confederation of Kilkenny, 181-2
  fears of Catholic army, 87-8
  parliamentarian, 179
  on Protestant 'massacre', 181-2
  sends secret message to London, 171
  support for Gaelic Irish, 104-5
  and Ulster Rising, 133-5, 139-40, 149,
    170, 216
  under Charles II, 236
  and Wentworth, 54-5, 101-8, 109,
    113-14
Protestant ethic, 117
Protestantism, 1-3, 207-8
  differences from Catholicism, 63-4
  no attempt to convert Ireland, 16, 64
  in Scotland, 59
Protestants, Irish 224-5, 242
  act of attainder against, 247
  ascendancy, 225, 251
  attitude to Old English, 37
  in Irish parliament, 46, 47

'massacre' stories, 151, 160-1, 165, 182
  and William of Orange, 249-50
Puritanism, 8, 55, 57, 66, 68, 87, 123
  in Church of Ireland, 57, 58
  'Independents', 183-4, 195
  and Ireland, 105
  and New English, 74, 75, 113-14, 117
  opposed to monarchy, 170, 195
  'Presbyterians', 183-4
  revolution, 206-7
Pym, John, 120

Radcliffe, Sir George, 49-50, 51, 55, 96
Rathmines, Battle of, 217
Rathmullen, Co Donegal, 26
rebellions, 3, 27, 70
  1641 *see* Ulster Rising
  loyal rebellions, 8-10
recusancy, 13-15, 32
  fines for, 34, 37, 39, 42, 43, 191
  tacitly ignored, 126
  in the towns, 33-4
  see also Old English
Reformation, 85, 176, 177, 182-3, 191,
  204, 212
  in England, 1, 2, 119
religion
  controversies over form of worship,
    63-4
  expropriation based on, 3
  and loyalty, 1, 2-3, 6-8, 11, 13-16, 18,
    74-6
  in Scotland, 59-60, 61, 64-5
  and the Stuarts, 59-62
  see also under specific religions
republicanism, 3-4, 73, 173, 217
  birth of, 208, 224
Restoration, 66, 180, 195, 204, 222-3, 235
  constitutional questions, 228
  and Ireland, 220-1, 236
  land settlements, 247
revocation, act of, 65
Richard I, 21
Ridgeway, Sir Thomas, 17-20
Rinuccini, Giovanni Battista, 86, 187,
  192, 205, 217, 218, 250
  arrives, 193
  Callaghan's attack on, 219-20
  constitutional question, 208, 248
  imprisons Supreme Council, 199
  influence of, 214, 216, 238
  and O'Neill, 173, 202
  opposition to censures, 233-5
  and Ormond treaty, 196-9, 200

revokes Glamorgan treaty, 193-4
uses excommunication, 198-9, 201, 219-20
Vatican support for, 203, 219, 233-5
leaves, 204
Ripon, Treaty of, 125
Robartes, Lord, 228, 236
Roman Catholicism, 39, 176-7, 190
  Anglicanism form of, 122-3
  and Charles I, 75-6, 101, 109, 116, 170
  Counter-Reformation, 85-6
  Declaration of Indulgence, 230-1
  differences from Jansenism, 210
  differences from Protestantism, 63
  English fear of, 239, 244-5
  in France, 226
  influences of, 68-9
  in Ireland, 172, 176-8
  mediation through ritual, 122
  religious freedom demanded, 189-91, 194
  in Scotland, 59-60
  and sovereignty, 176, 250
  struggle for political control of, 221-3
  and the Stuarts, 2, 36, 66, 203-4, 244-5, 248-9
  universalism of, 212-13, 214
Roman Catholics, English
  loyalty of, 6, 155, 231
Roman Catholics, Irish, 73, 214, 215, 225, 245
  after Restoration, 220-1
  Ardpatrick synod regulations, 243-4
  army for Charles I, 87-8
  barred from parliament, 30-2
  and Charles I, 124
  clergy banished, 12
  concessions to, 32
  Convocation of, 189-91
  and Counter-Reformation, 77
  divisions among, 68-9, 124, 173, 176-8, 201, 208, 232, 238-42
  effects of Nine Years' War, 5-8
  excluded from legal settlement, 141
  Glamorgan treaty, 192, 197
  and James II, 245, 246, 247
  land forfeited, 169
  loyalty of, 125-8, 155, 233-7
  no attempt to convert, 15-16, 64
  Oath of Association, 173
  Oath of Supremacy, 11-12
  political allegiances, 228-9, 248
  political power removed, 141, 208, 215

post-Confederation, 201, 208, 216-17, 222-3
  relations with Vatican, 228-30
  see also Gaelic Irish; Old English
Roscommon, Co, 171
  plantation, 46, 56
Rowe, John, 219
Ryswick, Treaty of, 251

St Andrews, Archbishop of, 67
St John, Sir Oliver, 33-4, 35
St Leger, William, 185
St Ruth, General, 253-4
Salisbury, Earl of, 14, 20
Sarsfield, Patrick 252
Scarampi, Pier Francesco, 182-3, 192
Schomberg, Duke of, 251
Scotland, 75-6, 99, 109, 112, 120, 195
  Catholicism in, 67
  and Charles I, 57, 65-8, 85, 98, 102, 114-15, 120, 121-2, 207-8
  Charles I surrenders to, 180, 194-6
  and Charles II, 225
  church administration, 61-2
  and France, 59-60, 64-5, 120
  and Gaelic Irish, 68, 69
  invades England, 125
  and James I, 62-3
  need for viceroy, 116
  no religious compromise, 59-62
  opposed to English parliament, 205-6
  rebellion 1614-15, 70
  religious divisions, 2, 8-9, 61, 64-5
  Solemn League and Covenant, 183-4
  and Ulster, 76, 99, 109-11
  and Ulster Rising, 78-84, 93-6
  undertakers from, 28-9
Scottish General Assembly, 102, 118-19
search and confiscation, rights of, 17
Shelton, Alderman, John, 11-12
ship money, 120
Sigginstown, Co Kildare, 183
Sixtus V, Pope, 86
Sligo, Co, 52, 171
  plantation, 46, 56
Sligo, Co Sligo, 254
Solemn League and Covenant, 183-4
  and Ulster Scots, 185
sovereignty, 3, 169, 195, 228
  Cromwell's claim to, 207
  divine right of kings, 9, 61-2, 85, 245, 248-9
  and finance, 115
  Louis XIV's view of, 221

problem of, 89, 174-5, 190
and Roman Catholicism, 176, 250
divided between king and parliament, 131
and theology, 209-26
Spain
    dangers of Calvinism, 87
    decline of, 36, 211
    and England, 35, 38, 109
    and Ireland, 56, 68, 177
    and Netherlands, 73, 85, 249
    Roman Catholic influence, 58, 71, 72, 88
    and the Vatican, 71, 72, 86, 187
    Ulster Rising, 90, 141, 142
Spanish Succession, War of the, 251
statute of limitations, 47, 131
Stewart, Sir Robert, 182
Stewart, Sir William, 154, 161
Strafford, Earl of *see* Wentworth, Thomas Viscount
Stuarts, 45, 46, 61-2, 66, 206
    ideology of, 59-76
    importance of Scottish monarchy, 75-6
    and Roman Catholicism, 2, 36, 66, 203-4, 244-5, 248-9
surrender and regrant, 1, 26, 33
Synod of Kells, 172

Talbot, Peter, Abp Dublin, 231, 233-5
Talbot, Richard *see* Tyrconnell, Earl of
Talbot, Sir William, 12
Tandragee, Co Armagh, 131
Thomastown, 9
Thomond, Earl of, 51
Thornton, Sir George, 9-10
tonnage, 20
Tories, 221, 246
tories, 232, 241, 243
towns, 7-8, 45
    antipathy to Gaelic Irish, 8
    Catholic revolt of, 8-10
    independence threatened, 10-11, 15-22, 33-4
    and Nine Years' War, 6-8
    revolt of loyal towns, 4
    threat to port towns, 17-18, 21-2
    trading rights threatened, 16-22, 45-6
trade, 16-22
    limited, 226
    loss of trading rights, 45-6
    privileges attacked by Wentworth, 48-50

transportation, 33, 208
Trent, Council of, 233
Trim, Co Meath, 181
Trinity College, Dublin, 28, 57
Trinity guild, 20
Tuam, diocese, 227, 238
Tudors, 2, 59, 87
Tyrconnell, Earl of (Rory O'Donnell), 4, 84, 85
    defeat and flight of, 23, 24-6
Tyrconnell, Earl of (Richard Talbot), 246, 251, 252, 253
    death, 254
Tyrone, Co, 28
Tyrone, Earl of (Hugh O'Neill), 4, 82, 95, 175, 204
    and English law, 174
    flight of, 23-6
    as Gaelic Irish, 72, 73, 202-3
    military defeat, 22, 23, 88
    motives of, 5-8
    and the Vatican, 70-1
Tyrrell, Patrick, Bp Clogher, 231-2, 241

Ulster, 5, 31-2, 47, 185, 251
    armed, 111, 125
    and Confederation of Kilkenny, 184
    Gaelic Irish in, 22-8, 202-3, 232
    politics of, 68
    proclamation to, 24
    resistance, 73, 75-6
    and Scotland, 76
    see also Presbyterians, Ulster; Ulster Plantation; Ulster Rising
Ulster Plantation, 22, 28-32, 44, 51, 173
    land grants, 28
    native Irish, 28-9
    servitors, 28-9
    success of, 251
    undertakers, 28-9
Ulster Rising, 4, 70, 77-108
    arrivals from Scotland, 109
    beginnings, 131-2
    course of, 169-72
    and Gaelic Irish, 92-3, 96-7, 142
    and New English, 118
    Old English involvement, 103, 113-14, 132-3, 140-6, 149, 169-72, 215
    parliament punishes, 169-72
    and Wentworth, 99-108, 113
undertakers, 33
    Ulster plantation, 28-30
United Irishmen, 224
University of St Andrews, 63

Urban VIII, Pope, 70, 187
Ussher, James, Abp Armagh, 38
Utrecht, Peace of, 248

Vane, Sir Henry, 98, 99, 107, 110, 111, 113
  appeal to parliament, 120
Vatican, The, 59
  and Confederation of Kilkenny, 180-1, 182-3, 187, 189-91
  Counter-Reformation, 123
  and England, 117
  and France, 86, 211, 228-9, 242-3, 245
  Franciscan influence, 85-6
  and Ireland, 71, 204, 222-3, 228-30
  papal monarchy, 174
  power struggles in, 177
  and Rinuccini, 203, 219, 233-5
  and Spain, 71, 72, 86, 187
  supports William of Orange, 223
  supremacy of, 214, 216, 218, 221
  and Ulster Rising, 176
  views on Jansenism, 237

Wadding, Luke, 180-1, 182
Walsh, Peter, 217, 219, 222, 227, 233, 235
  influence of, 239
  Loyal Remonstrance, 229, 236, 242
Wandesford, Christopher, 127
wardships, control of, 35
Waterford, Co Waterford, 9, 20, 21
  charter, 10, 34
  Synod, 196-9
Watson, James, 49
Webb, George, Bp Limerick, 57
Wentworth, Sir George, 80
Wentworth, Thomas Viscount, 42-57, 100-1, 185, 205
  army for Charles I, 80, 82-3, 88, 125-6, 142, 168
  assessment of, 42-3, 45-6, 101-2, 112-14, 130

created Earl of Strafford, 98, 105, 118
  economic policy, 51, 197-8
  execution, 105, 130
  Irish policy, 44-6, 117-19
  and New English, 44, 54-5, 101, 102
  and Old English, 43-4, 46-7, 51-4
  and parliament, 118-19, 121, 127-8, 129-30, 141
  plantation policy, 51-4, 131
  Privy Council appeal, 113-14
  relations with Charles I, 42, 46, 57, 78, 82-92, 96-8, 101-2, 112-14, 129-30
  religious policy, 57-8
  successes of, 114, 115-16
  summons Dublin council, 102-8
  trial, 151
  Ulster crisis, 77-108, 109-12, 143-4
  waning influence of, 98-9
Westmeath, Co, 32-3
Westmeath, Earl of, 38, 143
Westphalia, Peace of, 220
Wexford, Co
  plantation, 32-3, 46
Wexford, Co Wexford, 9
  Cromwellian massacre, 205, 216
Whigs, 221, 246
Whitfield, Serjeant, 152, 155, 158, 162, 163
  addresses Maguire jury, 164-5
Wicklow, Co, 171
Wild Geese, 250-1, 254-5
William of Orange, 195, 206, 248, 249-50
  constitutional monarch, 248, 250
  proclaimed king, 246
  Vatican support, 223
  war in Ireland, 252-5
Wilmot, Charles Lord, 40-1
Wilmot, Sir Charles, 10
Windebank, 90, 91, 92, 100, 125
Woodcock, John,
  and Maguire trial, 155-7, 161
Worcester, Battle of, 205
Wordrose, Mary, 164